# Frontiers of Anthropology

# Frontiers of

AN INTRODUCTION TO

ANTHROPOLOGICAL THINKING

# Anthropology

**MURRAY J. LEAF**
*University of California, Los Angeles*

*with*

**BERNARD G. CAMPBELL**
*University of California,*
*   Los Angeles*

**CONSTANCE CRONIN**
*University of Arizona*

**GEORGE A. De VOS**
*University of California, Berkeley*

**WILLIAM A. LONGACRE**
*University of Arizona*

**MARLYS McCLARAN**
*University of California,*
*   Los Angeles*

**FRED T. PLOG**
*State University of New York,*
*   Binghamton*

**JACK H. PROST**
*University of Illinois,*
*   Chicago Circle*

**ROY WAGNER**
*Northwestern University*

D. VAN NOSTRAND COMPANY
*New York   Cincinnati   Toronto   London   Melbourne*

Cover designed by Debra Malian

D. Van Nostrand Company Regional Offices:
New York  Cincinnati  Millbrae

D. Van Nostrand Company International Offices:
London  Toronto  Melbourne

Copyright © 1974 by Litton Educational Publishing, Inc.

Library of Congress Catalog Card Number 74-4535
ISBN: 0-442-24720-6

Published by D. Van Nostrand Company
450 West 33rd Street, New York, N.Y. 10001

Published simultaneously in Canada by
Van Nostrand Reinhold Ltd.

10 9 8 7 6 5 4 3 2 1

# Preface

To describe anthropology as "the science of man," as if it were already established in this role, is to rob it of much of the excitement it has for modern anthropologists. Such a description may lead to a misunderstanding of the peculiar character of most anthropological arguments and debates. The fact is that anthropology, in the eyes of most leading anthropologists, is not an established, stable discipline of the sort suggested by many introductory texts. There is no agreed-upon framework within anthropology that gives it a single, unitary pattern, one set of goals, and one set or system of conceptual and methodological tools or empirical findings. Rather, it presently involves the fluid and dynamic interchange among people and groups as to whether such a unified discipline is possible and what its goals and structure should be. Some anthropologists take part in this broad discussion by presenting their versions of the theory and goals of the discipline as if describing some sort of fact. They and those who read them understand, however, that they are merely making a recommendation, and all would normally recognize that there are many anthropologists who do not agree—at least with any scheme so far proposed. Other anthropologists take part in the debate in other ways. Sometimes they discuss several competing theories of the discipline in a broad theoretical comparison—(Nagel's *Foundations of Social Anthropology* is an excellent example). Sometimes people offer what they consider to be specific tools or problems and solutions that suggest a general orientation, but they leave the task of systematizing that orientation for others. This is the kind of argument most often found in the scholarly journals of the field. But always, no matter what the vehicle, the arguments reflect the fact that anthropology is not a discipline "in being" but rather one "in the process of becoming."

Textbooks have played a fairly important and rather special role in the overall pattern of anthropological debate. They have been a major means by which programmatic conceptions of the discipline have been advanced. They often have been used by their authors to present statements about what anthropology *should be* in the disguise of statements about what it *is*. This presentation has consistently involved the idea that anthropology should have a single pattern and/or a single unifying theme, even though no such theme or unity in fact existed. Unfortunately, introductory textbooks have not made their purpose and context clear in this respect, and students have often been misled. In upper division or graduate studies, a student may find that many things he had been taught as simple truths that everybody believed were in fact highly debatable opinions and that professional anthropologists agreed on only a few major issues and problems that were not only different in substance but often in kind. Generally speaking, anthropologists agree not on any particular proposition about the general features of man or society, but rather on certain rules of the game for discussing such propositions.

This introduction to anthropology attempts to avoid the pitfalls of single-authored texts by having chapters by nine anthropologists representing current developments in the four traditional subfields of anthropology: archeology, social and cultural anthropology, physical anthropology, and linguistics. In addition, Chapter 1 provides an historical overview of the field, while the concluding chapter tries to identify underlying themes and issues in the research and to project them into the future in the context of other likely developments in the field. All of the chapters were written for this volume and, except for the conclusion, all are based on the current research interests of the authors. The spread of chapter topics within the subfields and within the discipline as a whole is intended to suggest the full range of concerns of anthropology. The fundamental idea, however, is not to provide a survey of anthropology as if seen from afar, but rather to provide a text presenting the different ways anthropology appears to researchers in different positions within the discipline.

Each chapter following the historical introduction uses a general format designed to combine the professional sophistication of scholarly articles with the straightforward and comparatively simple presentation required of a textbook. Each essay begins with a brief theoretical review of the issues it deals with. It then presents an example of an empirical test of these theoretical conceptions and describes the implications of the tests for the theory and for future research.

Although the order of discussion within each chapter is arbitrarily uniform, it is not artificial. The authors of the essays agree that four components are the basis of anthropological inquiry: assembling theory, making informed interpretations of it, inventing dramatic and clear observational tests that challenge its underlying assumptions, and then making careful, justified interpretations of these tests. Although most anthropologists have for some time agreed in principle that these are the steps analysis should follow, they have engaged in many types of activity based on quite different plans—from highly impressionistic grand theory without clear empirical pertinance to supposedly unpretentious, "pure" description without clear relevance to any set of theoretical problems. Most especially, textbooks have not been built along experimental lines, even if their authors avowed such aims within them as general principles.

It is intended that the instructor who uses this book will take the role of advocate of yet another position, parallel to those presented. Hopefully, this approach will eliminate the unhappy choice imposed by overly simple treatments between parroting the text or dwelling on what is wrong with it and will encourage the instructor to express his own research commitments in their true professional context contrasted with other working formulations.

## DEVELOPMENT OF THE PROJECT

I should begin by noting that, strictly speaking, I did not originate this textbook. The main impetus for the project came from Mr. Hyung W. Pak of D. Van Nostrand Company.

Like many anthropologists, I had been asked to write or edit textbooks on a variety of subjects, and like most anthropologists I regularly declined such requests. It is difficult to recall why I deviated from my usual policy in this case, but, briefly, I did not reject the idea flatly but rather offered a counter-proposal consisting of the case-study format that has been used. Mr. Pak considered the idea, liked it, and began to urge the project strongly. After some intervening difficulties I began to contact "young" scholars whom I thought had new and potentially important things to say.

Of the present authors, those contacted during the first round of exploratory discussions were people I knew personally: Professors Constance Cronin, William Longacre, Marlys McClaran, and Roy Wagner. I had known Professors Wagner, Cronin, and Longacre when we overlapped as graduate students at the University of Chicago in the early 1960s and had followed their work since. I knew that their interests and accomplishments were diverse, but that at the same time they shared an underlying concern with rigorous proof and concrete issues that would be of interest to the introductory student as well as to the discipline as a whole. Professor McClaran had been at Chicago as a graduate student during the same time that Wagner, Cronin, Longacre, and I were there, but we had not met. I came to be acquainted with her work at UCLA and became convinced that she represented a necessary next generation building on the "radical," "new" ideas (now nearly twenty years old) of Noam Chomsky and his associates and was returning to some of the older issues that are still outstanding, especially in relating linguistic form to meaning. Since my estimation was shared by several major anthropological linguists, I asked Professor McClaran to represent linguistics in this project.

Discussions with Professors Cronin, Longacre, McClaran, and Wagner convinced me that the project would be generally feasible; I then had the problem of finding a representative of physical anthropology. In this one instance I determined in advance the type of study I wished to include and the type of issues that I wanted to raise—a decision that to some extent avoids current trends. The dominant interests of physical anthropology at the moment seem to lie in genetics, studies of primate social behavior, and to a lesser extent in studies of primate physiology and neuroanatomy. My own feeling is that in the immediate long run—roughly the next twenty-five years—the first two of these will not be as productive as present investments should indicate. I cannot, for example, foresee any major contribution from advances in genetics to our understanding of cultural behavior. At the same time, studies of social organization of primates, like baboons, never had been given a powerful theoretical framework, and when all is said and done there is and will be no obvious connection between baboon bands and human groups unless we learn of it directly from a more advanced understanding of human groups. Neuroanatomical studies will have a more direct contribution, but for the most part I felt that studies in this area were too technical for this text.

Since I did not personally know any suitable representative of the field, I asked Professor F. Clark Howell (presently at the University of California, Berkeley) to suggest someone in physical anthropology who viewed the human body as a "thinking machine" and studied the physiological basis of apparently "cultural" activity. Of those he recommended, Professor Jack Prost seemed the most appropriate, and after discussing the project with him he agreed to join.

The above contributors provided studies representing the four traditional subfields of anthropology and accomplished the main purpose of providing case-studies illustrating the range of ways anthropologists were trying to identify and think through important new problems.

However, I still felt it was necessary to identify gaps in the coverage and find additional contributors to cover other topical areas.

Professor McClaran called my attention to an earlier paper by Professor Bernard Campbell on language acquisition in primates and indicated it would complement her own study. I was familiar with his textbook and felt his treatment in general would complement but not .duplicate Professor Prost's. We eventually discussed the idea and he agreed to join.

I had followed Professor Fred Plog's work for some time, beginning when he was at UCLA. Initially it had seemed too technical for inclusion, but as Professor Longacre's project became clearer it appeared that alone it would not present a wide enough range of new archeological research for an introductory text. After some initial conversations with Professor Plog at his field site in Arizona, it seemed that the fact that Plog and Longacre both worked in the Southwest might provide more insight into archeology in general than studies from disparate areas. The two studies would convey a sense of the different ways a single problem area can be approached by people whose interests and goals are similar. Professor Plog agreed to write on an area that would complement Longacre's chapter, and his interest would raise some issues in ecology and social adaptation that have general anthropological importance.

It also seemed desirable to include a section on culture and personality. The faculty of UCLA is very strong in this area, but those whose interests seemed appropriate were unable to contribute because of other commitments. Their recommendations and those of Roy D'Andrade of the University of California, San Diego, whom I knew to be sensitive to a wide range of issues in other areas, led to the selection of Professor George De Vos.

The initial plan was that all contributors would meet for a few hours at the annual meeting of the American Anthropological Association in New Orleans at the end of November, 1973. It was hoped that prior to that time all would have submitted drafts of their chapters and that we would be able to discuss them. At the time of the meeting, Professor Cronin was in Iran, Professor Campbell was in San Francisco, and only four chapter drafts had been submitted, but six of us did meet with Mr. Pak one evening. Up to this time, no contributor knew more than two or three others, in addition to myself.

It was at this meeting that we discovered that we predominantly represented a Chicago-Oxford/Cambridge-Harvard axis, as much in style and approach as in actual scholastic background. In our discussions, it began to appear that we had, and that the chapters would show, a convergence of interest and orientation. Although no one could predict what it would be, it became apparent that we shared a common commitment toward more technical expertise than most of our forebears, even though at the same time we did not consider that this commitment amounted to an orientation toward "specialization" as opposed to an orientation toward a broad, integrated discipline. It turns out, as the conclusion indicates, that this is only the beginning of the agreement that has emerged.

Murray J. Leaf

# Contents

# Frontiers of Anthropology

## Chapter 1

# The Development of Modern Anthropology

**Murray J. Leaf**

Anthropology is among the youngest academic disciplines. The first university departments of anthropology were founded in the 1890s. By contrast, law, medicine, logic, theology, and languages have been part of university programs since the first European institutions were founded in the beginning of the thirteenth century, and the natural sciences have been part of the program since the time Galileo taught in the sixteenth century. Yet for all its newness, modern anthropology is a thoroughly academic set of concerns, and it cannot be explained or understood apart from its academic context.

Speculation, and even highly sophisticated analysis, on man and society is ancient and worldwide. What is unique about modern academic anthropology is not so much that its ideas on these topics are new or better but that its organization of inquiry is far more massive and efficient than any previously developed. Ideas that have been available for centuries can only now get a thorough test and review.

In addition to a characteristic organization, there may be a characteristic anthropological attitude or style, as many anthropologists like to believe. Certainly, most anthropologists like to think of themselves as fairminded and universalistic, careful to avoid imposing the values and ideas of their own cultures on others and striving for a balanced, comparative perspective that treats each social or cultural viewpoint and idea equally. Whether anthropologists actually succeed in this, however, is best left to the student to judge on his own.

The organization of anthropology as an academic discipline is complex and constantly changing. For purposes of discussion it can be initially divided into two spheres: the first can be called the professional sphere, the second the intellectual.

1

## THE PROFESSIONAL ORGANIZATION OF ANTHROPOLOGY

The professional organization of anthropology is the system of formal positions that individuals occupy in their capacities as anthropologists, either for pay or voluntarily. The professional organization has three main components: (1) academic positions that anthropologists occupy and administer in museums, universities, and some research organizations, (2) positions in professional organizations, generally including relations to various professional journals and other serial publications, and (3) positions on various agencies that provide funds for anthropological research and research-related activities, generally government agencies and private, nonprofit foundations.

### Academic Positions

By far the greatest portion of the personal income of anthropologists comes from salaried positions in universities, colleges, and, secondarily, museums. In most cases, university and college positions are in departments of anthropology, but there are also many programs in anthropology and many joint departments, most often combining sociology and anthropology. Generally, the designation "department" means that that body supervises the awarding of a degree in anthropology. In a college, the degree would be baccalaureate, usually bachelor of arts, while in a university, degrees may also be at the master's or doctoral level.

In North America, the first university department of anthropology was founded in 1887 by Franz Boas at Clark University in Worchester, Massachusetts. Clark was then a very ambitious university attempting to develop in the natural and social sciences. The first degree was a doctorate, given at Clark in 1892 to Alexander Chamberlain, who remained at Clark and continued the program. Boas, who became one of the major figures in anthropology, moved after a number of on-and-off situations to Columbia University. He started teaching a general course in physical anthropology there in 1896 and became Professor of Anthropology, with a department that conferred doctorates, shortly thereafter. This was the first major continuing program. Harvard University had developed a program in anthropology, primarily archeology, just prior to this time, and it too began awarding doctorates. In 1902 the third major department was founded at the University of California at Berkeley, mainly by A. L. Kroeber. In 1927 the fourth of the historically most prominent programs was founded at the University of Chicago, after a number of smaller programs had been initiated. Up to the end of the Second World War, these four departments at Columbia, Harvard, Berkeley, and Chicago produced almost all of the American doctorates in the field. They still tend to predominate in both numbers and acknowledged quality.

In Britain, the programs at Oxford University and the London School of Economics have similar histories and roles.

The years of the Second World War formed a watershed for the growth of academic anthropology, both in terms of numbers of institutions and of persons. Before this time, growth was steady but slow in the United States, the British Commonwealth, and Europe. It was fairly evenly distributed between museums and universities and was primarily in graduate rather than undergraduate studies. During the war, anthropology in Germany was almost wiped out, and in France it was inoperative. But in this same period, for a complex of reasons, interest in anthropology in the United States and the British Commonwealth became much more widespread. After 1945, growth of new departments was almost explosive, especially in colleges and universities and especially at the undergraduate level. Since then, anthropology has become an important course in general undergraduate curricula.

In 1973–1974, eighty-four years after the first program was founded, the American Anthropological Association listed, in its official *Guide to Departments of Anthropology*, 276 institutions in the United States and Canada that had students enrolled in either graduate or undergraduate programs in anthropology. Over 3,800 people were listed as being employed in various capacities in the institutions reported on—departments and museums. Although it must be recognized that some of these were not full-time research anthropologists, the number is as good an approximation of the present size of the discipline in North America as any.

The total number of undergraduate degrees awarded in 1972–1973, according to the *Guide*, was 6,121 (up from 4,057 two years before). There were 886 master's degrees awarded in the same year (up from 821 two years before) and 295 doctorates (up from 209 two years before). This annual output almost certainly amounts to more degrees than were conferred in the first four decades of the century combined. Anthropology has not reached the height of popularity of sociology or psychology, but it has reached a level sufficient to alarm many serious anthropologists who fear premature routinization, erosion of critical standards, and loss of effective communication within the discipline.

Doctorates in anthropology are presently awarded in almost all European countries and in many countries of Asia and Africa. The pattern of growth in Britain, Australia, and South Africa has not been quite as marked as in North America, but it has generally followed along the same lines. France and Latin America also show growth, as does Germany to a lesser degree, but in these countries, for different reasons, lines of development have not followed the North American or Commonwealth patterns.

An anthropologist who is a faculty member at a major institution, especially one with a graduate program, is normally expected to teach, supervise student research, share part of the administrative responsibilities of the department (such as recruiting new faculty, selecting new graduate students, awarding financial aid, and deciding curricular policy) and, by no means least of all, to engage in his own original research and publish his results. This last requirement makes up the much-discussed "publish or perish" syndrome—often cited by students as the cause of indifferent teaching and often defended as the only reasonable way to be sure that what is being taught is current and forward-looking. Whatever the merits of the debate may be, the fact is that when hiring faculty leading departments of anthropology are primarily influenced by the ideas the person has advocated and his standing in the field.

The desire for faculty who are active in research, and to a lesser extent the desire to make teaching programs responsive to professional developments, brings the work of the departments, indirectly, into rather close relationship with the activities of the second major component of the professional organization of academic anthropology, the recognized professional associations.

### Professional Associations

The professional associations that anthropologists belong to have four major functions. They generally own and operate scholarly journals that anthropologists use to communicate their research and ideas to each other. They sponsor annual meetings that serve as the principal site of employment exchange in the field. The annual meetings also provide the opportunity for anthropologists from diverse regions to come together and exchange views and ideas (and renew old acquaintances). And fourth, they represent their membership to the general public and governments. This last function often includes nominating some of their members to serve on policy-making and resource-allocating bodies. In hiring an anthropologist, academic departments generally take into account the roles he may play in any of these capacities in the professional association (or associations) he belongs to.

In view of the close relationship between associations and departments at the present time, it may seem strange that the associations represent a much older form of anthropological organization. In the 1830s there developed a number of local societies in North America concerned with the protection of Indian culture, understanding Indians and getting along with them productively, and seeing that treaties were enforced equitably and justly. One of the first of these was the Algic Society founded by Henry Rowe Schoolcraft in 1832 and based in

Washington, D.C. Similarly, in London, England, the Aborigines Protection Society was founded in 1837, and the Société Ethnologique de Paris was founded in Paris. In 1843, The Ethnological Society was founded in London, and many similar institutions sprang up in other European cultural centers. These were precursors to the present professional associations, which are national and international rather than local and which are more concerned with academic and scientific policy than with legislation and public opinion.

The Algic Society no longer exists, but the American Ethnological Society, founded in 1842 by Albert Gallatin in New York City, is very much alive and publishes an important monograph series. In 1873, the Anthropological Society of Washington, D.C. was founded by Major John Wesley Powell, who had explored the Grand Canyon and founded in 1879 the Bureau of American Ethnology, the first anthropological institution of the United States government and part of the U.S. Geological Survey. The Bureau still exists and is important, though much less now than formerly.

In a series of events beginning about 1898, the American Ethnological Society (AES) merged with an anthropological club in New York City that had been founded by Franz Boas and with the Women's Anthropological Society of America based in the same city. This greatly strengthened the AES, which had become quite inactive due partly to disagreements reflecting abolitionist issues. The AES then sent delegates to a meeting attended by members of the Anthropological Society of Washington, under the auspices of the American Association of the Advancement of Science (which had, and still has, an anthropological section). The arranged purpose of this meeting was to create an anthropological organization of national scope, along the lines of the previously established Chemical and Geological Societies.

In a series of actions at this and several subsequent meetings, the journal of the Anthropological Society of Washington entitled *The American Anthropologist* was reorganized to reflect the interests of a more broadly selected editorial board. It was retitled *American Anthropologist new series*, and the volumes were started with number 1 in 1898. In 1902, Articles of Incorporation for the new society were drawn up and a constitution was adopted. The organization was to be called the American Anthropological Association. Today, it is the largest such body in North America and the world.

At the time it was founded, the Association had eighty-seven members. The American Anthropological Association was not intended to absorb the local societies but rather to provide a wider organization to coordinate some of their activities and communications. In fact, however, the center of anthropological activity rapidly shifted to the national or-

ganization, and active local associations, apart from the recently developing regional adjuncts of the national bodies, became almost nonexistent.
Even the AES is no longer a local body and is now a smaller national
association.

The membership of the American Anthropological Association has
increased at least as rapidly as the number of anthropologists and anthropological programs in universities, colleges, and museums in North America. As of January 1, 1973—seventy-one years after the organization was
founded—the American Anthropological Association had 1,915 fellows,
153 foreign fellows, 2,757 voting members, and 3,520 corresponding members. The grand total of memberships in all classes is 8,345. In the four-
year period from 1967 to 1971, the total membership increased by 34 percent or about 8.5 percent a year. This compares with an average increase
of about 6 percent per year for the period from 1910–1940 and shows
clearly that the postwar acceleration of growth is continuing. In its first
meetings at the turn of the century, all the members of the Association
came together in a single room. Now, the estimated attendance at the
annual meetings is over 3,000, and it is not possible for them to meet in
a single hotel. There is some feeling, however, that the rate of expansion
should begin soon to decrease, chiefly because sources of support for
graduate students have been drastically cut since about 1968.

In Britain and the Commonwealth the predominant anthropological
association, closely paralleling the AAA, is the Royal Anthropological Institute of Great Britain and Ireland, based in London. The Institute was
formed in 1871 when the Ethnological Society of London was amal-
gamated (or reamalgamated) with the Anthropological Society of London (the Ethnological Society previously had broken away from the Anthropological Society in 1863 over racial issues). In 1965, the Institute
combined two previous journals into a single journal entitled *Man*, which
they began to renumber from that year. This journal has the same broad-
stated purposes as the *Anthropologist* and is of very high quality—probably the most prestigious of any—although it should be noted that the
range of viewpoints it represents within the area of cultural anthropology
is somewhat more restricted than those of its American counterpart. In
addition to the journal, the Institute publishes special series of several
sorts, including occasional papers. It also maintains a library that is open
to fellows and dispenses certain prizes, research funds, and fellowships.
Its function of representing anthropology in relation to the British government scientific organizations is precisely parallel to that of the AAA.
At present, the RAI has about 1,500 members.

Despite the national character of the names of both these associations, neither of them restricts its membership on the basis of citizenship.
The AAA is as much Canadian- as United States-oriented, and Austral-

ians, Canadians, or French do not hesitate to join the RAI. Many Americans are fellows of the RAI, just as British and French scholars are members and fellows of the AAA. There are no Latin American, European, African, or Asian anthropological organizations of the prominence and size of the RAI or the AAA, and these two bodies and their journals tend to predominate in the old and new worlds respectively. There are many other bodies with journals, monograph series, occasional papers, and meetings that are often very important regionally or in a particular subfield, and some of these carry materials of high quality and broad importance. Two very important European journals are *Ethnos*, published in the Netherlands, and *L'Homme*, published in Paris, both of which are multilingual. Examples of journals of specialized interest are *Language*, the journal of the Linguistic Society of America (founded by Franz Boas in 1924), *American Antiquity*, the journal of the Society for American Archeology, and *Ethnology*, a journal founded in 1961 and guided by Professor G. P. Murdock and devoted to cultural and social anthropology primarily.

In addition to journals whose contents are determined by theoretical ideas of fields and subfields, anthropologists normally serve on the boards of and write articles for journals concerned with different geographical areas. Many anthropologists, for example, belong to the Association for Asian Studies, hold office in it, and use its journal. In this, they work together with historians, political scientists, sociologists, geographers, literary scholars, and others concerned with the same region. In many respects, an anthropologist defines himself professionally by the professional associations he works in, belongs to, and publishes with.

In addition to the indirect relations between university and college departments of anthropology and the professional associations that come about through the departments' consideration of professional associations in hiring and promotion, there are often more direct relationships that come about through formal institutional affiliation between a university and an association. Many small journals are permanently or semipermanently attached to specific universities. Departments are quite often willing to provide office space and a modicum of salary support for such a periodical in exchange for the recognition it brings and its help in attracting superior students or faculty. Academic presses often attempt to attract major monograph series in an effort to establish their importance and draw attention to less well-known projects. Since the journals normally depend financially on the income from membership dues for their support, they are generally in need of additional aid and often welcome such institutional affiliation.

Departments often try to develop a distinct flavor or style of anthropology, and occasionally a local journal or monograph series can be an important aid to this, both as a means of making the ideas of the group known in the profession at large and by attracting the notice and interest of sympathetic people elsewhere. On occasion, a department will attempt to hire a prominent anthropologist with the object of becoming the home of a journal (or section of a journal) he is responsible for. Conversely an anthropologist committed to a publishing activity will often choose a department in part because of the aid they are willing to supply.

## Funding Agencies

The third type of organization that anthropologists work with is agencies that provide funds for conducting research. These organizations and their policies are at least as dynamic as the professional associations —and probably more so.

Anthropologists commonly expect to draw small amounts of funds from within their university. In addition, they have recourse to a wide variety of programs from a wide variety of national and international, governmental and nongovernmental, sources. Among the best known international sources is the Wenner Gren Foundation for Anthropological Research. Important funds open to citizens or permanent residents of the United States or Canada come from the American Council of Learned Societies (ACLS) and the Social Science Research Council (SSRC). These funds are restricted largely to cultural and social anthropology. The ACLS is nongovernmental, although some of the money it disburses comes from government sources. The American Anthropological Association, as one of the constituent organizations of the ACLS, regularly nominates representatives to it and the SSRC. Among governmental agencies in North America, the United States' National Science Foundation supports major research in all branches of anthropology. Different divisions of the National Institutes of Health have also been a major source of funds for research proper and for graduate student training, although this role has been cut back since about 1968. In Canada, the Canada Council, which reports directly to Parliament, is the predominant supporter of research in all branches of the discipline, and the proportion of projects supported out of those submitted is quite high—funding 55 percent of the projects proposed in 1971–1972, for example. In the major American programs, initial screening eliminates almost half the applications before serious consideration even begins.

In almost all cases, proposals submitted to funding agencies are processed in what is called "peer review," in which, in principle, each proposal is evaluated by knowledgeable specialists in the same area of work. Because funding agencies cannot be permanently staffed by a wide range of experts, the regular staff of the funding organization is usually responsible for locating reviewers and coordinating and evaluating their responses. Most commonly, reviewing is done by one or more panels of prominent anthropologists who are hired by the agencies on a consulting basis. The panelists come together several times a year to review proposals. In addition, proposals are sometimes sent out to two or three anthropologists in the field of specialization for analysis and recommendation. Generally, the procedures that provide the most uniform review for all proposals do not supply the best technical competence for each proposal, and vice versa. Because of differences in the ways agencies try to combine technical competence with uniformity of criteria and simple differences among the personnel of each board, no two agencies will see the same proposal exactly the same way at any given time.

From the time he is a graduate student, applying for funds is a major concern of any serious anthropologist. Service on the panels of funding agencies, by the same token, is among the most serious responsibilities a senior anthropologist can have.

## THE INTELLECTUAL ORGANIZATION OF ANTHROPOLOGY

Departmental decisions and the actions of the professional associations and funding agencies all have reference not only to each other but also to the fourth type of organization of anthropology—the intellectual organization. This is often described by anthropologists as the field as a whole which in turn is divided into subfields or subdisciplines.

The intellectual divisions of anthropology could be described by one current group of scholars as *ideal types*. Others could describe them as a *mythological charter*. However, whichever term one uses, the main point is that even though the divisions are often spoken of as if they segregated people, they are in fact acted upon as divisions among problems and theoretical persuasions.

The intellectual divisions of the field provide one of the conceptual tools that departments use to plan their programs with a sense of completeness and comprehensiveness and that professional organizations and funding agencies use to define and communicate their aims and purposes.

As one would expect from a set of categories that is used primarily to divide tasks and responsibilities from one another, the concept of the totality—the whole field of anthropology—is not particularly well developed. About the only definition of the field that most anthropologists can be counted on to accept is the one imbedded in the etymology of the word *anthropology* itself: from *anthropos*, Greek for man, and *logos*, a Greek word with a long history including the idea of form, scientific law, and study. Anthropology, literally, is the study of man.

This definition strikes many anthropologists as too broad, for it fails to distinguish the way anthropologists study man from the way psychologists, sociologists, economists, and biologists do. While there is some sense to this objection, it seems obvious that one of the most distinguishing characteristics of the anthropological approach is precisely its broadness. Some anthropologists take an approach much like that of sociologists, others like those of psychologists, economists, or biologists. Yet all their efforts ultimately are more akin to each other than to any other field. The desire to approach man on a broad front, integrating many perspectives, and to avoid focusing on one aspect to the exclusion of others, is a persistent characteristic of anthropology that marks it off from other social and behavioral sciences.

At the present time, it is generally accepted that anthropologists consider the field as a whole to be divided into four subfields: physical anthropology, archeology, cultural and social anthropology, and linguistics.

### Physical Anthropology

Physical anthropology is the study of man in his biological aspect—the study of human anatomy, physiology, and the biological bases of behavior. There are two major divisions within physical anthropology. Comparative morphology (from the Greek *morph*, meaning form) is concerned with the form and function of the human body, its evolution, and its patterns of growth. The second division, designated by the terms *human genetics* or *human population genetics*, is concerned with the biological mechanism of reproduction and with models of the transmission of genetic materials in human populations over time. The division between the two areas of study corresponds to and reflects gaps in our theoretical knowledge.

At one time, comparative morphology was the most characteristic interest of anthropology. It was this interest that marked anthropology off from other types of evolutionary concerns in the later nineteenth century and distinguished it from history, natural history, linguistics, and sociology. In much of Europe even today, the word *anthropology* conjures up immediate visions of calipers, measuring tapes, and cases of human skulls. Such implements and artifacts came into prominence as part of an effort to define the races of mankind and to state their historical and evolutionary relationships.

During the first part of the nineteenth century there was great interest in the question of whether modern varieties of humans all descended from one or several ancestral groups. This set of concerns had a clear relevance to the morality of slavery and colonial domination and to the dispute between monogenist (single original population) and polygenist (multiple original populations) positions. After the widespread acceptance of Darwin and Wallace's conceptions of evolution by natural selection (published in 1858), interest in the polygenist position faded. In the course of this development, most scholars came to believe that the broad and obvious differences between the major human races reflected different evolutionary histories—diverging from some original ancestral group under different adaptive conditions. It was believed that knowing the evolutionary circumstances that caused the differences between races would explain the physical form of the major races and that the form in turn would be shown to be connected with habits, learning abilities, and eventually even cultural forms and predilections. The concern with calipers and tapes was part of the underlying effort throughout this whole sequence of arguments to come to agreement on what the larger races actually were and to refine the analysis by making more exact measurements of racial features and defining more specific racial types in order to relate them to more specific histories and environmental settings. Since most estimates of the total age of human history (projecting beyond the estimated ages of then-known human fossils) ranged between five and, as E. B. Taylor said, "tens of thousands of years" (1911: 115), it seemed that such projection on the basis of measurements of modern and historical human remains might extend back to the very beginning. In the context of this hope or plan, a major reason for the concern with body structures was that such structures were the best ways to connect the obvious modern races with the older types that in most cases were known only from skeletal remains. At first, the task seemed to be to connect skeletal races with races defined by the more common marks: skin color, hair form, size, and general appearance. Soon, however, it became clear that it was almost impossible to define a race by skeletal form.

While a few indices turned out to be relatively stable (like the cephalic index, the ratio of head width to head length), most of the effort to find skeletal indices of race led only to more disputes, and the finer the measures were drawn, the more it turned out that the exact races corresponded to no reasonable intuitive populations, coherent in space or time. This kind of result might have led eventually to death by exhaustion (although one still finds some measurement going on), but three developments at the turn of the century robbed the activity of almost all of its theoretical basis and importance and brought it to an abrupt halt.

The most anthropological of these developments was an extended criticism of racial ideas by Franz Boas, beginning about 1899. Part of this argument was based on a study of immigrant populations in New York City, with a view toward the then current discussions pertaining to laws to limit immigration into the United States. His findings, using the standard measurements, were that all children of different immigrant populations changed from the parental type and that all changes were toward the American national averages (implying that the direction of change was not controlled by racial inheritance). Further, some of the changes were so great that according to some criteria children could be classified in different races from their parents. Boas concluded from this that environmental factors were more important than any purely hereditary factors and that studies of environmental influences had to take precedence over evolutionary reconstruction. *Nurture* was more important than *nature*. Others went further and saw in his work a reduction to absurdity of the whole effort to find progressively finer and more exact racial characteristics and even of studies of race in any form.

Boas' conclusions in America and the implications they had for the concept of race were supported in Britain by the results of the Torres Straits Expedition, organized and led by A. C. Haddon in 1898. This was the world's first scientific expedition that was purely anthropological. When it set out from England, one of its major purposes was to find possible physiological or "racial" bases of cultural differences. The Torres Strait separates Australia and New Guinea, and the natives of its islands lived with a very rudimentary cultural "tool-kit" and appeared to be among the most primitive human groups in the world. It was hoped that by measuring the reaction times, reflex times, discriminating abilities and the like of these natives, some physiological correlates of their cultural level might be found. The study was carried out with great thoroughness and scientific rigor. But it was found, as for example in the work of C. S. Myers, that "the sense perceptions of the Islanders hardly differed from those of Europeans, and that differences were personal rather than racial" (Penniman 1965:99). In addition to Myers, Haddon was accompanied by W. H. R. Rivers and C. G. Seligman who became two of the most influential teachers of the next generation of British anthropologists —the generation which radically separated physiology from cultural studies.

The second development was the rediscovery, in 1900, of the work of Gregor Mendel on heredity. In 1865, after eight years of experimental work crossbreeding common peas, Mendel had published a paper describing his discovery that certain inherited characteristics (1) were clearly independent of other inherited characteristics, (2) appeared in fixed ratios within a population, and (3) clearly *were* controlled by mechanisms in the reproductive apparatus (rather than the environment) and once lost would not be spontaneously recreated. The characteristics he had in mind were, for example, whether a pea had wrinkled or smooth seeds or was tall or dwarf. In crossing varieties that otherwise bred true, Mendel found that certain characteristics like tallness were what he called *dominant*. A cross from a tall and dwarf pea would produce a second generation of tall peas only. But as the seeds from this generation in turn were collected and sown, it was seen to produce a third generation of peas that grew dwarf and tall in the ratio of 1 to 3. The new dwarfs would in turn breed true, but the tall peas of the third generation did not breed true. Some did, producing all tall offspring, but others produced dwarfs and tall peas in the ratio, again, of 1 to 3. Counting the tall parents that bred true and those that acted like the second generation hybrids, Mendel found that the ratio was 1 to 2.

Mendel brought his results into a single, coherent pattern with the idea that each characteristic of each individual plant is controlled by two factors, but that in sexual reproduction the factors are separated and each *gamete* (the sex cell, a grain of pollen in the case of the male pea) carries only one. Then one gamete from the male and one from the female combine to produce the new characteristic in the new individual. *Pure strains* are those where each individual has only one type of gamete per trait, so any male gamete will form the same combination with any female gamete. Hybrid strains are produced by systematically putting the pollen from one pure strain on the flowers of another (or some similar process), so all hybrid individuals have one trait from each strain at each point. If one trait is *dominant* (it shows its characteristics in the adult plant when combined with an unlike gamete) and the other *recessive* (it does not show its characteristic in the combined form), all will exhibit only the dominant trait. But in their offspring, because half their gametes will represent each characteristic, there will be the same kind of distribution we would have if we took an urn filled with black and white balls in equal numbers and grabbed them out two at a time. One-fourth would be the pure strain of the recessive (two dwarf gametes, for example, or two black balls), two-fourths would be mixed (one black and one white, or one tall and one short), and one-fourth would be pure dominant (white or tall).

These results give Mendel's observed ratios. Since all the individuals that receive either or both dominant gametes will show the dominant trait, the ratio of plants with recessive to dominant characteristics will be one-fourth to three-fourths, or 1 to 3. But since among the carriers of the dominant characteristic only those with both gametes showing the dominant trait will breed true, the ratio of those that will not breed true to those that will is two-fourths to one-fourth, or 2 to 1. Mendel called the particles of inheritance *characters* ("*Merkmal*," Sturtevent 1967:12). His theory, in effect, was of the control of inheritance (1) by the reproduction and random independent assortment of characters, (2) given that two characters control each contrasting characteristic of an individual, but (3) that only one of the pair appears in each sex cell that the individual produces, and that (4) combines with the sex cell of another individual to produce a new individual.

In 1865, Mendel did not know what physical objects might correspond to his characters (later renamed genes) except that they presumably were contained within the reproductive cells. Shortly after he was rediscovered, a series of workers filled out the picture dramatically. A connection was made between the predicted properties of genes and the observable activity of chromosomes, long bands of material within cells which evidently split themselves lengthwise when a cell divided. From there a further connection was made between the characters and very small chemical bands upon the chromosomes that themselves split when the chromosomes divided. Since there were only a few dozen chromosomes in most cells, but very large numbers of such bands, the bands became the natural candidates for the role of Mendel's genes. By 1933, when Thomas Hunt Morgan received the Nobel Prize in Medicine for his work with inheritance among fruit flies, the actual chemical and physical basis of Mendelian distributions of characteristics was known.

In one sense, Mendelism showed how Darwin's natural selection could work. Genes that produced desirable characteristics would stay in a population and be passed on, and genes that produced characteristics which prevented their carriers from reproducing their kind would be reduced in a population. But in another way, this set of ideas completely changed the frame of reference and emphasis in evolutionary study and superseded several of Darwin's basic assumptions. Mendel's idea of the discontinuity of traits—the lack of intermediate types—was flatly in contradiction to Darwin's idea of a kind of natural tendency for intermediate types to develop in each generation. This tendency was the basis of his conception of variability of species form and the variability it produced was in turn precisely what he saw natural selection as operating upon. In addition, Mendel's sharp distinction between the outward physical form and the underlying genetic form of a feature made Darwin's type of anatomically based comparison a secondary rather than a primary form of analysis.

After Mendel, genetics properly became more an aspect of biochemistry than of comparative morphology. Conversely, comparative morphology of humans and their evolutionary kin became detached from genetics and placed in a cultural and behavioral setting concerned more with the relation of the form of the organism to its behavior and environment than to its genetic constitution. In a way, the outcome of the acceptance of Mendel's ideas reinforced the conclusions of Boas, driving a second wedge between the study of the development of biological races and species on the one hand and the study of organic form and its relation to culture on the other. The study of "nature" became concerned most strictly with what are called *genotypes*, and the study of "nurture" became a major part of the study of the developed, physical *phenotypes*.

The third development began with the discovery of radioactivity in 1896 which radically increased nineteenth-century conceptions of the age of the earth. Before this time, Lord Kelvin had calculated that, based on known rates of cooling by radiation of heat into space from a molten state, the earth could not be more than twenty million years old (although geologists and biologists held out for much longer times). This made known history a very large fraction of the total earth history— about one three-thousandths. It followed from this that prehistoric human and animal remains were relatively close in absolute time to historic periods. Kelvin subsequently revised his estimates upward to as much as 200 million years, but this is still far less than present estimates. The discovery of radioactivity meant that the earth had been heating itself throughout its life even while it was using heat through radiation. Therefore a rate of cooling alone could not be used to estimate its age. Ultimately, corrections for heating from internal radiation led to an estimate of about 3.3 billion years, with the absolute age of known history staying the same and therefore becoming an insignificant proportion of the total. This meant that the human fossil remains that had been placed geologically in the upper Pleistocene era (the "ice age" of periodic glaciations) were not thousands of years old but rather many tens of thousands. Newer finds, lower (earlier) in the Pleistocene and possibly at its beginning, could on the new scale be easily two million years old. The original branching-off of the human stock, naturally, would have to be much earlier still. This made it impossible to believe that known associations between racial types and historical cultures had any evolutionary significance or could be used to infer anything about the original state of man or his culture. It became clear that the evolution of biological species occurred on a much larger time scale than the evolution of distinct cultures and states, and, therefore, understanding the processes of one type of development could not necessarily lead to understanding of the others.

With these three developments, the post-Darwinian hope of an all-encompassing evolutionary explanation of human history faded into oblivion, at least so far as leading thinkers were concerned, and comparative anatomy for a while was reduced to a relatively unimportant area of investigation.

In the 1930s, 40s and 50s, comparative anatomy was an area of interest restricted primarily to what is now called *paleoanthropology*—literally *old anthropology*, or the study of ancient man. "Ancient" in this case did not mean what it previously had meant—the study of such types as Cro-Magnon (a modern type) or Neanderthal or of time levels believed to be just beyond ten thousand years ago. It meant, rather, the study of what we might easily call "pre-men," like Australopithecus (literally "south-ape") or Sinjanthropus, often broadly classed as *Homo erectus* and distinguished *as a species* from *Homo sapiens.* The remains of these types are from 350,000 to the above mentioned possible two million years old. At these time levels, the physical differences between one group and another and between these groups and modern man are large enough so that criticism of the over-fine racial measurements does not apply with great force. Gross anatomical comparisons—of tooth shapes, head size, and general skeletal form—are generally considered quite adequate for determining their interrelationships, even in the absence of knowledge of how such differences come about genetically. The problem is not in distinguishing groups of men like modern races from each other, but rather in distinguishing pre-apes from pre-men—differences at the species or genus level rather than the racial or varietal level.

Further, because it is impossible to recover genetically simple features, like blood types, from the kinds of remains that are found, there is no method other than that of comparative morphology to fall back on when reconstructing evolutionary history, so the method has to retain respectability.

In the last two decades, there has been an expansion of research in comparative morphology, accompanied by some important revisions of the basic orientation of theory in this area. The reorientation reflects increased knowledge of human development and manages to combine in an interesting way some of the old interest in evolutionary reconstruction with the Mendelian ideas of the discreteness of genetic characters.

The new approach in comparative morphology is sometimes called the *biological systems approach* or the *functional* or *functional systems approach.* Basically, it involves abandoning the habit of thinking of bodies as divided into different classes of tissue—the skeleton, the musculature, the nervous systems, etc.—and thinking of them instead as functional groups of muscles-plus-bone-plus nerves and transport mechanisms. In humans, the hips and legs make one such major system, the shoulders and arms another, and the head another. One reason for separating the parts of the body this way is that they actually appear to have evolved separately system by system in time; for humans the shoulders were first to attain their present form, then the hips, and last the head. Another reason, related to the first, is that the final shape of the bone in one system in any living individual is strongly related to the action of muscles and several other tissues around it as it grows, and muscle growth in turn is related to bone insertion and use. In short, the morphology of each specific unit of each kind of tissue is influenced most directly by the other types of tissue immediately around it and much less by similar tissues elsewhere in the body. These influences go system by system, with considerable independence between systems.

The biological systems approach has been employed in an increasing range of studies of the relationship between human bodily form and behavior and nonhuman bodily form and behavior. These include experimental and behavioral studies of apes and other primates, as well as studies of many nonprimate species. They blend into ethology, the general study of animal behavior. Studies of modern apes have been especially important in both laboratory and field contexts. Such studies cast light on what the behavior and social organization of early hominid forms must have been. From there, they help us understand in one of the most direct ways possible the biological basis of human development and behavior. Some of the important questions pursued in this connection have been: What is the relationship between head position, head growth, and brain size in man and apes? What is the relationship between the brain and behavior in man and apes? How do apes actually behave, and how and what do they learn? What kind of movements and actions in the human body do we need to attribute to cultural learning and what can we find to be physiologically determined? What have been the relationships between physiological development, diet, and patterns of geographical movement in human populations as we reconstruct them? When did humans become strongly carnivorous, unlike most great apes? When did humans become territorially wide-ranging, in contrast with the narrowly restricted territorial habits of the larger apes?

The purpose of these questions is no longer to find the evolutionary basis of cultural differences, but rather to understand (1) what aspects of human behavior can be attributed to the form of the human organism, (2) to what extent the form of the human organism represents a special adaptation to the use of language and other cultural tools, and (3) to find a better and more exact sense of the way the capacities for culture that are built into the organism are actually utilized. By understanding what aspects of behavior do not require or are not susceptible to cultural control, we can better understand where cultural learning fits into the larger behavioral picture. By understanding what cultural learning does *not* do, we can focus more sharply on the complementary area where it does operate. This will add great precision to our knowledge and understanding of culture itself, as well as to human physiology and its immediate consequences.

The theory of anthropological genetics is the same as that of population genetics in biology. Physical anthropologists concentrate on developing the implications of genetic theory in order to better understand human adaptation and development. They have been concerned with a wide range of problems, from the influence of culturally significant patterns of marriage choice on the patterns of genetic combinations in a population to the dynamics of inheritable diseases and immunities. Such studies have shown, for example, that variations in skin color and body form that exist between high and low castes in some parts of India, variations that early writers often attributed to different racial origins, can result entirely from culturally defined selective breeding within a single population (identifying light skin with beauty and matching beauty in marriage).

With respect to immunology, investigations of sickle cell anemia, a hereditary disease, have illustrated the way in which a genetic trait can give a population an advantage in surviving in a specific environment. Sickle cell anemia is controlled by a single recessive gene at a single locus. When two recessive genes occur side by side (call it $ss$), the result is sickle cell anemia, a fatal condition in which red blood cells are small and sickle-shaped and unable to carry adequate oxygen for the body's needs. When two normal dominant genes are found at this locus ($nn$), the blood cells (hemoglobin cells) are normal. People with normal blood are susceptible to malarial attack and in areas where this disease is present a significant percentage of those with normal blood will be killed by the disease before they reproduce. When the recessive gene occurs with a normal gene ($ns$), the blood cells are not quite normal but not dangerously anemic. Such persons have considerable immunity to malarial attack, and roughly 24 percent more individuals of this type will reproduce in each generation than individuals with normal blood. As this works out, in nonmalarial situations the sickle cell gene is rapidly reduced to very low levels in the population because of the death of those affected with the anemia, although a small reservoir of the genes remains in the $ns$ individuals. But in malarial areas, because of the rapid diminution of $nn$ individuals at equal or greater rates than the $ss$ individuals, the gene builds back up to high levels (approaching 50 percent) in the population in a few generations. If such genes are confined to a single cultural group, that group—and the culture—would have an obvious survival advantage in malarial situations apart from whatever the culture's intrinsic properties might be (see Allison 1954).

Such studies continue the important movement away from the early type of evolutionary theory, and from the early concept of race, toward a fuller understanding of the dynamic range of phenomena that can affect human biological development. Yet despite this and the fact that the theory of genetics is probably the most sophisticated and well-developed of any anthropological theory, the results of this branch of research have not been particularly exciting to anthropologists in general and, for example, not nearly as exciting as the recent studies of primate behavior and social organization. This occurs because the genetic studies do not have direct implications for other types of studies.

Selective mating, with its consequent changes in gene pool configurations, is undoubtedly interesting in its own right, but it does not make any clear contribution to a social explanation of marriage rules. Nor, conversely, do social studies of marriage rules have any clear implications for the genetic studies—in fact, quite the opposite. Social analysts are now inclined to regard social marriage rules as not directly affecting or controlling concrete individual behavior, but rather as providing important "symbolic" concepts. It is not at all clear what social mechanisms a genetic model of selective mating would correspond to, to say nothing of inherited biological immunity to diseases.

Eventually, the situation will have to be corrected. But for the present, genetic problems are cut off from other types of physical problems and from other branches of anthropology by a wall of unknowns that people are only beginning to cut through.

## Archeology

The second major group of anthropological problems is archeology, literally the study of ancient objects, but understood more precisely to be the study of remains of former human communities and activities.

In the first half of the nineteenth century, archeology developed as a branch of classical history. Then, after Darwin, but while the whole of human history was still thought to be on the order of 20,000 to 40,000 years old, archeology became closely intertwined with studies in comparative morphology. Now, however, archeology and physical anthropology only overlap for the very earliest time levels—the paleonanthropology mentioned above. At these early time levels, there was little regional variation in cultural traditions that was not associated with variation in physical type. Also since there are comparatively few types of cultural artifacts, skeletal remains loom relatively large in the archeological inventory. There is thus little purpose in separating cultural artifacts from physical ones, so they are studied in a package.

For more recent time levels, however, beginning about 100,000 years ago just after the middle of the geological period of recurrent glaciations called the Pleistocene, this picture changes rapidly. The number and variety of cultural artifacts increases greatly, and the changes in the groupings of artifacts from place to place and time to time no longer varies with changing physical remains. Professor S. Washburn describes the general situation by saying that in the earlier cases we have instances of human *culture* while in the latter we have human *cultures*—distinct

and independent cultural traditions. This point is added to purely anatomical considerations which some physical anthropologists and paleoan-
thropologists follow when they group the early remains as one genus (not
just species) and the later as another—called *Homo erectus* and *Homo
sapiens* respectively (see Campbell 1966: Ch. 11). The modern physical
type—whether classed as genus or species is really unimportant—is therefore not associated with any one cultural type but rather with a generalized ability to have *and to alter* culture; and culture, by the same
token, develops to a point of complexity where it assumes its own special
kind of autonomy. That fact of human evolution necessarily creates a
separation between the study of modern man from an anatomical point
of view and from a cultural point of view. The distinction between cultural dynamics and physiology and between physical anthropological
studies and archeology becames more pronounced as one moves closer
to the present.

Archeologists working on the period of about 70,000 to 30,000 years
ago when the first modern physical forms and distinct cultural traditions
appear are often competent in anatomical analysis and include detailed
anatomical descriptions in their reports when such materials are found.
Archeologists working in early farming sites in the Middle East generally
do not pay much attention to physical analysis and do not include detailed descriptions of skeletal remains in their reports. They worry about
the sex and social status of burials, for example, but not cranial capacity,
dental growth patterns, muscle insertions, gross estimated body weights,
suture patterns and the like—which generally fall to more specialized
physical anthropologists if they are of concern at all. There are no detailed anatomical descriptions of the differences between Assyrians and
early Hittites, and no interest in making such comparisons. Perhaps more
to the point, the amount of material recovered at these time levels is so
great that one is forced to specialize. There is simply more culture to be
studied when investigating a more recent site, such as Jericho for example, than when studying an early cave shelter. Given that one must
specialize, the lack of relationship between physiology and culture makes
choosing between cultural and anatomical studies a likely first way to
narrow one's interests. In addition to concentrating on cultural rather
than anatomical remains, archeologists generally specialize by time level,
geographical area, and sometimes by the type of cultural system with
which they are concerned.

The same set of developments that separated the problems of physical anthropology into those of comparative anatomy and genetics, separated physical anthropology as a whole from archeology. The nineteenth-
century evolutionary theories that assumed a short total chronology for
human development necessarily saw a close relationship between schemes

for classifying cultural remains into developmental stages and theories of racial development. As it became clear that cultural and physical developments occur on very different time scales and that most cultural development has occurred in a period of little obvious physical change in the human organism, the broad evolutionary scheme failed to justify archeological research. By the 1920s and 1930s, the evolutionary idea of societies as expressions of racial characteristics ceased to be related to the everyday problems leading academic archeologists had in interpreting their materials (although it did hang on longer in some regional traditions—as in the archeology of the American Southwest). In an important sense, this left archeology temporarily without a general theory for organizing its activities and for relating its results to other areas of research.

In practice, the absence of a theoretical framework did not greatly bother archeologists, and they have not made an effort to create alternative views of the reasons for social development and differentiation until quite recently. There were a number of reasons for this. In the first place, there were a great many important questions that more or less asked themselves and would have had to be answered regardless of what one's concept of an explanation was, or of one's idea of what had to be explained.

Archeology of the New World—North and South America and most of the surrounding oceans—was only developed in the last eighty-odd years. In approaching it, it was necessary to make a basic determination of what came before what, and what came after what. The way to do this was self-evident—by digging and seeing what was over what, and what was under, and then by coordinating the results over the widest possible area. Many kinds of objects had to be placed in such sequences —not only all the great ruins that were known or found ranging from the American Southeast to the Andes and all smaller ruins that commanded major attention (many are still untouched), but also the workaday objects that link one ruin to another: sculptural objects in different traditions, ritual objects, tools, fabrics, written materials, and, most of all, ceramics. In order to classify each object, it is necessary to reconstruct how it was made and, in the case of writing, what it means. Obviously, the amount of work involved was and is enormous, and even today it is far from finished. But it is easy to see how archeologists could reasonably have been content to discuss general and specific taxonomies and to let "more scientific" issues ride while the basic outlines of the chronology were being worked out.

The situation in the Old World was much the same. Although work had started there in the early nineteenth century, especially involving the deciphering of hieroglyphics on the Rosetta stone in 1821 and of cuneiform script in 1858, it had mainly concentrated on monumental sites like Mesopotamian temples, great walled cities, Roman and Greek ceremonial centers, and Egyptian pyramids. This is what is meant by saying archeology in this period was a branch of classics. The life of ordinary peoples was virtually unknown, to say nothing of primitive peoples, and it was not of interest. These areas became topics of concern when evolutionary theory became popular and continued to be of interest once work had started. Because the classical work was so restricted in time and space, the basic groundwork of establishing a chronology and relating the major forms of artifacts to it in this century turned out to be much the same in the Old World as in the New. In some ways, in fact, it was even greater and more pressing. The Old World has greater density of artifacts and the stages of its prehistoric development are more numerous and complex because its population was always denser and its technology more diverse. This work too is by no means complete. Important new discoveries that change our conceptions of the major lines of development and paths of influence are made almost every year.

In the mid-1950s most archeologists began to recognize a need for some theory other than lists of type-categories for artifacts and static cultural taxonomies. Some general conception of cultural development was again sought as a way to enable archeologists to digest the massive information on chronological sequences that was accumulating. In general, recent work in this area has followed two lines of development, which have not been mutually exclusive.

The first development has been a shift away from the interests in styles that dominated the chronology-building and toward a habit of speaking of societies and their productive systems. Taxonomies such as formative, preclassic, classic, and postclassic, which were logically circular schemes primarily concerned with classifying decorative motifs as they appeared in stratified sites, gave way to concepts like "the agricultural revolution" and "the urban revolution" that indicate a major shift in the way people organize themselves to exploit their environment, to work, and to live. The synthesizing work of Henri Frankfort (Middle East) and V. G. Child (Near East and Europe), in the late 1930s and early 1940s, have served as the model and inspiration for such theories, along with some more recent work in ethnology done under the label of "cultural ecology" (Steward 1957; Sahlins and Service 1962).

The second major theme has been in refining analytical methods to avoid arbitrary interpretation and to exploit more fully the material from a given site and a given amount of labor. Part of the motivation for this has come from the accumulation of contradictory interpretations of given sets of materials in earlier studies. Part has come from a widespread revulsion at the needless destructiveness in many excavations of major sites where large amounts of useful and crucial information were by-passed in a rush to get spectacular artifacts for museums or private collections that later turned out to be worth little once the circumstances of their recovery were lost. In archeology, as in all types of scientific inquiry, a sense of context is a sense of importance. However, archeology is unlike many fields in that there is little opportunity to correct mistakes in data collection.

There has developed an interest in carefully controlled statistical designs for research, largely with the aid of electronic computers. Modern archeologists no longer look for the most promising part of a site and burrow down into it or trench across it. In fact, they avoid doing so. They view a site as a region and try to arrange a minimal amount of excavation, on the basis of statistical sampling, that will give a full picture of the range of activities that occurred in the region and of the remains these activities have left. In deep sites, the sampling must be not only spatial but temporal, and this is not always easy to think out in advance.

Statistical thinking carries through from the research design into the description of the research results. Whereas formerly a site was characterized by certain artifacts that seemed to mark it off from other sites—like certain, but not all, pottery types or tool types—there is now an increasing tendency to think of a site in terms of the frequency of the types of artifacts recovered, of correlations between types of artifacts, and even of patterns of frequencies. At the same time, it is now clearly recognized that different artifact types alone, or even different frequencies, do not necessarily mark the differences between different cultures or groups. They may (if they are not chosen so arbitrarily that they mean nothing at all) mark only different but interrelated areas of a domestic unit or village—like the difference between a shopping area and a residential neighborhood.

### Social and Cultural Anthropology

The third major division of anthropology is the hardest of all to describe, principally because its major theoretical debates are concerned with the problems of saying what its subject matter actually is—and few seem to agree. It will follow majority sentiment, but satisfy no one completely, if we call this field as a whole *ethnology* and consider cultural anthropology and social anthropology as two partially distinct subdivisions of it.

Ethnology is concerned with individual human beings as social or cultural actors and thinkers and communicators rather than as physical organisms. It focuses on cultures or societies as systems of rules, rights, roles, and established relationships rather than as systems of physical remains of productive modifications of the natural environment with which archeologists are involved. At present, there is no logical relationship between ethnologists' conceptions of individual human beings and the conceptions of physical anthropologists and no clear relationship between ethnological conceptions of social groups and those of archeologists. Although ethnologists of all kinds, physical anthropologists, and archeologists all have opinions on these topics, the opinions do not agree and are not based on the same assumptions. To a large extent, the difference between their respective assumptions in approaching the general topics is the measure of the distance between these three subfields.

The modern distinctness of ethnology from the other three major subfields is in part a product of the same developments that separated physical anthropology from archeology—the events that destroyed the general concept of race as a unifying principle. The people who became the first ethnologists, cultural anthropologists, or social anthropologists responded to these developments in a very specific way. Unlike physical anthropologists, they repudiated biological influences in principle (not just race in the old sense), and unlike archeologists they repudiated historical study in principle (not just attempts at universal evolutionary reconstruction). They turned instead to the tradition that was called sociology in Europe in the nineteenth century, especially as this tradition was represented by the works of Herbert Spencer, August Comte, and a number of less philosophical writers including Max Weber, George Simmel, and Emile Durkheim. From these men, in different versions, they took the idea of society or culture as what philosophers would call a "thing in itself." The idea was that while a society was composed of individuals, it was not a mere aggregate. A social group had an organizing principle of its own, over and above its members, that was not reducible to its members, in the same way that a living organism was not reducible to its chemical substances alone and a chemical substance was not reducible to its physical elements alone (in their view).

Spencer called the special principle "civilization," and described it as "superorganic"—meaning "over the individual organism." He considered its study to be more general and encompassing than the study of the more specific levels of phenomena that made it up.

Comte called the principle "social" and coined the term *sociology*. He considered sociology a more specific and exact science than physics, chemistry, or biology because while all phenomena were physical, most were chemical, and many but not all of these in turn were biological, only a few very specific combinations of these took place in forms that were also social as well—in societies.

Some anthropologists followed each view, but it is easy to see that the agreements between them far outweighed the disagreements. Social and cultural anthropology proper were created when these sociological ideas were applied to the analysis of primitive communities that anthropologists had already been developing, replacing evolutionary ideas as the general framework. Where nineteenth-century anthropologists had looked at tribal organization in terms of the general level of development of its people (as racial/biological types), social anthropologists looked at it in terms of its own form of social organization, and cultural anthropologists looked at in terms of its own cultural patterns or cultural integration.

For the most part, the term *culture* was preferred by early anthropologists in Germany and America, while the term *society* was preferred in England and France. There were many small differences between cultural and social anthropology and a few large differences in emphasis, but for the most part they were two parallel developments trying to cope with the same changes in the overall intellectual climate of opinion in roughly the same way. By the mid-1930s, the positions of both cultural and social anthropology had crystalized substantially to the form they have today.

The dominant American position was represented in the opening paragraphs of Robert Lowie's *The History of Ethnological Theory* (1937):

> By culture we understand the sum total of what an individual acquires from his society—those beliefs, customs, artistic norms, food habits, and crafts which come to him not by his own creative activity but as a legacy from the past, conveyed by formal or informal education.
>
> . . . ethnography . . . is that part of anthropology (in the English sense of the word, the whole science of man) which is not primarily concerned with races as biological divisions of *Homo sapiens* and does not interest itself in the psychology of individuals except insofar as it reflects or influences society. (1937:3)

Lowie went on to indicate that when he considers the "raw facts" for "orderly arrangement and interpretation," "the descriptive ethnographer turns theoretical ethnologist"—that is, ethnology is theoretically oriented ethnography, so their subject matter is the same (p. 14). Lowie construed the "sum total" as a single whole. Lowie's work was rather like the origin myths of many primitive societies, and for that matter of many modern groups: in saying how cultural anthropology or ethnology arose, it defined what it *was* and created something where nothing had been before. It was really theory in the guise of history.

A comparable position for social anthropology was stated by A. R. Radcliffe-Brown in a 1935 article entitled "On the Concept of Function in Social Science" in the *American Anthropologist*. It began by recalling the ideas of Comte and Durkheim in saying that "The concept of function applied to human societies is based on an analogy between social life and organic life." It then discussed Durkheim's concepts of "needs" that a social institution fulfilled. Radcliffe-Brown argued that such needs were fulfilled in the institution's function and further that such needs or functions were to be construed as "necessary conditions for existence" of the institution to be "discovered by the proper kind of inquiry." This last phrase implies (what he elsewhere spelled out clearly) that the needs were to be identified by the analyst alone and had nothing to do with the felt or perceived needs of the people in the system. The full scheme of surrounding ideas was that:

> The concept of function as here defined thus involves the notion of a *structure* consisting of *a set of relations* amongst *unit entities,* the continuity of the structure being maintained by a life-process made up of the *activities* of the constituent units. (Reprinted in Radcliffe-Brown 1956:180)

Of course, describing function by linking it to other terms only forces us to ask what they, in turn, mean. Radcliffe-Brown tried to explain this in two subsequent essays, one in 1940 and the last, probably neatest, statement in 1952.

The 1940 article, entitled "On Social Structure," was delivered as the Presidential Address to the Royal Anthropological Institute and reprinted in its journal. In the article, he described social structures as the relations between persons. The idea of a person, in turn, he connected to the idea of a "social personality." Echoing Lowie, he made a radical separation between this social person and a biological individual:

> Human beings as individuals are objects of study for physiologists and psychologists. The human being as a person is a complex of social relationships. (1940:194)

This, of course, makes a "person" an aspect of structure, and, conversely structure is a set of relations among persons.

The circularity of these definitions—each term relying only on the others—was never resolved. On the contrary, it was defended in Radcliffe-Brown's 1952 continuation of the discussions with the philosophical idea that all scientific theories were necessarily circular—a "set of analytical concepts, which should be clearly defined in reference to concrete reality, and which should be logically connected" (1952:1). Abstract discussions established the concepts and their logical connections, while case studies, in this view, linked the theories to reality. This last was always a very weak part of the whole scheme.

In the same 1952 discussion, the "life process" idea was brought up again and defined in such a way as to make clear that it too applied only to abstract social structures and not to biological individuals. The process of social life in "regions" was described as the unit of investigation, but because it was too large and complex for direct description, the analyst had to abstract certain recurrent "forms" ("discoverable regularities") from it. On this basis, Radcliffe-Brown redefined "social anthropology . . . as the comparative theoretical study of the forms of social life amongst primitive peoples" (1954:4).

Although cultural and social anthropologists occasionally attacked each other in strong language, the points of agreement between Lowie's "wholism" and Radcliffe-Brown's "functionalism" (or "structure-functionalism") were fundamental while the differences were comparatively trivial—more in the way the ideas were put than in what the ideas were. Both agree that something social controls or patterns behavior and that this thing is a single organized whole. They agree that the individual lacks a comparable creative or directive role in relation to society, at least insofar as he is of interest to the analyst. Both contend that insofar as culture or society is manifested in individuals, that aspect of the individual is radically separate from the biological aspects of the individual, and from individual mental (psychological) processes. Both agree that culture or society is an abstraction—a product of the analyst's mental activity with no regular or necessary relationship to the ideas and beliefs of the people being studied. Both agree that theoretical analysis involves comparing several such entities (several things that are already abstractions) and finding commonalities. They also agree that there can be formulated apart from observation, and without experimentation, a very different kind of theory from the genetic conceptions of physical anthropologists, as one example.

Beneath these theoretical ideas are others that amount more to a philosophy of science. Both Lowie and Radcliffe-Brown shared the idea that by describing a human group one was somehow explaining the behavior of the individuals in that group. This reflects a common underlying adherence to "social determinism," the idea that society determines individual behavior, and it reflects adherence to an idea that scientific explanations must be deterministic in character—they must show that whatever happened *had* to happen. This point of view rules out chance, and in social analysis it also rules out free will. It is intimately related to the idea that the analyst deals only with his own observations and abstractions and not with the natives' needs or ideas of his culture or society. Durkheim expressed this concept very dramatically when he spoke of society as the "collective consciousness" (1918:230), "outside and above local contingencies" that imposed itself on individuals by its own authority (p. 17). In Durkheim's view, the general concepts of human reason were social in origin and could only be explained socially. Other authors, like Lowie and Radcliffe-Brown, had different views of what was social in origin, but they shared Durkheim's basic idea of what an explanation amounted to.

Although these theoretical and philosophical ideas have turned out to entail many serious difficulties, as will be indicated in several succeeding chapters, they had a serious and reasonable set of purposes behind them when they were offered.

One major purpose was to avoid racism. It must be remembered that despite the scientific abandonment of the idea of race the early part of this century saw increasing use of racist political ideologies to justify brutal and unjust internal policies, culminating in the Nazi policy of genocide and enslavement of Jews, Gypsies, Slavs, and other "inferior races." Anthropologists had generally opposed such policies even when evolutionary ideas seemed credible. Once the scientific value of racial ideas was removed, the majority of anthropologists undoubtedly saw the ideas of social determinism as an alternative position which would make it clear that they saw no scientific merit in the racial assumptions that were being made.

A second purpose, obvious from the quoted material, was to avoid theories based on psychology and psychological universals and to recognize in their place the importance of cultural or social contexts. Many anthropologists felt that currently popular psychological theories, especially introspective theories, explained too much. According to such theories, all men ought to be uniform in their actions and beliefs, which in fact they were not. Anthropologists, focusing on foreign groups and on a variety of groups, wanted to look at differences and inquire into their importance. They wanted to get at the question of human nature through an understanding of human differences. Theories that attributed universal attitudes or values to people at the outset were no help.

The importance of cultural differences was often expressed in the idea of "cultural relativism," which probably deserves to be called the characteristic anthropological attitude if any one attitude does. The attitude is both ethical and scientific. As the name implies, it is the idea that the actions of an individual are relative to his cultural surroundings. In moral terms a person's actions have to be evaluated in terms of the moral principles and beliefs of his society, or culture. In scientific terms they have to be explained and understood in the light of such cultural principles and beliefs. One cannot arrive at a proper evaluation of the actions of a person in another culture by imposing the values or beliefs of one's own culture upon them. A man who wears a skirt in Scotland cannot be understood in the same terms as a man who wears one in Hollywood.

Of course it is not always easy to avoid imposing one's own values, and anthropologists constantly struggle with themselves and with each other over it. For example, many anthropologists saw the ideas of cultural and social determinism as explaining and embodying the idea of cultural relativism. Others, however, thought that the radical division between the individual and society and the idea of determinism were ideas peculiar to European culture, and that these ideas necessarily distort the way other people see themselves and their worlds.

Finally, along with both the disavowal of psychology and the argument for the uniqueness and importance of culture (or society), anthropologists were interested in establishing a new academic discipline, distinct from psychology, economics, and sociology, yet important and academically respectable in its own right. Whatever the purely theoretical weaknesses proved to be, there can be no doubt that the ideas of social and cultural determinism, wedded as they were to the ideas of a primitive tribe or community, served these organizational purposes in a dramatic and effective form.

Deterministic theory was not unchallenged when it first appeared. In England, Radcliffe-Brown's functionalism was set against the functionalism of Bronislaw Malinowski—in fact, it was Malinowski who first used the term. He had borrowed it from functional psychology, which derived from the work of William James and John Dewey, among others. Malinowski also spoke of needs, but in his case they were explicitly described as individual needs. He described conceptions, but they were individual conceptions—not conceptions that originated in society alone. And he spoke of institutions, but they were related to individual purposes (and needs) and did not form a single social whole apart from individuals. He carefully emphasized field methods in his accounts, indicating where each type of regularity was encountered—whether in what people said, in ritual actions, or in his own impressions of behavior. He strongly argued for the necessity that psychological theory and anthropological theory be related, and he saw individual action not in terms of a dichotomy between the individual and society but in terms of the individual and his relation to other individuals and to his economic, material, and ideological surroundings. This was a nondeterministic conception that focused on the observable individual and his setting rather than a deterministic conception that focused on society as an abstraction apart from the individual.

In the United States, Franz Boas's position was very much like Malinowski's, focusing on the individual and seeing culture not as something apart from individuals but rather as something implicit in and manifested through their actions and the products of their actions. Boas never opted for any kind of determinism and specifically spoke of "contradictory attitudes" in single cultures (1932 reprinted in Boas 1965:256).

He never argued specifically against Lowie, his early student, friend, and supporter, and Lowie explicitly credited Boas with his own "totalitarian" conception of culture (1937:151). But this was wrong, and Boas forcefully rejected similar views as they had been advanced by Alfred Kroeber and Robert Redfield, as well as Radcliffe-Brown. He called their views "the new speculative theories based on the imposition of categories derived mainly from our culture upon foreign cultures," and declared that he was fighting them as he had fought the "old speculative theories"—the evolutionary theories that they had replaced (Boas 1936 in 1965:311).

The tradition was allied through the psychology of Wilhelm Wundt with the pragmatic philosophy of William James and, ultimately, with the critical philosophy of Immanuel Kant. In this tradition, society, moral principles, values, and the like are viewed as products of human history and human invention, and largely as matters of belief. The explanatory effort focused on accounting for these beliefs, explaining why people had them and what they did; the explanations revolved around ideas of human purposes and needs. This orientation was almost the exact reverse of Comte's and Spencer's efforts to take society, moral principles, and the like as timeless, explanatory entities like the forces of physics and to apply them as explanations to human behavior.

In any event, between 1940 and 1950 the deterministic position won out. It was advanced and accepted that Malinowski, who died in 1939, and Boas, who died in 1942, had both been primarily field workers and that Lowie, Kroeber, Redfield, Radcliffe-Brown, and others were not so much presenting radically different theoretical views but rather more sophisticated versions of the same general type of theory. Many of the differences were never really discussed in an orderly way at all.

Acceptance of the idea of social determinism shared by Lowie and Radcliffe-Brown led to a wide range of activities in the wartime and postwar periods that played out the themes they had proposed. Following the idea that theory was a logical system of statements, there were many efforts to provide hypothetical schemes upon which empirical analyses could be based. Following the idea of social determinism, and the related idea that only one social system could control behavior, there were many disputes over just what type of system was the real basis of behavior—religion, economics, kinship, political structure, psychoanalytic symbolisms, and ecology all have been proposed. Many subfields of cultural and social anthropology are defined by precisely such arguments. Each group focuses on one more or less clear set of phenomena, argues that it is the underlying structure or that it represents that structure, and offers its ideas of how it all comes about.

Since a theory that is circular and depends on the analyst's own categories, prior to application and apart from rigid empirical standards of verification and proof, cannot be rejected in favor of another theory constructed along the same lines, these arguments of deterministic theory have naturally come to be quite frustrating and, ultimately, self-defeating.

Experience has shown that no social group has a single, uniform religion, culture, or structure in any of a number of senses, or a single set of symbolic predilections. There are always contradictory values, ideas, and principles of organization, and among individuals there is always conflict. Consequently, all analyses that attempted to show a single underlying determinant of all action had to ignore some data. Ethnologists recognized this, and often developed elaborate rationales to the effect that "the more exact is the structure the more difficult it becomes to fit it to reality" (Bailey 1960:12–13). But even if they could agree on this, they could not agree on which data could be ignored, or how much. Every major monograph, in presenting a description of a social group, also included its own arguments on the selection of data. Contradictory analyses of the same or similar groups (and there were many) presented contradictory views of these issues. Arguments for one type of subfield (such as ecology or economics) often involved the claim that the particular phenomena in question were more objective than others, as well as more powerful in determining action.

Important works of this period in cultural anthropology included Melville Herskovits's *Economic Anthropology* (1940), Clyde Kluckhohn's *Navaho Witchcraft* (1944), Ruth Benedict's *The Chrysanthemum and the Sword* (1946), the English translation of Max Weber's *The Protestant Ethic and the Spirit of Capitalism* (1948), Robert Redfield's *The Primitive World and its Transformations* (1953), and as a sociological work that served many anthropologists as a model of general theory, Talcott Parsons's *The Social System* (1951).

Representative influential works in social anthropology include E. E. Evans-Pritchard's *The Nuer* (1940), S. F. Nadel's *A Black Byzantium* (1942), Meyer Fortes's *The Web of Kinship Among the Tallensi* (1949), Claude Lévi-Strauss's *Elementary Structures of Kinship* (1949), and Fred Eggan's *Social Organization of the Western Pueblos* (1950).

While it is possible that, in terms of numbers alone, a majority of anthropologists still accept the ideas of social determinism and are still seeking to find the one real basis of cultural behavior, an alternative position began to develop among the acknowledged leaders of the field in the mid-1950s. In many respects, this represented an attempt to reincorporate the ideas of Malinowski and Boas.

At first, the revisions focused on the need of the wholistic theories to sacrifice large amounts of obvious data and on their natural tendency to produce models of society that, because they were tightly integrated and self-contained, seemed also static and unable to recognize the actual facts of change and development that one finds in all societies. In social anthropology, a watershed work in this respect was Edmund Leach's 1954 *Political Systems of Highland Burma*—quite probably the most influential single ethnological work to date.

Leach described the social structure of the Kachin of highland Burma as involving not one structure but two—or rather two versions on one fundamental plan. He attempted to retain the idea of determinism by arguing that there was an automatic relationship between the two. One structure was held to be a democratic or anarchic, while the other was more aristocratic, and there was supposed to be an automatic tendency for power to consolidate in an increasingly aristocratic structure until a point was reached where, in effect, a rebellion was precipitated which led to a return to the anarchic condition. Thereupon, the cycle started again. Built-in constraints kept the aristocratic form of the system from stabilizing permanently in the manner of the ethnically distinct lowland people in the same region.

This analysis not only incorporated change into a deterministic structure, it also incorporated contradictory data that could not all have been included in a more static account and, equally importantly, the argument was conducted with an attention to very high fieldwork standards for the period. All this was far more reminiscent of Malinowski and Boas than of Radcliffe-Brown and others. Equally reminiscent of Malinowski was the strong suggestion that the structures were not only analysts' abstractions but were in fact both real for the natives and consciously exploited by them.

Leach made many explicit criticisms of the preceding works, but the most effective criticism was made by doing what others had declared, with force and authority, to be impossible.

Similar points were made in cultural anthropology in two major areas: (1) in some attempts to describe acculturation and culture change, and (2) in some work in the area of culture and personality where the wartime deterministic efforts to equate personality structure with cultural patterns gave way to attempts to see some sort of interaction between individual cognition and cultural activity. Beginning with a revision of Herskovits's *Economic Anthropology* in 1952, there was also increasing interest in attempts to accord theoretical recognition to some sort of universal rational or calculating behavior, which might conflict with "traditional" societal or cultural rules or principles.

In the last few years, this line of development has grown to include explicit arguments for the idea of multiple independent social structures within single communities (Bailey 1960; Leaf 1972), and a large number of explicit attacks on the idea that such structures were purely analysts' models in favor of the idea that they are native products and tools for communication—"social symbols" of some sort.

The cultural and social anthropological chapters in the present work represent the latter lines of development, although, as will be seen, they are not by any means uniform in their approach or in the defects they recognize in the older tradition. It should be noticed that in rejecting wholistic determinism the authors do not abandon the idea of the independence of anthropology as a scholarly discipline. They also retain the antiracial position of early anthropologists and the commitment to a social science that does not use one culture as the standard by which others are to be measured.

## Linguistics

At the present time, ethnology is most closely allied with the fourth major subfield of anthropology—linguistics, or more strictly, anthropological linguistics.

Following current usage, the field of linguistics includes studies ranging from the descriptive analysis of modern languages through the reconstruction of past languages and linguistic relations up to quite abstract concerns with the theory of grammar and of language analysis in general. Anthropological linguistics is best regarded as an area of overlap between anthropology and linguistics whose practitioners regard themselves as anthropologists as well as linguists. The group of people who consider themselves anthropological linguists in this sense is decreasing in size relative to anthropologists proper as well as to linguists proper. Fewer and fewer departments of anthropology consider it necessary to have linguists on the staff or to offer courses in linguistic analysis or the structure of many exotic languages. Linguistic departments, which formerly concentrated on classical and European languages, are now offering courses in such areas as Bantu, Mayan, and Polynesian languages. However, the role of linguistics in relation to anthropology as a whole is greater than the present rather small number of anthropological linguists might suggest, in both an historical and a theoretical sense.

Historically, it is reasonably accurate to say that linguistics was the first of the anthropological subfields to develop, and was the special historical starting point for anthropology as a whole. In an historical sense, the racial theories of the later nineteenth century are actually an outgrowth of linguistic evolutionary theories of the early nineteenth century —before Darwin.

The modern history of linguistics dates from 1796. In that year, Sir William Jones introduced the discovery of Sanskrit to European scholars, arguing that it was:

> more perfect than Greek, more copious than Latin and more exquisitely refined than either; yet bearing to both of them a stronger affinity, both in the roots of verbs and in the forms of grammar, than could possibly have been produced by accident; so strong, indeed, that no philologer could examine them all without believing them to have sprung from some common source, which, perhaps, no longer exists. (Quoted in Jesperson 1924:34)

There are many important aspects of this statement. In the first place, the idea of such an old, original common language was itself revolutionary since it was known and assumed that Latin and Greek were ancestral to most European languages and were older than the earliest history and literature. Second, the geographical spread of the new language family thus envisioned reinforced the idea of an ancestral culture of great antiquity and further suggested to many the idea that a very large portion of the world's history would be encompassed in unraveling the historical developments Jones suggested. But startling as they were, his two points were only the surface marks of a much more fundamental development.

Although Jones did not say so, his perception of the perfection and elegance of Sanskrit was due to the work of an Indian grammarian of the fifth century, B.C., named Panini. In order to preserve the important religious and philosophical texts that were old even in his time, Panini developed a system for breaking them apart sound by sound and grammatical unit by grammatical unit so that the parts could be arbitrarily memorized by several people independently and later fit together in such a way that alterations could be discovered and corrected. This system worked for many centuries and ultimately was committed to writing. Panini's system of analysis had been preserved by Sanskrit, just as it had preserved the ancient Sanskrit. This system—Panini's "metalanguage" or language for talking about language—is what permitted the revolutionary break with past traditions of linguistic analysis.

Finally it should be noticed that Jones' references to what "chance alone" would have produced along with the references to roots of verbs and grammatical forms implies a very definite conception of historical language development and of linguistic analysis that in many respects closely parallels the methods of comparative morphology. There is a sense of random variation that will occur in any two languages and will produce accidental resemblances between them, and there is a sense that some aspects of a language are more fundamental and less subject to nongenetic forces that produce such divergence. For Jones, roots and grammatical forms are better evidence of historical connection than, for example, recurrent sounds, common words, or seemingly important words with similar meanings (like words for Gods). This set off lines of thought in many directions, most of which converged rapidly in late nineteenth-century anthropology.

One of the subsequent developments was the search for fuller knowledge of Sanskrit and for other ancient languages as they might be discovered in ancient texts. This was precisely the line of development that led to the decipherment of hierglyphic and cuneiform, and, in effect, to archeology in its first form as an extension of classics.

The second line of development was the search for ancient survivals of language and culture in modern tongues, mainly European at first. This tradition focused especially on literary texts (oral and written) in the popular traditions, like ballads and epic poetry. It included especially the famous *Kinder und Hausemarchen* (children's stories) that was first published in 1812 by Jacob and Wilhelm Grimm.

In addition to the excitement of finding an important new field of scientific inquiry, the work by the Grimm brothers commanded considerable attention because it had, at the time, certain important political implications. Following the French revolution, an important argument had been developing in Germany. Its subject was the proper kind of a constitution for the state and the proper kind of political structure to go with it. One important camp, corresponding to the Bonapartists in France, argued that law had to be codified on the basis of universal rational principles and imposed by an aristocratic class informed of those principles. This was the Hegelian position. The opposite position was that law had to grow out of the life of the people and could only reflect what they believed and wanted. This corresponded to the British conception of a constitution and was the liberal, and Kantian, position. An important figure in this latter movement was the legal scholar Friedrich Karl von Savigny, who was Jacob Grimm's teacher when he studied law. Many people saw the Grimms' work as providing a new scientific method for investigating the natural growth of law in this sense.

An 1885 description of the work of the Grimm brothers said in part that:

> . . . In the hands of the two Grimms philology became national and popular; and at the same time a pattern was created for the scientific study of all the people of the earth and for a comparative investigation of the entire mental life of mankind, of which written literature is nothing but a small epitome. (Quoted in Jesperson 1924:41)

In effect, this says that the method of historical linguistic analysis that began with Jones' notification of the importance of Sanskrit became the basis of the comparative evolutionary ethnology of the late nineteenth century.

This is the same ethnology that has been described above as involving a blending of physical and archeological ideas under the broad idea of race and racial evolution. This may sound strange or contradictory to us now, when our ideas of race and language do not convey at all the same meanings. But in the nineteenth century, before Mendel, it was much different. A racial group was usually identified by common language and a shared language was often considered a mark of racial identity and common racial history. It was felt that if the first language was reconstructed, it would also show us, by its inventory of words and concepts, the first civilization of the original human group as well. As late as 1907, the famous scholar William Robertson-Smith said:

> As a rule, therefore, the classification of mankind by language, at least when applied to large masses, will approach pretty closely to a natural classification [racial classification]. . . . Where we find unity of language, we can at least say with certainty that we are dealing with a group of men who are subject to common influences of the most subtle and far-reaching kinds . . . the continued action of these influences has produced a great uniformity of physical and mental type. (1907:7)

The reason for the close fit between racial ideas and ideas of language is quite simple: the ideas of race, and the idea of biological evolution itself, were both patterned after the ideas of linguistic evolution suggested by Jones.

When Jones first articulated his conception of a tree of languages branching by descent from a common original parent language, there was no equivalent idea in biology. On the contrary, biologists, following the great work of Linnaeus (1766) were consistently and stoutly maintaining that each natural species was a unique and separate creation of God and that the broader classes of species were pure arbitrary inventions of the biological classifiers. The first major biologist to advance the idea that all divergent biological forms might have developed from a common origin was Jean Baptiste Lamarck in 1815—not only after Jones but also after Grimm and several equally important and well-known linguists. At the time, however, Lamarck's ideas were rejected in biology, partly because the mechanisms he proposed for such divergent development were unconvincing and partly because his writing style in general was speculative and diffuse and he failed to make a definitive empirical case for the issue.

Darwin's own contribution was not the idea of evolution itself, but rather the idea of natural selection as the mechanism that explained how such evolution operated in the realm of biology. The idea of inherent species variability that he used to explain how traits originated for selection to operate on was a direct borrowing from linguistic theory. Darwin makes a specific comparison between a language and a species in the *Descent of Man*, chapter VI, saying in part that they "are curiously parallel" (1936:465), and others who spoke for him pointed out the parallels at greater length.

Once the close relationship between racial and linguistic ideas in the late nineteenth and early twentieth century is understood, it should not be surprising that the last major reorientation in the development of anthropological linguistics took place in the same upheavals surrounding the rejection of the concept of race that so greatly altered physical anthropology, archeology, and ethnology, and gave them their modern form. Nor should it be surprising that one of the major figures in this change was Franz Boas.

In the introduction to the *Handbook of North American Indian Languages* (1905), Boas argued that people could not dependably be "classified" in the same way by physical type, culture, and language. That is, people who had the same type of culture need not have the same language or physical type; people who have the same physical type need not have the same language or culture; and people who had the same language need not have the same culture or physical type. In this, Boas was already making a very important distinction between a language as a system of symbols—especially a *spoken* language—and the ideas that language conveys, the texts and oral traditions that embody it and, of course, the people who speak it. Boas was not original in this. He was aware of a number of European scholars in all branches of work who had refused to be seduced by the evolutionary promises. But he was especially forceful and energetic, and his voice prevailed strongly in the period of change through the 1920s and 1930s. The distinction between written and spoken language, and between a language and what it is used to convey, is fundamental to modern theory, which concentrates almost exclusively on spoken language.

In 1937, many of the techniques and ideas that Boas and his students represented were embodied in a major theoretical synthesis by Leonard Bloomfield, published under the title *Language*. However, Bloomfield departed from the broad Kantian framework that Boas had shared with Grimm and many of the major European analysts and adopted instead the general conceptions of language that were associated with positivistic philosophy—the same conceptions that were shared by Radcliffe-Brown, Lowie, A. L. Kroeber, and most of their contemporaries in social and cultural anthropology. Just as Radcliffe-Brown approached the analysis of society in terms of a theoretical division between his analytic categories and other peoples' objective behaviors, so Bloomfield approached the analysis of language on the basis of a theoretical division between his analytic categories and the physical sounds other people made in objective situations. Meaning, as an aspect of words and linguistic constructions that was neither physical sound nor analyst's theory, was left out of Bloomfield's analysis entirely.

The second chapter of *Language* is devoted to a stimulus-response theory of language learning and language use that is intended to serve as a substitute for theories of meaning, purpose, or reference. The idea is that a linguistic utterance is produced in a situation. If it is rewarded, it is repeated; if not, it is dropped. In a more complex case, linguistic symbols themselves can serve as substitutes for practical responses. This idea was very popular for a number of years, and still has some adherents. Recently, however, it has come under severe attack, mainly from Noam Chomsky. The same chapter dismisses written language from consideration on the grounds that it is merely a set of graphic symbols for conveying the spoken language.

With meaning and writing thus eliminated, Bloomfield had to deal with a seemingly much restricted problem. Since speech (if not thought or writing) occurs as a sequence of distinct sounds in time, the main problem seemed to be that of identifying recurrent patterns in such sequences. Bloomfield's solution to it involved three general levels of analysis: phonology, grammar, and the lexicon. Each involved a different set of criteria for dividing the flow of speech sounds: a different set of concepts for units into which the flow was divided and their rules for combination. The levels were hierarchically arranged.

Phonology for Bloomfield meant the study of the sounds of speech and was subdivided into three major areas. What he called "laboratory phonetics" pertained strictly to the acoustical aspects of the production of speech sounds by the human vocal apparatus. This was, and is, of comparatively small importance in linguistics, and is more a part of physics.

Above the level of laboratory phonetics, Bloomfield placed what he called "practical phonetics." This focuses on the description of certain sounds that are especially significant in each language and is pertinent, for example, to the development of useful scripts for linguistic transcription and language teaching. Of all the speech sounds that can be produced, each language normally selects only a few and uses them to produce clear and regular contrasts among the units of speech. For example, in English (and most languages) there is a sharp contrast between sounds that are voiced and sounds that are voiceless. This is, for example, the difference between the initial sounds in the words *din* and *tin*. There are also normally quite clear zones where "stops" (sounds produced by completely interrupting the flow of air from the lungs—like the *t* and *p* in *stop*) are produced in each language, and these tend to be regular distances apart. For example, in English stops are made by bringing the

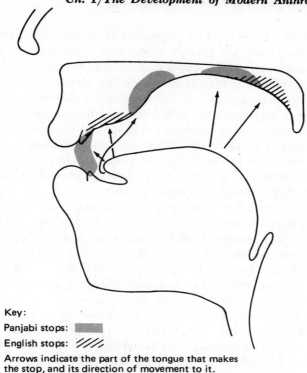

Key:

Panjabi stops: ▨

English stops: ////

Arrows indicate the part of the tongue that makes
the stop, and its direction of movement to it.

**Figure 1.1** *Different points of articulation of stops in Panjabi and English.*

tip of the tongue in contact with the area around the back upper edge
of the teeth and alveolar ridge (the *t* and *d* sounds), and by bringing the
middle portion of the tongue in contact with the palate (the *k* and *g*
sounds), but not in between. In Panjabi, by contrast, stops are made
with the tip of the tongue against the back of the teeth and with the
underside of the tip against the inside edge of the alveolar ridge, but not
in either of the English positions (see Figure 1.1). It also happens that in
Panjabi each such stop involves not only the contrast between voicing
and lack of voicing, as in English, but also a contrast between what is
called "aspiration" and "nonaspiration." In the English word *tote* the
first *t* sound has a slight puff of air after it while the second does not.
The first is aspirated, the second is unaspirated. In Panjabi, this would
make a difference between two significant elements. In English, it does
not. The sounds are simply two versions of one element and reversing
them would sound strange but would not change the meaning (function)
of the word. Systematic isolation of the significant sound contrasts of a
language are extremely important in a practical way and also provide
data for consideration in terms of theories of minimal perceivable differences in communication systems.

Bloomfield's third level of phonological analysis was "phonemics." Seemingly forgetting his general theoretical commitments, Bloomfield defined a *phoneme* as "the smallest units which make a difference in meaning" (p. 136). His idea in distinguishing phonemics from practical phonetics was that as minimal units making a difference in meaning, phonemes of a language can be isolated and designated with arbitrary symbols and their rules of combination described without knowing what the actual sounds involved are. They are functional units, rather than substantive units. We can know that in spoken English the words spelled *bow, toe, dough* all end with the same functional element without regard for the way that element is actually produced by the vocal apparatus.

Once the combining sound units of a language are delineated, generally about thirty-five or forty in number, everything seemed to Bloomfield a matter of providing rules for their combination. This is what he called grammar, which, like phonology, covered a number of different levels of analysis. The most fundamental level is that of the *morpheme*, defined as the minimal unit of language that can have a grammatical role, and also as consisting of one or more phonemes. The form *a* (as in *a car*) is a morpheme, as is *car*. The form *running* is a complex form consisting of two morphemes, *run* and *-ing*, each of which can be recombined with other elements and one of which, *run* can also stand alone. Forms that can stand freely are called *unbound* forms, and those that only occur in combination are called *bound*.

Discovering which sets of phoneme sequences are morphemes in a language necessarily leads to the second step of grammatical analysis, delineating the morphemes and basic morpheme classes. This arises from determining the bound forms and finding out what they combine with. It would normally give such classes as the noun, verb stems, possessive markers, negation markers, and tense markers of language: the rules that say that *happily* is legitimate, but *happies* is not, or more correctly, a morpheme that appears in combination with the bound form *-ly* (an adverb) cannot appear with the bound form *-s* (a plural morpheme for a noun), and vice versa.

The catalogue of morphemes for a language is its "lexicon." Above the rules for combining the bound forms, the next level of analysis involves what is usually called "syntax," the rules for combining the resultant morpheme constructions (roughly, words) into phrases, clauses, and sentences. At this level—the analysis of sentences—linguistic interest generally ceases.

Since Bloomfield, the various levels of analysis have consistently been more clearly and fully separated and the analytical methods associated with each have been more fully articulated. At each point in its development, linguistic theory has served as a model for theory in ethnology. Bloomfield's original formulations and the practical success of the linguistic efforts they synthesized in describing the world's languages and in forming the rationale for teaching programs in the Allied countries during the Second World War lent powerful support to the related positivistic theories of Radcliffe-Brown, Lowie, Kroeber, and many like them.

In the 1950s several new treatments focused on the more abstract concepts of the levels of analysis themselves, especially the differences among phonetics, phonemics, and morphemics. They concentrated on stating generalized methods for differentiating levels and defining units in the data—general ideas of a frame or environment and of the types of comparisons that defined the elements that varied within them. Many linguists, and anthropologists after them, thought they saw in this the possibility of a parallel approach to a general theory of culture—not by saying what culture was, but rather by saying what methods of procedures of discovery would reveal its units and the boundaries between the units at different levels of analysis. Kenneth Pike's *Language in Relation to a Unified Theory of Human Behavior* (1954) was an especially notable work in this regard.

At about the same time, the exclusion of meaning by Bloomfield and his immediate followers came to be recognized as both arbitrary and unnecessary, and there was some effort to return to this aspect of language in a discussion of what was called the "Whorf hypothesis" or the "Sapir-Whorf hypothesis."

Edward Sapir had been a student and colleague of Boas, older than Bloomfield, and had never accepted Bloomfield's conception of meaning. Instead, he tried to see language as a kind of template for culture—as separate from culture (following Boas) but at the same time embodying basic categorical distinctions through which the user saw his world.

Benjamin Lee Whorf was a highly independent thinker. He had received his formal training with Sapir at Yale in the early 1930s and followed his ideas more than anyone else's. Although his interests were narrower than Sapir's, he was more careful than Sapir in some important respects in his formulations. Whorf tried to define new types of word classes on a conceptual rather than purely functional (grammatical) basis—like "nouns of substance" as opposed to simply "nouns that take the bound form *s*" or something similar. He then went on to ask if the configuration of concepts found in such classes of words in a language influenced or corresponded to other aspects of the culture—if the way, for example, the Hopi regarded time in their habitual action corresponded to the temporal categories embedded in the word classes of the Hopi language. This, too, created (and still creates) a certain amount of interest among ethnologists, and they joined the linguists who were trying to come to some reconciliation of this type of question with the seemingly more rigorous, and certainly neater, theory that followed in Bloomfield's line proper.

Finally, the last development has been in what is called generative-transformational analysis, connected with Noam Chomsky. Strictly as a linguistic matter, this type of analysis introduces a technique for the generation of complex sentence structure from the operation of a very few simple combinatorial rules. For example, a verb phrase must combine with a noun phrase and not another verb phrase to make a sentence. These rules can operate recursively to embed sentences inside other sentences. For example, a verb phrase plus a noun phrase can in turn serve as constituents of a verb phrase in a more complex sentence, and so forth. This introduces far more order into the analysis of grammar than previous systems had, and brings this difficult area of analysis up to the same level of explicitness as phonology. Chomsky and many of his followers have argued that the rules for generating sentences are also rules of thought and embody fundamental characteristics of human mentality. In this respect, they also claim to have brought about at least some reincorporation of meaning into rigorous theory. This, too, has created considerable interest among ethnologists. Some analysts of kinship terminologies and native systems for the classifications of natural and social phenomena have attempted to organize their material with generative (recursive) rules patterned after Chomsky's analysis of English syntax.

These issues, especially the larger ones relating language structure to meaning, thought, and action, are still hotly debated, and it is by no means clear how they are going to be resolved. As yet, no satisfactory conception of the relations between language and culture or society has been developed, although it is increasingly clear that we must do so.

## INTERACTION OF PROFESSIONAL AND INTELLECTUAL ORGANIZATIONS: THE WAY RESEARCH IS DONE

Reports published in journals and monographs generally convey the impression that research is conceived and carried out only in relation to the intellectual organization of the field. The announced aims of research generally are to extend the range of currently-known phenomena which have not yet been theoretically accounted for or to question and alter the basic assumptions and thereby to change the boundaries of the subfields. But these announced aims and the theoretical interpretations of the research that are reported in print do not convey the whole picture. In fact, quite commonly they hide the most difficult and interesting part. They treat the research as something accomplished, a deed that is done.

The major excitement of research, and the part most difficult to describe, is in the very early stage—the selection of the research area and of the project within it.

It is not easy to change the subdisciplines within a field or the assumptions that create them. One cannot redo all the work of the field, or even a small part of it. A project has to be selected which is small enough for one person to control and complete so that the conclusion of the researcher can be seen to be the best possible interpretation. At the same time the research should be clearly pertinent to the major assumptions of the subfields in question. The results, in an important sense, should speak for themselves so that other scholars can look at them and see the relevance for their own work, even if those scholars might not share the language, theoretical commitments, or skills of the designer of the project. It is fairly easy to develop a research project that can be carried to completion within a reasonable amount of time and resources and whose interpretation can be seen to give reasonable assurance of exhausting the data and excluding other interpretations. It is also reasonably easy to think of projects that would resolve the great issues and change the boundaries that presently divide issues within the discipline. But it is difficult to do both at once.

On both the practical and the theoretical side, the person designing a research project has to take into account all aspects of the discipline that he can be aware of and assess: the intellectual organization and the theories that structure it, the professional organizations, the funding organizations, and his own academic setting. Any given theoretical purpose, if it has general implications, necessarily can be accomplished in a variety of ways. Selecting one possibility out of the others often turns on such factors as funding, time, colleagues who might participate, and likely places where different research reports might be published. In practice, all these considerations interact to form the final project and its results. At the same time, however, it should be added that crucial research projects have changed the configuration of resources in the past and will undoubtedly do so again. The factors that have to be taken into account in constructing research projects are constantly being changed not only by outside forces but also, and to a very great extent, by the research projects themselves.

Partly in the belief that the art of choosing research projects and interpreting their results is going to be constant and important when present theoretical issues have long been transformed into something quite different, and partly because it is where a good part of the real adventure of anthropology lies, the following chapters depart from the usual style of research reports by the inclusion of additional information on these topics.

The research described in the following chapters is not intended to be a representative sample of all work now going on. Although it is spotted widely throughout the discipline, it is work that in the opinion of the contributors will be exceptionally important in the years to come. It is intended as leading work whose consequences are at present somewhat risky and uncertain—this too being part of the adventure it presents. Each problem dealt with draws on a different theoretical area and often makes very different criticisms, at least on the surface.

After the individual research cases are presented, we will conclude with a kind of simulation of the sort of interaction among research problems and solutions that constantly goes on in the discipline. We assume that the ideas advanced in the several papers will be accepted to some degree by others, and on this basis we will ask how they will interact to produce possible alterations in the present state of the art. What are the likely organizational and intellectual effects? If some of the ideas presented take hold, what will anthropology be like in another twenty-five years—in the year 2000 A.D.?

## SELECTED READINGS

### History and Professional Organization of Modern Anthropology

Helm, June, ed., 1966, *Pioneers of American Anthropology*. American Ethnological Society Monograph No. 43. Seattle: University of Washington Press.

A set of essays focusing mainly on women who were influential in the developments in American ethnology at the turn of the century. The essays are interesting and provide many personal insights into the politics and personal relationships of the period, involving both major men and women.

Kardiner, Abram, and Preble, Edward, 1961, *They Studied Man*. Cleveland: World Publishing Company.

Interesting biographical sketches of a number of people of importance in the formation of anthropology, giving a good sense of their personal and professional lives, as well as of their intellectual interests.

Penniman, T. K., 1965, *A Hundred Years of Anthropology*. London: Gerald Duckworth & Company.

The most comprehensive and useful review of the authors and works that have formed the major anthropological traditions of the nineteenth and early twentieth centuries.

Stocking, George, Jr., 1968, *Race, Culture, and Evolution*. New York: Free Press.

This is a collection of essays on the emergence of the modern concept of "culture" primarily in relation to the work of Franz Boas and E. B. Tylor. It is the best documented historical writing on the period. The essays often deal with relationships between anthropological, literary, and social events not normally touched on in histories of anthropology.

## Physical Anthropology

Campbell, Bernard S., 1973, *Human Evolution*. Chicago: Aldine.

A well-written textbook which provides a good overview of the area.

Dobzhansky, Theodosius, 1956, *The Biological Basis of Human Freedom*. New York: Columbia University Press.

A discussion of the major discoveries in physical anthropology and their general intellectual and philosophical implications, written for a popular audience by one of the leading geneticists of this century.

Leakey, L. S. B., Prost, Jack and Prost, Stephanie, eds., 1971, *Adam, or Ape: A Sourcebook of Discoveries About Early Man*. Cambridge: Schenkman.

A fine, comprehensive selection of papers that have been of major significance in the development of our present understandings of human evolution, ranging from the reports of discoveries of the first Neanderthal remains through the summations of the prosecution and defense in the Scope's "Monkey trial." The essays include an historical overview by Professor Prost and an "Epilogue" by Dr. Leakey, looking ahead to the work still to be done. The selections are not too technical for undergraduate readers.

Morris, Desmond ed., 1967, *Primate Ethology*. Chicago: Aldine.

A collection of papers by major workers in this area, dealing with learning, communication, and social behavior among nonhuman primates. The contributions carry on the tradition of Conrad Lorenz's well known *Solomon's Ring*, but with somewhat more care for scientific control over the interpretations and observations. The papers are rather technical, but very stimulating.

## Archeology

Adams, Robert McC., 1965, *The Evolution of Urban Society*. Chicago: Aldine.

An archeological case study which is well written enough to be handled by beginning undergraduates, but it is theoretically and conceptually sophisticated.

Deetz, J., 1967, *Invitation to Archeology*. New York: Natural History Press.

A provocative and insightful discussion of the principles of archeology focusing on major concepts.

Fagan, B., 1972, *In the Beginning*. Boston: Little, Brown & Co.

A comprehensive discussion of the practice of archeology in the field, in the laboratory, and in the mind of the archeologist.

Hole, F. and Heizer, R., 1973, *An Introduction to Prehistoric Archeology*. New York: Holt, Rinehart, & Winston.

This book covers the same ground as Fagan's but at a more advanced level. It is stronger on recent innovative trends in archeology. The bibliography is excellent and should be consulted in pursuing any specific topic of research in archeology.

Leone, M., ed., 1972, *Contemporary Archeology*. Carbondale: Southern Illinois Press.

An excellent anthology of readings in the practice of archeology, including both theoretical articles and case studies. The best available work for the study of recent innovative trends in archeology.

### Social and Cultural Anthropology

Benedict, Ruth, 1959, *Patterns of Culture*. Boston: Houghton Mifflin Co.

A major attempt in relatively nontechnical language to present a coordinated idea of culture as a basis of social organization. This marked a major synthesis of past efforts to construe culture as an alternative to "social structure" and the beginning of the tendency to see the two concepts as overlapping.

Firth, Raymond, 1961, *Elements of Social Organization*, third edition. Boston: Beacon Press. (First published: 1951)

Like Benedict's *Patterns of Culture*, this too was a relatively simply written but important work, marking a change in orientation. In this case, the move was away from the social determinism that dominated social anthropological thought at the time of the Second World War, toward a fuller recognition of individual activity as an independent variable in social analysis.

Nadel, S. F., 1951, *The Foundations of Social Anthropology*. London: Cohen & West.

A wide ranging discussion of major conceptual problems in social anthropology, probably the best informed and most mature of its kind. This book deserves careful reading by everyone seriously concerned with social theory, although it will make more sense if the reader is at least acquainted with a few major monographs of specific social systems.

Tax, Sol, ed., 1962, *Anthropology Today*. Chicago: University of Chicago Press.

A selection of articles from a larger work published in 1953, edited by A. L. Kroeber. These are the articles that aged best, and many of them are still quite adequate. Each article is intended to cover a major topic area and is written by a leading scholar in that area. They are presented as a general survey—abstract summary rather than new case studies—and they concentrate on laying out major understandings and conceptual problems.

Wax, Rosalie H., 1971, *Doing Fieldwork: Warnings and Advice*. Chicago and London: The University of Chicago Press.

There have been a number of good books recently describing fieldwork experience, and in my opinion this is the best. The author is theoretically astute and fully aware of the complexities of her situation in a scientific sense, yet does not lose sight in her description of the emotional, "human" aspects of the situations she describes—some of which were quite sticky. This book does a fine job of recreating the full range of perceptions and emotions involved in this "trial by fire" of all ethnologists.

### Linguistics

Gleason, H. A., 1961, *An Introduction to Descriptive Linguistics*. New York: Holt, Rinehart, and Winston.

A very influential and clearly written textbook, oriented toward anthropological linguistics.

Hymes, Dell, ed., 1964, *Language in Culture and Society: A Reader in Linguistics and Anthropology*. New York: Harper and Row.

A good comprehensive reader, including some more unusual papers. Hymes' introductory remarks to the various sections are excellent.

Whorf, Benjamin Lee, 1956, *Language, Thought, and Reality*. Selected writings edited by John B. Carroll. Cambridge: M.I.T. Press.

A collection of papers dealing mainly with the structure of language and its relation to thought, especially with the problem of how language can be said to embody thought. These papers raise questions that remain as outstanding problems for modern theory, and the concepts employed stand as a major alternative to those used in most other types of modern linguistic research.

# Archeology

## Chapter 2

# Kalinga Pottery-Making: The Evolution of A Research Design

**William A. Longacre**

This chapter describes the evolution of a research project which is presently in its beginning stages. The research focuses on pottery and other material items being made and used by the Kalinga, a tribal people living in the mountains of northern Luzon, the Philippines. The results of this work should have direct relevance to archeological methods for inferring patterns of behavior and organization of peoples who existed in the past.

It may seem odd that an archeologist is beginning a field project among living peoples, and perhaps even stranger that an archeologist who has done most of his excavation in the southwestern United States is working in the Philippines. Perhaps the most perplexing fact is that somehow these interests, southwestern archeology and Kalinga ethnography, are intimately related. The purpose of this account is to reveal the link through a presentation of the gradual development of the research project.

In the process, we will be exploring the ways in which archeologists have attempted to infer various aspects of the organization and behavior of peoples who existed in the past. Archeologists have long been interested in these nonmaterial aspects of extinct societies, but the problem has always been in determining them from only material remains. How can one study the means of reckoning descent, for example, or the rules for establishing residence after marriage using archeological data? What can the ruins of houses or fragments of pottery reveal about social organization? How does the archeologist use them to infer behavior?

51

## BACKGROUND TO THE PROJECT

Archeology is hardly over 100 years old as a systematic field of study. From the beginning archeologists have made inferences about human behavior. During the past century, the ways in which archeologists have approached the problem of inferring behavior from prehistoric materials have changed, and it is instructive to examine the different approaches in some detail. To do this, we will focus on the southwestern United States, an area that has been the scene of active archeological work since the 1880s.

### Ethnographic Analogy

Interestingly, the earliest workers in the Southwest were equally at home conducting ethnographic field work among the various American Indian groups living in the area as they were undertaking excavations of prehistoric sites. They saw archeology simply as the extension of ethnology into the past. Since they were interested in the organization and behavior of American Indian societies, they turned to archeology as a means to develop historical perspective for these peoples.

They noted that the prehistoric villages they excavated were quite similar to the villages of the living peoples. Pueblo peoples, like the Hopi and Zuñi Indians, were therefore thought to be direct descendants of the peoples who built the prehistoric Pueblo communities in the area. Since the prehistoric styles of architecture and pottery were similar to their modern counterparts, the early archeologists assumed that aspects of social organization and behavior must be similar as well.

By learning about modern Pueblo social organization, for example, these archeologists thought they would be able to interpret the social organization of past Pueblo peoples. They noted the association between certain styles of buildings among the modern Pueblo Indians and various divisions of the society. They tried to identify the numbers and kinds of rooms utilized by a single family. They observed that special ceremonial structures (kivas) were used by social groups larger than the family, such as "clans." Then when they excavated prehistoric Pueblo sites, they used these observations to discuss prehistoric families and clans. This approach to inferring behavior and organization archeologists call ethnographic analogy. In a sense it involves the use of knowledge about the present as a means of interpreting the past. Things found by archeological investigation that had similar counterparts among modern peoples were assumed to have had the same significance or meaning in the past as they have in the present. This approach is based on the assumption that there has been little or no change from the past to the present. Thus, if kivas are associated with clans among contemporary Pueblo peoples, then they must indicate clans in the prehistoric sites where they are found.

Today, these early attempts to infer social organization from prehistoric remains appear somewhat simplistic. Though the questions that were being asked did focus attention on these important nonmaterial aspects of past societies, the method of obtaining answers was inadequate.

Most of the early workers were not academically trained in anthropology. Formal education in the discipline was not available in this country until the latter part of the nineteenth century. Some of the workers were zoologists and botanists with a background in natural science, but lacking formal training in anthropology. When the first anthropologically trained archeologists appeared, there were enormous changes in the direction of prehistoric research in the Southwest.

Some writers have referred to the period from about 1910 to 1925 as a time of revolution in American archeology. There was a new, systematic emphasis on defining prehistoric cultures and placing them in time and space. Archeological cultures in this framework were defined on the basis of certain observable features or traits, such as styles of pottery and houses. Precise methods were developed to place the cultures so defined into their proper relative chronological order.

This body of newly rigorous research quickly demolished the rather uncomplicated view of prehistoric Pueblo culture that had permitted direct analogy with living peoples. Aspects of prehistoric peoples that could not be directly observed in the archeological record came to be ignored by archeologists on the grounds that they required speculation rather than objective appraisal of facts. With methods of data collection then in use, one could not observe social organization in a prehistoric ruin; one saw, handled, and photographed only the material items that survived, such as ruined houses, pottery, and other physical artifacts.

The period from roughly 1910 to 1950 was a productive one for historical studies in the Southwest. Great amounts of research were conducted and the complex outlines of Southwestern prehistory gradually emerged. Important historical events and processes, such as the change from hunting and gathering subsistence to agriculture, were identified. Techniques for dating prehistoric sites were refined, and workers attempted to offer explanations for historical processes they inferred from the archeological record. It was discovered, for example, that large portions of the Pueblo area were abandoned by 1300. Explanations ranging from extreme droughts to foreign invaders were offered to account for this depopulation.

Concern with the development of Pueblo society, however, had not disappeared from all anthropological studies in the American Southwest.

Cultural anthropologists were still interested in the development of social institutions and other nonmaterial aspects of Pueblo culture. Interesting hypotheses accounting for the modern form of Pueblo societies were presented by a variety of cultural anthropologists, but Southwestern archeologists tended to focus on their own interests in historical recon- struction of "objective" prehistory.

Around the time of World War II, the archeological world was shaken by several scathing reviews of current work. One was written by an archeologist (Taylor 1948) and the other by a cultural anthropologist (Kluckhohn 1940). They pointed out how archeology had diverged from the mainstream of modern anthropology and argued that nonmaterial aspects of past peoples had to be studied in order to understand clearly what happened in the past.

By the 1950s archeologists in the Southwest once again began to offer inferences about the behavior and organization of past societies. But they made these inferences largely on the basis of ethnographic analogies, much as the workers in the 1890s had done. Some workers even accepted the hypotheses offered by the cultural anthropologist as "true" and used them to interpret the prehistoric communities.

## Alternative Approach

By the early 1960s some archeologists were again becoming dis- satisfied with this approach to the study of the past, but this time their criticism took a new direction. They pointed out that, if we use the present as a means to interpret the past as is done in ethnographic analogy, then we are saying that we have nothing new to learn from the past! Some method was needed that would allow the past to speak for itself. Could we not develop the method and theory that would enable us to *test* hypotheses about nonmaterial aspects of past societies? Follow- ing this possibility, concern began to focus on developing a means to evaluate possible alternative explanations of past behavior.

Several important research projects were completed during the 1950s and 60s. They proposed a method to examine organization and behavior of peoples who existed in the past which used archeological materials such as pottery and arrowheads and which was not directly dependent on ethnographic analogy.

One of these projects was completed in 1960 and involved the analy- sis of several early historical villages occupied by the Arikara Indians in South Dakota (Deetz 1965). Other analyses involved prehistoric com- munities located in Arizona and will be described below. All of the projects had two basic assumptions in common. The first assumption is that the materials in an archeological site are highly structured and patterned. Many of these patterns are extremely subtle and difficult to detect. The second assumption is that the patterns are the direct result of the behavior of the people who made, used, and discarded or abandoned the materials. Of course, many of the material items that once existed are no longer available for study, for they have been destroyed by time and the elements. But enough material items usually survive to enable the archeologist to search out patterns that relate to the hypotheses about behavior and organizations which he is trying to test. Nonetheless, one must always be on the lookout for distortions of original patterns in the archeological record caused by natural processes (erosion, rodent activity, and so on) or even human behavior (such as reburial of human remains or transportation of materials to new locations).

If these assumptions are correct, then we have a means for testing the hypotheses we can generate about past behavior. Different kinds of behavior and organization will produce different kinds of subtle patterns in the archeological record.

*Arikara Society.* The early historical Arikara village that Deetz excavated was occupied largely during the eighteenth century. During the time that the village existed, the Arikara Indians underwent a number of profound changes, which are documented in travelers' accounts and other such historical materials of the period, independent of the archeological record proper. They experienced a rapid population decline and there was a major economic change. At the beginning of the eighteenth century, the Arikara economy was centered on productive agriculture, largely the domain of female labor. By the latter part of the century, the Arikara were drawn into the fur trade, and wealth began to result from the trading activities of males.

This economic shift had profound effects on Arikara social organization. During the early period, the Arikara were strongly matricentered in their organization: descent was traced through the female line and residence after marriage was with the wife's family (uxorilocal residence). Because of the changes in the economy and the population decline, the social system gradually became more flexible. The importance of males in the economic system led to a breakdown of the earlier pattern of uxorilocal residence after marriage.

Deetz wondered if these changes would be reflected in the archeological materials recovered at the site. He focused on patterns in the decoration of pottery produced by the women when the village was occupied. Since mothers or grandmothers taught daughters the art of pottery making, Deetz argued that, through time, microtraditions of pottery styles should result. If related female potters tended to live together as would result from uxorilocal residence rules, then these microtraditions should be localized in various discrete parts of the village over time. As the change toward male-dominated productive activities developed, these patterns of localized microtraditions of ceramic styles should break down with the disintegration of the system of uxorilocal residence.

Deetz considered a variety of decorative features of the pottery in his analysis. He hypothesized that these features should form clusters during the early periods and that during the later period the decorative features should be distributed more randomly within the village. He used a computer for the analysis and was able to demonstrate that the decorative features in the ceramics did in fact cluster during the early period but not during the later period of the village's occupation. This demonstration confirmed the hypothesis, and the study shows the value of the underlying assumption of a relationship between the behavior of people and the subtle patterns present in the materials they made and used.

*Cronin's Study.* At about the same time, an independent analysis of prehistoric pottery styles was undertaken by a cultural anthropologist (Cronin 1962). Taking part in a series of research projects sponsored by the Southwest Expedition of the Field Museum of Natural History, Cronin was working with ceramics recovered from several contemporaneous prehistoric communities located in east-central Arizona. The pottery consisted of several distinctive styles of decorated black-on-white wares, and each village produced all the different styles of decoration. All the pottery she had to work with was in the form of broken pieces, called sherds. But there were decorations on the pottery fragments, and she focused her analysis on the decorative features or elements that occurred on each sherd.

The original intent of her study was to assess the degree of similarity among the different styles of pottery produced in eastern Arizona at the time the communities were occupied (about A.D. 900). In the course of her work, however, she noticed that there were more similarities in decoration among the different styles of pottery found at any one of these sites than there were within a single style produced at all of the villages.

This finding had some interesting implications. If the pottery had been made by the women, it suggested that women were remaining in the village over time. If several generations were involved, there might be a subtle microtradition of ceramic decoration present at each village. Further, the clustering of decorative features by village may reflect aspects of a tradition based on descent.

Those of us associated with the Southwest Expedition were greatly stimulated by the results. We decided to design some projects that would refine the method of investigation and augment our understanding of the evolution of culture in east-central Arizona during the several centuries after A.D. 1000. We were particularly interested in this period because from the prehistoric record a number of major changes appeared to have occurred at that time. It was a time of population aggregation in the area, for example. Prior to about 1000, the region was the scene of many small Pueblo hamlets from 1 to perhaps 15 rooms. Then relatively suddenly, these small villages were abandoned and people began to aggregate into much larger towns. By 1300, some towns had as many as 100 rooms.

We were attempting to understand the reasons for this process of population clustering and the emergence of large towns. We were also concerned with identifying the enormous social changes that must have accompanied the joining together of diverse groups of people to form a single large community. Cronin's research offered a means of exploring aspects of organization and behavior during this period of change in the nature of communities in the prehistory of east-central Arizona.

We focused our research on two prehistoric sites in the area. One, the Carter Ranch Site, was occupied at the beginnings of population convergence (about A.D. 1100–1225). It is a Pueblo community of about 40 rooms with several ceremonial structures (kivas) and a large trash mound. The other site, Broken K Pueblo, was occupied during the later period (about A.D. 1150–1280) and, with 95 rooms, is more than twice the size of Carter Ranch Pueblo.

*Carter Ranch Site.*   A plan or map of the Carter Ranch Site is presented in Figure 2.1. Site plans such as this are useful to the archeologist in planning research and an important way to present basic information resulting from the excavation of a site. Usually the map is prepared by the archeologist himself using surveying equipment and it is therefore necessary to develop surveying and cartographic skills in training to become an archeologist.

Traditionally, such maps were prepared as the excavation was carried out and site plans were viewed as a result of excavation. More recently, reasonably accurate maps are being produced prior to major excavations as a helpful device in planning the research. This is especially true for work in Puebloan sites in the American Southwest.

Corners of all the rooms in such a site are excavated to the point where the nature of construction of the corners can be observed. Revealing the corners permits an accurate, room-by-room map to be drawn and enables the archeologist to determine the sequence of construction of the rooms and groups of rooms at the site. When the map and analysis of the corner constructions of rooms is completed, the archeologist can determine the frequency of variously sized rooms in the site as well as the relative time each was built. Such information is critical to selecting rooms for excavation.

The Carter Ranch Site consists of a U-shaped block of rooms which

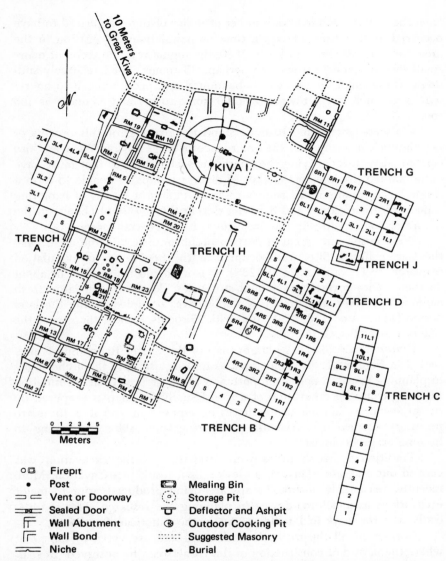

**Figure 2.1** *Plan of the Carter Ranch Site, East-Central Arizona. (From* Fieldiana: Anthropology, *vol. 55, p. 16; Chicago, Ill.: Field Museum of Natural History, 1964. Reprinted by permission.)*

face a courtyard or plaza with various activity areas, such as cooking and storage facilities and ceremonial structures. A large trash mound is located in front of the site. This mound contained a number of human burials, which formed three clusters: one at the north end of the mound, one at the south end, and one in the middle. The burials in the northern cluster were oriented east-west; those in the southern areas were oriented north-south; and the burials in the central area were mixed with respect to orientation.

Our preexcavation research design involved the formulation of testable hypotheses and the generation of test implications or data expectations for them. Extending Cronin's method, we hoped to investigate the intrasite structure to see if we would discover meaningful divisions within the community.

For example, one hypothesis was formalized as follows: if there were a residence rule that led to related females living in the same locale through several generations, then ceramic manufacture and decoration would be learned and passed down within the context of this residence unit (assuming female potters). Nonrandom preference for certain designs might reflect this social patterns.

One hundred and seventy-five design elements and element groups were defined using more than 6,000 sherds and a number of whole vessels. A computer was used to assess the distribution of these decorative features in the pottery, and several spatial clusters were defined. One cluster encompassed a group of adjacent rooms at the south end of the pueblo and a second included a block of rooms at the north end of the pueblo with an adjacent kiva.

The ceramics associated with the burials were analyzed to see if the burial clusters could be related to the architectural units of the site. Our results suggest that the northern burial area had pottery with designs that occurred in the northern rooms at the site, and the southern burial group was similarly linked to the southern rooms. The central burial cluster was mixed with respect to design distribution.

The burials in the central part of the trash mound were quite different from the other two burial clusters. In addition to being mixed in orientation and in the distribution of design elements and element groups, this central cluster of burials contained almost all of the ceremonial items included as grave offerings. There was a greater concentration of pottery vessels in the central cluster than we would expect by chance—almost one and a half times as many vessels per burial.

|  | North | Center | South |
|---|---|---|---|
| Vessels | 19 | 32 | 20 |
| Burials | 8 | 9 | 8 |

The pattern suggests that the central cluster represents "high status" individuals drawn from the residence units. It would appear that each of the residence units maintained its own burial area but that a separate portion of the cemetery was reserved for relatively "high status" individuals.

On the assumption that the females were the potters, the patterned distribution of ceramic decoration in contiguous groups of rooms, kivas, and trash deposits argues for postmarital residence in the vicinity of the wife's female relatives, with ceramic decoration learned and passed down within the residence unit. The localization of females in architectural units at the site over a period of several generations suggests in turn that nonportable objects such as rooms and access to a specific mortuary area were inherited within the residence units and that this inheritance was probably in the female line.

The Carter Ranch Site stands as a turning point in the prehistory of this particular region of the Southwest. The occupation of the site by two residence units began in an era of population aggregation in the area. Prior to this—over a period of more than 500 years—villages consisted of small groups of people approximating the size of one of the residence units of the Carter Ranch Site. This striking shift in the structure of population culminates in a pattern of fewer but considerably larger towns during the fourteenth century.

The process of aggregation coincides with the onset of a period of environmental stress and would seem to be an adaptive response on the part of these extinct societies. The initial set of adaptive changes appeared in the area by 1300. Many of these changes seem to be in the direction of a form of cultural system similar to that of the modern Western Pueblo peoples (Longacre 1970a).

*Broken K Pueblo.*   In an effort to refine and expand the method and theory behind the work at the Carter Ranch Site, we next turned our attention to Broken K Pueblo. Broken K is located in the same valley as the Carter Ranch Site. It is the latest site in the immediate area and was occupied from about 1150 to 1280. Directed by James N. Hill, the work at the site employed a number of important innovations in archeological method and theory. These included the application of sampling design for the selection of rooms to be excavated based on statistical probability theory, and the use of fossil pollen recovered from the floors of rooms to determine the range of activities carried out in the rooms as well as to assist in the relative dating of the rooms at the site.

Hill was able to demonstrate the presence of five uxorilocal residence units at the community, and these were grouped into two larger, more inclusive units. The five residence units at Broken K Pueblo were similar in size to the two units discovered at the Carter Ranch Site, which suggests that the whole community was perhaps equivalent to one of the major groups at Broken K Pueblo. This finding sheds light on the process of aggregation, and Hill (1970:107–8) was able to suggest that, as villages increased in size, there were probably more of the larger groupings per village.

Hill made this inference on the basis of sophisticated statistical tests run with a computer program designed to assess patterns in the distribution of a wide range of cultural materials at the site. One of these studies involved the distribution of design elements and element groups in the ceramics at Broken K. Hill also used other kinds of data to augment the findings based on the patterned array of decorative features on the pottery.

Hill's results complement and generally extend the findings at the Carter Ranch Site. The addition of a second major study in the same area based on the basic assumptions we have described adds strength to our feeling that the assumptions are probably correct. My own current archeological research is focused on another prehistoric community in the American Southwest, the Grasshopper Pueblo, located about 25 miles south of the Carter Ranch Site and Broken K. The preliminary results from this study also support our belief in the validity of these primary assumptions. Indeed, we can continue to attempt to assess their validity by treating them as law-like generalizations and deducing testable hypotheses about aspects of behavior and organization of extinct communities. As more studies are carried out whose results are positive and internally consistent, our confidence in the validity of the assumptions will continue to grow.

## THE PRESENT PROJECT

There is another approach to this problem that might be more efficient. This approach would involve undertaking field work in a situation where both the patterns of material culture and the behavior and organization of a society were observable; it would mean doing field work in a living society. Great care would have to be exercised in selecting a society in terms of the particular aspects of behavior and organization that one wanted to explore. For example, if I wanted to examine the degree to which subtle variability in pottery decoration reflected the learning framework and the effects of coresidence on potters, then I would have to choose a particular type of society to study. It would obviously have to be a society which makes and uses pottery on a large scale. In addition, the pottery-making must be an activity carried on throughout the society and not by only a small group of specialists. Also, the pottery must be made by the people for their own use and not as a commercial product to sell to tourists or to supply regional demands for pottery in a market. In these latter cases, pressures would be exerted on the potters to produce wares that would "sell," which would probably distort the more subtle effects that would produce microtraditions in a nonmarket economic system.

As one might imagine, finding such a society is difficult in this age of mass-produced metal and plastic containers! Nonetheless, I wished to undertake field work in such a community which made and used pottery on a household basis. Further, I hoped to find a group that had been studied by a cultural anthropologist. This would make the sociology of the group available to me, allowing me to study directly the connection between variability in the material culture produced and used by the group and its organization and behavior.

Does such a society exist in the world? I began my search close to home. There are American Indian groups in the southwestern United States who make pottery today. These include the various Pueblo peoples such as the Hopi and Zuñi as well as groups like the Navajo, Pima, and Papago. In all cases, however, these peoples are producing pottery almost entirely for sale to tourists and not for their own use. Throughout Mexico, pottery is produced and used on a large scale, but it is made by specialists for sale in the market. I could find no society close at hand that suited my research intersts.

Finally I learned of a group in the Philippines that sounded ideal for my purposes. These people are the Kalinga and live in the mountains of northern Luzon. They had been studied in the 1930s by cultural anthropologists and as recently as 1965 by the late Dr. Edward P. Dozier of the University of Arizona, whose book presents an anthropological description of Kalinga society (Dozier 1966). The Kalinga live in small isolated villages in the Kalinga-Apayao Province in northern Luzon. They are rice agriculturalists, and, traditionally, they make and use pottery on a household basis. Also, in some of the Kalinga areas, there is a tendency toward uxorilocal postmarital residence.

Do the Kalinga still make pottery for their own use or has "civilization" caught up with them? Professor Dozier told me he thought there were pottery-using villages in the more remote Kalinga areas. I tried to find out by writing to anthropologists who had worked in the Philippines. I contacted a number of American and Filipino anthropologists at the University of Philippines and at the Philippine National Museum. No one could tell me the current situation; I could not find out if any of the Kalinga villages still made and used pottery on a household basis.

In order to undertake the kind of research project I felt was necessary, I would have to spend about a year living in a community. I would need to make detailed studies of the pottery-making in a number of households throughout an annual cycle. I would have to study how pottery-making was learned, and who taught whom. I would want to collect detailed information on the uses of pottery by the society and the native system of classification. I would also have to record carefully the disposition of pottery and other items of material culture made and used by these people. To accomplish all this, I would have to obtain a rather substantial research grant, probably from the National Science Foundation. But how could I submit a detailed proposal to such an agency when I could not determine if an appropriate field situation existed? And even if there were Kalinga villages which made and used pottery, would I be welcome to live with them for a year and undertake such a study?

I decided that the only way I could answer these questions was to go to the Philippines and visit the more remote Kalinga villages myself. Toward that end I applied for a University of Arizona Institutional Grant for funds. I described my project as a feasibility study to see if the larger project I wished to undertake were possible and referred to this first stage in my research as "Phase I." I was awarded a grant of one thousand dollars to help cover my expenses.

In the late spring of 1973 I made extensive contact with friends and colleagues in the Filipino anthropological community, telling them that I wished to visit the Kalinga and what I hoped to accomplish. They were encouraging in their responses and promised whatever assistance they could offer. On July 1, 1972, I left San Francisco for Manila by air.

I arrived in Manila early in the morning on July third. During the next week, I spent much of my time at the National Museum and the University of the Philippines discussing my project with colleagues and seeking advice and aid in making essential contacts. With their help, I hired a Kalinga guide who agreed to take me to a remote area of Kalinga villages where pottery was supposedly still being made and used.

I traveled north from Manila by bus to Baguio City in the Mountain Province where I met my guide. From there we traveled northward by bus for two days into the Kalinga-Apayao Province. We left the bus at the small Kalinga town of Lubuagan and from there hiked for half a day on the mountain trail to the village of Dangtalan. I stayed in Dangtalan for about one week and from there visited other Kalinga villages in the Pasil Municipality.

These villages are remote and somewhat cut off from the outside world. Nearly everything the Kalinga need they grow or make themselves. They grow rice in a complex system of irrigated terraces surrounding the villages, and they raise pigs, chickens, dogs (a source of meat on certain occasions), as well as carabao and some cattle. Only a few staples are brought in from the outside: salt, sugar, tobacco, and occasionally dried fish and cooking oil.

Of greatest interest to me was the pottery. It was abundant and conspicuous in everyday use. In Dangtalan, pottery is used to cook with, to store food, to brew *Basi* (a sugar cane wine), and to transport and

**Figure 2.2**  *A woman at work making pottery.*

store water. Every adult woman in the village makes pottery for her own family, a skill that is learned from her mother. I was able to observe a great deal of stylistic and functional variability in the Kalinga pottery.

I was in Dangtalan during the rice-planting season, and most women were busy in the fields. No one was making pottery. I was able to spend one day, however, observing a woman making pottery in the nearby village of Puapo. I recorded basic technological data on Kalinga pottery-making and checked their validity by asking my hosts in Dangtalan about the accuracy of my notes. I also was able to take a number of photographs illustrating the various stages in pottery manufacture.

In addition, I obtained basic information on the Kalinga classification of their own pottery. They classify their pottery on the basis of the design of the container in terms of its projected use. This functionally based classificatory system focuses on such features of the ceramic vessel as size, shape, presence or absence of a slip (a thin wash of finely ground clay), and other features.

During the week I spent with the Kalinga at Dangtalan, it became clear that I had found an ideal situation to carry out the research project I had in mind. But would I be welcome to come back at some future date for an extended stay?

The Kalinga are warm and generous people. They welcomed me to their village and treated me as a relative rather than as an outsider. They respected my interest in their pottery-making and did everything they could to facilitate my inquiry during my brief stay.

On one day during my stay in Dangtalan, a funeral was held for a child who had died a few days earlier in a nearby village. I was invited to attend the funeral along with a delegation from Dangtalan. A number of villages also sent delegations, so when we arrived there was a considerable group of people present.

At Kalinga funerals, the women gather in the house of the deceased while the men sit in front of the house. The men drink *Basi* and discuss a variety of topics. Discussion takes the form of speeches and responses by individuals addressed to the entire group. All of the village leaders were present at this funeral, and it was a time of discussion of topics of interest to all the Kalinga villages in the area.

There was a certain amount of polite curiosity about me and my reasons for being there. I was asked to explain myself to the entire group. Further, I was asked a number of other questions. For example, they were curious to know how American funerals compared to the one I was attending. They were also interested in the recent moon-landings they had heard about. They wanted to know if America had really landed men on the moon and how, in fact, I knew this to be true. They were curious to know my feelings about styles of government and various political matters. And they asked probing questions about my research interest in Kalinga pottery. At the end of this rather lengthy public discussion, a senior headman rose and made a speech indicating that they were pleased with my answers and especially with my interest in the Kalinga people. He said I would be welcome to return to undertake my research and that he and his people would help me in any way they could. After this we drank more *Basi*, and then a carabao was slaughtered and butchered and all of us present were given some meat to take home to our villages for the evening meal. I felt then the way was clear for me to return to Dangtalan to undertake the research project over an extended period of time; I would be welcome.

I left Dangtalan and a number of new friends at the end of the week. After hiking out to Lubuagan, I took the bus south making a detour to Banaue where I visited the famous Ifugao Rice Terraces. From there I returned to Baguio City and then to the town of Calasiao in Pangasinan Province on the coast, north and west of Manila. I spent several days in Calasiao visiting barrios and observing domestic pottery in use in these low land communities.

I returned to Manila where I spent several days discussing my experiences and plans with my Filipino colleagues at the University and the National Museum. During this period I presented a public lecture at the National Museum and conducted a seminar for anthropology students at the University of the Philippines. I also spent one afternoon at a commercial pottery-making factory in Maybunga in Rizal Province. This provided interesting comparative perspective.

The next step will be to undertake the actual research and that, of course, requires a great deal of careful preparation and planning. I am now at work developing a fairly detailed research design that will guide my planned field work among the Kalinga. This work will focus on the degree to which stylistic variation in the pottery reflects the way in which pottery-making is learned by Kalinga potters and the effects of living and working together in the same household. When I return I will have two major tasks: (1) to develop fine scale measures for recording stylistic variability in Kalinga pottery and (2) to understand and record the social context of pottery-making.

My work will include making a map of each of the pottery-making Kalinga villages, showing every house, and doing a census of each village to determine the exact genealogical relationships of the members of each household and the relationships between and among households. Using this information, I will select groups of related potters (probably mothers and daughters) and potters who are not related but who consistently work together in making pottery. Such individuals would have learned the art of pottery-making from different teachers. The pots made by these groups will be carefully analyzed and stylistic variability will be recorded. After analysis I will then measure the degree of similarity in the pottery made by each group of potters. Some of the variables in the pottery to be measured include: the design attributes selected by each potter for decorating her pots; the exact color of the pot (primarily the result of the temperature and the length of time of the firing of the vessel); the number, size, and placement of "firing clouds" on each pot (a blackened area caused by the combusting fuel actually touching the pot during firing); the thickness of the vessel wall for each type of pot; the degree of curvature of the flaring rim for each types of vessel; the size of each category of pot; the size of the aperture of each vessel; and other additional features.

I hope to work with a minimum of 100 vessels for each potter in my sample and plan to record 40 to 50 observations for each pot. I hope to work with at least 25 potters from each of three villages. This research will form the core of the project, but other aspects will also be investigated such as observing and recording the "life spans" of pots in everyday use. I hope to determine how long different types of pots used in various kinds of activities survive and to study patterns of disposal of broken pots and other household debris. I plan to record basic technological data on Kalinga pottery-making in order to present a detailed description of the ceramics.

I anticipate that the results of my archeological project will support my theory that the subtle patterns I now believe exist in Kalinga pottery do indeed relate to the social organization and behavior of the Kalinga people. If I am successful in detailing this relationship, the results should be of great use to archeologists interested in studying the ceramics of a people in order to better understand the organization and behavior of people who lived in the past.

## SELECTED READINGS

Binford, S. R. and Binford, L. R., eds., 1968, *New Perspectives in Archeology*. Chicago. Aldine Publishing Co.

A series of essays that will augment aspects of the method and theory discussed in this chapter with numerous examples.

Deetz, James, 1965, The Dynamics of Stylistic Change in Arikara Ceramics. *Illinois Studies in Anthropology*, no. 4. Urbana: University of Illinois Press.

Reports the details of the author's research briefly described in this chapter.

Dozier, Edward P., 1966, *Mountain Arbiters, the Changing Life of a Philippine Hill People*. Tucson: University of Arizona Press.

A full description of Kalinga society and culture with a number of photographs.

Hill, James N., 1970, "Broken K Pueblo, Prehistoric Social Organization in the American Southwest," *Anthropological Papers of the University of Arizona*, no. 18. Tucson: University of Arizona Press.

A full description of the research briefly described in this chapter.

Longacre, William A., 1970, "Archaeology as Anthropology: A Case Study," *Anthropological Papers of the University of Arizona*, no. 17. Tucson: University of Arizona Press.

A description of the research carried out at the Carter Ranch Site.

Longacre, William A., ed., 1970, *Reconstructing Prehistoric Pueblo Societies*. Albuquerque: University of New Mexico Press.

Focuses upon additional research carried out in the Southwest designed to investigate aspects of prehistoric social organization.

Martin, Paul S. and Plog, Fred, 1973, *The Archeology of Arizona: A Study of the Southwest Region*. New York: Natural History Press.

An excellent general survey of the prehistory of the Southwest.

# Chapter 3

# Settlement Patterns and Social History

**Fred Plog**

The work of the archeologist in attempting to understand man's past is firmly identified in the minds of most individuals with excavation, or digging. The laboratory, where artifacts are cleaned, conserved, analyzed, and interpreted, is usually considered a second major area of work in archeology. This essay is concerned with neither excavation nor laboratory analyses, but with a third basic activity of archeology: surveying by observing artifacts and features present on the surface of the earth.

Surveying is the activity of finding prehistoric sites. The survey has a history in archeology that is at least as long as that of excavation, but because many archeologists view it secondarily, as simply the finding of sites for the purpose of excavating them, the survey has never drawn the kind of attention that excavation has. Typically, an individual conducting a modern survey must deal with materials as diverse as historical documents and accounts of travelers that mention the locations of sites or ruins, verbal accounts of living individuals, myths and traditions concerning the past dwelling places and migrations of native populations, aerial photographs and the complex techniques required to identify possible site locations from these photographs, and his own notes. If digging is physically demanding, so is walking many miles in an effort to locate sites. Furthermore, surveys result in the same quantities of materials for laboratory analyses that excavations do. Surveys are, in short, as physically and intellectually demanding as excavations.

In this chapter I will discuss some of the reasons why archeologists undertake surveys, the major concepts used to understand survey data, some difficulties with these concepts, and a newer approach that I have found particularly useful in resolving these difficulties.

## WHY ARCHEOLOGISTS SURVEY

In a concise and comprehensive account (1966), Reynold Ruppé suggests that archeologists undertake surveys for four reasons. The first is to build an inventory of sites. A list of site locations in a given area is often a necessary first step in a project that will primarily involve excavation. In some instances, an excavation project begins with a focus on one particular site. More typically, however, an archeologist begins work in an area because its prehistory is unknown or because some important aspect of its prehistory is unknown, and so he is often uncertain which site or sites will yield the desired information. The archeologist therefore investigates the range of sites that exist within the area in order to make an informed decision in selecting one or more sites for excavation. A survey is undertaken to define acceptable alternatives.

In recent years, surveys intended to build an inventory of sites have been undertaken for the additional purpose of locating sites to prevent their destruction. The rapid growth of our society, especially insofar as it has involved construction projects which significantly modify the surface of the earth, has had a destructive effect on archeological sites. More and more archeologists have invoked a variety of state and national laws covering the preservation of antiquities in order to ensure that such construction efforts will not destroy their ability to understand the prehistory of the affected area. Surveys in areas that are to be disturbed or destroyed have been undertaken with a view to salvaging by excavation evidence from at least some of the sites. The inventory has provided a basis for estimating the extent of the damage that a construction project is about to cause and has permitted the archeologist to make informed decisions as to which sites will most economically provide information on the area's prehistory. In both these cases, the primary purpose of carrying out the survey is to build an inventory of sites and so ensure that an excavation to be done in the future has a high probability of success.

The second major reason archeologists survey is to obtain background information that will aid them in interpreting materials uncovered through excavation. While survey work typically precedes excavation, excavation does sometimes lead to survey. In the course of excavating a site, an archeologist may encounter problems whose solutions require the collection of survey data. For example, in excavating a stratified site—a site on which different prehistoric occupations are stacked on top of each other—the excavator may discover that some occupations are well represented at the site while others are not. A survey may serve to fill in these gaps. Similarly, an archeologist might find a series of artifacts that do not seem to have been made at the site he is excavating and undertake a survey in order to discover their origin. He might also find that the settlement he is excavating was surrounded by pallisades and undertake a survey to determine if there are other pallisaded settlements in the area. Finally, archeologists often begin surveys to obtain a larger collection of artifacts to compare with those they have already excavated.

During the last two decades, more and more archeologists have surveyed for the purpose of obtaining survey information independent of excavation. A part of this recent development, the third major reason archeologists survey is to define the spatial and temporal boundaries of a prehistoric culture. Archeologists define prehistoric cultures on the basis of distinctive associations of artifacts and artifact styles. For many investigators it is important to know the extent of the terriory occupied by a prehistoric culture, defined in this sense. Such information is obtained not by excavating a single site or even a few sites, but rather by surveying a region in an effort to find the limits or boundaries of the material patterns used to define the culture. If similar information is desired concerning related populations or populations who occupied nearby areas, a survey may be used to investigate the expansion and contraction of the populations' territories over time. Similarly, given that an archeologist has some way of distinguishing sites of different time periods, he may undertake a survey to arrive at an estimate of the temporal boundaries of a prehistoric culture.

The fourth major reason for surveying, which is also independent of excavation, is to understand a prehistoric population's organization and/ or adaptation to its environment. Ruppé defines this last type of survey in terms of its emphasis on collecting all of the kinds of data that can be recovered from the surface of sites. But what he has in mind is collecting all of the kinds of recoverable data that will be useful in understanding the organization/adaptation of the populations that inhabited the sites.

It should be noted that while the third type of survey focuses on survey work rather than excavation, it does not focus on the sites per se. It treats the sites as mines from which information relevant to the definition of spatial and temporal boundaries of a population is taken. But when a survey effort focuses on a population's organizational and adaptive problems, the characteristics of the sites themselves are important as well as the artifacts collected from them.

As Ruppé suggests, such surveys typically involve the collection of many different kinds of data. As in other types of surveys, collections of artifacts are made at each site. In addition, a record is made of a variety of characteristics of each site itself—its size, its shape, and the presence/ absence of rooms. If architecture is visible on the surface, the record will generally include a map of the site. Finally, information is recorded that locates the site with respect to critical natural resources and other sites.

Surveys undertaken to collect space/time data and those undertaken to obtain organizational/adaptive data are sometimes based on the argument that the prehistory of an era can best be understood by collecting large quantities of survey data and supplementing them with the more detailed information that can be obtained by excavation. In other words, unlike the first two types of survey, these are based on the notion that survey is the primary archeological tool and excavation secondary. At a minimum, such surveys are undertaken in the belief that they can provide a range of information concerning the prehistoric past that cannot be obtained in any other way.

## THE SETTLEMENT-PATTERN CONCEPT

The nature and variety of the materials collected in the last two types of survey are complex. This complexity has led archeologists to search for conceptual models that can be used to organize survey data. Over the past twenty years, the single most important concept used in organizing and interpreting survey data has been the *settlement pattern*. As it is used today, the concept is employed in referring to: (1) the distribution of different site types with respect to each other and with respect to natural environmental zones; (2) the design or layout of habitation or dwelling structures; and (3) the layout of settlements (the configuration of different kinds of activity space on a site). The first referent of settlement pattern is the most important for interpreting survey data.

### A Brief History of Settlement Studies

The settlement-pattern concept began to be developed clearly in Gordon Willey's survey work in the Viru Valley of Peru (1953). Willey describes the purposes of this research effort as follows:

> First, to describe a series of prehistoric sites with reference to geographic and chronologic position; second, to outline a developmental reconstruction of these prehistoric settlements with relation to function as well as sequence; third, to reconstruct cultural institutions in so far as they may be reflected in settlement configurations; and fourth, to compare the settlement story of the Viru and other regions of Peru. (1953:1)

Willey employed two key concepts in his study—site type and settlement configuration. For Willey, site types are defined on the basis of different activities that are carried out at them, that is, on their prehistoric function. Functionally different sites are not randomly distributed over the landscape, but form a particular configuration or pattern. Thus, settlement pattern refers to the distribution of different kinds of sites with respect to each other and the natural environment.

Willey's work provided a beginning in modern settlement studies. Subsequent developments have followed two major lines Along the first line there have been a series of attempts to refine his methodological categories and, thereby, make the analysis applicable to a wider range of societies. This is exemplified by Stuart Struever, K. C. Chang, and Bruce Trigger. The second line involves extending the concept of the settlement pattern to new theoretical areas. The work of Robert M. Adams will serve as an important example.

Struever's work in the Illinois River Valley focused on those aspects of settlement patterns which relate to a population's interaction with its natural environment. Struever argues that variations in the distribution of artifacts, dwellings, and work structures within sites can be used to define "activity areas" and "areas of social distinction" within sites. Site types are then to be defined on the basis of different configurations of activity areas and areas of social distinction at different sites. In brief:

> All sites in which a particular configuration of exploitative and mainte-
> nance activities were carried out will disclose a similar structure of mate-
> rial elements, and thus become examples of a single site type. (1968:287)

In looking at a region, Struever argues, the distribution, kind, and number of sites and their relationship to natural resource zones can be used to define a *subsistence-settlement system*. Thus, Struever speaks of settlement types such as shoreline settlements, bluff camps, bluff base settlements, summer agricultural camps, regional exchange centers, and mortuary camps.

It is important to note the differences between the ways Willey and Struever use the site-type concept. Willey defined site types on the basis of their observable major attributes: their size, the presence or absence of temples, temple mounds, public buildings, cemeteries, and so on. Struever, working with the remains of a far more primitive people, could not employ these criteria. While attention is given to the layout of sites, crucial to Struever's type definitions are the artifacts and patterns of artifacts found at sites, the ecofacts (subsistence remains), and the location of the sites with respect to natural resources. Struever's approach reflects his ultimate concern with resource extraction within an area and the exchange of resources between areas. Thus, Struever has developed a particular interpretation of the settlement-pattern concept which reflects the characteristics of the archeological data he deals with and concentrates on the natural environment and its effect on settlement patterning.

Chang, like Struever, has worked with archeological data left by societies that were less complex than those of the Viru (1967, 1968, 1972). While he has by no means ignored the natural environment or problems of resource acquisition, his own interests have led him to a greater concern with the relationship between settlement patterns and cultural institutions than is reflected in Struever's work. His greatest contribution has been in the area of making institutional inferences from settlement data.

For Chang, the settlement is the primary analytical and interpretive unit of archeological research. He argues that the layout of sites reflects the social organization of the population that inhabited them as well as land-ownership patterns. Chang describes, for example, the neolithic period (the prehistoric period of transition from a hunting-gathering to an agricultural resource base) in terms of changes from nonlineage, unplanned villages to planned villages where a single lineage resided and finally to planned, segmented villages where several lineages resided.

Like Struever, Chang is working with a site-type concept that departs from Willey's original notion. The important characteristics of a site in Chang's view are those that allow the archeologist to describe the community that once existed at the site, specifically to determine whether the settlement was planned or unplanned, segmented or unsegmented, and whether it was the residence of an aggregate of individuals, a lineage, or several lineages. Having described the organization of the community that existed at the site, Chang sees the archeologists' attention turning to the ties among different communities within a region. Thus, Chang's approach permits the archeologist using information left by primitive societies to achieve a more refined understanding of the manner in which settlement patterns reflect cultural institutions.

Bruce Trigger (1968) has effectively summarized the state of settlement pattern studies at present. On the one hand, he considers a large list of "determinants" of settlement patterns that archeologists have now identified. These are natural and social environmental factors that cause a particular settlement pattern to take the form that it does. On the other hand, he lists a variety of topics that archeologists use settlement data to learn about:

> . . . individual structures furnish information about family organization, craft specialization, and perhaps the relative importance of different aspects of the social structure; the layout of shrines or temples may elucidate religious rituals; community plans have yielded useful information about lineage organization and a community's adaptation to its physical and cultural environments; and real (regional) patterns reflect a good deal about the social and political organization of complex societies as well as about trade and warfare. (1968:74)

These developments mainly extend and refine Willey's original descriptive intent, but they do not apply the concept of a settlement pattern to other than descriptive uses. Now, however, the concept is also used to test theories of how particular structural-functional configurations came into being and how they developed.

The first major use of the concept in this context was by Robert M. Adams (1960, 1965). Adams used the concept to test Wittfogel's (1957) argument that the appearance of complex state and urban societies in some parts of the world was precipitated by the need for bureaucratic and political institutions that could manage the complex irrigation networks on which the success of agriculture in these societies was based. Adams's survey work near Baghdad sought to determine whether the scale of irrigation networks and the relation of settlements to the networks supported Wittfogel's theory. He found that they did not.

> The main towns . . . do not form the hubs of radiating canal networks along which the subsidiary villages are strung. . . . The subsistence requirements for the existing, still comparatively small, population could have been met with flood irrigation based on temporary dams and small ditches to direct the water, supplemented with, or perhaps increasingly replaced in time by small canal systems that grew slowly by accretion but that never were extended more than a few kilometers inland from the streams. In the context of Mesopotamian conditions, it has recently been shown that this kind of irrigation is well within the capabilities of local groups without state intervention. Elaborate control works to regulate the water supply certanly were not necessary for so rudimentary an irrigation system. Hence it is difficult to see the emergence of the towns as a consequence of any monopolistic control of the water supply of surrounding villages, and still more difficult to imagine the growth of their political institutions as a consequence of a need for a bureaucracy concerned with canal management. (1965:40–41)

Paradoxically, both these lines of developments and their contributions to our knowledge raise questions about the value of the concept of the settlement-pattern itself. The concept has been valuable, but might not another concept be more valuable and fit the data better? Specifically, since archeologists recognize a number of cultural patterns that can be inferred from survey-settlement data, is the settlement-pattern concept the best concept for organizing archeological materials to facilitate such inferences? Moreover, since archeologists recognize a substantial number of natural and social environmental variables that affect the kinds and distribution of settlements in a given region, is the settlement-pattern concept the best concept for representing configurations and kinds of sites?

## Settlement Patterns and Specific Inferences

Everything we have said so far suggests that one can use survey data to make inferences concerning specific prehistoric organizational and adaptive patterns. But is the settlement-pattern concept *necessary* for using survey data to make inferences about the organizations of prehistoric societies? The answer to this question—a resounding no—is based on a reasonably simple argument. Using the settlement-pattern concept commits the archeologist to collecting survey data on a wide range of cultural patterns. If an archeologist is interested in some specific organizational pattern, however, he is better off concentrating on those survey data that are relevant to the particular pattern he wishes to understand rather than studying the settlement pattern as a whole. Thus, an archeologist interested in understanding prehistoric religious behavior is likely to focus on sites and architecture associated with this phenomenon. There is no good reason why, for example, he should study seasonal fishing camps. Furthermore, if he is interested in prehistoric fishing techniques, there is no reason why he should be concerned with religious architecture. Yet the settlement-pattern concept would commit him to such an undertaking. For an archeologist interested in a particular cultural pattern, it is not worthwhile to allocate equal time and effort to examining the whole complex set of survey data needed to define a settlement pattern. Let us look at an example.

Mark Leone, an archeologist working in the American Southwest, set out to examine a particular pattern of change in the Hay Hollow Valley of Arizona. He was interested in the effect of the adoption of agriculture on social organization. Leone chose as the focus of his research a particular hypothesis: ". . . increasing dependence on agriculture increases the social distance between minimal economic units" (1968: 1159). He reasoned that the increasing economic autonomy of communities that is associated with the adoption of agricultural subsistence strategies should lead to increasing social autonomy. Social autonomy in turn should involve greater community endogamy, meaning fewer marriages that transcend the boundaries of the community. Cronin's study mentioned in Chapter 2, for example, demonstrates how patterns of decoration on pottery can be used to make inferences about prehistoric Pueblo communities' social organization, especially in regard to postmarital residence rules. These inferences are successfully made without reference to Pueblo settlement patterns. Leone extended the same assumptions and made them applicable to survey work. He collected a very large quantity of ceramic data from several hundred sites in Hay Hollow Valley. He used the ceramic collections from a number of these sites to demonstrate that social autonomy (endogamy) increased as agricul-

ture became more important in the area. (We should note in passing
that the chain of argument upon which such organizational inferences
are based has been questioned in recent years. In particular the assumption that endogamy, matrilocality, etc. are actual patterns of behavior in
which all or most of the inhabitants of a prehistoric community partici-
pated has been challenged as an oversimplification of behavior and a
confusion of social behavior and social concepts.)

This shows how ceramic surface collections can be used in making
inferences about prehistoric social organization. But it should be seen
that the conceptual model on which our discussion has focused—the
settlement-pattern model—is in no way necessary to the success of the
effort. Had Leone undertaken a study of Hay Hollow Valley settlement
patterns, he would have become involved in a study so complex that he
would probably not have found time to concentrate on the hypothesis
that was the focus of his research.

Archeologists are always in the position of having to choose between
approaches that are satisfying because they offer some insight into a
broad range of phenomena and approaches that are satisfying because
they offer a great deal of insight into one or a few phenomena. In choosing to employ the settlement-pattern model, an archeologist commits
himself to making a broad range of inferences about each site he is
studying in order to define site types and then settlement patterns. This
is a time-consuming, expensive, and difficult task, but it does result in
some information concerning most sites and a large number of cultural
patterns. When an archeologist is attempting to understand some particular pattern, however, a limited inference about each site may serve
him better than the complex of inferences that the settlement-pattern
model demands.

The difference between these two approaches to the problem is perhaps clearest when we are talking about site types. One cannot employ
the settlement-pattern concept without defining the types of sites that
make up the pattern. In early settlement-pattern studies, when site types
were defined on the basis of gross features such as the presence/absence
of a temple, this was a relatively simple task. But, in later studies, done
in simpler societies and with a concern for greater ecological sophistication, defining site types has become an expensive and time-consuming
task. This temporal and monetary cost becomes important when we
realize that the definition of site types may seldom be essential to understanding particular cultural patterns. For example, the settlement-pattern
model now demands that the archeologist detail at least some ways in
which the organization of populations inhabiting two sites differed. But,
for the study of a particular pattern, it may be sufficient simply to say
that the organization was different or that interaction between inhabi-

tants of the two sites was minimal. Similarly, it is not always necessary to establish that one site was a seasonal fishing camp and another an agricultural camp. It may be sufficient to say that artifacts found on the two sites indicate that the activities carried out there were different. Such an approach would suffice, for example, were an archeologist concerned with the elaboration of activity-specific sites in a population. In short, the settlement-pattern model commits archeologists to many complex inferences. When an archeologist is interested in some specific pattern, he can almost always undertake the understanding of that pattern by employing concepts and models that require fewer and more limited inferences.

### Settlement Patterns and Holism

Many archeologists would agree that the settlement-pattern concept is of limited utility in attempting to make specific inferences but that it is useful for holistic studies.

Most archeologists who attempt to explain prehistoric organization through settlement patterns employ a particular process of reasoning which involves defining settlement patterns for two different areas or two different time periods in the same area and comparing these settlement patterns, noting their similarities and differences. It should also involve attempting to show why these similarities and differences exist. In fact, however, most settlement-pattern studies never proceed to the final point of explanation; most do not even go beyond the point of defining settlement patterns. The failure to go beyond definition and description directly reflects the complexity of the tasks that the settlement-pattern model demands. Unfortunately, the complexity of the concept has led to efforts to simplify it which limit the archeologists' ability to understand prehistoric organization.

First, the site types used in settlement-pattern studies often refer to abstract characteristics which offer little insight into on-the-ground behavior and organization. This problem exists, for example, in Chang's definition of site types based on lineality. The concept of a lineage community is an intuitively appealing one, but such a conceptualization of social organization grossly betrays the complexity of behavior which characterizes most of the populations that anthropologists have studied. The ethnographic literature contains few, if any, descriptions of communities whose inhabitants are all descendants of a single ancestor. It does contain many studies in which descent from a common ancestor is claimed by the inhabitants of a community, whatever their actual genealogical relationship. In this latter situation, lineality is a concept or model that individuals use in discussing and organizing their activites; it cannot be equated with real behavior. Yet, it is precisely lineality as real behavior which underlies Chang's notion of a lineage community

A second difficulty occurs in efforts to make the settlement-pattern model manageable. Most efforts to compare and contrast settlement patterns concentrate not on the pattern itself, but on particular elements of the pattern. For example, pattern X has sites with temple mounds, pattern Y does not. Pattern Y has sites which are fishing camps, pattern X does not. If settlement patterns can be compared only at the level of their elements (site types), there is little utility in building a theory that concentrates on overall configurations.

The settlement-pattern concept is fundamentally synchronic: it is a way to envision a culture—or a set of cultural remains—representing one point in time. When using such a model to deal with change over time, one must organize the data into a series of discrete stages or states. These are then compared and contrasted to determine what has changed from state to state. Such an analysis is still basically comparative or static. It focuses on what has changed, not on the pattern of change.

Finally, it is easier to define a settlement pattern for a period of relative stability than for a period of more rapid change. When site locations last for a reasonably long time and the organization of activities on sites is reasonably constant, it may be possible to define a settlement pattern. When a society is undergoing immense changes, the definition of a settlement pattern will be difficult as preferred site locations and the organization of activities on sites changes. If we are interested in the study of change, we will find only limited utility in a concept that works best when a prehistoric society is changing least.

Settlement pattern models are, then, descriptive functional models with only limited explanatory value. They are models for describing and organizing survey data in order to provide insight into the manner in which prehistoric societies functioned. They are unlikely to lead the archeologist to an understanding of how a particular distribution of sites came to be, how it changed, or why it changed.

## An Alternative Approach

Recently, new conceptual tools applicable to survey data have been developed by a school of geographers who take as their focus topics such as the spatial organization of society and/or spatial behavior (Haggett 1966; Chorley and Haggett 1968; Morrill 1969). They study the location of human settlements and the way that location affects interaction between these settlements. Their approach reflects a much heavier emphasis on the distribution and aggregation of population and the interaction between population aggregations than does the approach of settlement pattern archeologists. This "locational analysis" approach has received some attention in the archeological literature already (see Chang 1972; Hole and Heizer 1973), but to date, most archeologists have viewed it as a source of new ideas to try out in the framework of a more traditional settlement-pattern approach. I want to suggest here that locational analysis is at least potentially a source of a great deal more than isolated new ideas, although it will certainly have to be modified before it is fully developed as an archeological tool. But when it is, it seems very likely it may replace, and go beyond, the idea of a settlement pattern. Let us examine the use of locational techniques in archeological surveys.

When an archeologist begins a survey, he defines a particular territory he will cover. Usually his initial boundaries are culturally arbitrary; they are not defined so as to correspond to some organizational unit that existed in prehistory. Often they are set at the limits of some convenient geographical unit, such as a drainage, a valley, or in the case of salvage work, a highway right-of-way. The first decision made is whether to survey the entire region or some portion or sample of it. Then the crews set out to collect surface artifacts, map sites, note other features of interest such as soil types, vegetation types, available resources, and in general collect the information considered necessary for a general survey of the specific problem at hand. Even a moderately thorough survey can result in a large quantity of artifacts and information.

Using the resulting survey data, one might define settlement patterns for the region. The locational approach suggests an alternative that is much simpler. This approach treats the sites as remains of a *population*, with certain demographic and organizational characteristics, instead of a "culture" or a "society." It identifies a number of population-related characteristics that are known to vary from region to region and that have been shown to reflect organizational variability between regions. Each such characteristic can be expressed directly with straightforward numerical indices for the survey region, avoiding the tedious middle step of deliniating overall patterns. Among the most important characteristics are the following, derived largely from the geographical literature, partly from the archeological literature, and partly from my own organization and codification of earlier work.

A first and most obvious characteristic of any group of sites in a region is its *density*. Density is the number of sites or rooms per unit area. While density is an important characteristic of a population of sites, it is an average figure for an entire survey unit. There are sometimes important variations in patterns of density from area to area within such units. One measure of such variation is *evenness*, which may be defined as the extent of variation in average density from area to area within a survey region. If sites are evenly spaced, there will be little such variation, and the distribution will be even. If there is a tendency for sites to cluster, the distribution is uneven.

A third characteristic, related to evenness, is the *agglomeration* of a site distribution. Agglomeration is a measure of the extent to which a population in a region is distributed evenly among all sites or concentrated in a few sites. It can take a number of forms: there can be regions in which only a few large sites along with many smaller ones but no intermediate sizes are found, for example, or in which an even gradient of site sizes from very small to very large is represented. The *hierarchy* of a distribution is a measure of the extent to which a pattern of agglomeration is associated with a full continuum of site sizes.

So far, these characteristics of the sites of a region all concern the distribution of rooms, the sites themselves, and, inferentially, the spatial distribution of the human population that occupied the area. Other characteristics pertain to activities, or functions. A particular population of sites may be characterized by one or many different kinds of sites, where a kind of site is defined in terms of the activities carried out there. *Differentiation* is a measure of the number of different kinds of activity sites in a population of sites. A population with only a few kinds of sites is undifferentiated; one with many kinds is differentiated. Activities, like population, may be more or less evenly distributed and more or less agglomerated. Thus, it is useful to consider *functional evenness, functional agglomeration*, and *functional hierarchy*, where these terms are defined as above except with reference to *kinds* of sites rather than *sizes* of sites per unit area.

The archeologist can also investigate the *integration* of a population of sites. Integration is a measure of the extent to which the sites in a population of sites are connected or tied together. Following long established archeological tradition, the best way to determine the extent of integration is to investigate the sharing of styles in the manufacture of artifacts among the sites. *Integrative agglomeration, integrative evenness,* and *integrative hierarchy* are important considerations and can be defined along the lines suggested above.

Once these characteristics of a population of sites have been identified, the archeologist is in a position to define one or more spatial clusters which reflect organizational units that existed prehistorically. There may be, for example, regional clusters of sites separated from each other by a few miles, local clusters separated from each other by a mile or so within regional clusters, and site clusters within local clusters. Each cluster so defined has a territory, and the *extent of territory* can be estimated and compared from cluster to cluster and time period to time period within clusters. Similarly, the *symmetry of clustering* can be discussed. Are the site, local, and regional clusters replicas of each other (symmetrical)? Are there no important clusters (nonsymmetrical)? Or are the clusters very different from each other in respect to the characteristics we have been discussing (asymmetrical)?

These characteristics of a population of sites are not final or exhaustive, but they do represent a way of organizing the products of survey research that avoids many of the pitfalls of the settlement-pattern approach. Each of the characteristics, for example, calls for a direct and limited inference from the initial data. Also, each characteristic can be used directly in plotting time trends, without having to build total "stages." Most importantly, each characteristic is an aspect of the population of sites of the overall region, and each site contributes to the character of the population. Thus, although there is no concept of a cultural whole, patterns for the population can be described and different survey areas can be compared without decomposing the pattern into lists of parts. In this framework, comparing two areas does not mean asking whether both have fishing camps or temple mounds. Instead it involves comparing density, differentiation, and a series of other shared and comparable regional characteristics—which can ultimately provide a great deal more insight into the patterns of the areas in question.

## TWO TEST CASES

Testing these ideas, I have used a locational approach in the analysis of survey data in two different areas of eastern Arizona: the Upper Little Colorado and the Chevelon Drainage. The Upper Little Colorado region has been the center of archeological research for the Southwest Archeological Expedition of the Field Museum of Natural History, directed by Paul S. Martin. It is an area of roughly 1300 square miles in east-central Arizona. Since 1960, the work of the Expedition has been concentrated in Hay Hollow Valley. As our first test case we will examine survey data collected during the summer of 1967 from a 5 square-mile area in a savannah environment along Hay Hollow Wash.

The Chevelon drainage has been the focus of research for the Chevelon Archeological Research Project directed by myself and Professors James Hill and Dwight Read of the University of California, Los Angeles. It is a triangular area of roughly 1000 square miles. During the summer of 1972, a 3 square-mile block of the woodland community lying between Purcell and Larson Washes was intensively surveyed, and for our second test case we will concentrate on this locality.[1]

In both the Chevelon and Upper Little Colorado regions, the pre-

1. The bulk of the research done in both of these localities has been made possible by the National Science Foundation, whose support is gratefully acknowledged.

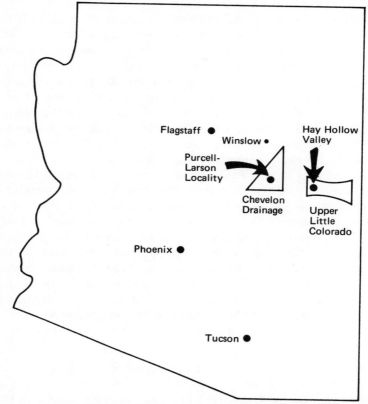

**Figure 3.1**  *The Chevelon and Upper Little Colorado regions and the Purcell-Larson and Hay Hollow localities in Arizona.*

historic record begins in Paleo-Indian times and lasts until around 1400–1500 A.D. Hay Hollow Valley was first populated by Desert Culture groups at about 1000 B.C. The prehistory of the Purcell-Larson locality does not begin until about 500 A.D. Therefore, in comparing the two localities, I will begin at this later point in time.

Environmentally, the two areas are quite different. Hay Hollow Valley is in a savannah community, while the Purcell-Larson area is in a woodland. Hay Hollow is a broad valley bounded on either side by steep ridges. The Purcell-Larson topography is a series of small ridges separated by narrow and shallow stream valleys. Hay Hollow Valley has deep alluvial soils, while those of the Purcell-Larson locality are thin and derived more directly from bedrock. Annual rainfall is somewhat higher in the Purcell-Larson locality than in Hay Hollow Valley.

In both localities, the survey techniques used to record information on sites were intensive. The localities were thoroughly traversed by teams of archeologists walking 10 to 30 feet from each other. Extensive notes were made about the characteristics of each site that was found, maps were drawn, and samples of pottery and chipped and ground stone artifacts were collected.

This technique of surveying is far more intensive than those which have been used in many areas of the Southwest. As a result, the data from the two localities show five to ten times the number of sites than is typical for most Southwestern research areas. But since we found many more small sites using this approach, average site sizes are five to ten times larger in the other areas. Thus, the prehistoric records in both the Hay Hollow and Purcell-Larson localities appear superficially to be very different from the records in other parts of the Southwest. But it is unclear whether this discrepancy is due to an actual difference in the prehistory of these two localities or to a poor understanding of the prehistory of other areas of the Southwest because of the casual survey techniques through which it is known.

The locational characteristics of the populations of sites that were recorded in the two areas are as follows.

*Density.* In the overall pattern of density over all time, Hay Hollow Valley had somewhat more sites, with more rooms, but fewer sites with rooms. Purcell-Larson had fewer sites, slightly fewer rooms, but more sites with dwelling units. The five square-mile locality in Hay Hollow Valley contained 251 sites. The three square-mile Purcell-Larson locality contained 117 sites. Thus, the density of sites for all time periods in Hay Hollow Valley was about 50 sites per square mile, while that in the Purcell-Larson locality was 39 sites per square mile. Of the total sites found in each locality, 77 Purcell-Larson sites and 68 Hay Hollow sites had one or more dwelling units. Thus, the density of these habitation sites was 26 per square mile in the Purcell-Larson locality and 13 per square mile in Hay Hollow Valley. There were 56 habitation rooms per square mile in the Purcell-Larson locality and 61 per square mile in Hay Hollow Valley.

The figures for habitation sites per square mile are shown in Table 3.1. To standardize comparisons from time period to time period, the figures are per 75-year time block. Thus, the initial site totals for the period 500 to 850 have been divided by about 4.5 since there were that many 75-year units between 500 and 850. Later periods which are 75 years in length required no such division. Table 3.1 shows that the density of habitation sites in the two areas was very similar during the first two time periods. But between 1050 and 1125 there were more than twice as many habitation sites per square mile in Hay Hollow Valley as in Purcell-Larson. Then, during the final two time periods, the number of sites per square mile is much higher in Purcell-Larson than in Hay

**Table 3.1**   *Density of habitation sites per square mile per 75-year time block*

| Time Period (A. D.) | Purcell-Larson | Hay Hollow Valley |
|---|---|---|
| 500– 850 | 0.3 | 0.8 |
| 850–1050 | 2 | 3 |
| 1050–1125 | 2 | 5 |
| 1125–1200 | 7 | 1 |
| 1200–1275 | 8 | 1 |

**Table 3.2**   *Density of rooms per square mile per 75-year time block*

| Time Period (A. D.) | Purcell-Larson | Hay Hollow Valley |
|---|---|---|
| 500– 850 | 0.7 | 6 |
| 850–1050 | 6 | 7 |
| 1050–1125 | 5 | 9 |
| 1125–1200 | 13 | 22 |
| 1200–1275 | 24 | 8 |

Hollow Valley. Moreover, there is a substantial increase in the habitation sites per square mile in Purcell-Larson at about 1100 which does not occur in Hay Hollow Valley.

Table 3.2 summarizes information concerning the number of rooms per square mile. Population as reflected in room density is much larger at the beginning of the sequence in Hay Hollow Valley. Then, in both areas, the number of rooms increases substantially in around 1100. With more tightly defined time periods we would see that this is the culmination of a growth process that had been proceeding for several centuries. In Hay Hollow Valley, this population peak is a short-lived one, while in Purcell-Larson growth continues for at least another 75 years. In fact, a higher room density is ultimately reached in this locality than in Hay Hollow, reversing the earlier trend.

*Evenness.*   Locational geographers use a statistic called "the nearest neighbor" to characterize variation in the evenness of density in a region. When a population of sites shows a tendency toward clustering and there is substantial unevenness, the statistic has a value near zero. When sites are evenly dispersed over an area and there is little area-to-area density variation, it tends toward a value of 2.15. When a distribution shows a complex mixture of clustering and dispersion, the figure tends to be around 1. The figures for most time periods in Hay Hollow Valley tend to be about 1. Those in Purcell-Larson vary around .5. Thus, Purcell-Larson shows a substantially more uneven or clustered distribution.

*Agglomeration.* The data in Table 3.3 show variation in the average number of rooms per site in the two areas. A number of differences between the two localities are indicated. At the outset of the sequence, sites in Hay Hollow Valley are, on the average, larger than those in Purcell-Larson. Between 850 and 1125, the two localities are very similar. Thereafter, sites are again much larger in Hay Hollow Valley. The trend in Purcell-Larson is extremely stable—there is no significant variation in average site size. In Hay Hollow Valley, by contrast, there are substantial increases and decreases in average site size.

More information on this emerging pattern can come from considering the percentage of rooms that occur on the largest sites in the two localities. It is, however, difficult to decide on a single definition of *large* that can be used for comparative purposes. In Purcell-Larson, a large site is one with more than four habitation rooms. In Hay Hollow Valley, sites of this size are rather ordinary—a large site is one with 15 or more habitation units. The two localities are described using both definitions in Tables 3.4 and 3.5. Again, Purcell-Larson looks rather stable, except for the 850 to 1050 time period. Hay Hollow Valley, on the other hand, underwent substantial changes in agglomeration: there was an early period of agglomeration followed by two periods of dispersion and then agglomeration again.

*Hierarchy.* In Hay Hollow Valley there were at least a few large sites in all time periods. In the early periods, these were associated with

**Table 3.3**  *Average number of rooms per site per 75-year time block*

| Time Period (A. D.) | Purcell-Larson | Hay Hollow Valley |
|---|---|---|
| 500– 850 | 2.5 | 7.5 |
| 850–1050 | 1.5 | 2.0 |
| 1050–1125 | 2.5 | 2.0 |
| 1125–1200 | 2.0 | 22.0 |
| 1200–1275 | 3.0 | 14.5 |

**Table 3.4**  *Percentage of all rooms occurring on sites with five or more rooms per 75-year time block*

| Time Period (A. D.) | Purcell-Larson | Hay Hollow Valley |
|---|---|---|
| 500– 850 | 60% | 87% |
| 850–1050 | 00 | 44 |
| 1050–1125 | 40 | 17 |
| 1125–1200 | 38 | 100 |
| 1200–1275 | 46 | 100 |

**Table 3.5**  *Percentage of all rooms occurring on sites with fifteen or more rooms per 75-year time block*

| Time Period (A. D.) | Purcell-Larson | Hay Hollow Valley |
|---|---|---|
| 500– 850 | 00 | 36 |
| 850–1050 | 00 | 00 |
| 1050–1125 | 00 | 00 |
| 1125–1200 | 00 | 82 |
| 1200–1275 | 00 | 69 |

many small sites. In the last two time periods, one finds only large sites in the Valley. In Purcell-Larson, while there were large and small sites, there was always a substantial number of medium-sized sites, a full continuum of site sizes.

*Differentiation.*  Unfortunately, analyses of the Purcell-Larson data have not proceeded to a point where a detailed comparison of the organization of activities in the two areas can be made. It is possible, however, to note one significant difference between the two areas. One hundred and eighty-three nonhabitation or "limited activity" sites, 37 per square mile, were found in Hay Hollow Valley. By contrast, only 13 per square mile (40 in all) were found in Purcell-Larson. The Purcell-Larson sites were also typically much smaller than those in Hay Hollow. This difference suggests that the peoples who inhabited Purcell-Larson carried on a much greater percentage of their work at their habitation sites, while in Hay Hollow Valley a significant percentage of the activities was carried out at limited activity loci, away from the habitation sites.

*Integration.*  Integration can be approached on the basis of the sharing of stylistic elements between sites within a region. The reasoning begins with the assumption that sites that are close to each other are more likely to share design styles than ones that are far apart. This type of sharing does not have important organizational implications since it only shows that prehistoric peoples interacted with their neighbors. Significant inferences can be drawn from deviations from the expected sharing: from nearby sites with substantially different design styles (indicating boundaries) or distant sites with very similar design styles (indicating continuities). If the sharing of design styles is only proportional to the distance between sites, then no particular organizational pattern is implied.

S. Plog (1973) has worked with ceramic materials from both Chevelon and Hay Hollow Valley. In Chevelon, the sharing of painted design style elements on ceramic *jars* is highly correlated with the distance between the sites from which the samples were taken. Elements on *bowls,* however, show a significant pattern of sharing, a correlation from site to site that is far stronger than one would predict on the basis of distance alone. In Hay Hollow Valley, S. Plog finds no correlation of any sort between distances between sites and the degree to which they share design styles. This pattern may reflect either a complex set of boundaries and continuities in Hay Hollow Valley or the failure to control for jar as opposed to bowl designs, since this distinction was crucial in understanding Chevelon. Possible implications of this difference will be mentioned in the next section.

Turning to architectural evidence of integration, we observe that both the Purcell-Larson and Hay Hollow Valley localities have large ceremonial loci called Great Kivas. Though there are only a few of these in each locality and they tend to predominate in later time periods, the Great Kivas in Purcell-Larson tend to be associated with clusters of sites while in Hay Hollow Valley it is not atypical to find adjacent sites with Great Kivas or to go for substantial distances from the sites without observing any Great Kivas at all. Again, the implications of these data are not obvious in isolation, but seem to fall into a larger pattern when taken with other data, as will be indicated below.

*Clustering.* I suggested that a final task in the analysis of survey data should be the definition of site clusters that have some organizational reality. Data are not yet complete for either Purcell-Larson or Hay Hollow Valley, but a few preliminary conclusions can be made.

In the Purcell-Larson locality, strongly developed site clusters are typical for most time periods. These usually have a single large site surrounded by a number of smaller and medium-sized ones. The clusters typically have Great Kivas. In Hay Hollow Valley, clusters are far more difficult to define. Over most of the prehistory of the Valley, there were a few large sites, but it is not possible to associate these large sites with a clearly bounded cluster of sites. The distribution of Great Kivas also does not suggest any clustering pattern.

In Purcell-Larson, the clusters are substantially symmetrical—the composition, and, inferentially, the organization of any one cluster is much like that of any other cluster. Hay Hollow Valley is either asymmetrical or nonsymmetrical; to the extent that clusters exist at all, there do seem to be important discontinuities in composition and organization from cluster to cluster.

These locational characteristics move us in the direction of asking and answering important questions about the differences in organization and adaptation in each area, and these answers in turn shed considerable light on the general forces that were operating in the prehistory of the region.

## ANALYSIS: WHY ARE THE LOCATIONAL CHARACTERISTICS DIFFERENT?

Let us begin to draw the larger picture by returning to the first characteristic that we considered: density. The average density of habitation rooms, and inferentially of population, for all time periods is about the same in the two areas. Moreover, the peak of room density reached in each of the two areas is very similar, as noted. This means that we have no basis for arguing that the differences between the two areas were caused by overriding demographic variables. The population of Hay Hollow Valley was larger in early time periods than that of Purcell-Larson. The longer period of time during which the Valley had been inhabited probably causes this difference. In fact, if one looks at savannah areas in Chevelon, that is, areas outside of Purcell-Larson, one does find an early demographic situation very similar to Hay Hollow Valley.

We noted a more stable rate of population growth in Purcell-Larson than in Hay Hollow Valley. This difference probably reflects the respective biomass/productivity characteristics of the two plant communities in the localities. Biomass is a measure of the total quantity of flora and fauna in a community; productivity is a measure of the ability of that biomass to increase rapidly in response to more favorable conditions, or vice versa. Biomass is somewhat higher in Purcell-Larson, but productivity is much lower. The combination of these two environmental factors would suggest a limit on the rate of human population increase in Purcell-Larson that would not have existed in Hay Hollow Valley. Thus, the more stable rate of population increase in Purcell-Larson is a product of this environmental limit.

We observed that density was less variable from area to area in Hay Hollow Valley than in Purcell-Larson, that Purcell-Larson sites were more clustered. When the difference between the two localities is considered in terms of the evenness of population density, the reason for the difference seems obvious. In Purcell-Larson, most resources are distributed homogenously throughout the region, with one major exception—soil. There are two different soil groups in the Purcell-Larson area: a deep, red, sandstone-derived soil and a shallow, grey, alkaline, limestone-derived soil. The former is quite suitable for the practice of agriculture, while the latter is not. Moreover, the distribution of these two soils is patchy—the red soil occurs in limited geographical areas within an overall limestone-soil zone. During the time periods we are discussing, Southwestern populations were practicing agriculture, and it is in these areas of rich red soil that Purcell-Larson sites concentrate. Such patchiness is not characteristic in Hay Hollow Valley. First, resources are not homogenously distributed. Second, they tend to occur in broad cross-cutting zones. Thus, any given location in the valley is likely to be very different from a whole series of other locations with respect to a large number of desired resources.

These different patterns merge as we try to imagine what strategy must have been followed by prehistoric populations who were deciding where to locate their fields and settlements. People would have sought to locate their settlements at sites that were within easy distance of all the agricultural and nonagricultural resources they needed. In Chevelon, this would have been an easy task—find the red soils. Those soils were critical for agriculture, and since all other resources were homogenously distributed, selecting a site on the basis of soil automatically left the settlement in a desirable position with respect to the other resources it needed. In Hay Hollow Valley, the situation was not so simple. A location that was desirable for one resource was likely to be less desirable for others and undesirable for at least some. Thus, alternative site locations in Hay Hollow Valley were only relatively better or worse than each other. As a result, settlements in Purcell-Larson cluster around areas with good soil. Sites in Hay Hollow do not cluster because most site locations were average ones—they were good locations with respect to some resources, poor locations with respect to others, and average with respect to the majority. There was no resource zone in Hay Hollow Valley around which it was *especially* desirable to locate sites.

This same consideration probably accounts for the differences in agglomeration that we observed between the two localities. Under the environmental circumstances we have just discussed and given population growth, it would have been as convenient for individuals in Hay Hollow Valley to remain at a natal site as to move to a new one. Given population growth in Purcell-Larson, individuals had to disperse—the small patches of good argricultural soil could not support greater populations, even in the short run. Productivity was probably a complicating factor in Purcell-Larson: the local vegetation would not have been quick to recover from the effects of a large, concentrated human population.

We may also consider the differences in the pattern of resource distribution in the two areas as underlying the differences in the organization of work. Given the homogeneity of resources in Purcell-Larson, one would not expect a large number of limited activity sites. If prehistoric peoples located settlements with respect to areas of high quality soil, then most other resources were available virtually at their doorsteps. In Hay Hollow Valley, the complex and heterogeneous distribution of resources meant that wherever settlements were located, a number of desired resources would be some substantial distance away. Thus, the larger number of limited activity sites in that area—locations that were specialized for processing resources for short periods of time—is a direct result of this uneven distribution of resources.

Finally, we may turn to integrative differences between the two areas. In Purcell-Larson, the sharing of design elements on jars was proportional to distance and indicated no strong pattern of integration. The bowls did indicate wider interaction, but it is evidently of a comparatively specialized sort. The bulk of the evidence suggests that the site cluster, centered in a zone of good agricultural soil, seems to have been the major effective unit of integration in this area. In Hay Hollow Valley, the pattern was far more complex. The pattern of a few large and many small sites typically occurs when there is some centralization of integrative activities within a society. (Whereas a generally even distribution of site sizes such as that in Chevelon only suggests that the somewhat larger sites simply grew a bit more than the others.) The sharing of design elements and the distribution of Great Kivas also suggests a fairly complex integrative pattern in Hay Hollow Valley. Given the problems of human interaction that arise in an agglomerated population, the problems of organizing work activities at spatially disparate activity loci, and the problems of competition for resources and resource allocation in an environment where those resources are heterogeneously distributed and where sites cannot be clustered so as to define "territories" of resource utilization, it is reasonable to interpret this design element as indicating some sort of social organization on a wider scale than the site cluster, perhaps a system of dispersed clans centering on the kivas.

## CONCLUSION

I began this chapter by noting the growing importance of surveys as a means of making research more efficient and of providing a fuller context in terms of which excavated materials could be understood, and by discussing the development of the *settlement-pattern* concept to describe this context. I argued that as surveys became more important and the data they produced more substantial, the settlement-pattern concept began to show its faults. On the one hand, it was too cumbersome to facilitate asking direct questions and testing specific hypotheses. On the other, it oversimplified behavioral reality and was in terms of both time and money too costly for most archeologists to afford.

In the locational approach we are offered an alternative way of conceptualizing archeological data which remedies some of these deficiencies. We can conceptualize the products of survey data as populations of sites, identify and measure discrete locational characteristics of those populations, and use those characteristics to investigate the history of the prehistoric peoples we are studying. This approach still leads to important questions about economic and social history, the organization and adaptation of prehistoric populations, but it can attempt to answer these questions in terms of characteristics that require more direct and limited inferences from the archeological record and more limited expenditures of time and money. Moreover, I would argue that these limited inferences are more in keeping with the weight of inference that the archeological record of most areas of the world actually can bear. The cost of such an approach is giving up the familiarity of ethnographic description—of lineal communities, matrilocal pueblos, and spring fishing camps. The benefit is a far more efficient understanding of prehistory even when holistically conceived.

## SELECTED READINGS

Adams, Robert McC., 1965, *The Evolution of Urban Society.* Chicago: Aldine.

A discussion of the origins of urbanism and state level societies. He relies heavily on survey and settlement-pattern data from both Meso-America and Mesopotamia in his discussion. The work illustrates the uses of such data in a fully elaborated social history.

Chang, K. C., 1966, *Settlement Archeology.* Palo Alto, Calif.: National Press.

This book contains a number of excellent settlement-pattern studies as well as a good discussion of the history and current status of the settlement-pattern concept.

Martin, P. S. and Plog, F., 1973, *The Archeology of Arizona.* New York: Natural History Press.

A discussion of the prehistory of Arizona with a focus on many of the issues considered in this chapter. Survey data is used heavily in addressing many of the problems.

Morril, R., 1969, *The Spatial Organization of Society.* Belmont, Calif.: Wadsworth.

Morril places the locational literature in geography within a coherent theoretical framework and discusses many of the locational characteristics that are used in this chapter.

# Ethnology:
# Social Anthropology

# Chapter 4

# Are There Social Groups in the New Guinea Highlands?

**Roy Wagner**

The study of man's social arrangements—his relationships with his fellow man and how he conceives of those relationships—has traditionally been the province of cultural anthropology. This does not mean that social relationships and what people think of them are not important to archeology and physical anthropology. It simply means that society and social relationships, rather than man's physical constitution or the record of his development through time, are a part of the basic subject matter of cultural anthropology.

Cultural anthropology is almost as large and vaguely defined as anthropology in general. Since cultural anthropology can and does include studies of everything from poetry to plowing fields, anthropologists have often distinguished the study of social arrangements as social anthropology, a particular subfield of cultural anthropology. This designation tends to be misleading, for it suggests that the difference between social anthropology and the other aspects of cultural anthropology is mainly one of subject matter. In fact this is not so. Traditional social anthropology is based on some very special assumptions about the importance of society —assumptions that are not necessarily shared by other cultural anthropologists—and it contains a large body of theory developed on those assumptions. What those assumptions are and whether we are justified in separating the study of society from the rest of cultural anthropology is the subject of this chapter. In order to answer it, however, we shall have to turn from this ambiguous and confusing realm of definitions and examine the historical development of the concepts involved. After all, the only excuse for recognizing some particular kind of anthropology at all is that there is a body of theory that enables us to do that kind of anthropology.

In order to more fully understand social anthropology, we must first attempt to answer some basic questions: What is the rationale for social anthropology, the anthropology of society? Where did its assumptions come from and where did the questions and answers about these assumptions come from?

## THE DEVELOPMENT OF SOCIAL ANTHROPOLOGY

In many respects the assumptions of social anthropology are the legacy of Emile Durkheim, the brilliant French social thinker of the late-nineteenth and early-twentieth centuries. Durkheim addressed himself to man's moral and collective life—the forces and influences that hold human beings together, their "groupiness" in all of its aspects—as a phenomenon for scientific investigation. His writings so exclusively emphasized the basic importance of the "social," the collective and moral aspects of human life, that it is easy to base a social determinism on them or accuse Durkheim of "reifying" society—making society into a "thing." What he achieved was the foundation for a science of social integration focusing on how human associations and society itself, that most "permanent" of associations, are put together and what keeps them together. This concern with "integration" was the rock upon which social anthropology was founded.

Following Durkheim, the "problem" of society was taken up and developed by two distinct national traditions. In France Durkheim's collaborators and students founded a symposium for theorization around a journal called the *Année Sociologique*. Much of this work, especially that of Durkheim's nephew, Marcel Mauss, formed the groundwork for the later structuralism of Lévi-Strauss. But it was in England, and wherever else abroad that the influence of A. R. Radcliffe-Brown penetrated, that the descent theory had its first and most telling successes.

These successes were generally called *functionalism* (though Radcliffe-Brown himself shied away from the title), and functionalism provided the theoretical core for the classical social anthropology that developed in England in the thirties, forties, and fifties of this century. Functionalism was grounded in the notion that no matter how bizarre or peculiar the practices and "institutions" of a people and regardless of how they had got that way, the important question was how they *worked*. Furthermore, though there were a great many ways in which they might work or not work, there was always one more or less central function, that of keeping society together, something that the social anthropologists always insisted was a "political" or "politico-jural" matter.

The "politico-jural" assumption was the contribution of a very secular and pragmatic British turn of mind to Durkheim's original problem. And it was Radcliffe-Brown who chose the realm of jurisprudence, with its fine distinctions and its painstaking adjudication of "rights," as a model for thinking about the moral collectivities of society. Of course, the tribal societies of the sort studied by Radcliffe-Brown, Evans-Pritchard, Fortes, Gluckman, and other social anthropologists did not have politics in our sense, nor did they have laws, though many of them held courts and engaged in litigation. Furthermore, the emphasis on "rights" led naturally to a consideration of rights of inheritance and a concern with "property," although .the property in question was in most cases valued precisely because it was exchangeable for people, something that is almost never true of property in our society.

Social anthropology gradually evolved into a kind of game of heuristic pretending: concepts with a very broad base of acceptance and understanding in Western society, like "politics," "law," "rights," and "property," were applied to the collective usages of tribal peoples, with a sort of implicit "as if" attached to them. As long as the players in the game kept the "as if" in mind, their use of the Western concepts to translate the native customs into the kind of rational and legal consistency that we expect of our own institutions was accepted, even though it cast the native subjects in the unseemly roles of barristers and bewigged judges and made their collective existence into a droll parody of the Bank of England.

However, the game could not be played in a vacuum. It was first of all descriptive anthropology, and it had to come to terms with the customs of the people it described. And this is what the problems and concepts of social anthropology are all about. If the Southern Bantu or the Nuer or Tallensi did not have laws as such, then analogous collective usages would have to be found to take their place. The analogies were in fact drawn with the regularities (or as a later generation would call them, "norms") that govern kin relationships, and the game became one of turning kinship into jurisprudence and corporate economics, the study of "descent systems" and of the "institutions" formed in tribal societies by the descent of rights and property. Social anthropology became the science of descent groups, and descent groups and their constitution came to be crucial issues in accounting for the core function of integrating society and keeping it together. The more emphatically the investigators insisted on the importance of definitions, rationality, and their own conceptions of law and property, the more substantial and strictly bounded the groups became. They became, in short, much more like the consciously organized, planned, and structured groups of Western society in spite of a lack of any kind of evidence that natives actually thought of them in that way. "Groups" were a function of *our understanding* of what the people were doing rather than of what they themselves made of things.

The science of descent groups met its severest test in dealing with the ways in which native usages *did not* correspond to its theoretical expectations. There were instances where kinship usage flatly contradicted the expectations of an institutional model of society. In the tribal societies that social anthropology chose as its subject matter, such instances were neither uncommon nor trivial. The refinement of the so-called "descent theory" was accomplished through the ongoing effort of dealing with such contradictions. The beginnings of this are evident in the classic papers of Radcliffe-Brown reprinted in *Structure and Function in Primitive Society*. They deal with the right of a southern Bantu youth to "snatch" food and possessions belonging to his maternal uncle, normally a member of a different descent group, and with the peculiar "joking" and "avoidance" relationships found among many tribal peoples in which participants engage in banter that seemingly violates the relationship or avoidance that seemingly negates it. Radcliffe-Brown chose to interpret all of these phenomena in terms of what he called "alliance or consociation." In the face of tensions resulting from the divergent interests of different intermarrying groups, including conflicting claims on or expectations of a single person, these inexplicably "contrary" practices served to maintain social order and solidarity ("integrate the society") where nothing else could. In the words of Radcliffe-Brown:

> The alliance by extreme respect, by partial or complete avoidance, prevents such conflict but keeps the parties conjoined. The alliance by joking does the same thing in a different way. (1965:103)

The apparent antisocial character of "snatching" or joking and avoidance relations could thus be explained by the necessity to integrate groups themselves (ally them) into a larger social whole. Any evidence to the effect that kinship usage did *not* have the effect of promoting group solidarity could be explained away as building the solidarity as a whole through alliance.

The science of descent groups defended itself against ethnographic exceptions by assuming that society itself was just a bigger and better descent group with its own laws and means of operation. It was not necessary to stop believing in social groups or solidarity; all one had to do was admit that solidarity was sometimes achieved indirectly. It was this ingenious formulation by Radcliffe-Brown, snatching group solidarity from the jaws of frivolous irrationality, that Meyer Fortes used as a foundation for his theory of descent and filiation. To begin with, if the "descent" that anthropologists had been using as a kind of legal basis for the constitution of groups was not the only principle in operation, then a more general one had to be devised. This was "filiation," a kind of two-way descent based on the ties of an individual with each of his parents. Descent, figured through the mother or father, corresponded to what

Fortes called the "socially weighted" form of filiation, whereas the other kind, relating the individual to those outside his descent group, was called "complementary filiation." The former provided the juridical or "politico-jural" basis for groups, whereas the latter furnished a means for intergroup alliance (though it was supplemented by such things as ritual).

At first sight, this strategic maneuver by Fortes seems to have solved the social anthropologists' dilemma of having solidly bounded descent-group "institutions" and allowing for the interests of the greater social whole at the same time. But the solution cost a certain amount of internal contradiction, for what filiation gave with one hand it took away with the other. It moved the theoretical center of gravity away from the straightforward rationalism of Durkheim and Radcliffe-Brown, so much so that when later descent theorists such as Goody wanted to establish a definition of the "corporate" descent group, they were obliged to invent concepts like "shadowy claims" and "submerged rights" to explain the workings of complementary filiation. These refer to weak claims on property or rights in his mother's natal group that a man can exercise by virtue of the fact that "his mother might have been a man." If his mother were a man, he would be in her group because of patrilineal inheritance of "rights" (of membership). If the claims were clear-cut rather than shadowy, and if the rights were to surface, then the boundaries of the corporate descent groups, which were fixed by precisely those kinds of rights and claims, would be eroded and compromised. And if this happened, social anthropologists would have to admit that groups as they had conceived of them did not exist.

Shadowy claims and submerged rights were simply a way of saying that relations (of "alliance or consociation") among groups were just not as "real" as the groups themselves. This peculiar shadowy status was reserved for everything that moved between and mediated among the hard boundaries of groups, including "ritual" (religion). (Everybody knew that ritual dealt with insubstantial and supernatural things like ghosts and gods, whereas groups involved substantial things like people and cattle and homesteads.) In this way the social anthropologists tended to make their groups solid and substantial by sacrificing the reality and substantiality of everything else.

But the shadowy and insubstantial world of rights and claims moving unaccountably between groups still posed a major challenge to the science of descent groups. Its very in-betweenness and insubstantiality was provocative, and so a great deal of theoretical effort was devoted to deriving some kind of justification from the realm of the insubstantial, which of course made it more necessary, more provocative, and more important. Solidarity came to be explained through antagonism, rather than being defined in contrast to it, and society was eventually understood in terms of antisociety.

Gluckman's theory of "rituals of rebellion," reflected in many aspects of African social life, marked a further step in this direction. Gluckman maintained that the institutionalized public dramatization of a mock rebellion against the ruler enacted regularly in some African societies served to strengthen the ruler's position. By setting up a sort of "false negation" of the ruler's authority, a kind of collective political joking relationship, and then overcoming the negation, the social order became what it was by failing to achieve the opposite. The importance of his theory lies in its reliance on contradiction as a basis for explanation. Although firmly committed to the functional integration of society, it is indicative of a radical shift in the theoretical center of social anthropology.

By now the way was cleared for a social anthropology that addressed itself largely to the realm of ritual and the "betwixt and between." This is the course taken by two modern social anthropologists, Mary Douglas and Victor Turner. In her book *Purity and Danger*, Douglas stressed the central position of contradictory or paradoxical situations in human society and related these to the notion of pollution. Turner, building on Gluckman, focused on the ritual process and the significance of transition (liminality) between social and ritual states. Although the social retains its preeminence in the writings of both, their increasing reliance on the contradictory corresponds with another important departure: instead of functional integration, their explanation comes to rely more and more on meaning and conceptualization as expressed in symbols.

If this emphasis on contradiction and the "betwixt and between" reduced the science of descent groups to a kind of absurdity with respect to its former position, the interest in symbols and native conceptualization had a similar effect on the heuristic game of understanding native usages as if they were Western institutions. We might conclude that social anthropology was teased into its opposite by the exigencies of dealing with its subject matter. But by this time its opposite (in the sense of its major emphases) had already come on the scene in the form of Lévi-Strauss's "structuralism," and had prosecuted a very successful running debate with descent theory under the guidance of Edmund Leach and Rodney Needham.

Claude Lévi-Strauss's structuralism is the "opposite" of traditional Radcliffe-Brownian social anthropology: it addresses itself to the oppositions and contradictions within the social order—with an eye toward resolving them as a part of its explanation—rather than to its legal regularities and integrated harmonies. Lévi-Strauss's work emerged from a different tradition in anthropology that was founded by Durkheim's students and followers in France who had developed a body of theory about society along the conceptualist lines of Durkheim's own work rather than the legalist and materialistic ones of British social anthropology. They wrote on the subjects of "primitive classification," dual organization, the concepts of self and society, and on forms of gift exchange. Perhaps the best known of their works is Marcel Mauss's superb *Essay on the Gift,* a book which, like Mauss himself, exercised a strong influence on Lévi-Strauss.

Gift exchange, or reciprocity, is where structuralism begins. Or rather it is where functionalism ends for the structuralists, for reciprocity between individuals and between groups is the structuralist answer to the functionalist question "What integrates society?" Assuming the universal presence and significance of reciprocity, structuralism took as its major problem that of how society and its parts are conceptualized. Thus it completely reversed the orientation of functionalism, which took this kind of conceptualization for granted and focused its attention on the problem of integration.

Beginning with Lévi-Strauss's *Les Structures Elémentaires de la Parenté (The Elementary Structures of Kinship)*, published in 1949, the social group took on a new and radically different aspect for some anthropologists. It was described in conceptual ("ideal") and symbolic rather than legal and materialist terms. Instead of on cows, compounds, and rights *in rem* and *in personem,* groups and group structure were based on cosmological dualities: right versus left, water as against land, the above in opposition to the below, etc. Instead of actual, physical groups "on the ground," there were hypothetical units reconstructed according to the roles taken in reciprocity—"wife-givers," "wife-takers," "cycles" determined by marriage rules, and so on—social constructs of the analyst devised to implement native ideology.

Since these constructs were intended to replicate something in the native's "mind," rather than something a fieldworker could draw a map of, like a compound, it would be inaccurate to call them "groups" in the same sense as the constructs of social anthropology. And yet, in spite of this increase in sophistication, the constructs were no less "groupy" in many respects than the descent groups of British anthropology. The major difference was that *these* descent groups existed in the native's imagination, regardless of what they looked like "on the ground." They were descent groups for precisely the same reason that Radcliffe-Brown's basic units were—because Lévi-Strauss, like the British anthropologists, took kin relationships to be the locus of "law" or "rules" in tribal societies.

Characteristically, however, he did not begin with rules of inheritance or the ownership of property, but rather with the incest taboo, which he saw as the archetypical marriage-rule. It was from this taboo, according to Lévi-Strauss, that the "universe of rules" that constitutes human society descended. And it was from the taboo, with its implied necessity for reciprocity ("If I can't marry my sister I'll exchange her for someone I can marry") that he derived the basis for descent: "The positive aspect of the prohibition is to initiate organization" (Lévi-Strauss 1969: 43).

"Organization" turned out to be an incorporation of descent in all of its traditional forms and varieties ("patrilineal," "matrilineal," and so on), with the exception that it was significant in conceptual rather than in material terms. And although this borrowing of traditional terminology may not have been necessary for a theory which needed groups only as a kind of "anchoring" framework for reciprocal relations, order and organization of some kind was necessary to structuralism, for it shared with functionalism the view that a culture or society represents a systemic order of some kind, a "system."

Both British social anthropology and Lévi-Straussian structuralism take as their task the discovery of some kind of systemic order within the subject culture, an order that they identify with the way in which that culture "works" (functionalism) or is articulated conceptually (structuralism). We have seen that social anthropology first attempted to discover this order within the data themselves, postulating the existence of self-evident descent groups and the like, but gradually worked itself around to the position that the basic problems were conceptual and interpretational. Like structuralism, in other words, it came to acknowledge the importance of building models of the "native system" and verifying these as a mode of explanation.

This procedure amounts to observing something and then describing it systemically or else contriving a system and then demonstrating that it is "out there," or closely resembles what is "out there." In practice it generally includes a bit of both. In either case, however, it involves the invention and projection of an "order" on the part of the anthropologist, one that is a function of his process of understanding. And so if we choose to challenge this systemic mode of explanation, we can pose the question of whether descent groups and their associated paraphernalia of social order do in fact exist apart from the anthropologist's need to explain things in terms of them. Is there something about tribal society that demands resolution into groups? Or is the notion of "groups" a vague and inadequate description of something that could better be represented in another way?

## CHALLENGING THE "AS IF" ASSUMPTION

Our first step in trying to answer these questions must involve a frank assessment of what we are looking for. For if we approach the matter with the outright intention of finding groups or with an unanalyzed assumption that groups of one sort or another are essential to human life and culture, then nothing will keep us from finding groups. And if a frank assessment is in order, then we must also be clear about what we mean or expect in the way of groups. Do we mean the strict, empirical, and material "corporate groups" of the social anthropologists, the genealogically based, flexible, inclusive social gradations of a segmentary lineage-system, or the totally conceptual constructs of the structuralists? First and foremost we should try to answer the crucial question of why we need to explain social structure by groups at all.

We live in a culture in which founding, joining, participating in, and integrating groups is a deliberate and important matter. The constitutional charters of our nations are founded on a notion of a "social contract," a conscious act or event of some kind which initiated the existence of society. Citizens are members of these colossal "descent groups." Those who are not "born to" them or within their clan territories must be "naturalized," much as children may be legally adopted by foster parents. A society which emphasizes the citizen's duty to vote and be vigilant on behalf of his country is certainly insisting on conscious participation. And by making belonging to and participating in society conscious, this particular social form also makes it problematic. The problems of recruitment, participation, and corporateness (economics) are *our* problems, but we take them with us when we visit other cultures, along with our toothbrushes and favorite novels.

Nations, societies, and groups are the *social* form or manifestation of the reliance on order, organization, and consistency that pervades our whole approach to collective doing and understanding as an unquestioned assumption. The suggestion that our ideas of order, organization, and consistency may be open to critical review, or in the social realm that groups may not be the most important consideration, appears to many as a betrayal of our social and scholarly ethic. Yet all we are doing is challenging the "as if" of systemic anthropology, the attitude of the British social anthropologists and French structuralists which says, "Let's assume that the natives are like us so we can understand them." And we are challenging this assumption in order to avoid an anthropological perspective that inadvertently makes our own cultural assumptions a part of "the way things are," the way in which all mankind thinks and acts.

Anthropologists have an ethical responsibility to deal with other peoples and other conceptual worlds on a basis of equality and mutuality. When an anthropologist sums up the lives and imaginations of his subjects in a determinist "system" of his own contriving, trapping their fancies and inclinations within the necessities of his own economies, ecologies, and logics, he asserts the priority of his mode of creativity over theirs. He substitutes his own ("heuristic") *making* of groups, orders, organizations, and logics for the way in which "the natives" make their collectivities. And it is this "native" mode of *making* society, rather than its curious similarities to our notions of groups, economics, or consistency, that compels our interest here. The understanding of this creativity per se is the only ethical *and* theoretical alternative to those patronizing efforts that would "civilize" other peoples by making over the remains of their own creative efforts into hypothetical groups, grammars, logics, and economies.

In asking whether there are social groups in the New Guinea Highlands, I am concerned not with what kinds of "groups" best describe the local communal arrangements, but rather with the way in which the people there create themselves socially. The answers to this question may help to tell us whether the "models" of the corporate group, the segmentary lineage system, or the conceptual "structural" unit have any particular relevance to the situation, and they may tell us much more. We have all sorts of ways of defining groups—residential, genealogical, political, economic, and so on, just as we have many kinds of definitions for groups, including those mentioned above as well as marginal or negative ("groups" that are not groups) constructs called "kindreds," "quasi-groups," and "networks," but we have virtually no thorough-going alternative to the concept of a grouplike collectivity. What is worse, we have no set of criteria for determining when such a concept is applicable and when it is not.

Since the notion of the group is our own, the problem of finding such criteria rests with us. Since a deliberate collective focus, a sense of common participation and awareness, lies at the core of our notion (and of our motives for finding groups), our criteria ought to emphasize this factor. Other means of grouping people on the basis of shared similarities, whether they specify common or contiguous residence, economic or ecological cooperation or involvement, genealogy, or political behavior, can easily become devices for making groups out of people who would never do it that way (or perhaps do it at all) themselves. A people have groups to the extent that, and in the way that, they conceive of such things; otherwise the anthropologist simply "has" the people, by foisting his idea of "groups" upon them.

How, then, do the peoples of the New Guinea Highlands create their sociality? What are the "facts" as the natives make them? Do they have a "problem of society" and a systemic solution, or are their problems conceived in a totally different way, which relates only indirectly to social grouping? Can we learn to understand or simulate their creation of social "facts" without making them pawns in a game of our own? One way to attempt to answer these questions is to approach a specific people from as many viewpoints as possible, with a certain naiveté especially regarding groups and systems, as a fieldworker might approach them. Let us approach the Daribi, a people of the eastern New Guinea Highlands among whom I did fieldwork, in this way.

## DARIBI SOCIALITY

If we could go back and visit Baianabo, the site at which I lived during much of my first period of fieldwork (1963–65), in 1950 or so, ten years before the Daribi people were "pacified" by the government, we would find gardens and a small settlement there. You might not recognize the gardens as such, for they would be of the "swidden" or "slash-and-burn" variety, with dead, bare-limbed tree trunks standing upright or lying about where they had been felled, covered with the vines of sweet potato (the staple food). Nearby would be stands of "second growth": former gardens in various stages of growing back to bush, and perhaps also the clearings of new gardens being cut. Surrounding all of this, on a broad, flat volcanic plateau about 3,500 feet above sea level, is a mature tropical forest, many of its white or gray barked trees five or six feet in diameter at the base.

About four or five adult men live here with their families. The oldest is a short man with graying hair named Buruhwạ.[1] We ask him who his "house people" are (a local idiom); he hesitates, muttering "my house people," and then says "Weriai." Talking to him, we discover that he was born at a place called Awa Page (he gestures off to the southwest), among some people he calls "Noru," and then went to live with the Weriai (except that now he qualifies this term and calls them "Kurube") at a place called Waramaru. Then his sister married at Peria, a large complex of houses and gardens about a mile north of where we are standing, and he moved here to Baianabo "to be near her."

It sounds as though we have stumbled into one of those situations known often in social anthropology as a "special case," but actually this kind of personal history is common among the Daribi. We ask the other men about their "house people" and places of birth, and it turns out that they are "Weriai" or "Kurube," born at Waramaru. Where do the other Weriai live? A few, it turns out, live in a house just nearby, a great many live at Waramaru, with the "Noru people" or "Sogo people," and others, many more, live with some people called the "Nekapo." Eventu-

---

1. I have written the Daribi terms cited here in a standard Latin orthography in which each vowel is given its own distinctive sound (for instance *e* is pronounced like our *a* in "gate," *u* like the *oo* in "boot") and the *r* is lightly trilled. In general the words are pronounced as they would be in Spanish. The apostrophe (as in mama') indicates high tone, and the hook (as in Buruhwạ) denotes nasalization.

ally we discover that Waramaru is a good, hard day's walk to the west, with many other peoples in between, and that the Nekapo people live perhaps a half day's walk beyond that. If the Weriai are indeed "house people," they are certainly spread over an appreciable chunk of landscape; and if some live with the Peria, others with the Sogo or Nekapo, they seem to be quite well partitioned, too. Is this a "group," a "tribe," a "nonlocalized clan?" And whatever it may be, what is Kurube? Is it perhaps another name for Weriai? But before we get out copies of *Notes and Queries in Anthropology*, the standard fieldworker's guide in situations like this, to search for an appropriate definition, we should remind ourselves that we are deliberately *not* trying to play the "heuristic" game of calling unfamiliar socialities "groups" in order to salve our sense of explanation. A pat, group-centered definition just won't do, at least until we have learned more about these people.

General terms like "house people" and specific ones like Weriai, Kurube, and Noru are part of the extensive and ever expanding means that Daribi use to make social distinctions. The latter are called *bidi wai'*, "man-ancestors," and are characteristically based on the names of genealogical ancestors, though this is not always the case. Sogo, Weriai, and Kurube are names very likely borne by actual forebears ("Kurube" was developed from Kuru, said to be another name of the man called "Weriai"); Noru and Nekapo are probably not. Mama' Di'be and Huzhuku Di'be ("light" and "dark" Di'be, respectively) distinguish the Di'be people who live near the "light" river from those who live beneath the "dark" mountain.

If we were absolutely committed to "finding" groups, it would be no trouble to assume that these distinctions are descriptions or definitions of concrete, bounded, and empirically existing groups. The fact that some of them include others—Weriai, Daie, Sizi, and others are said to be Para, issue of certain sons of a man named Para, and Kurube were Weriai living with Sogo, Noruai were Weriai living with Nekapo, and so on—could be taken as evidence of a "segmentary lineage system." This amounts to a hierarchical arrangement of progressively more inclusive groups, based on genealogical reckoning and standardized into levels with corresponding labels, so that Para might be considered a phratry, Weriai a clan, Kurube a subclan.

The hierarchical order necessary for such a model is certainly there, implicit in the fact that the terms can be seen to include, exclude, or contrast with one another. Yet, we would be well advised to take the distinctions at face value, as distinctions only and not as groups. They only group people in the way that they separate or distinguish them on the basis of some criterion, and we cannot deduce from the conceptual distinctions an actual correspondence of the terms with discrete and consciously perceived groups of people.

The terms are names, rather than the things named. They differentiate, saying "These are of the river, those are of the mountain," or "These are the issue of Weriai, those of Daie," and they are significant not because of the way in which they describe something, but because of the way in which they contrast it with others. In his masterful analysis of "totemism," Lévi-Strauss concludes that *"It is not the resemblances, but the differences, which resemble each other"* (1962:77). Thus although Weriai means "blinded" in Daribi and Daie means "to be thoroughly cooked," neither is intended literally; they are just names, and in this capacity the content of one differentiates as effectively as that of the other.

As names used to draw distinctions, these terms are very flexible. "Para," for example, is a contraction of *pariga* ("ribcage") and is sometimes used as a nickname indicative of laziness ("He is called 'ribs' because he lies on his ribs all day"). Whether for this reason or some other, the name became associated with a man alleged to be the originator of a great many lines of paternal substance, a common *bidi wai'*. The name may be used to distinguish *all* of these lines from other complexes like Noru or Di'be, to distinguish *some* of them from parts of the latter (at Waramaru, Weriai called the Sogo people "Noru"), or to distinguish some of the Para lines from others. Those who call themselves Sizi, Warai, Ogwanoma, or Siabe are often referred to as "Para" in contradistinction to Weriai, for instance, or Daie, although the latter are otherwise just as much Para as they are.

There are good reasons behind these seeming irregularities. For one, Daribi tend to use the broadest and least specific terms possible in most situations. For another, the Sizi, Warai, and Ogwanoma peoples remained behind at Boromaru, the traditional home of Para, while the other lines moved away. But in spite of these, Para can scarcely be said to represent a group, for it is impossible, given the range of usage, to determine which of the applications is the "correct" one. Para is a name, not a group; it is a means of distinguishing, of including and excluding, and thus merely a device for setting up boundaries.

Such a device can be used very flexibly, now drawing this distinction, now that, without ever being tied to a particular element or a bounded definitional "domain." This "broad" or "hyperbolic" use of terms might better be exemplified in the Daribi distinguishing of colors. When shown a dark brown, green, or blue object, the Daribi will identify it as *huzhuku*; when shown something that we would call red, scarlet, crimson, or even light brown, they will call it *mama'*; our yellow or yellow-green are *sewa'* to them. And yet in speaking of the fruit of the pandanus tree, most varieties of which are scarlet to dull rose, though one is mustard yellow, they will refer to the former as *huzhuku* and the latter as *mama'*! The contrastive qualities of the terms (dark/light) turn out to be more significant in this context than the more specific ("color") values.

What are the social effects of this kind of usage? Drawing boundaries by creating contrasts has the effect of *eliciting* groups as a sort of general context of one's expression, alluding to them indirectly rather than consciously organizing or participating in them. The things we imagine to be "groups" take on a continuous and almost invisible quality, like our notion of "time," which we likewise try to elicit and compel by the arbitrary contrasts and distinctions of our clocks and calendars.[2]

The elicitation of social collectivities by indirect means is more than a mere rhetorical device among the Daribi; it is a style or mode of creativity that pervades the whole range of their activities. A man who has been wronged, for instance, will frequently rage and shout, deliberately pushing his anger to the limit—and if he provokes an opponent into angry rejoinder, so much the better. He is trying to elicit a collective response in the form of conciliation, peacemakers who will arrange a negotiated settlement of his grievances in the general interest (and to stop the hideous racket!).

Names simply outline a mode of creativity whose most serious aspect, in native terms at least, is that of the exchange of wealth. This exchange in turn derives from a further use of contrast and distinction to elicit social relationship—in this case the very basic one between men and women. The men emphasize their "maleness" in opposition to the women who assert their "femaleness" in return, each drawing a "response," and a complementary aspect of the social whole, from the other. Women are valued for their productive and reproductive capacities, the ability to do female work and bear children, a creativity to which the men respond by taking control of it. Control is achieved by negotiating "exchanges" of women (as well as their progeny, their "products") in return for products and implements of male creativity—the axes used in gardening, meat (including pigs) which is believed to augment spermatic fluid, and pearl-shells that create the assertive male image. Such exchanges actually constitute a "substitution" of male creativity for its female counterpart.

Every legitimate acquisition of a woman and, since all human beings are born of female creativity, every acquisition of a person must come about through this kind of exchange. Accordingly, every Daribi has *page-bidi* ("people at the base") who are entitled to receive male wealth in

---

2. It is scarcely surprising, in the light of this, that Leach and others have introduced the concept of "social" or "genealogical" time as an explanatory device. Even the images chosen by Melanesians—"lines" in Pidgin, "ropes" in many local idioms—emphasize continuity rather than discrete groupiness.

**Figure 4.1** *A Daribi bride-price: pearlshells, axes, bushknives, shell jewelry, and trade-cloth. (Masi, 1968)*

exchange for his custody or affiliation. *Pagebidi* include the brothers and other close kin of a woman and the close maternal kin of a male or unmarried girl. All people must be "paid for" in this way, and every act of exchange draws a contrast between male and female.

Thus every exchange in which a woman or child is "acquired" by a man amounts to an act of differentiation, a separation of wife from kin or of child (and sometimes adolescent) from maternal kin, effected through the giving of male wealth. And just as everyone has *pagebidi*, who must be compensated in this way, so everyone also has *be' bidi* ("house people"), centering on the husband or paternal relatives, who do the compensating. This distinction, plus the differentiating exchange through which it is made, is *in itself* the most important consideration in Daribi social life. In an important sense it *is* Daribi social life, for its consequences and implications are respected regardless of other factors and

**Figure 4.2** *A Daribi bride standing next to members of the "groom's party" who are wearing their traditional attire: cassowary plumes, white shells, faces and bodies blackened with soot. (Masi, 1968)*

circumstances. *Be' bidi* must always be kept distinct from *pagebidi*, so that even if closely related people decided to marry (as they sometimes do), their relatives—even if they all live in the same house (as they sometimes do)—would have to subdivide into these two categories for the occasion. Moreover, in this or any other instance, the *be' bidi* are absolutely forbidden to share any of the meat given by the latter to others.

Daribi themselves say that they marry the sisters and daughters of those to whom they "give" meat, and may not marry among those with whom they "eat" (or "share") meat. Thus the explicit distinction drawn in any exchange is one between those who *share* meat or other wealth and those who *exchange* meat or wealth. Every such act and distinction draws a boundary. But since the distinction itself occupies the central focus, this boundary is actually more significant than the things it differentiates.

It may, for instance, come to pass that some people who have formerly identified with each other now want to intermarry; this will be condoned, though it may be inconsistent with earlier relationships, *provided that a suitable and clear-cut differentiation is made among them.*

As in the case of names, the specific (definitive or descriptive) content of the things referred to (the social "units," the categories *be' bidi* and *pagebidi*) is left implicit: what is made explicit is the distinction that separates or differentiates them. Hence just as names may be said to "elicit" social collectivities in the act of distinguishing them, so the exchanges that allocate rights to a woman or child can be seen to elicit specific instances of *be' bidi* and *pagebidi*. By virtue of the restrictions that must accompany such exchanges, every exchange will create its own social circumstances in this way. Even though one does not "start out" with groups, since these are never deliberately organized but only elicited through the use of names, one always ends up with specific bunches of people as *be' bidi* and *pagebidi*. It is an "automatic society," one that suddenly appears in concrete form wherever the right distinctions are made. What we might want to call the "permanent" sociality exists as an associational context flowing from one such *ad hoc* occasion to another.

Except for the ongoing restrictions regarding the sharing and non-sharing of the continuing gifts of meat that follow marriage and the birth of children, which tend to "freeze" the distinctions and categories, the groupings are no more completely consistent with one another than those elicited by naming. Nodes of people appear, in varying degrees of informal inclusiveness which I have termed *zibi*, clan, and community (Wagner 1967), based on the overlapping of sharing restrictions. (Since male reproductive fluids are believed to be increased and augmented by meat, a father and his children are automatic "sharers of meat.") And yet these by no means form a rigid hierarchy, an organization for the proper sharing and exchanging of meat. A clan is made up of consituent *zibi*, all of which tend to cooperate in sharing and speak of their mutual association in this way, but it is not unheard of for them to intermarry and thus "exchange." A community is made up of clans that have, in most cases, intermarried, and thus exchanged with each other; nevertheless they speak of their association as one of "sharing meat." Consistency is not always maintained from one nodal "level" to another, and therefore any attempt to put together the whole as a "system" or "order" is invariably compromised.

Thus *zibi*, clan, and community are not groups in the sense of deliberately organized or ideologically regularized constructions. Terms like "clan" and "community" may be helpful ways of referring to these associational groupings, provided that we keep in mind they have generally denoted fairly "unintentional" associations of this kind and that we do not try to make them into representations of our own corporations and consciously sociopolitical bodies. They are human sociality and relationship without inherent distinctions, and this is why people have to make the distinctions themselves, though of course in the act of making the distinctions they also elicit the sociality. In this respect they are the opposite of our Western forms, where people make the groups through deliberate participation and thereby elicit the "class" and "national" distinctions.

It is somewhat pointless, in tribal societies, to ask where the groups themselves are, for they never really materialize. What we see in the form of a village or a communal gathering is just a close approximation, an *ad hoc* representation of an abstraction, one that "will do" for the situation. Sociality is a "becoming," not a "become," thing, and its elicitation resembles the concept of "deficit spending"; people draw boundaries, compel, and elicit, and the relationships take care of themselves.

## EFFECTS OF WESTERN CONTACT

When the white men first came to Karimui they felt a strong obligation to discover groups. They were administrators, faced with the task of building an interface between the native's "institutions" and their own, and intent on resolving a confusing array of names and settlements into groups that could serve as the final (local) constituents in a political chain of command. They were heirs of a self-conscious "colonial" tradition, and many of them had taken courses in "the science of descent groups" as a part of their training. They knew, in short, how native society was supposed to be set up. And they also had explicit instructions as to how to deal with groups: in each (named) local group a leader, or Tultul, was appointed, and each Tultul was entrusted with the safekeeping of the "village book," in which census records were entered. Presented with a bewildering chaos of scattered homesteads and overlapping names, they reacted in the only way they knew how: they made groups.

They may have enlisted the help of the people themselves in doing this, bringing together all people identified by the same name (if there weren't too many) and ignoring any contradictions they could not handle, for they were content to let the boundaries of the group take care of themselves. In any case, the people, who had been living in single-story or double-story longhouses (housing anywhere from 2 to 60 people) scattered among their shifting garden-sites, were obliged to abandon the traditional pattern and settle in nucleated villages. (This concept was completely new to Daribi, who still use the word *be'*, "house," in reference to these complexes.) Such a reorganization into villages is characteristic of administrative control and policy throughout Papua-New

**Figure 4.3** Be'bidi: *Tua people in their* sigibe', *a two-story longhouse (1963).
Men live on the upper floor, women on the lower.*

Guinea. Various reasons have been given for it: it is said to make the
people easier to census, for example, and to be more healthy than aboriginal arrangements. But in fact it has one overriding advantage which
removes the most important ambiguity facing these outsiders—it makes
"groups" visible to people who simply cannot conceive of human sociality
in any other way.

Most of the villages at Karimui were formed in 1961–62 (Russell
*et al.* 1971:83), though a few stragglers were living in the traditional
pattern as late as 1969. By late 1963, when I first arrived at Karimui,
villages were a characteristic part of the local landscape; the natives
were in fact living in these clusters, regardless of who made them. But
is this sufficient reason to regard them as groups? The question is not
an easy one to answer, and a good answer requires our consideration of

the evidence. Let us take a close look at the resettlement of Buruhwą's Weriai people.

The patrol officers who encountered the Weriai in the middle 1950s were probably bewildered by the scattering of these people. In order to straighten things out—and incidentally strengthen the potential local labor force—they requested that all the Weriai relocate at Baianabo. (This was not as extreme as it might sound; the Kurube people claimed they were "coming slowly" to Baianabo anyway, and this kind of "slow motion" was actually highly characteristic of such demographic movements.) In about 1960, all of the Weriai people from Waramaru, as well as a number who had recently settled at a place called Suguąi, had joined Buruhwą's people in a single two-story longhouse at Baianabo. A number of other Weriai from Nekapo had moved into similar houses on an adjoining tract of land, called Sonianedu.

Shortly afterward, the Weriai were prompted by the government (with the strong urging of a fundamentalist mission) to construct rows of Western-style single family dwellings, or "line houses." These were abandoned by 1966 because they were nuisances and health hazards, but the people never went back to the highly concentrated longhouse occupation that predominated before Western contact. Thus the "village"

**Figure 4.4**  *A view of Kurube (settlement C) in 1964. Although the "line houses" are falling into disrepair, the grass has been cut and the road ditched in anticipation of a visit by the Patrol Officer.*

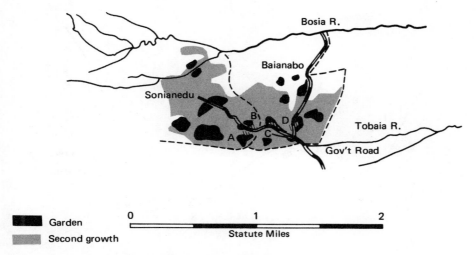

Garden

Second growth

Statute Miles

**Figure 4.5** *The Baianabo-Sonianedu region, 1968.*

as it appeared in 1968 took the form of a straggling line of houses, with noticeable "nodes" of concentration, scattered for a half mile along a cleared track that is locally known as "the big government car road" (Fig. 4.5). The nodes or settlements (designated A through D in Fig. 4.5) probably represent people who would share the same longhouse under precontact conditions.

The people themselves have no general term for these settlements; though they may be referred to as *be'*, this word is more often used in connection with actual houses, and the usage is thus ambiguous. Furthermore, although settlement A is often spoken of as Kilibali *be'*, B as Noruai *be'*, and either C or D (or both) as Kurube *be'*, any of these names may be used in reference to the village or complex as a whole. Sometimes the term Weriai is applied to the whole complex, but this is seldom done within the village itself. More commonly the complex as a whole is simply not referred to at all. Within it, terms like Kilibali, Noruai, and Kurube can be used to draw distinctions, though these characteristically do not take account of the small but noticeable flow of people from one settlement to another. Indeed, settlements C and D, which were formed by the splitting of a larger settlement since 1966, have not yet found an effective verbal means of differentiating themselves: members of each call their own "Kurube" and improvise a name for the other on the spot.

A glance at the actual distribution of houses (Fig. 4.6) shows that the nodes themselves are not very distinct. For one thing a number of people who might otherwise live in A and B spend most of their time in

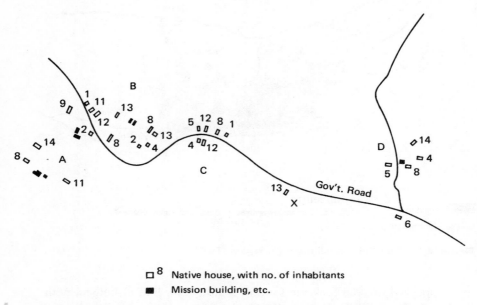

□ 8   Native house, with no. of inhabitants
■     Mission building, etc.

**Figure 4.6**   *Houses and settlements at Baianabo-Sonianedu, 1968.*

smaller houses located in their gardens. But even on the map there is
the curious anomaly of the house marked X. It seems to sit exactly in
the middle, between C and D. There is a very good reason for this. Of
the two men who live there with their families, one is closely related to
the people of D, but he obtained his wife by stealing her from the most
powerful man in D. The other man is related to the people in C, but he
has been looking after the aged mother of his housemate as well as some
of the men in D. If we speak of discrete "groups," it is difficult to decide
what affiliation to assign these people, but fortunately, for them at least,
the problem never comes up.

These "acculturated" settlements are no more literally and deliberately constituted groups than the more scattered ones that existed
before government control. They blend together as a continuous sociality
which seems to cry out for the distinctions that effectively elicit it. It
is a sociality adapted to the natives' way of dealing with it (which is
actually a way of creating it), and it will come into being whenever and
wherever people choose to deal with it in that way. If this particular
form seems to be adapted somewhat to the white man's notion of society,
it is only because the people themselves were under a strong coercion to
make it look like that. They also have a habit of wearing Western-style

clothing, which originated partly because outsiders wanted them to dress like Westerners. This does not mean, however, that they wear their clothes in the way that Westerners do, treat them the way Westerners do, or think of them in that way.

Nevertheless, if we look at the people in a certain way, ignoring or not seeing significant differences, they will look like Westerners. Similarly, if we look at their social life in a certain way, we will see "villages," groups, corporations, or jural systems. Because the native sociality is not the result of deliberate "grouping," however, but rather the outcome of indirect elicitation, it will take on a different appearance with every change in the observer's perspective. We have been examining the actual layout of the houses on the ground, and have found it to be only vaguely representative of "grouping." If we choose to differentiate the settlements according to the customary native distinctions (Table 4.1), we find that approximately 80 percent of the residents can be assigned to a Weriai *be'* —about 40 percent each for Noruai and Kurube (ignoring the fact that the latter actually comprises two nodes, or *be'*). But if we undertake an investigation of the paternal ancestry of the male household heads (remembering that they are "automatic" sharers of meat with their offspring and hence also with their own fathers), we find a rather different situation (Table 4.2). Only about half of the people are Weriai *be' bidi* in

**Table 4.1** *Collective identities at Baianabo-Sonianedu (1968) according to place of residence*

| Terms of Reference | Number of People | Percent of Total |
|---|---|---|
| Kilibali | | |
| settlement A | 33 | 14.1 |
| in garden houses | 13 | 5.6 |
| Total | 46 | 19.7 |
| Weriai | | |
| Noruai | | |
| settlement B | 83 | 35.4 |
| in garden houses | 13 | 5.6 |
| Total | 96 | 41.0 |
| Kurube | | |
| settlement C | 42 | 17.8 |
| settlement D | 37 | 15.8 |
| house X | 13 | 5.6 |
| Total | 92 | 39.2 |
| Total | 188 | 80.2 |
| Grand total | 234 | 99.9 |

**Table 4.2**  *Collective identities at Baianabo-Sonianedu (1968) according to genealogical identification of male head of household*

| Terms of Reference | Number of People | Percent of Total |
|---|---|---|
| Para | | |
|   Weriai | | |
|     Kurube | 60 | 25.7 |
|     Noruai | 59 | 25.2 |
|     Total | 119 | 50.9 |
|   Yao | 4 | 1.7 |
|   Total | 123 | 52.6 |
| Nekapo | | |
|   Kilibali | 67 | 28.6 |
| Noru | | |
|   Dogwaro-Hagani | 28 | 11.9 |
|   Sogo | 10 | 4.3 |
|   Total | 38 | 16.2 |
| Masi | | |
|   Yasa Masi | 3 | 1.3 |
|   Maina | 3 | 1.3 |
|   Total | 6 | 2.6 |
| Grand total | 234 | 100.0 |

this respect, Noruai and Kurube each accounting for approximately 25 percent of the total, whereas most of the remainder are not even identified as Para.

These discrepancies are the direct result of a naive and literal-minded approach to phenomena that are elicited indirectly by their creators. Although accurately documented, they suffer from a certain misplaced focus; right answers to the wrong problem. If brought to the attention of a native they certainly would not trouble him very much. While residence and the sharing of meat with one's *be' bidi* are crucially important considerations to the Daribi, neither is employed as a program for the deliberate formation of groups as such—they are not parts of a consistent effort at building society and will not show the kinds of consistency that we expect when we assume that they are.

Discrepancies of this kind show up very often in the anthropological literature on the New Guinea Highlands, and because most of the writers dealing with the area have shared a faith in the necessity of groups, the discrepancies are often introduced as evidence of an important problem. Because the highlanders do not seem to pay much heed to what are assumed to be "dogmas of descent" they are said to be "pragmatists," or it is assumed that the "real" dogmas are those of residence (de Lepervanche 1967). And yet it would seem to be the anthropologists, rather than the natives (to judge from the statistical records), that have brought dogmas onto the scene. The alternative to the "dogma" approach has been the assumption of "loose structure," groups with a certain strategic or pliable "give" in their organization (Pouwer 1960)—in short, another arrangement for having your groups theoretically and eating them pragmatically. Others have gone further and suggested an improvisatory basis of action on the part of Melanesians (Held 1951, Wagner 1972), or postulated a conception of society itself as a flux (Watson 1970) as I have done here.

Clearly if capable, experienced administrators, armed with a United Nations mandate and .303 rifles, have not been able to rearrange these people into clear-cut, Western-style groups, we would be asking rather too much of scholars by expecting them to do so with pen and ink and definitions. The problem is misplaced if we imagine "grouping" (that is, the deliberate construction of society) as a task of the native when it is actually our own. It is *our* job to account for the discrepancies, not the native's, since they are not discrepancies to him. It is also our job to explain just why they should be regarded as discrepancies, or as irrelevant, for in determining what our initial assumptions and problems will be, we also determine what kinds of evidence will be relevant and admissible.

## CONCLUSION

For many people, it is far easier to assume the existence of groups than to try to understand the subtleties of how the natives conceptualize their sociality. "Groups" and "society" form a kind of modern shorthand idiom for certain social phenomena; they exist as part of the "subject matter," as "facts," for those who believe in them or need them. The question of whether such facts exist wherever they have been postulated, however, whether "the social" exists as an objective level of phenomena, is a matter of which theory we elect to follow. We have a habit of confusing *the ways in which we study phenomena,* the theories through which we understand them, with the phenomena themselves. Thus we speak of "the chemistry of the body," "the biology of human reproduction," "the ecology of a forest," talking about the world (quite understandably) in the ways we have come to know about it.

Models are ways of *making* (or, as the language of science would have it, of "discovering") the various phenomenal "levels," by creating the characteristics in terms of which we perceive them—the science of descent groups is a set of models for making social interaction into descent groups. The analyst may have certain predispositions as to how he would like to make the world of his investigation in this way, or he may want to try to work on several "levels," but once he has committed himself to a certain model, his conclusions are to a certain degree predetermined.

The issue of social groups and their "reality" may or may not be a significant one, depending on what kind of anthropology one is interested in. But the implications of what the anthropologist does when he assumes the existence and the necessity of groups are essential matters for all anthropologists to consider. They suggest that *we* are creators no less than the peoples we study, and we must take heed of our own creativity as well as theirs. To put it somewhat differently, the assumption of creativity puts the anthropologist on a par with his subjects; the native, too, is an "anthropologist," with a "working hypothesis" of his own regarding his way of life. And regardless of how we wish to put that way of life together, we must come to terms with its own "theory" as a matter of professional and ethical obligation.

This kind of science, which treats a subject matter of the same order of phenomenal existence as its own hypotheses and conclusions, is a comparative latecomer. When it finally arrived on the scene, all of the more established disciplines had already developed a notion of "science" based on the "determined" nature of its subject matter. The idea of nature as a mechanistic (or behavioral) system with a precise, determinate and uniformitarian constitution made it possible to conceive of an "exact science" whose job it was to know or predict that order. This gave scientists an ideal of absolute certainty that was scarcely shaken by Einstein's "theory of relativity" or Heisenberg's indeterminancy principle, for however indeterminate nature might ultimately be, its indeterminancy and relativity could be measured in an exact way and made into a principle. Taking (believing, proving, verifying) the model to be identical (or very nearly so) with the subject matter amounts to the "style" of making phenomenal reality under the impression that one is discovering or predicting it.

But an anthropology that is under obligation to consider every cultural operation (whether action or experience, whether its own or its subjects') as an act of creativity can ill afford the luxury of attributing "reality" value to any of them. For this is precisely the decision that removes them from consideration as relative and creative acts. If the anthropologist is fallible the native cannot be infallible; if the native is fallible then anthropology stands to gain little indeed from the adoption of a determinist ideology.

## SELECTED READINGS

Glasse, M. and Meggitt, M. J., eds., 1969, *Pigs, Pearlshells, and Women: Marriage in the New Guinea Highlands*. Englewood Cliffs, N. J.: Prentice-Hall.

A collection of eleven short papers dealing with marriage in various highlands societies, with an Introduction by Mervyn Meggitt. This book invites theoretical as well as ethnographic comparisons among the different viewpoints and societies represented.

Leach, E. R., 1966, *Rethinking Anthropology*, London School of Economics Monograph in Social Anthropology No. 22. New York: Humanities Press Inc.

This collection of provocative essays may seem difficult to the beginner, but it is an excellent way of experiencing firsthand the impact that Leach and his structuralist colleagues had on the world of British social anthropology. Beginning with a valuable general introduction, Leach goes on at some length to discuss his structural interpretation of some classical functionalist problems and winds up with an excursion into symbolic anthropology.

Lévi-Strauss, C., 1963, *Structural Anthropology*, tr. C. Jacobson and B. G. Schoepf. New York: Basic Books.

A collection of essays on a broad range of subjects, subdivided into sections corresponding to Language and Kinship, Social Structure, Magic and Religion, Art, and Problems of Method and Teaching. This book presents Lévi-Strauss at his most approachable and comprehensive level, and its essays do a lot to explain some of the more difficult aspects and implications of his mode of theorization. An interested reader might want to supplement this book with *Claude Lévi-Strauss* by Edmund Leach, New York: Viking Press: 1970, Modern Masters Series, a more ambitious attempt to present Lévi-Strauss's line of theoretical argument in a systematic (though often heavily biased) way.

Mauss, Marcel, 1954, *The Gift: Forms and Functions of Exchange in Archaic Societies*, tr. I. Cunnison. Glencoe, Ill.: The Free Press.

An anthropological classic that has had a profound influence on modern thinking, this book is extremely readable and abounds in ethnographic examples. The reader might like to supplement this book with a more modern treatment of the subject, "On the Sociology of Primitive Exchange," by Marshall D. Sahlins, in ASA Monograph No. 1: *The Relevance of Models for Social Anthropology*, ed. M. Banton, New York: Frederick A. Praeger: 1965.

Radcliffe-Brown, A. R., 1965, *Structure and Function in Primtive Society*. New York: The Free Press.

This classic of social anthropology brings together various approaches by its author that figured prominently in the development of a functional "science of descent groups." Much that is implicit elsewhere in the writings of the British social anthropologists owes its origins to the essays collected in this volume.

Schneider, David M., 1965, "Some Muddles in the Models: Or, How the System really Works" in ASA Monograph No. 1: *The Relevance of Models for Social Anthropology*, ed. M. Banton. New York: Frederick A. Praeger.

An analysis and clarification of the two dominant bodies of theory in social anthropology, "descent theory" and "alliance theory," with particular attention to the crucial conceptual differences that separate them. Although somewhat advanced, the exposition is clear and forceful enough to repay close reading and careful attention with some real insights into a significant theoretical crisis.

# Chapter 5

# Ritual and Social Organization: Sikh Marriage Rituals

### Murray J. Leaf

Rituals are referred to in drawing inferences about a wide range of phenomena—society as a whole, kinship systems, political systems, religious systems, cultural beliefs, and personal values and desires. This variety of treatments of ritual means that there is no single organized approach to the analysis of ritual at present. It also means that if such an approach could be developed, it would have broad implications in many theoretical areas.

## A BRIEF HISTORY OF RITUAL STUDY

In the nineteenth century, rituals were of interest as likely places to find "survivals" of previous forms of the culture or society—conservative elements from which early stages of development might be reconstructed. Most of this nineteenth-century interest was organized around the concept of *totemism,* a supposed universal or near-universal early form of religion uniting religious and social rules in a single symbolic system expressed through the identification of human social groups with animal species or quasi-species. The key idea was the *totem* itself—a term and concept borrowed from Northeastern American Indian usage around the turn of the nineteenth century. The definition by Andrew Lang, one of the most important scholars on the subject in the latter part of nineteenth century, reflects the way this idea was debated and used:

> In stricter terminology "totem" denotes the object, generally of a natural species, animal or vegetable, but occasionally rain, cloud, star, wind, which gives its name to a *kindred* actual or supposed, among

many savages and barbaric races in America, Africa, Australia, and Asia and the isles. Each child, male or female, inherits this name, either from its mother ("female descent") or from its father ("male descent"). Between each person and his or her name-giving object, a certain mystic *rapport* is supposed to exist. Where descent wavers, persons occasionally have, in varying degrees, the totems of both parents. (1911:28,79)

The term "kindred" refers to an organized division of kinsmen. The terms "savagery" and "barbarism" refer to what were considered separate stages of social development, and the descent rules refer to basic principles along which societies were supposed to be organized. Mystic rapport was supposedly expressed by prohibitions on eating or killing, by ceremonial representations of the animals, by use of animal names, by the possession of special songs about animals, or in fact by any mention of animals or the other types of objects regularly made in connection with any social group. Many of the various cultural usages pertaining to animals or plants were interpreted as evidence of totemism—if not in a fully developed form then at least as a remnant of a fuller past version.

William Robertson-Smith and Sir James Frazer are also associated with the study of totemism. Robertson-Smith viewed the religion of the early Semites (the supposed group ancestral to both Hebrews and Arabs) as basically totemic (think of the food taboos). Frazer thought magic, including magic found in modern European religious beliefs, derived from an early totemistic cult that gave rise to the classical pantheisms of both Greeks and Romans.

The last major work in the totemistic tradition was Durkheim's *Elementary Forms of the Religious Life*, published in 1912. Durkheim's analysis concentrated on accounts of Australian rituals which he considered expressions of the "collective consciousness" (society), the basis of human thought and action. Rituals were direct manifestations of principles of social order; these principles, because they were social, formed the basis of the general concepts that individuals used in ordering their worlds. Rituals were thus considered the means by which concepts originating in society were impressed upon individuals.

One of Durkheim's ideas that has been influential in the modern period is that rituals are universally characterized by being "sacred," as distinct from wordly objects which are "profane." According to Durkheim, this sacredness is a direct expression of the social character of ritual, whereas the profane is associated with particular and individual matters. A second influential idea is that the contents of a ritual include the congregation which attends and its members' actions. A good part of Durkheim's proof that rituals are expressions of the society rests on demonstrating that rules for ritual behavior create social categories for persons who should and should not participate in the ritual.

By the time Durkheim's work was published, however, the idea of totemism had been largely discredited. In 1910, Alexander Goldenweiser had published "Totemism, an Analytical Study" in the *Journal of American Folklore*. This essay was an extended criticism of virtually every characteristic that had been attributed to the "totemic complex" by Frazer, Lang, Tylor, and others. It is argued that the different characteristics did not in fact go together with any significant regularity and that there were real and important differences among the totemisms of each major continental area which made them incomparable. The conclusion was drawn that totemism existed only in the minds of anthropologists, not of natives—a conclusion that obviously undermined Durkheim's claim to have found the way society universally presents itself in individual mentality. Goldenweiser's conclusions were subsequently endorsed and summarized by Franz Boas in 1916. Boas said totemism lacked "psychological reality," by which he meant both that it lacked subjective integrity for the natives who were said to adhere to it, and that it lacked *historical* integrity for them (Boas 1916:320).

Although the force of Boas's and Goldenweiser's critique was felt, Boas's alternative criteria were not accepted. In an effort to replace totemism, theoretical interest in ritual analysis after the publication of *Elementary Forms of the Religious Life* went off in several more narrowly focused directions. The direction that was initially most influential, especially in England, was begun by Arnold Van Gennep.

Van Gennep's *Rites de Passage* was published in 1909. It represents a general orientation toward defining classes of rituals more narrowly than totemism had done. These classes are still thought of as universal types, however, and as basically expressing social relations. "Rites of passage" are rituals that define or mark a change in an individual's social status—preeminently those rituals marking birth, marriage, and death. Once a class of rites is defined, the rites can be seen to have clear relations to the structure of the society and, insofar as they are rites at all, to distort the representation of the structure in some way while marking the change that the individual is undergoing. Van Gennep argued that such rites involve universal symbolic devices, including symbolic modifications of the normal flow of time. Symbolic stages in the rite beginning with the suspension of the initiate's former status and a period of ritual impurity are followed by assumption of the new status, purification, and resumption of the new role in nonritual space and time. Van Gennep also formulated a rudimentary theory of the kind of changes in status such rituals mark. His treatment inspired analyses of rituals of rebellion, rituals of succession, and some aspects of rituals of pollution and purification—all of which were recently grouped together in an important collection called *Essays on the Ritual of Social Relations*, edited by Max Gluckman (1968).

A second major direction away from totemism, especially pursued in the 1950s, can be traced back to Marcel Mauss. Mauss was not as concerned with ritual per se as was Van Gennep, but he shared Van Gennep's generalizing and symbolic orientation. In his book *The Gift (La Donne)*, Mauss argued that gifts are not simply a crude form of economic action but the basis of all social order. The argument was based on the idea that a gift consists not only in the object given, but also in the relation it marks. A gift is between people in social capacities, and as such it symbolizes those capacities and their interrelationships.

In 1949, Claude Lévi-Strauss extended Mauss's schema to an influential general theory of social structure for kinship-based societies by considering marriages as gifts of women between groups. The theory applies to group relations, myths, and rituals. In the main, his technique of analysis was to find systematic sets of "binary oppositions" in social, mythical, and textual materials. His fundamental concept of binary opposition is vague, essentially meaning that he can find a contrast between two elements, but not three. These elements may represent the distinction between wife-givers and wife-takers in social organization, between Gods and mortals in myth, or between different kinds of food in culinary practice and in ritual. To arrange these in a single series, Lévi-Strauss and others argue simply that the contrasts from one sphere are either associated with or analogous to the contrasts in the others. Often the evidence is that the two contrasts occur together in ritual or myth; sometimes the evidence is unclear. In the end, a list of paired, contrasting terms is produced, which is taken as showing the specific form of the dualistic principle that underlies the society in question, and as suggesting the general content of the supposed universal laws of thought themselves.

The third major line of analysis was most dramatically articulated by Gregory Bateson in his 1936 book titled *Naven*. Naven is the name of an initiation ritual of a tribe in New Guinea. Bateson did not treat this ritual in connection with other rituals and usages to find conceptual patterns or category oppositions which corresponded to structural relations between groups. Rather, he looked at it in isolation—as if it were the only ritual the people in the tribe had, and it is frankly taken as an embodiment of the *ethos* and *eidos* of their culture—a general spirit or outlook on life and society.

Bateson described the ethos and eidos in terms of the older idea of a *zeitgeist*, or "spirit of the age," evidently trying to develop a type of analysis that would have had "psychological reality" in Boas's sense. Consistently with this, his concept of a culture was very well thought out as something ideational or thematic that *could* be represented in a ritual, as for Durkheim.

Bateson attempted to use known psychological processes to account for the impact of the ceremony on those who attended it, in place of Durkheim's mystic communion. This attempt involved focusing on many "odd" behaviors—especially what appeared to be dramatic reversals of normal roles. Respected people were treated with disrespect, men were substituted for women and women for men, people normally held in reverence wore disgusting clothing, obscene and intimate acts were performed in public, and so forth. To account for these, Bateson tried to relate them to the creation of the cultural outlooks at first with a modification of psychoanalytic theory and later with some form of communication theory. Though he did this only in a sketchy and programmatic way, the fact that he tried to do so at all made his work very nearly unique.

Bateson's overall approach permitted the use of thematic materials from the ritual and the surrounding activities without arbitrarily saying that the themes had to be interpreted in terms of totemism, binary opposition, or any other universal, a priori, categories. But there was arbitrariness in Bateson's analysis on another level. To prove that the ethos and eidos of the culture were reflected in this one ceremony, he would have had to look at several ceremonies that were different on their face and show that they did not in fact project wholly different general outlooks for the culture. This he did not do. He should also have looked at nonceremonial usages to show that the ethos and eidos they embodied were in fact the same as in the ceremony. He did not do this either. To complete his argument properly, Bateson would have needed a much clearer and more exact conception of the crucial variables: what a ceremony was, what a culture was, what an ethos and eidos were, and what, in each case, where the methods of analysis and description that were appropriate. These problems are conceptual and theoretical, and Bateson did not resolve them.

In the 1950s and 60s, these three approaches were combined with each other and with other developing interests in social organization and religion especially. The literature that resulted was highly sophisticated, but it demonstrated very little concrete progress over what was obvious to Durkheim. Anthropologists knew that society in some sense is reflected in rituals, and as such society is some kind of mental or intellectual entity —something to be learned, rather than some brute pattern of behavior that only an analyst can detect from a distance. Moreover, there is something odd about ritual symbolism, but this oddness when looked at in detail makes sense. Rituals have to be seen in terms of where they occur in a person's life and in the conceptual framework of the people who put them on. They must be viewed not only in terms of the declared purposes of the ritual (like initiation or divination), but also in terms of the conceptual categories in which these purposes are framed as well as of the audience and participants who attend and use those categories. These observations did not add up to a theory, however, and all the efforts to tie them into one simple and coherent notion of what a ritual is and does raised more questions than they answered.

## SELECTING A RESEARCH PROBLEM

In the early 1960s, I chose not to engage in research to find new classes of rites of passage or another universal type of ritual, to find binary relations or another universal type of formal pattern, or to find a new and better way to infer a whole culture from a few details of a single ritual. Enough had been done along these lines by good scholars to make it clear that one more such effort would not be useful, and that to make any real progress it was necessary to start out on a new approach.

The best starting point seemed to be a consideration of the nature of the actual data we had, and this in turn seemed to mean that we would mainly consider not what was unique about ritual so much as what was obvious and objective. What was most obvious was that rituals were *textual,* in two senses. First of all, a ritual was generally like a play: it had a cast of characters, a theme, and a plot. Secondly, as rituals appeared in anthropological literature they were most often texts and no more: transcriptions of what one or a few informants said, whether or not the performance described was ever actually seen.

Of course, taking rituals as textual materials does not differentiate them in any major way from the rest of the materials anthropologists normally deal with. Informants' descriptions, verbal or written, are in fact the principal source of data for almost all cultural and social anthropology, even when the subject is verified by field observation. This point was not unwelcome, for it fitted with a major theoretical trend then developing in social structural analysis. In 1961, E. R. Leach had described certain important kinship structures as "organizational ideas that are present in any society." Several anthropologists, partly agreeing with Lévi-Strauss but reacting against his solipsism, had been speaking of culture and society alike as "symbol systems," or "codes" in some sense (see Schneider, 1965 for an important review of part of this development). In this framework, rituals were considered specially designated embodiments of the general social symbols; they were particularly dramatic presentations of these symbols, but not different from them in kind.

Working with Professor David M. Schneider, I tried to develop the idea of a symbol system or code into something more exact and powerful by combining the anthropological ideas and methods with an older tradition of analysis equally adapted to a conception of society as something fundamentally textual. This was the tradition of "social contract theory" that had dominated social thought in the seventeenth and eighteenth centuries, but had been largely neglected in the nineteenth and twentieth centuries. This tradition was strong precisely where social theory in anthropology was weak. It incorporated a reasonable view of human motivation. Furthermore, it showed how society as a system of texts nevertheless was forceful and convincing to those people who reported them. There were two fundamental premises to the tradition. The first was that society was an "artificial" body, a conventional creation of human beings. The second premise was that people created such a body in order to pursue their own perceived self-interests.

The idea was that native descriptions of their societies (or, in the language of the time, the constitutions of states) were "contracts," in two senses. The first was that such a description was a contract between a group of people and one or a few of their number whom the people established in the form of a government to guarantee their individual rights. Classically, in this analysis, the people gave up a portion of their liberty in exchange for a type of security. In the second sense, the form of government, whatever it was, was then implied in any private "contracts" among people in a state thus established. The state existed in consensus and agreement. These contracts—interactive agreements among people—reinforced the consensus by the very act of depending on it.

To apply this concept to the range of phenomena anthropologists had in mind under the heading of "symbol systems," it would be necessary to find some uniform and plausible way of interpreting informants' reports and rituals in the areas of religion and kinship, as well as in politics, economics, and other such systems. These reports and rituals would have to be seen as expressing self-interest on the one hand and as implying the existence of sanctioning authorities on the other.

The approach I took in developing these initial formulations into a theory of ritual was threefold. One aspect was to treat rituals as "contracts" which people entered into out of their own interests and which reflected the larger social structures that provided the sanctioning power behind agreements and rights. Besides analyzing rituals themselves, I necessarily had to analyze social structures independently and, finally, to develop a scheme organizing a complete economic census at the individual level so that individuals' interests could be objectively determined. The three analyses together could be used in predicting the configuration of interests that would be represented by the actual persons attending a series of real ritual performances.

The theory could presumably have been put into effect in any geographical area, but a number of extrinsic considerations based on accessibility, the quality of the literature, and historical importance of the area led to the selection of a Sikh village in North India, which I call

Shahidpur. On the basis of this choice, the main ritual to focus on had to be marriage. Marriages are the most important rituals these villagers normally engage in. In addition, the developed literature on Indian marriages embodied a conclusion quite the opposite of what was predicted: rather than promoting the individual's self-interest, marriage rituals were considered to work counter to his interests. Weddings in India have generally been described as irrational expenses, a major source of rural debt, and an indication of subservience of individual rationality to traditional and counterrational social pressures. For example, a study of a village in another part of India by Scarlet Epstein, published just as my own project was being thought out, stated flatly, "Every wedding involves the wedding household in expenditure which is excessive in relation to its income. Even the magnates had to borrow to meet their wedding expenses" (1962:105). A standard work on the Panjab states of all Indian peasants that:

> In a good year his [the cultivator's] ignorance and improvidence make him spend the whole of his surplus on marriages and festivities, and his extravagance on such occasions often leads him even in good years to the doors of the money-lender. A ryot would stop at no extravagance in marrying one of his children or performing any funeral or social ceremony to show more ostentation than his fellows. (Darling 1947:53)

My project was funded by the National Institute of Mental Health in 1963. I arrived in India in the spring of 1964.

Research in India went generally according to plan. The description of Sikh social structures turned out to be easier than I had expected. On the other hand, the description of individual interests turned out to be more difficult. With a relatively small number of crucial cases, it was possible to establish the general thesis for the dissertation. To develop the thesis more fully through a more precise assessment of individuals' interests, however, it was necessary to work out a system of computer analysis of legal records, my own censuses, and other data that pertained to individuals in order to put them into an accessible system of individual socioeconomic profiles. This was finished in 1971.

In 1972, the basic analysis of structures that provide the background for the ritual analysis was published, in a more refined form than the dissertation. The refinements reflected the computer analysis of individual interests and strategies. More importantly, they involved a newer and broader theoretical framework based on a modification of information theory (Shannon and Weaver 1964). In the final formulation, the general idea of an "information system" as a culturally established set of constraints upon, and resources for, the formation of recognizable and repeatable communicative actions was used to incorporate both what would formerly have been called social structures on the one hand, and ecological, economic, and resource management systems on the other. The general idea is that the more highly organized a system is, and the fewer elements it has, the less potential information can be conveyed by its messages. Low information messages have little power to direct specific sequences of behavior. A message from a low information source reflects few choices, so it can only direct few choices.

There are six cultural information systems in wide use in Shahidpur. Three are very highly organized, with few elements. These systems, which I call "conscious sociological models," have the character of rigid ideologies, general conceptual formulae which can be applied to a wide number of actual behavioral circumstances. The remaining three systems have more elements, and allow more choice. Their elements in use appear to be more "concrete," and their behavioral implications more specific.

The conscious sociological models in order of increasing complexity are (1) the concepts of factions, (2) the basic concepts of the Sikh religion, and (3) the kinship terminology and a related concept of property. Fundamentally, each of these systems can be represented by a simple image, although each has many implications for those that have learned its meaning.

The image for the factional, or "party," conceptions, as it was drawn by a villager, was:

| Party | A | B |
|---|---|---|
| Position | Yes | No |

The vertical line represents a conflict between two groups of "enemies" who are each attempting to "dominate" the other over an issue of "principle." "Yes" and "No" represent their respective stands, and it is generally understood that the "issue" is the election of one of two opposed leaders to a major position of power. The image, with the special words and concepts it defines and interrelates, is referred to in abstract discussions about parties in the village, and is also seen as the "meaning" or social foundation that underlies actual cases of party activity. Villagers act out party conflicts by using words and other symbols of the ideas in this model, and they do this consciously and deliberately. By talking and acting as if the party model described some independent reality, villagers create parties, but the parties do not in fact exist apart from such communicative actions that embody the model, and are in that sense shaped by the model.

The religous image has many pictorial forms. One common and general one is that of a fish in a pool of water. Another is that of a man "in the cool shade of a mango tree." The idea is that the fish (or the

man) survives and thrives because it is unlike the surrounding medium
and because it is smaller than it. If the fish were to be like the water in
substance or size, it would cease to survive as a fish. God, considered as
Truth and the basis of human perception, is like the water, the sustaining
medium. The worshipper—"Sikh" actually means "student" or "learner"
—is like the fish. The truths that the religion attempts to present are
understood as being basic to practical action in the world, necessary for
individual survival. It is said that the truths of the religion, in this sense,
are the "patrimony" of the Sikh gurus who tried to teach them. They are
the useful property that one has inherited from the first teachers just as a
person inherits farmland or capital from his own father and uses it to
sustain himself in his life. Abstract as they may sound, these ideas also
are used in daily communication on a moment-to-moment basis, and in
this sense they are as viable as the parties, and the entities they describe
are as "real" as the parties to the same degree and in the same way.

The kinship terminology is more complicated—a bit too complicated
to be fully represented here. The best simple way to picture it is in the
shape of a butterfly, with "ego," the user of the system, at the center.
Looking "up," ego has superior kin divided into two exclusive wings:
those related through his father and those related through his mother.
Each set has its own distinct set of names. The word for the "uncle" who
is mother's brother is different from the term for father's brother. The
terms for father's father and father's mother are different from the terms
for mother's father and mother's mother, and so forth. At each generation level above ego, the terms are divided into two contrasting sides.
On ego's own level, of course, there are no divisions: his mother's children and his father's children are classed together, as in English. But also
classed with them are all people who would be called "cousins" in
English as well: a "brother" is any male child of any relative of the
father's and mother's generation. Below ego's own generation are the
reciprocals of the superior terms. That is, there is one "nephew" term
that goes with the terms for mother's brother, and another that goes with
the terms for father's brother, and so forth.

The special concept of property that goes with the kinship terms is
often rendered in the legal phrase "ancestral property," which means inherited property that a group of kin depends on for its common liveli-
hood. Concepts of different specific types of kinship groups are derived by
combining specific groups of terms with specific senses of "property." The
"family" is the group centering on a father and mother who share a
physical household and its goods. A "caste" is a group taken to be descended from a group of similar people who have in common a similar
*kind* of property, like land or masonry tools, and so on. Five major named
types of group-concepts are generated in this way, as well as an indefi-

nite but large number of minor conceptions—like "mother's side" and "father's side." It is precisely the larger number of elements, and the larger number of combining possibilities, that gives the kinship system the highest information potential of the three conscious sociological models.

The other three, more "concrete," information systems are the economy, the division of labor, and the ecology, still in order of decreasing organization and increasing information value. The economy is the system of monetary values and the marketing practices that apply them to certain specific goods in certain specific ways—to wheat by weight and not bulk, and not to dogs at all. The division of labor consists in the concepts of control and ownership and the mechanisms that symbolize their use: gates, locks, legal records, the strength of actual individuals, and the like. Finally, the ecology is the system of biological populations in the community—the cows as a population, wheat as a population, and so forth.

Each system uses a different set of elements, a different number of elements, and a different formal arrangement of elements. Within a system, there are necessary relations among elements. To change the meaning of the concept of God is to change the meaning of the concept of a disciple. To change the price of one good will have necessary repercussions on other prices. But across systems, the relations are loose and dependent. Currency reform may or may not have an effect on cattle raising or religious thought. People related to each other in kinship terms may or may not share religious ideas, and a change in kinship terminology may or may not go along with change in religious conceptions.

Now, working back from the idea of an information system, it is possible to restate the original view of ritual and its analysis, and to reformulate the original problem. A sample of the analysis here will indicate the general line of argument and the kind of results that will be achieved.

## MARRIAGE RITUALS IN SHAHIDPUR

Information systems and rituals have different relations to behavior. A highly organized information system consists of a set of definitions and symbols for their use—for example, the definitions of terms that one applies to kinsmen. Although the terms are often used in behavior, they do not indicate behavioral sequences. In English, a "cousin" is a son or daughter of a sibling of a parent, but this definition does not imply any actual sequence of action among those who use the term. The definitions of social information systems are as timeless as the definitions of mathematics and logic.

By contrast, rituals *are* sequences of behavior. They have a well-defined conceptual component, which we can call the "script" of the ritual. This conceptual component specifically calls for individuals of certain classes to execute certain acts in a certain sequence. It calls for a cast and a performance. For this reason a ritual, like a story, can be analyzed into plot elements and role relations.

Marriage rituals used by peasant farmers and other relatively well-off groups in Shahidpur, as elsewhere in North India, are long and complex. They begin with the selection of a spouse and end with the transfer of the bride to her husband's village—following the custom that is almost universal in South Asia. The villagers of Shahidpur describe their normal marriage rituals as involving three major stages, each with a number of segments that vary according to the caste and tastes of those putting on the affair. The stages are *mangnā, shādī,* and *maklāva.*[1] We will concentrate on the middle stage.

*Mangna* is generally translated as "engagement." It begins when the girl's father assembles a group of "close people" to go "look at" the prospective groom in his village. If he "likes" the boy, he places one rupee in his hand. (The rupee is the basic unit of Indian currency, approximately equivalent to 20 cents at the time of the study.) If the parties remain agreeable, there is an exchange of ritual gifts and countergifts which ultimately results in setting the date for the next major series of actions: *shadi.*

*Shadi,* generally translated as "wedding," takes place in the village

---

1. Panjabi vowels as represented in print in this chapter each have one single value as follows:

| | |
|---|---|
| a | The so-called short *a*, pronounced like the vowel in *but*. |
| ā | The long *a*, pronounced like the vowel in *pot*. |
| i | The short *i*, pronounced like the vowel in *bit*. |
| ī | The long *i*, pronounced like the vowel in *feet*. |
| u | The short *u*, pronounced like the vowel in *put*. |
| ū | The long *u*, pronounced like the vowel in *boot*. |
| o | Pronounced like the vowel in *ought*. |
| e | Pronounced like the vowel in *bet*. |
| ai | Pronounced like the dipthong in *hair*. |
| au | Pronounced like the dipthong in *shout*. |

Consonants as represented have approximately their English values, except that capital letters are used to distinguish a retroflex series (T, Th, D, Dh) from a dental series (t, th, d, dh). The retroflex series are pronounced slightly behind their English counterparts, with the underside of the tip of the tongue contacting the back of the alveolar ridge (see Fig. 1.1 in Chapter 1, page 39). The dental series are pronounced forward of their English counterparts, rather like the stops of Castilian Spanish, with the tongue nearly between the teeth.

Consonants written with following *h* are aspirated, which means they are followed with a slight release of breath leading onto the vowel that follows. Other consonants are pronounced without such a release. Generally the consonant written *j* in Panjabi can be pronounced with either an English *j* or *z* value.

of the bride and is the part of the marriage ritual usually described in connection with supposedly lavish expenses and display. *Shadi* involves two major subsegments and a number of minor rituals and rituals within rituals. The two major subsegments are *milnī* and *anānd kāraj. Milni* literally means "meeting," and it involves the coming together, theoretically for the first time, of the families of the bride and of the groom. *Anand karaj* (literally "making joy") involves the actual union of bride and groom. *Maklava*, the third stage of the ritual, covers the removal of the bride to her new home, and begins right after *shadi*.

### Shadi

*Shadi* normally lasts two days and one night, beginning one afternoon and ending on the next. *Milni* takes up the first evening and has three major subdivisions: arrival of the bride's mother's kin and formation of the bride's wedding party; arrival of the groom's group and welcoming; and tea, dinner, and entertainments.

Although the arrival of the bride's mother's kin follows a fixed order, it is generally a jolly and casual-seeming occasion. The women arrive first in a procession through the village gate (see Fig. 5.1). Then, with men and women both present, the mother's brother sets out on display the gifts the family is giving to the bride. Afterwards all the women leave to begin their own sequence of rituals and preparations, and the men prepare to await the arrival of the groom's party.

The bride's or groom's mother's relations are called *nānke*, from the kinship term *nānā* ("mother's father"). The actual *nana*, however, does not attend. *Nanke* are expected to attend weddings. In fact, if a girl's father dies or is otherwise unable or unwilling to put on her marriage, her mother's brother is expected to assume the responsibility.

In addition to *nanke*, each wedding group contains the bride's or groom's father's kin. These are called *dādke* for a man (after *dādā*, "father's father") and *piuke* for a woman (after *piu*, "father"). Together with other members of the same caste, these two groups make up the *meli* of the bride or groom. The *meli* in turn, together with the *lagis*—families of other castes attached to the family of the bride or groom—finally make up the entire group, which is called the *janj*.

Within the ritual, certain members of the boy's *janj* have special roles and are marked with symbolic clothing. Their roles give the group as a whole a specific type of ritual structure. The groom is called *lara*, and he carries a sword and piece of cloth and wears a garland. His father or mother's brother—whoever is sponsoring the rite—is marked by a piece of cloth he carries over his shoulder. The *lara* is accompanied by a *sirwala* who wears a similar but smaller garland. *Sirwala* literally

**Figure 5.1**   *Arrival of women of the bride's* nanke.

means "keeper of the head." The underlying idea is that if the *lara* should die, the *sirwala* will inherit his responsibilities to the bride.

Outside the *meli*, several of the *lagis* are also marked. The *Brahmin* (described by some as "not really" a *lagi*) who accompanies each group is generally recognizable by clothing and turban. Others of lower rank are occasionally marked in different rituals as will be noted. The Barber in particular is conspicuous and marked by special terms and by his action. He is called *raja*, "king." The Barber is the master of the ceremonies, saying what should be done, summoning the parties to each segment, and deciding disputed points. His wife is called *rani*, "queen," and has a parallel role among the women. In actual fact, the one Barber who lives in Shahidpur earns a substantial part of his income from managing weddings in this way.

In the girl's group, of course, the *lara's* marking does not exist, and the girl's father, while always conspicuous, does not carry a cloth. Whoever is sponsoring the bride, father or mother's brother, is called the *korum* of his counterpart sponsor of the groom. The bride, called *lari,* wears special clothing when she appears. She is accompanied by an "elder sister" who contrasts with the *sirwala* of the groom. All other roles are the same.

Each *janj,* but especially that of the groom, is described as a group of warriors. The groom has come to capture the girl, and the girl's group tries to protect her. The ritual structure and martial aspects of the two groups is briefly but concisely enacted in the ritual of *milni* proper.

*Milni.* After the groom's group arrives and settles in the place it will be staying, its *raja* meets with the *raja* of the bride's group. When they determine both groups are ready, the groom's *janj* assembles outside the village gate (see Fig. 5.2). Following its band and the *raja,* who "knows the way," it enters the village and goes to the "house" of the bride's family (which may be any place they have decided to hold the rituals and which has been arranged accordingly). The bride's group is waiting in front for them. The groom's party approaches and stops a little way before the girl's group, facing it. In the front rank of the groom's group will be the groom, the *korum,* probably the mother's brother (if he is not the

**Figure 5.2** *Groom's* janj *assembled to enter bride's village for the first time.*

*korum*), the *sirwala*, and the *raja*. In the girl's group are the *korum*, the *raja*, any brothers, and the mother's brother (if he is not *korum*).

As the parties face each other, the two *rajas* come together between them. They first agree between themselves that each person in the two groups is the right person. This done, the *korum* of the groom's group comes forward, and the *raja* of his side says to the other and the company, "This is so and so" (name and description of the *korum*). Then the other *korum* stands out and is introduced by his *raja* in the same way. The girl's group's *korum* takes a rupee, passes it around the head of the *korum* of the boy's group, and gives it to the *raja* of the latter's group. Then the *korum* from the boy's side gives a rupee to the *raja* of the girl's side in the same way. The two *korums* then present each other with a rupee and a piece of cloth, such as a turban or a *chadar*—a wrap used generally as a kind of skirt, but noted proverbially for its versatility. The value is said to depend on the wealth of the giver. Finally, the *korums* embrace each other. It is said that each will try to lift the other, but if neither succeeds, the girl's side's *korum* is supposed to give up and allow the boy's side's *korum* to win. No other persons are introduced. It should especially be noted that the groom is never introduced to anyone, and specifically not to the brother of the bride (his logical counterpart). *Milni* is complete when the two *korum* have embraced.

Immediately after the formal embrace, the girl's father invites the boy's group in for light refreshment, generally tea and sweets. In stereotypic verbal descriptions, it is said that he "brings" the refreshment and serves the boy's group. Because of the substantial size of the groups, which averaged about 80 people in the summer of 1965, this is not practicable in fact. As the tea is first served to the boy's group, the men of the girl's group stand aside and watch. This is the most elaborate service, with careful attendance to the needs of the guests and a plentitude of sweets of many kinds. When they have had "all they want," they leave and, led by the band, go back to the place they are staying. (The band has also had tea at the same time and in the same way.) Then tea is given to the members of the girl's group who want it. This is generally to the people who have come from outside the village. The service is much less elaborate, with more self-help and fewer kinds of sweets. Whereas rented china might have been used to serve the members of groom's party and they might have been seated, the *meli* of the girl's father will take their tea standing, in glasses or brass tumblers, the normal items used in the village. The *Harijan lagis* of the father may be given tea next. ("Harijan," a polite term coined by Ghandi for the groups formerly referred to by the British as "untouchables," is identified in Shahidpur with two caste-names: Weaver and Leather-Worker. Both are described as laborers.) They will have to bring their own tumblers, and the sweets will be given into their hands or put upon a cloth they bring themselves. Whereas the *meli* might have drunk standing at the tables, the *Harijans* will be served seated on the floor to one side. When tea is finished, preparations are immediately undertaken for serving dinner.

Dinner is the first of two major meals for the *janj* of the boy. It is an important ritual in its own right. The *lagis* have traditional roles in the preparation of the food, but the actual cook may be hired from outside. When the food is ready, the servers first take around the sweets, which are served as long as they are in demand. Next the meat and whatever vegetables will be eaten are served with the bread. One goat provides one meal for about 130 people. Tea and some spicy or salty savory finish the meal. The servers are "volunteers" from the village, not *lagis*.

At each meal, a place is set aside and laid with carpets. While the groom's party eats, this area is occupied by a group called the *panchāyat*. The *panchayat* includes the father of the girl and prominent villagers in his *janj*, such as members of the actual village *panchayat* or village *lambardārs* (tax collectors). *Panchayat* is a traditional term for a village judicial body and signifies that these men are acting as official witnesses of the proceeding. The father of the girl directs the proceedings through the *raja*.

*Anand Karaj.*   *Anand karaj* which creates the marriage bond between the bride and groom takes place the morning of the second day. It is said that the rite must take place before noon. The rite occurs in the same place as the eating, but it is arranged differently. If tables and chairs have been used for the meal, they will be removed.

Early in the morning, after sunrise, the Guru Granth Sahib (Sikh sacred scripture) is brought to the ceremonial area, which thus automatically becomes a Gurudwara (Sikh temple). The Granth is positioned on a dias near a wall, where its reader sits facing the assembly. The *āsā di wār* (literally "song of hope"), the regular morning prayer of Sikhs, is then sung. During this, the boy's group remains in its rest area, and the bride is not present.

As the regular service ends, the "boy and some of his men go to the girl's house," summoned by the Barber. They enter and take their places. The band remains outside the house. The men sit in a body facing the reader's left-hand side. The groom sits before him, slightly toward the left. The girl's party then collects, enters, and takes its traditional place: the men of the girl's group sit in a body on the right-hand side of the Granth opposite the boy's group; the women sit directly in front of the Granth, behind the groom's back, and between the two bodies of men. Then the bride enters, accompanied by her sister, and is seated directly at the groom's left hand, on the side of her own group of men. Her

**Figure 5.3**   *Bride and groom at beginning of* anand karaj.

"sister" is close behind her, generally whispering to her and guiding and comforting her.

For *anand*, the groom leaves behind the sword he otherwise carries. He has in his hand only the piece of cloth, and he continues wearing the garland. The bride wears a red outfit with a red shawl; the color is said to be very "joyful." Over this is a white mantle, generally a sheet, that covers her completely (see Fig. 5.3). White is associated with passivity and is often worn by religious people. She cannot see ahead and must be guided. The bride and groom are seated before the Granth. They are connected to one another by someone (generally the sister) who puts a free end of the cloth the groom carries into the hand of the bride. The ceremony begins promptly.

The person who has read out the *asa di war* will often have been specially invited for the occasion. He instructs the seated couple briefly on their obligations and duties as a married couple toward each other and their relations. This finished, he prepares to read the special four couplets which form the basis of the Sikh rite of marriage. The bride and groom will circumambulate the Granth four times while the four traditional couplets are read out of the Granth. One circumambulation occurs to each couplet. As the reading starts, the male relatives of the bride line up around the perimeter of the open space that the reader and the Granth occupy. The sister of the bride helps her rise to her feet beside the boy who also rises. The couple then sets off clockwise around the Granth. The boy leads and the girl follows, connected by the cloth. Her "sister" goes with her, still supporting and guiding. As they pass around the Granth, they move inside the circle of men. The men pass the girl and her "sister" along from hand to hand. Each man supports them by taking the "sister" by the shoulder as she comes by and steadying her until she comes near the next man. The bride keeps her head down and her face covered by her veil and mantle (See Fig. 5.4). At the end of the second circuit, the bride and groom stop before the Granth and bow to the floor facing it, in a token of respect. They then resume their walking and complete the four circuits, while people throw flowers upon them. When they finish, they sit again in their former position. The bride's relatives resume their places in their group. This concludes what is

**Figure 5.4** *Circumambulation of Guru Granth Sahib by bride and groom.*

generally said to be the only essential part of *anand*, which is itself described as the only essential part of the Sikh rite of marriage. However, in the description of the weddings usually given as well as in the performances, there is more.

From the four circumambulations, the service moves into what is called *sikhīa*, "instruction." For *sikhīa*, the Granth is covered and various people step forward to lecture the congregation. For weddings, their remarks are aimed at such matters as family structure, the importance of the family, and religious duty. During these lectures, people come forward with garlands and money for the bride and/or groom. If money is being given, the giver passes it around the heads of both the bride and the groom and then either puts it in a pocket or else gives it to the groom. I did not confirm the identity of the givers, but the only people I directly observed doing this were from the groom's party. Often the givers tease the groom. The attitude of the bride and groom throughout is attentive but passive, with the appearance of shyness. They remain connected to each other by the cloth.

After the *sikhia*, the reader of the Granth leads the *ardās*, a prayer which occupies in Sikhism a place analogous to that of the Lord's prayer in Western Christianity. As the people stand for the ending of the *ardas*, the bride and groom rise with them. With the conclusion of the prayer, they take leave of the Granth, bowing first in respect. The groom joins his group sitting at one side. The bride is escorted by her sister out of the room entirely. She is generally described as going "into her house, alone." The congregation then resumes sitting for the distribution of *deg*, a ceremonial food that always concludes a Sikh service.

After the distribution of *deg*, the groom's group rises and leaves. As it is going, "some old person" steps forward to the groom and detains him. The groom is asked to come into another part of the house. There he is asked to sit on something on the ground, and the women and girls of the bride's side, her friends and sisters, come and walk around him. They pass money over his head and put it in his pockets. They joke with him, tease him, and play tricks on him. He is at the same time given sweets to eat. All of his new *sālīs*, wife's sisters, are present for this. In fact, almost all the women seem to be there as well. The only people obviously absent are the bride and probably her mother. The women seem to enjoy this ritual behavior and the special songs they sing in the presence of the groom on this occasion are considered quite entertaining, though unfit for mixed company. While this small rite is going on, the men of the girl's side are clearing out the area, returning the Granth to its usual place, and setting out what will be needed for serving the tea which will follow.

When tea is ready, the boy's *janj* is notified through the Barber, and it comes through the gate with the band. According to the descriptions, some of its members come and take back the groom just before this. In any case, the groom is present with his group and is once again in possession of his sword. After tea, the *janj* retires to await lunch.

At the regular time for lunch, about one o'clock in the afternoon, the *janj* is notified through the Barber that the meal is ready. It comes, as usual, escorted by the band (see Fig. 5.5). When the *janj* arrives at the house for this meal, it does not immediately sit down and eat as before. Before the *janj* takes its place, the groom's father meets the girl's father and says that since the girl is now his daughter-in-law and "belongs to him," she must eat his food. He takes a vessel, fills it with sweets, and puts in some money—"any amount" up to ten rupees. He then covers it all with a cloth and sends it to the bride. The idea is that the vessel,

**Figure 5.5** *Groom's* janj *coming to lunch after* anand.

**Figure 5.6**   *Groom's* janj *eating lunch, being watched by* panchayat.

money, and cloth will more than offset the cost of the sweets (which actually come from the kitchen of the girl's father). Therefore, in a sense, the food (the sweets) has been purchased by the groom's father and represented as a gift. This small rite is called *patal*. After the food has been sent to the girl, the *janj* is again invited to eat by the girl's group. This time it accepts and starts to eat. The meal and the service are exactly the same as in the previous dinner (see Fig. 5.6).

When the *janj* is finished and has risen to leave, the father of the boy throws some coins on the tenting that covers the eating area. Children and others scramble after the coins, and a scene of happy confusion is instantly created. The explanation for this and other coin-throwing is that the giver is "happy."

### Maklava

After the meal, the area is cleared and rearranged in preparation for the final rite, called *khaTh*. This is described as a combination of two rites: the giving of *dhej* to the boy's group, and *maklava,* the rituals that mark the parting of the girl to her new house.

Between *anand* and *khaTh,* two minor but "necessary" actions take place. The girl's father first gives *lāg,* a rupee and some cloth, to each member of the groom's band. These are either collected by the band at the house of the girl or taken to the band by the Barber. The girl's father then shows to the *pioka* (the entire paternal group of kin) of the girl those gifts he is personally presenting to her. The gifts generally consist of clothes, jewelry (gold), henna, and other such things for adornment.

The place of the rites is prepared for *khaTh* by arranging tables (or beds) on one side and placing on them all the gifts to go with the girl to her new house. Nearby, rugs are laid out for a large sitting area. Somewhere near the middle of this a cushion is placed for the groom. When everything is ready, the *janj* is called as usual. The members come and inspect the gifts. Then they take seats on the ground on one side of the groom's cushion and across from the girl's group, which is already seated. The stage is then set for giving *dhej,* which is a series of gifts to the different members of the boy's party.

The father of the girl first gives a gift to the groom, usually a gold watch and some cash (see Fig. 5.7). Next, from a brass tray ready at hand, the father takes some cooked rice and some turmeric. Crushing them together into a paste between his fingers, he solemnly puts a mark

**Figure 5.7**  Korum *(in this case the bride's mother's brother) giving a watch to the groom at* khaTh.

on the forehead of the boy. From the same tray he takes a piece of a sweet, called *laDu*, and places it in the boy's mouth. He next takes up a second tray, also ready at hand. In it there is a substantial amount of money, containing some number of rupees such as 101, 201, 501, and so forth. He rises, takes this tray to the father of the boy, who also rises from his seat, and offers it to him. The boy's father "can" accept it, but generally does not do so. He takes one rupee instead and returns the balance. This gift is called *dhāt*, or *dhanj*, meaning "metal." Each father then resumes his seat, and the last set of gifts is given out.

The Barber (generally of the boy's group for convenience) and some respectable or literate person act for the father and distribute single rupee notes to the *nazdīkī*, "close people," of the groom. The literate person has a list of those who are "close" which has been previously prepared with the help of the Barber of the groom's group (see Fig. 5.8). He reads each name off the list, and as he reads it he puts a rupee in the Barber's tray. The Barber immediately takes the tray to the person named, who takes the note from it. The money is called *vaDiai di rūpaie* (roughly, "the rupees of the respectable people who have come"). It is said the money is given "to show respect."

**Figure 5.8**   *A "respectable person" of a bride's group reading the list of those who will be given rupees by the father of the bride.*

When the rupees are given out, the boy's group leaves and the girl's group follows. The boy is expected to remain in place. The women of the girl's house then come out and gather around him. The mother puts a mark on his forehead, and others after her put sweets in his mouth from a tray they have brought. On this tray is also a coconut wrapped with a red yarn or piece of cloth, which is a conventional symbol of sacrifice. In all this the women make a great commotion, with laughter, ribaldry, singing, and general merriment, until the boy is led out by the Barber or until they are called away by business. The bride herself is not present.

Shortly, the baggage of the boy's group and that of the girl, which was on display, is packed on the vehicles. The *janj* takes its place on the vehicles, and the presence of the bride alone is awaited. The departure of the bride is one of the most dramatic scenes of the whole ceremony.

With the vehicles waiting, the bride emerges from her house in the midst of a throng of women. Close to her are her mother, who generally supports her, her sisters acting in like manner, and the wife of the Barber, who will accompany her to her husband's village as a chaperone and guide. The bride wails loudly. It is said that if she did not do so, "there would be something wrong." All around her are her close associates, friends, relations, and wives of the *lagis* of the house. These last carry marks of their relationship: the potter woman may carry a small pot, the water carrier will carry a pitcher of water, and the sweeper will be identifiable from her broom. Someone will be carrying a tray with sweets, brown sugar (a traditional gift to the bride), and the coconut with the red yarn around it.

The group moves slowly toward the vehicle with much wailing, condoling, and singing of songs. The bride enters the vehicle with the wife of the Barber and the tray with the sweets and the coconut. On this occasion the bride is dressed in red with a red veil over her face. Once in the car, the whole procession is ready to leave. The women gather around the vehicle in which the bride and the Barber's wife are riding and begin to push it. They push it far enough to signify that they themselves have propelled it out of the village, starting the bride on her first journey to the house of her in-laws. Then the vehicle starts under its own power and continues on.

To the outside observer, this scene appears to be of mixed and conflicting emotions. Close friends and kin of the girl show grief at her loss. Others show happiness with the romantic aspects of the situation. There is despair at her removal from the privileged life of a maiden of the village, and satisfaction in her having been established in a house with good prospects of future security. Concern with her welfare conflicts with personal desire for her presence, and the desire to make her happy and secure in life conflicts with sympathy for her tense and difficult immediate situation.

After witnessing such a parting scene, the outsider is surprised to learn that the bride will be back the next day, still in the company of the Barber's wife, and will remain in her own village after that for an indefinite period of time, from months to years. Thus ends the major rituals of of marriage, although the continuing shift of the girl's loyalties to her new family and village is represented in a continuing series of rituals, including a number of annual rituals calling for women at different stages in their life cycles.

It should be pointed out explicitly that there is no ritual analogous to those in Europe concerning the first sexual intercouse between bride and groom. In a very important sense, this is not what Sikh weddings are concerned with—that is considered a private affair between bride and groom which hopefully will evolve after marriage. The marriage itself is concerned with the change of residence of the girl and the transfer of responsibility for her care.

## ANALYSIS

Many of these rituals are self-explanatory: the significance of the ritual is clearly stated and understood, and the individual actions that make it up have an obvious bearing on that significance. The use of caste symbols and participation by *lagis* where they are called for shows the girl's household's place in the overall village social system and verifies the way they represent themselves in that regard. The contest of lifting and the defeat of the girl's father by the boy's obviously signifies the defeat of the girl's group by the boy's in the idiom of war parties. The giving of food and gifts by the girl's group to the boy's group, but not the reverse, signifies consistently the idea that the girl herself is a gift and is not being "sold" or exchanged for any kind of consideration. The use of the cloth to link bride and groom in *anand karaj* brings these two themes together. The cloth is to bind the captive. It is soft, however, and the bride holds it by herself—a willing captive, whose bondage will be gentle. The witnessing of the *panchayat* signifies that accepting the generoisity of the girl's group imposes an obligation on the boy's group, and the giving of food by the boy's father to the girl after *anand* signifies acceptance of that obligation, part of which is to treat the girl herself as respectfully and generously as the girl's father has treated the boy and his father's group. The gifts of the girl's father and her kin to the girl herself—which make up by far the largest single item of expense—are intended to make the daughter a valuable addition to the husband's household immediately, and also to carry through the theme of the other gifts by providing further assurance that the father of the girl is not receiving anything in exchange for her—he is not even being immediately relieved of the expenses for maintaining her. Yet interpreting such relatively obvious symbolic acts as these does not provide major insight into the theoretical questions concerning the analysis of rituals: the difference between rituals and ordinary behavior, the relation of rituals to social organization, and the way in which rituals represent social structures and/or general cultural themes or ideas.

The difference between rituals and ordinary or nonritual actions is easy to see when we look at the ritual script as a whole. The difference is not that rituals are sacred; we cannot see sacredness and it is, in any event, difficult to view all the actions of the wedding as sacrosanct. Rather, the difference is that the ritual acts are performed by a specially designated system of groups whose function is defined as being *only* ritualistic. These roles of the ritual are *defined* as being fulfilled by people with other, different roles in daily life: *lara* is defined as the ritual counterpart of the young man who wants a wife; *lari* is defined as a girl who will be a wife; *korum* is defined as the parent of the *lari* or *lara* who will marry one's son or daughter, and so on. The ritual actions are specified for the ritual roles *and not the other roles*. Thus, it is within the specifications of the ritual that a distinction is made between ritual roles and nonritual roles.

The relationship between ritual and ordinary social roles follows closely from the way ritual roles are supposed to be filled. If ritual roles are specified in terms of ordinary roles, then putting on the ritual and filling the ritual positions affirms the reality and importance of the ordinary roles. When one agrees to be a ritual *korum* because one is the father of the boy who will marry, one is affirming the existence and power of the nonritual role of father. Filling the ritual positions also affirms the identification of the specific people who take the ritual roles as occupiers of the ordinary roles as well. The person who plays *korum* agrees that he is "in fact" a father or mother's brother. The person who plays *lara* agrees, before witnesses, that he will "be" husband in fact. In this sense rituals are social contracts: they specify by implication who occupies ordinary roles, or systems of interrelated roles, and what the obligations or duties are in those roles.

On the basis of the links drawn between ritual roles and their nonritual counterparts in the script for the ritual, the symbols of the ritual indicate the content of those ordinary roles. They do this by a kind of symbol synonymy, by using symbols whose meanings rest on the concepts that are used in defining the analogous roles in ordinary life. This is where the information systems enter the analysis, because they are the systems of concepts that define such ordinary roles. Therefore they are also the concepts that supply the meanings for the ritual symbols. Major examples of such symbol synonymy, based on reference to the current information systems, have already been indicated.

The watchful, concerned relationship between the *korums,* each "respecting" the other, each showing concern for the children, but each ready to challenge the other to enforce what is proper, corresponds exactly to the way the relationship between fathers-in-law would be described in ordinary life. The ritual relationship also corresponds to the actual relationship between one's father and one's mother's brother, who has to acept the responsibilities of the father if the father fails to perform them and who therefore will enforce the father's acceptance of those obligations if he can.

The ritual relationships between *lara* and *lari* correspond to the ideas defining the relationship between husband and wife in ordinary life. He leads her but is not physically tied to her save through a common sharing of property (symbolized both by the cloth and the religious ideas, as will be explained). The *lari* is supported by her relatives and consoled by her "elder sister" (who in terms of the ordinary kinship information system would herself have been married just previously). And by being together, each brings benefits to the other.

The larger ritual relationship between the two groups of men, with the women in the middle, corresponds to the general relationship between men and their kin in other villages in terms of the ordinary rules of inheritance. Since men are linked to their own villages by the inheritance of property from their fathers, men in different villages can be linked to each other only through their mutual links to women, who are not similarly fixed to property. Women, conversely, depend on men— their fathers, brothers, and husbands. It is precisely this dependence, in common ethical thought, that obligates the men to care for them.

The relationship between the ritual *panchayat* and the guests they watch reflects the relationship in ordinary life of the people involved to other villagers. Along with other duties, members of the actual elected *panchayat* of the village (some of whom each father tries to have in his group) act as official witnesses in legal cases involving villagers. Similarly, village *lambardars,* tax collectors, who are also desired for ritual *panchayats,* act as official witnesses in the village. Furthermore, witnessing and giving other support in court and in village conflicts is a major function attributed to village factions, and it is understood that the ritual *panchayat* membership reflects the factional alliances of the father of the bride. In fact, in ordinary affairs it is understood that factional relations underlie the ways in which *panchayat* members and *lambardars* use their powers as witnesses, and so the three roles interwined in the ritual *panchayat* are equally intertwined in nonritual conflicts organized by factions.

These interpretations, perhaps seemingly arbitrary, are arrived at by two simple and replicable techniques and are supported by field verification. The first technique may be called the method of generalized restatement. The second is the method of hypothetical substitution.

The technique of generalized restatement has already been demonstrated. It consists simply in redescribing a specific ritual action or object with a term (with a native translation equivalent) somewhat more general than the most precise one available. The meaning of passing the bride's sister from hand to hand in *anand karaj* emerges when the action is more generally described as the men helping and supporting the daughters and their husbands as they go on their way. The meaning of the father putting *laDu* in the groom's mouth emerges when the action is rephrased as the father giving the boy something sweet without the boy's doing anything, and so forth. Once the technique was consciously formulated and carefully applied, it seldom failed to produce interpretations villagers would agree to as legitimate or appropriate. That is, it produced interpretations that were "psychologically real" for the villagers in at least one of Boas's senses. They had subjective integrity in terms of the categories and values of the villagers themselves.

The technique of hypothetical substitution was developed to elicit general formulations without first proposing one and was used, for example, when there was resistance on the villagers' part to the idea of stating one outright. It consists in offering alternatives to some specific object or action and asking if they would be more-or-less acceptable as the original object or action.

This method relies directly on the properties of a "message" in information theory. By asking if variation would be allowed in different elements of a ritual, one finds certain areas where the expectations are very rigid and minor variations are considered significant and other areas where there is great flexibility. In information terms, the rigid areas are part of the "message" and changing them changes the message. The flexible areas are more like part of the channel. Changing them will change the "noise" in the ritual, perhaps add a distraction, but it will not alter the meaning. Systematically applied, the method of hypothetical substitution is a way of probing for the significant patterns that the native perceives in an objective flow of activity.

The cloth the groom carried attracted my interest because, in all cases I observed, it was a common hand towel. The villagers denied, however, that such a towel had any particular significance. By proposing substitutes, I found that it only had to be a cloth and not a hard object or a rope, but that it was no special ritual cloth. Finally, an informant said "any clean cloth" would do. This is a point of little significance. Similarly, I asked if the *sirwala* could be older, married, or unmarried, and from this questioning I learned that he should be younger and unmarried while the bride's sister was older and married, as indicated. This is a point of considerable significance.

As one elaborates the ideas of the script by generalized restatement and hypothetical substitution, a pattern of redundancy becomes clear which increasingly reduces the possibility of arbitrary interpretation. It becomes evident that each ritual segment uses a small number of ideas, defined together in the established information systems. Further, the ideas used in the different segments contrast with each other just as the segments themselves contrast with each other. For example, it should be noted that all the meals used the notions of caste, faction, and households—the general ideas that are brought together in organizing a man's role as head of a household of the village in terms of the division of labor. The relationships used in the ritual roles, from preparing food to witnessing the service, are the same as those a farming household in the village would use to organize its productive activities, which also consist in the creation and distribution of food. By contrast, neither caste ideas nor factional ideas are used in the ritual of *anand karaj*. Moreover, the two groups of men do not confront each other as power blocs in this ritual. In this respect the absence of the sword is significant. My suggestion, as a hypothetical substitution, that a sword be carried was firmly rejected.

All these usages in the ritual are consistent with each other as symbols of ideas of the Sikh religion. The Sikh religion specifically prohibits caste observances, emphasizes equality and brotherhood among people, and stresses that religion itself is a guide in ordinary life. All members of the Sikh religious community, men and women both, are equally "sharers of the guru's patrimony." This is the major theme in the wedding rites. In effect, the ritual performance says that the leadership of the husband, who also will hold his own patrimony, is like the leadership of the guru, and that the husband will take the guru's leadership of the Sikh community as the model for his household and will rule with fairness, wisdom, and principle.

The "old man" who summoned the groom after each *anand karaj* in the village was in fact the village Barber. But labelling him "Barber" on this occasion was rejected by all villagers questioned, indicating how conscious people were of the completely religious framework of the action. As a caste name, "barber" itself was literally out of place.

The relationship between the fathers as shown in *khaTh* approximates the relationship between *nanke* and *pioke* as shown in the initial ritual assembly of the girl's *janj* on the first day. In this assembly, the *nanke* come and give gifts, but take nothing in exchange. In *khaTh*, the father of the girl (who will be *nana* to her children) similarly gives gifts to the groom and his group and takes nothing in exchange. (The reason the *nana* himself is not mentioned in the bride's group is that, stereotypically, he is so careful about receiving anything in exchange that he never visits his daughter's husband's village, wanting to avoid taking even a single meal there. In effect, the father is establishing the new relationships of respect (remember the gift of the single rupee as the start of "engagement"). He is creating or expressing the basis of a new *meli* that will center on the new couple and will serve for their children, just as his *meli* served for him and the boy's father's *meli* served for him. *KhaTh* is by that token signifying the creation of a new bilateral kinship group. The ritual shows this structure as it appears from a point of view inside it, where each individual is conscious of the contributions of others.

The last ritual, the departure of the bride, uses ideas from the standard conception of a woman's life cycle, which is another, distinct derivative of the ideas of kinship and the related rules of inheritance. The rules of inheritance give each man from birth a full equal share with his father in all of the family property. Women do not inherit. However, it is considered that a man owes his strongest obligation to his mother. Thus as a man has more sons, his own share relative to the family as a whole diminishes proportionally, while the position of his wife becomes proportionally stronger and more secure. The contrast between the weeping bride and her consoling mother in the procession to the vehicle that will take her to her new house illustrates both ends of the cycle. The bride is starting out totally propertyless and totally dependent. Stereotypically, she is crying because she is afraid of her new mother-in-law, who will be the domineering head of her new house. The bride's mother represents precisely a person like her mother-in-law—a senior woman with grown children, the master of a house in the village and an employer of *lagis*. The ritual send-off and the final return of the Barber's wife make the point dramatically that the servants are indeed her mother's, and not the bride's.

The relationships portrayed among the various roles in rituals provide the rationale for the expenditures by those who occupy the roles. Expenses fall into two distinct groups: those by the girl's group and those by the boy's, and these are not intermixed. The expenses of the girl's group are far greater than those of the boy's, and they are divided into three major subcategories: gifts to the girl herself, expenses of the ritual, and gifts to the boy and his group. The expenses of the boy's group are largely for transportation to and from the ritual, the incidental expenses for the band, gifts to *lagis*, and the like. The gifts to the girl remain her personal property and will come back with her if the marriage does not work out. The gifts to the boy's group are not returnable in the same way.

In the first and costliest wedding of the season, the gifts to the girl were valued at Rs. 6,220. The ritual costs were not more than Rs. 350, and the gifts to the boy and his group were not more than Rs. 300. These same proportions generally held in subsequent weddings, although the total expenditures were less (Rs. 4,000–5,000). An acre of good agricultuarl land in the village at the time of the weddings was valued at about Rs. 5,000, and its output, if converted wholly to cash, would be worth from Rs. 1,737.60 to Rs. 4,593.60 (but averaging about Rs. 2,000) depending on the crop. The total land value of the farmer who put on the most expensive wedding was about Rs. 45,000 and the annual value of his crop was about Rs. 11,400. In addition, he had a salary as an officer in the Indian army. The family whose wedding cost about Rs. 5,000 owned very little land, worth only about Rs. 9,600 but as a tenant it farmed a larger amount, about 4.17 acres, whose annual return was worth about Rs. 8,340. Generally, a farmer's land is about equal to half his total capital worth, for to farm, say, five acres efficiently, requires a barn, storage area, and housing for his family whose market value would be just about equal to that of the five acres themselves. This means that the average cost of a wedding in the village was about one-sixth the average value of the land of the farming family sponsoring it, and therefore one-twelfth the value of its total holdings. The cost of the wedding was equal in value to about one-half the annual income from farm operations.

These figures are consistent with a local rule of thumb. This rule was occasionally mentioned in passing, but people were embarrassed to state it to me "for the record," because no one wanted to imply that he could put a price on a sister or daughter. The rule is that the girl is entitled to about what she would get if she were a son and the land were divided. (On the average there are about six children per family among farmers.)

In practice, several factors reduce the burden of these expenses below what it might appear to be. First, many families do have cash income from sources other than farming in the village—such as the officer's salary mentioned. Second, wedding costs may be shared by several related houses. Finally, there is a regular system of customary exchange of "help," called *niūnda*. In this system, families officially contribute to each other's weddings, keeping records over the years so that they can call upon these debts when they have weddings of their own. In the first wedding, the *niunda* amounted only to token payments of Rs. 454— largely contributed by close kin and friends who would have felt embarrassed if they could not help in this way. In another wedding it amounted to about a third. In still another it amounted to about a half of the total expenditures.

Is the wedding expenditure high in relation to income, as has often been claimed? There is no governmental system of social security or even unemployment insurance at any level in India. In old age, a person must depend on precisely those relationships and concepts portrayed in the marriage ritual: friends, brothers, sisters, but most of all sons and the property one inherits. A man, like the ritually absent *nana*, depends on his sons to carry out the obligations he assumes and to execute his orders. A woman, like the mother of the bride, depends on sons to manage the property that gives her household the wherewithal to hire her servants and marry off her daughter. Beneath both these expectations lies the fact that sons inherit property with the father. Because the sons can be depended on to protect their own interests, this inheritance is precisely what secures the land of the father and the authority of the mother. In this context, the wedding expenses have two major functions: they provide the daughter of the house with her only really dependable chance for a secure and full life, and they clear the ground in the father's house so that the sons can themselves be married and have children of their own. (It would be awkard in India, as it would here, to try to incorporate new wives into a house where the sisters were still in residence. It is understood that if one did *not* provide for the marriage of one's daughter or sister one would have to support her anyway.) The money is laid out for its purpose in a way calculated to guarantee success, and if the expenditure is successful I am sure most or all villagers would say it was worth the cost.

The issue of debt, as such, is a red herring. If the expenditure is reasonable, it does not become less reasonable if the father of the girl should elect to borrow cash and return it over time instead, for example, of selling off half his entire crop for the year. He would only have to buy back much of the crop materials at prices that would be relatively more greatly appreciated than the repayments including interest on a loan. (Although I must add that no one in Shahidpur to my knowledge actually did borrow money at interest apart from *niunda* exchange.)

## CONCLUSION

The more our understanding of the rituals of marriage gains "psychological reality" and approximates or conveys the villagers own conceptions of the rituals, the more clearly it appears that the ritual acts as a social contract. It states what the agreement is and who specifically is making the agreement. It provides sanctions and penalties for breaches of the contract. It implicitly reaffirms the nature and importance of the larger social body—both the relations referred to in the contract and the sanctioning bodies. Finally, like a contract, the ritual codes the agreement in a compact, symbolic language that marks the contract itself as a special document of a standard type, out of the ordinary, and as the proper instrument for making such agreements.

The ritual says so-and-so agrees to take the role of husband in relation to so-and-so who agrees on her part to take the role of wife, while so-and-so agrees to take the role of father of wife and *nana* to future children as may issue from the marriage, and so on. All such roles are defined with brief established formulae in the ritual and the whole is duly witnessed by those who attend. In the course of this, the rituals necessary impute the roles described to the "real" nonritual world that will continue to exist when the ritual has ended.

The idea of a ritual contract provides a theoretical bridge between the more traditional conceptions of ritual in anthropology and the general model of communication described in my 1972 monograph.

In the three major anthropological traditions described earlier, there are basically two underlying models of the way rituals arise and what they produce. One model sees rituals in relation to the social structure, the other in relation to the social status of individuals.

A general representation of the way rituals are related to social structure is:

Society becomes unstable ⟶ Ritual ⟶ Social stability is reestablished in consensus.

Ideas on the source of this instability vary greatly, as do conceptions of the actual content of the reestablished stability. But major theoretical attention has not focused on either of these issues so much as on the way ritual itself expresses both instability and, at what appears to be a deeper level, stability and order.

The general model now accepted for the way rituals arise in relation to individual social status is similar in form:

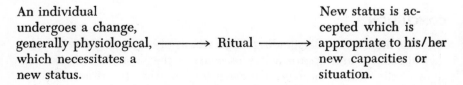

An individual undergoes a change, generally physiological, ⟶ Ritual ⟶ New status is accepted which is appropriate to his/her which necessitates a new capacities or new status. situation.

In this tradition, the ideas for the beginning and ending steps are better developed and more empirical. The accepted view is not only that when a person is born, dies, marries, has children, and so on, his own status must be altered, for this alone would not provide a strong reason for having a ritual. It is also that such changes in one individual have systematic effects on the status of others. When a man and a woman marry, it is necessary to mark not only their own new relationship, but also the many concomitant changes of the relationships among their formerly separate families and associates. When one thinks about the number of such changes and their interconnectedness, a ritual—a public symbolic act using agreed-upon shared social symbols—becomes not only a convenient device for doing what is needed, but even a necessary one. It is difficult, even impossible, to think of another way to get all the changes out in the open systematically so that everyone agrees to them and everyone knows everyone agrees to them.

Obviously, both these analytical traditions apply partially to the marriage rituals described above. They are often rather mixed together in the literature. But neither subsumes the other and, up to now, they have not been placed into an orderly theoretical relationship by being subsumed under a single larger model.

The general model of a comunication system that can incorporate them, and that underlies the present analysis, differs from the original model of Shannon and Weaver mainly in being cyclical where theirs was linear (like the above two conceptions of rituals). Linear models, in general, cannot account for the repetition and change in communication patterns or for the maintenance of the communication system itself. The general cyclical model for any message is:

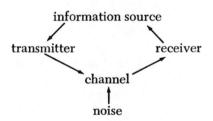

The arrows indicate the direction of transmission of the message. The information source, as indicated, is a set of socially organized constraints upon, and resources for, the organization of communicative behavior. The "transmitter," in this case, is a person who refers to the source in creating a message, assuming that such creation includes selecting the mode of transmission of the message. The channel is the means by which the message is conveyed. Noise is any additional input into the channel, not from the source, that confuses or erodes the transmission. The receiver is the person receiving the message, together with any devices that may aid him in this, and his action upon receipt that reinforces the structure of the original source.

The ideas of a message and a channel from this scheme can be applied to very large units of behavior or very small ones. The important thing is the constant relation of messages and channels to their source, transmitter, receiver, and noise input. If we take a ritual segment as a convenient unit to be represented in the model, then one representation of the "contractual" analysis is:

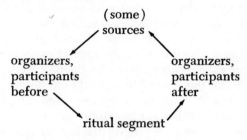

Message: *the contract segment*

This incorporates all the variables recognized in the first linear model, which sees rituals in relation to the rearrangement of individual relationships. This shows the major elements of the present analysis in their proper relationships to one another. The message, called here the "contract segment," is simply the aspect of the marriage that is being represented in the particular ritual segment: the separateness of bride's and groom's families at the beginning; the relationship of the bride to the men of her natal house on the one hand and to her husband's house on the other; the internal structure of a *janj*, or bilateral kingroup; the place of a family among caste groups; the relation between villages; or the career of a woman as bride and mother. As noted, such "contracts" often specify relations that are defined in terms of more than one system of information: economic and managerial as well as kinship and caste; religious, familial (but excluding caste), economic, and so forth. Each distinctive segment and type of ritual has its own distinct list of source elements. The distinction between the organizers and participants "before" and the organizers and participants "after" corresponds to the idea that the "message" of the ritual is received and will be sanctioned by the people involved in their new capacities as distinct from their old capacities: the father of the girl will exercise his obligations as father of a wife in another household, the boy as a husband, and so forth. In this specific sense, a ritual involves a group of people sending a message to themselves, and their action as receiver is what will reinforce the structure of the sources they utilize.

It may be a bit difficult to think of the ritual itself as a channel, although clearly it is not the message itself, and it has the property of being susceptible to noise. Probably, reflecting current orientations in symbolic analysis in social anthropology, there would be a strong temptation to call it a "code." The reasoning for the present analysis follows from the idea that the actual transmitter is the social group involved— the sponsors of the ritual. It is they who want to send the message. In this sense, the *raja* is not part of the group. They select the *raja*, who is therefore more analogous to a telephone or radio transmitter, and the ritual proceeds from the *raja* in turn. The ritual, performed according to the *raja's* instructions, conveys the message in the way that the electrical pulses on a telephone do, although the process is more available and transparent to the actual senders and receivers. Finally, the *raja* himself serves to "decode" the message that he sends, saying what has been done and what the next phase is.

We may want to consider that the knowledge of rituals that the Barber has, which enables him to perform as *raja*, is an information source for the general ritual that is not shared by the others, at least to the same degree, and in that sense the *raja* is a participant in a slightly different, overlapping, information transmission cycle. This type of technical elaboration would not contradict the basic system of analysis.

Two substitutions in this cyclical model (indicated in italics) change it to incorporate the tradition of analysis that sees ritual as springing from the social structure, reflecting social instability and permitting structural affirmation.

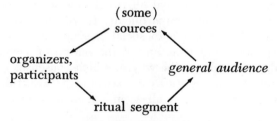

Message: *nature of social relations used in the contract*

This model does not contradict the first. It rather emphasizes a different, overlapping aspect of the total phenomena. It directs attention to the content of the ritual for the generality of those who come to see it, rather than just the participants who are "interested" in a more concrete sense. In this aspect, the ideas of the "contract" form only a general set of ideas about society, rather than something binding personally. The anthropological ideas of social instability and the reaffirmation of social order take their place here as possible components of the motivation for attendance and of the subjective impressions such attendance provides. To a certain extent, such feelings or perceptions may also provide motivation on the transmitter side as well, although obviously weddings, funerals, and the like are not put on merely as exercises in the promulgation of social ideologies by those who actually undertake the work and expense involved. There may be other significant configurations of transmitter, message, and receiver within ritual segments.

A complete analysis of a ritual segment would involve stating all combinations of transmitter/message/receiver that occur in it, down to quite minute details. But the aim of the theory is not to provide such a complete analysis, so much as the potential for it. This potential means that any aspect of a ritual segment can be selected and compared systematically with any other aspect. More than that, the same model permits orderly comparison of segments with each other (in which case the list of sources and the channels are what differs), and it permits whole ritual complexes to be compared—wedding rituals with funerals, for example. Finally, and most importantly, rituals can be compared with nonritual communicative behavior: the model makes especially clear how many points ritual and nonritual communicative behavior can have in common—sources, message, transmitters, and receivers. The difference could be one of "channel" only.

This approach does not produce an "essence" of ritual. It even suggests that there is none. Rather, it suggests that highly ritualized behaviors fade off into less ritualized behavior with the same meanings by degrees. But the approach does provide an important benefit not available in schemes that tend to seal off rituals and even aspects of rituals into their own watertight compartments. In showing ritual as a communicative process in relation to social message sources, it opens the door to an expanded understanding of the nature of social communication itself and, ultimately, to the way in which consensus on society and other important abstract entities can exist and be forceful, even though those entities may not exist at all as independent objects in their own right.

## SELECTED READINGS

Geertz, Clifford, 1957, "Ritual and Social Change: A Javanese Example," *American Anthropologist* 59:32–54.

This is an important attempt to overcome some of the problems in relating rituals to their overall social context. It takes account of the fact that rituals are sometimes disputed and sometimes involve manipulations of social conceptions, and it tries to place the analysis of ritual in relation to the question of the relationship between "society" and "culture" that was coming into focus as an important issue at the time the article was published.

Gluckman, Max, 1962, *Essays on the Ritual of Social Relations.* Manchester: Manchester University Press.

A good selection of contrasting analyses of rituals by four major social anthropologists: Daryll Forde, Meyer Fortes, Max Gluckman, and Victor Turner.

Leach, Edmund, 1970, *Claude Lévi-Strauss.* New York: Viking Press.

Not mainly concerned with ritual, this introduction to the ideas of Lévi-Strauss, as Leach sees them, provides a very clear and well-reasoned introduction to many of the ideas that anthropologists have been concerned with in the analysis of ritual and symbolism over the last ten to fifteen years.

Leaf, Murray J., 1972, *Information and Behavior in a Sikh Village: Social Organization Reconsidered.* Berkeley and Los Angeles: University of California Press.

Also not mainly concerned with ritual, this provides the analysis of information systems that underlies the present treatment of rituals. Chapter Nine on the analysis of behavior provides a general theoretical sketch of the way information would appear in rituals as well.

Miner, Horace, 1956, "Body Ritual Among the Nacerima," *American Anthropologist* 58:503–507.

An entertaining parody of ritual analysis that serves as a warning against over-zealous interpretation.

Peacock, James N., 1968, *Rites of Modernization.* Chicago: University of Chicago Press.

This extends the analysis of ritual symbolism to a form of drama in Indonesia, arguing both that such dramatic performances are indeed "rites" and that the ideas they promulgate have important social consequences. The general method of analysis has a good deal in common with the present treatment of marriage rituals, as well as with the work of Professor Singer listed below.

Singer, Milton, 1972, *When a Great Tradition Modernizes.* New York: Praeger.

Professor Singer's main focus is on the idea of civilization, not ritual, but in the course of his discussions he develops the idea of a "cultural performance" that is in a number of respects a generalized version of the idea of a ritual that most anthropologists use. He goes on to provide one of the fullest accounts of the way such rituals generate or create a sense of social reality for those who attend them.

Turner, Victor, 1968, *The Drums of Affliction.* Oxford: Clarendon Press.

An important full scale study of ritual symbolism and its appearance in ordinary behavior. Turner, in part, takes exception to Lévi-Strauss's ideas of universal conceptual pattern in rituals and stresses the uniqueness of the basic symbols and meanings he describes. He also pays considerably greater attention than is often done to empirical documentation of his analysis. Turner agrees with the present approach of seeing the rituals as repositories of ordinary social conceptions. But he stops short of saying exactly how those conceptions themselves are ordered, and he adheres to simpler rituals and simpler ritual themes than have been described in this chapter.

# Ethnology:
# Cultural Anthropology

# Chapter 6

# Social Organization and Social Change: Sicilian Peasants in Sicily and Australia

## Constance Cronin

The study of social change in social or cultural anthropology deals with alterations in value systems, institutions, and behavior patterns. Change is a process common to all societies in every time period, although the type and rapidity of the process can vary enormously: foreign colonial powers invade tribal areas, groups of immigrants move across oceans to new settings, major immigrant-receiving countries, such as Argentina and the United States, seem programmed for change, and even isolated tribal societies are now known to be characterized by change, albeit slow and intermittent. Change appears to be as characteristic of human society as families.

## THE STUDY OF SOCIAL CHANGE

Despite the near-universality of change in societies, there is no well-developed theoretical discipline which even begins to account for it. Most anthropologists and many scholars in related areas of other disciplines would agree with Edward Spicer that:

> The growth of a general understanding of cultural change among anthropologists has seemed slow and unsatisfactory. There is a widespread feeling that we have no really useful concepts, that there is no theory worthy of the name, for comparing and understanding the many instances of change with which we are acquainted. (Spicer 1961:517)

Why is the theory of social change so underdeveloped? Part of the answer lies in the broader development of theory in social and cultural anthropology as a whole.

The first anthropologists, the speculative analysts of the last century were primarily concerned with evolutionary change over long periods of time. Their sweeping theories of social improvement from savagery to civilization or from matrilineal to patrilineal to bilateral kinship structures, however, were based on scanty and poorly understood data. As more and better data were gathered, these grand conceptualizations based on Darwinian principles were quickly discredited. After a period of data collection and conceptual floundering, two branches of modern anthropology developed: social anthropology in Great Britain and cultural anthropology in the United States. While there were superficial differences between the two approaches, there was one basic idea underlying both. Anthropology was to be the study of models of society. These models are made up of institutions, such as religion and politics, and are based on two principles: (1) that each institution has its own structure, function, and value system, and (2) that all institutions are interrelated to form a whole society or culture which is a balanced, integrated totality. This view allows for no contradictions or imbalances, and any variation from the norm is labeled "deviant" and assigned to another field or ignored altogether.

According to this view, each society and its institutions have value systems which dictate the rules which, properly obeyed, will maintain the life and the uniqueness of the society. Society is dependent only on itself; it is above and independent of its human members. It has its own form, it is its own authority, and it makes and changes its own rules. It is, in other words, a unique creature with a life of its own. Humans are considered passive actors who simply obey the rules of the society and have no significant life, will, desires, or ambitions beyond those given to them by the society. Lacking the capacity to bend, alter, or break the rules of the society, individuals are "culture bearers" who "manifest the rules of the society."

Given these formulations, the proper unit of study can only be the creature called society itself. In order to be successful in this study, the anthropologist defines the social institutions, elucidates the rules of each, observes individuals in order to illustrate how the rules are carried out, and writes an analysis describing the structure and function of society at one point in time.

There are a number of important points in this approach to anthropology which must be recognized and remembered when one turns to change studies. First of all, these rules or value systems state what should be done, not what individuals are actually doing; they give the preferred pattern or behavior, not the range of behavior actually observed which conforms and does not conform to the rules. For example, writing of North American Indians Eggan states:

Each of these northern bands is apparently held together largely by the practice of bilateral cross-cousin marriage. This marriage was considered most correct, and over a third of the cases in the Barren Ground were of this type. (1955:522)

Note that two-thirds of the cases are simply ignored, as though irrelevant. Anthropologists neither deny that behavior based on a particular rule can and does vary nor reject the notion that a single rule may permit a range of different but nonetheless allowable behavior patterns. But most do deny the intellectual necessity to develop an approach that explicitly takes full account of the distribution of the actual ranges of behaviors.

In an important sense, this type of anthropological approach is descriptive and not explanatory. The researcher typically gathers whatever data seem pertinent to a well-rounded picture of the residential, economic, or status system of a society and presents it as if he or she is telling a story. There is no attempt to explain why the system is as it is, how it got to be that way, or which factors or variables are responsible. Early attempts by Radcliffe-Brown and others to move away from the difficulties of the early social evolutionists led them to an equally untenable position of implicitly denying causality, that is, they rejected all efforts to explain the causes of change in society. To quote again from Eggan:

This brief survey suggests the possibility that it may be profitable to deal with observed correlations between various aspects of social organization, not by considering one aspect as caused by another, but by considering them as variant manifestations of some more general factor or principle. (1955:73)

One of the reasons for this nonscientific, descriptive approach was precisely the very early emphasis on social institutions as the unit of study. Anthropologists defined the institutions (Eggan's "general principle") as their own theoretical constructs which bore no necessary relationship to the way the members of society themselves might define the critical units of their social surroundings. Anthropological monographs were designed to classify data according to such institutions as Environment, Family and Kinship, Ceremonial Cycle, Social Control, and, usually, Life Cycle to tie everything together, but they made no attempt to approach the data with questions or with a hypothesis based on testing the power and reality of social stratification, education, or age as independent variables. For example, the reader can find in these monographs descriptions of the rules by which a society is stratified, but there will be no mention of how the pattern or a change in the pattern of certain dependent variables (seemingly derivative and subordinate) such as husband-wife relationship or residence may be caused by social stratification (which seems a more important and all-encompassing phenomenon).

Another objection to the standard anthropological categories is that they were set up before empirical research demonstrated their value. Kinship systems, for example, were classed on the principle of descent they used, but they rapidly acquired secondary characteristics from which it is now impossible to divorce them. Today a reference to a "patrilineal society" automatically implies an entire social pattern which includes patrilineal descent, patrilocal residence, corporate property, patrilineal group inheritance, and so on. Yet few so-called patrilineal societies bear much relationship to this model. Moreover, we do not yet know that kinship is ever the one unifying principle of any human society.

Thus we have today backed ourselves into a corner made up of our own preconceived, untested, abstract ideas and theories. Though a great deal has been made known about thousands of separate, unique human groups, we do not know, nor given current thinking can we know, the actual principles, dynamics, and causal factors which would permit us to compare, draw general hypotheses, test, predict, and theorize.

Change studies reflect the early concern with abstract, nonexplanatory theory and the more recent concern with rethinking our categories in a more scientific way. American anthropologists such as Lowie, Eggan, and Tax in the 1930s and 1940s were engaged primarily in the study of American Indian groups. They were universally confronted with tribes which had been changed by the conquest and populating of the North American continent. Their early works and others like them were called "culture contact" studies, in which interest was focused solely on change which resulted from the arrival of European or American powers. They were not concerned with independent variables, the order of changes, which variables gave way easily and which resisted, or how subgroups reacted. Rather, their emphasis was on describing one society (or tribe) at two points in time: the first before contact, the second afterward. Both descriptions were standard ethnographic abstractions of societal models.

Sometime in the late 1930s the term "acculturation" came into vogue. While it is virtually the same as culture contact in its concepts, it did represent a broader substantive outlook. In the beginning only tribal groups were studied. Gradually the scope enlarged to include peasant societies and then immigrant groups. Today any instance of change which results from contact of any kind with another culture comes under this rubric: colonized societies, immigrants, migrants, urban dwellers, and developing societies.

In the most widely accepted general position paper on change studies in anthropology, acculturation is defined as "culture change that is initiated by the conjunction of two or more autonomous systems" (Barnett et al. 1954:974). The exact meaning of "autonomous cultural systems" is never made clear but presumably refers to traditional models of society. The argument then continues:

> The unit of analysis in acculturation studies is thus taken to be any given culture as it is carried by its particular society. It is recognized that individuals are empirically the culture bearers and that they are the mediators of any cultural process. Students of culture are, however, concerned with individuals as functioning members of a society and with the shared patterns of behavior constituting a body of customs. Consequently, while it is individuals who change their habits of doing and believing under the influence of alien forms, it is the body of custom of the society to which they belong that is said to be acculturating. (Barnett et al. 1954:974-5)

There is no real change at all, then, from culture contact to acculturation studies. The unit of study is still "culture" or the "body of customs," precisely as it had always been. The first step in acculturation studies is to reconstruct as near as possible the society as it was. The researcher then finds out about the "nature of contact," that is, the history of who came, what they did, and how they treated the people. Using the cultural model of the past as the base, he then turns to the present and describes the contemporary social system. Though there are a few methodological differences between the two kinds of studies, the major concern is still to describe the result of the meeting of two cultural systems.

Anthropology has not been the only discipline involved in the study of social change. Numerous sociological studies have been written on change situations especially in relation to urban situations. However, assimilation studies—the term favored in sociology—display the same lack of methodological ingenuity and the same contrast between a society at two points in time which are found in anthropology.

Through the years, sociologists have produced three major theories regarding change. The first is called Anglo-Conformity. This theory was based on the idea that the United States accepted newcomers provided they proceeded to turn themselves as speedily as possible into Yankee-Americans on the assumption that American democracy was fundamentally Anglo-Saxon. This idea coincided with the first great "immigrant wave" of Irish, Germans, and other northern Europeans. By about 1903 the second "immigrant wave" of southern and eastern Europeans led some Americans to evolve what became the second major sociological theory of assimilation, "The Melting Pot" theory. This phrase, taken from a popular Jewish play in 1908, symbolized the idea that everyone coming to the country deposited his ideas, customs, and beliefs with those of all others, including old Americans, where they simmered until a completely different distillation came forth which was entirely new and common to all. By the 1930s as data began to accumulate and as the second and third generation children of immigrants reached adulthood, it became apparent that neither of the existing theories had been correct. After a lull during World War II, immigrant and change studies again attracted the attention of sociologists. After reviewing field studies to that point, most agreed that what had actually happened was best characterized by the idea of "cultural pluralism":

> There was, however, general agreement on the concept of plurality plus adjustment, of a process towards uniformity at some levels but preserving differences at others. (Borrie et al. 1959:94)

But this is not a scientific theory, for it does not explain or predict. Rather, it is simply an abstract version of a common-sense statement which notes the fact that ethnics were the same as host country inhabitants in some ways and were different in other ways. This has nothing substantial to contribute to the problems in anthropology.

Acculturation and assimilation have never been defined to the satisfaction of a majority of scholars, and so it is simpler and clearer to use instead the phrase "change studies." A study of change is a study of process. Therefore the major focus should be on the process itself and not on the results of that process which are, at bottom, irrelevant. Within the context of the difficulties that carry over from anthropological theory in general, there are a number of specific criticisms of change theory and methodology which must be understood if the field is to move ahead. The first brings us back to the problem of unverified classes or categories: culture contact, acculturation, immigration, assimilation, urbanization. It has been assumed that these "types" of change are unique entities, each with its own history, impact, development, and style. This assumption has never been tested, however. Perhaps the parent-child relationship is different and changes in different ways depending on whether the individuals are immigrants, new urban dwellers, or contacted tribal peoples. But this assumption has never been tested either. It may be that the parent-child relationship always changes in certain directions under the influence of certain stimuli no matter what the historical situation is. The point is that we will never know the causes of differential change until we abandon these change "types" which permit comparison only within and not across types.

Another major problem with ordinary diachronic ("over a period of time") studies concerns process or time itself. There was a debate for years as to whether time was a necessary dimension in studies of change, but most anthropologists today agree that studies of change, by definition, involve time. This may be of varying lengths from a day to thousands of years. Therefore, we would expect all researches to be scrupulously concerned with controlling for the period of time over which the change is occurring. Unhappily such is not the case. Almost all social change studies use a before-and-after approach that does not accumulate changes through a specified period of time. Thus, if ten changes are found in the intervening period, for example, the reader will have no idea which changes came first, which influenced others, or how alterations built on themselves and spread out to induce yet other changes.

The next major problem concerns methodology or the way in which change studies are carried out in the field. There are four distinct yet interrelated problems in this area. The first problem derives from the tendency to work with cultures and not persons. It is never the case, for example, that whole autonomous cultures emigrate; rather, some members of the society emigrate. They may and usually do bring with them ideas and ideals about how societal institutions should be run but they do not bring their original institutions with them.

The Hungarian immigrant to Australia no longer lives within the framework of Hungarian political, economic, or religious institutions, but he may still retain his ideas concerning the proper functioning of such institutions, and these ideas may not at all be in accord with the Australian institutions. Thus adjustments or changes must be made by the immigrants. Immigrants have several choices open to them: they can refuse to participate in the Australian system; they can try to bring about changes in Australia which will make the system more like that of Hungary; or they can completely adapt to the Australian way. Whatever the varying individual reactions may be, it is not a matter of culture meeting culture but rather of some members of one culture encountering the individuals and the social institutions of another culture. Many anthropologists today believe that until both value systems and behavior systems are accepted as equally important and interdependent units of study no progress can be made in studies of social change. Conversely, just because the independence of values and behavior are so important and obvious in cases of immigration and change, this area provides especially clear tests of new formulations of potential importance in all aspects of cultural and social anthropology.

The second methodological problem concerns sample selection: the choice of persons who will be observed and interviewed and who will supply the raw data on which interpretation and testing will depend. The overwhelming tendency in immigration studies is to work with a visible ethnic or immigrant group. Suppose a researcher goes to Toronto and asks where immigrants from Poland live in the city. His resulting study of Polish persons in a Polish neighborhood in Toronto would actually show the process of social change then working on only a fraction of the total Polish population in the city. In other words, if the universe of study is Polish immigrants in Toronto, a continuum should be represented ranging from the least changed to the most changed persons. In our present state of knowledge, however, ghetto-dwellers (the term *ghetto* in sociology is used loosely for any culturally distinct residential area) appear generally to lie closer to the unchanged end of the continuum. Therefore looking only at them will systematically leave out the more changed or the most changed immigrants. In this sense, such a study would inherently present a false or skewed picture.

Another serious problem connected with sample selection is a lack of information on the socioeconomic characteristics of the sample. We must have a profile of the immigrants if we are to evaluate the data on them. For instance: How long have they been there? What are their ages? Are they rich or poor, men or women? Without this kind of information it is not possible to assess accurately the impact of change on the individuals or on the group. The basis on which change studies should rest is the fact that individuals react differently to the same situation and that we, as social scientists, must account for this diversity of reaction. We do this by testing certain independent variables such as sex, age, or education to see if they are causing subgroup differences within the population under study. Since this approach is generally not employed in social change studies, it is no wonder that we are today confused and bewildered at our lack of progress in elucidating general principles.

A final methodological point concerns the study of the pre-emigration social organization. Few of the authors on immigration have done field work in the original homeland, and often there is little, if any, published material on it. This problem is usually solved by interviewing the immigrants about what the old country was like before they emigrated. The flaw in this method is obvious: interviewing an immigrant who has been in the new country for forty or fifty years about his or her youth denies that any change has taken place in the perceptions and attitudes of this individual and obscures the fact that much may be forgotten, distorted, or never known in the first place. This practice is still more serious, of course, when the respondents are second or third generation residents. Clearly the researcher ought to find more studies of the homeland or go there himself. If this is not feasible (as in countries where foreign scholars are not welcome) another possibility is to conduct an interview with the immigrants which is designed to detect distortion, inaccuracies, or discrepancies among accounts, and then to publish this procedure in detail so the readers can evaluate for themselves whether these data are reliable or not.

## AN ALTERNATIVE APPROACH

My interest in immigration was to develop a diachronic study that would provide clear answers to the more general questions of social causality and process. The way to do this seemed to be to make an educated guess—an hypothesis—about some general causal relationships and then build the study around it. For example, "I hypothesize that when a family moves to an urban area where the husband has steady employment and the wife works outside the home, husband-wife relations will become egalitarian." The universe of the study is husband-wife pairs who have emigrated to a large city; the causal, or independent, variable is occupation; and the dependent variables, those through which we measure change, are factors in the husband-wife relationship which change as a direct result of immigration and the wife's occupation. It is then possible to interview a sample of spouses which includes working wives and nonworking wives. If the hypothesis is correct, it will be demonstrated in this way, and the correct choice of independent variable explains why the change occurred. The same researcher or others then can use the same construct in another area to test the cross-cultural validity of both hypothesis and variables.

When the time came to choose a doctoral dissertation topic, I decided to carry out a nondescriptive study of social change. One of the faults in most of the literature on the subject was an assumption that all areas of one's life are equal, both quantitatively and qualitatively. This notion I labelled the idea of unilinear change—that all immigrants stepped upon a conveyor belt at the moment of arrival in the host country and were then carried forward by the same process through the same steps to ultimate absorption. It seemed to me that in any group there would be differences based on socioeconomic and personality factors which would make for differences in the patterns of change exhibited by the subgroups. Further thought led to the idea that there were two major spheres in all our lives: the public sphere outside the home and the private sphere inside the home. Change might be observed in the workplace, for instance, because that setting demanded certain attitudes, behavior patterns, and perhaps the use of a new language. But inside the home, unless laws were broken, the immigrants were free to follow their own ideas as to how life should be lived. I therefore hypothesized that if the immigrant changed in both the public and the private spheres, deep-rooted change would be manifested; but if the change was limited to the public sphere, then a mere accommodation to the exigencies of living in a new country were demonstrated and change, what I thought of as "real change," was not occurring. For example, if an immigrant woman learned English so as to get a job in a department store but continued to use her native language at home, then some additional skills had been acquired by her but "real change" was not in evidence.

Since I also felt that pre-emigration socioeconomic differences would account for variability among members of any one national group, I chose three of the factors most used in descriptive studies and decided to consider them independent variables. The first was *age at emigration,* and I hypothesized that those persons who were young at emigration would change more rapidly and more completely than the older ones. This idea was based on research in psychology which reveals that the things learned earliest are the most difficult to change or give up. The second independent variable was *time in the host country,* and my hypothesis was that the longer the immigrant remained in the new country the greater the change. While I personally felt that the first hypothesis might be substantiated, I did not believe that the second would be proved true. I did not think time alone was a direct or a potent enough force to effect change when so many other factors were pressing on the individual. The third independent variable was *education,* and I hypothesized that the more educated immigrants would change more rapidly and more completely than the relatively uneducated. I was not at all sure that this idea was correct, but I felt strongly that the change patterns manifested by the two extremes of the education continuum would be very different. On this variable I had little prior research from which to make predictions, for the overwhelming tendency to work with visible ethnic groups in ghettos meant that only the relatively uneducated were ever studied. While we know from various statistical reports that many highly educated persons have emigrated, there are no studies that focus on them.

I decided to focus on Italian immigrants because the literature on them was more extensive than on any other single group. I then narrowed the choice to Sicily because, while the majority of Italian immigrants are from the south, it is difficult to delimit precise areas on the mainland. Sicily, an island, was ideal from that point of view. Moreover, the inhabitants in all parts of the island seemed to share in a common culture and society and therefore could be reasonably construed as a sociologically homogeneous population.

As I began to reread the relevant monographs more carefully, the first serious problem developed. Writers disagreed with each other, and often the same writer had contradictory statements in different parts of one book. For instance, while all agreed that children are under the domination of their parents until marriage, there was general disagreement about the nature of the family and of the husband-wife relationship. Roughly half the authors said that the family was limited to the nuclear family members, that is, father, mother, and unmarried children; the others stated that the extended family, which includes aunts, uncles, cousins, and others, was the important kinship unit. Many writers declared that the husband was an authoritarian figure who directed everything in the household. Others held that while the husband and wife were not equal in public they were completely egalitarian within the house. These contradictions turned out to rest on the fact that few of the researchers had worked in Italy. The few who had worked in Italy, along with most of those writing about Italy, were correct; the rest were wrong and had drawn their data, apparently, from other sources and from immigrant informants. Yet it was impossible for the reader who had not already done field work in Italy to judge which accounts were correct and which were not.

## PRE-EMIGRATION SOCIAL ORGANIZATION IN SICILY

Since the literature on Sicilians in Sicily was scanty and contradictory, I decided that it was imperative to begin my study of immigrants there. I firmly believed that it would be impossible to investigate change without understanding the pre-emigration social organization from which change came. Since I had not previously studied Italian, I first went for almost three months to the university for foreigners at Perugia, Italy. I had already selected the town of Nicuportu, Sicily as the place of study. It is a market town of 25,000 persons in the northwest corner of the island. It is considered a very traditional town and little changed from forty years ago. For many reasons it seemed ideal.

At the end of December 1963, I arrived in Nicuportu to find sunny Sicily bitterly cold, pouring rain, and shrouded in fog. These conditions lasted until March. I found a room in an abandoned nursery school and then passed the worst month of my life. Everyone in the United States and Italy had told me that I could not live and work in Sicily; it was dangerous and no one would cooperate with me. I brushed it all off until I arrived there. I reviewed the advice as I sat on the bed, the only piece of furniture in a bare frigid room, smoking cigarettes while wearing galoshes, watching the rain come through the pourous stone and collect on the floor. The outside seemed hostile and frightening. As I walked the streets people, all dressed in black, came forward to stare and glare. Never a smile, a welcome, or even the glimmer of a friendly face. Finally, making no progress by waiting but unwilling to quit, one morning I smiled at the women and said "Buon giorno." Open sesame. They rushed forward and flooded me with Sicilian-accented Italian, not a word of which I understood. But I did know they were friends and so they remained. Months later I asked why everyone had been so unfriendly when I arrived. They were astonished at my question, replying that it was not their place to approach the American "professor."

Nicuportu is relatively typical of Sicily. There are no tiny villages as we know from other parts of the peasant world; people considered a town of 5,000 too small for consideration. All of Sicily, with the exception of the eastern coastal strip, is classed as one of the most impoverished zones of Western Europe. Most of the inhabitants of Nicuportu are engaged in direct agricultural labor; but of the 21,485 working persons, 10,696 are hired day-laborers who work, in an average year, only 100 days a year. One of the principal characteristics of southern Italy is extreme fragmentation of land, which means that no one man or family has a single piece large enough to farm properly. In Nicuportu there are almost 11,000 farms. But of these, 2,102 are 0.5 hectares or less (a hectare is 2.2 acres); 4,535 are 0.5 to 2 hectares; and 2,204 are 2 to 5 hectares. Of those farms of 1 to 2 hectares, over 600 are composed of 2 pieces of land, over 500 are 3 pieces, almost 300 are 4 pieces, and over 100 are 5 pieces. These are very poor people who live with great expectation but little chance of bettering their lives. There is a middle class in the town made up of professionals such as doctors, lawyers, shopkeepers, and large landowners. Most of my data refer to the working class, but I will occasionally point out class-related differences.

I spent the first five months or so walking around town just talking to people, but I was always able to direct the talking to subjects of my choosing. This was easy to do because except in the short winter, women sit out in the street all day in groups, and when men come home from shops or fields they also join the groups. Life is dull and monotonous, they feel, and there is not much to talk about. So they were enthusiastic about my questions. During this period I took notes as soon as I got home. When I knew people a little better, I took notes in front of them. With the passage of time I had a fairly clear picture of the daily round of life, special occasions, and the people's attitudes about most subjects of interest to me. I also secured some information about inheritance, income, land tenure, budgeting, and tasks.

I then began a series of formal interviews with a selected sample of individuals from the larger group. I had made it a point to know persons from all class levels, income groups, occupational groups, and neighborhoods of town. The sample included a cross-section of these and other variables. The questions focused on family, kin, friends, child socialization, and attitudes toward change. They were open-ended schedules and demanded a great deal of time and some skill on both our parts. An open-ended question is broad and wide-ranging, such as "What are mother-daughter relations like here?" and are used by social scientists when they wish to delve deeply into one subject and also when little is known about the subject. During this time I continued the general conversations with a greater number of people. As I began to understand the family system better, I included conversations about that, too.

By the end of eight or nine months it was clear how the special topics were organized. Men did have, or were considered to have, greater power than women, and in public women always deferred to men. Both males and females believed that this was the way things should be, in reference to the value system. Given the problems of daily life, however, men could not actually make all decisions on their own, and couples felt that two heads were indeed better than one. All decisions were actually made jointly, though executed separately. While the value of male superiority and authority remained, it was clear to both sexes that males were not usually superior in fact. The "values" and the "behavior system" exhibited striking differences from each other.

The general agreement among earlier scholars on the place of children was borne out by my work also. While brothers are accorded higher status than their sisters, all children are in positions of complete dependence with respect to their parents. Children are trained to bring all problems to their parents, who then make the decisions. The North American and British insistence on early independence training for children who will grow up to be independent adults capable of making decisions and bearing the responsibility for them is totally lacking in Sicilian society. This early dependence on superior kinsmen is undoubtedly a factor in bringing husbands and wives together in problem-solving situations as adults, since neither probably has ever worked alone or was ever trained to do so.

The viable family unit turned out to be the nuclear family of parents and dependent children. More distant relatives live together only in cases of extreme emergency. With one exception they make no decisions together, and they generally have little contact except on ceremonial occasions. Most people distrust their relatives and compete fiercely with them for economic and social status.

The one major area in which distant relatives do think and act as a unit is when matters of "honor" are concerned. An extended family begins with honor and is accorded respect by the community. Honor can be lost, however. As the Sicilians say, it becomes "stained." A blot on the family honor comes from nonpermissible sexual activities of the women. If a girl is not a virgin at marriage or if a married woman is found in an adulturous situation, then the honor of the entire extended family is stained. People say that honor can only be washed away with blood; here lies the explanation for many vendetta killings and the numerous murders of young nonvirgins, their seducers, and the adulterous men who have cuckolded a husband. While the extended family exists in this state of dishonor it is not respected, business deals fall through, and the young men and women cannot marry. Therefore, the relatives bring pressure on the offending parties or their nuclear family to act so that a balance can be restored and honor washed clean. This set of concepts is clearly related to the general theory of male superiority and responsibility.

It became evident that while social status is a constant preoccupation with the people of Nicuportu, most of them can never improve their very low position so long as they remain there. Accordingly, most are not satisfied with life in Sicily and, from written reports, apparently have not been for at least a hundred years. Farm work is a despised occupation and way of life; an old proverb states that "a man who works the land is his own slave." The desire of most families is to educate their children for middle-class jobs or at least skilled workmen's positions, but very few are able to achieve this goal. The pressure for ready money is so intense that saving money to achieve status aspirations must be sacrificed. The seeds of discontent bloom, and the thought of emigration becomes more appealing.

## SICILIAN IMMIGRANTS IN AUSTRALIA

While in Sicily I began planning for the next phase of the study. I had chosen Australia because there are many Sicilian immigrants there, and they have been going there for a long time. Unlike the United States, however, their numbers were still small enough that the postwar immigrants would not be swallowed up in the millions who went before.

Once in Australia I decided, with the help of members of the Sociology Department at the Australian National University, to settle in Sydney as the site of my field work. Melbourne, the other main possibility, was at that time wracked by dissension in the Italian-controlled produce market, and another study of Italians had been done there. Sydney had the second largest number of southern Italians and was the kind of large metropolitan area they favor. I had originally planned to work, at least partially, with a random sample, but just as I arrived the Australian government banned the use of its records for purposes of contacting individuals. I therefore decided, in the absence of any lists of immigrants, to use a nonrandom sample which would be stratified acording to several of the independent variables of the overall research problem. I stratified time in five year cells from the present to 1896, the entry time of the earliest living immigrants. Each cell would contain the same number of persons. The same procedure was carried out with respect to age at emigration and education so that an equal number of respondents were available to fill the cells.

I next drew up two separate interview schedules. The first to be administered dealt solely with subjects in the public sphere: reasons for emigrating, immigration experience, job history, residence history, language history, and general satisfaction with the public institutions of Australia. The second interview concerned private sphere variables: family and kin relationships, friendships, child socialization, husband-wife relationship, and satisfaction with Australian people and their private-sphere way of life.

The first step in the city was finding a place to live. I did this the first day by going into an Italian coffee bar in an Italian neighborhood where I heard of a Sicilian family looking for a boarder. We liked each other and I lived and ate with them for the rest of my time in Sydney. My next step was to find respondents in a city of over two million inhabitants, with no lists or records to use. I had no idea how to go about this except that I knew I could not simply knock on doors and introduce myself, for Sicilians are suspicious in some ways. In addition, this method would only have been feasible in Italian neighborhoods, and the study was specifically intended to get away from a residential ghetto orientation. In the first weeks I began interviewing the relatives and fellow-townsmen of the family with whom I lived. Many of these interviews, however, were later excluded from the statistical analysis since they were too similar. I then decided that if I wanted highly educated professionals, I should go through the yellow pages listings for doctors, lawyers, dentists, and architects and pull out the Italian names and addresses. I wrote to those which the family I lived with judged to be perhaps Sicilian, explaining my background and the study and asking for their cooperation. I then phoned each a week later. Of a group of twenty-three, many were not even Italian and several were not Sicilian. Most were second-generation Sicilians. All who qualified, including the second generation, were willing to participate in the study. I began with them. I had decided to interview the second-generation Sicilians both because they were of interest in themselves and in order to meet first-generation individuals through them. I asked each person interviewed for names of others, and in this way slowly spread my net over the entire Sicilian population of Sydney. Since I recorded the geneologies of each respondent, I was able to ascertain after about ten months that I was covering all areas both of Sydney and of Sicily. After some months word of my work began to spread. A number of new people approached me to be interviewed. They felt they had things to tell me which were important for my work.

Each respondent was interviewed twice, about six months apart. None of those contacted refused: an important point since studies of sampling techniques have revealed that certain types of people refuse to cooperate in studies, and the omission of one or more of these may skew the data in such a way as to render the results invalid or questionable. There were, of course, some practical problems. Both men and women worked long hours and were often simply too tired to work again in the evening with me. In addition, no one would agree to an interview on a weekend, a holiday, or during the month of December, which is summer vacation time for most Australians. My notes show that almost fifty percent of the times when I went to a home for an interview, unexpected guests arrived and the interview was postponed. It often took three or four phone calls and several visits before one interview was completed. One of my greatest concerns over this was that the respondent would become annoyed at my constant pestering and break off relations. This never happened, however. Eventually I had to extend my stay two additional months to complete the second interviews.

Many of the questions were structured—they asked a specific question to elicit a specific answer; this was especially the case in the first interview with areas such as job and residence patterns. But many questions were open-ended because I did not have any clear advance idea of how they would be answered, such as "Tell me what your first year in Australia was like." Especially at the beginning mistakes were made, and one was a near disaster. I asked in the first interview, "Why did you emigrate?" Most respondents replied, "To better my future, to secure my family." With the first ten respondents or so I left it at that and went on to the next question. If I had been thinking sharply I would have realized that this answer told me nothing. It was a truism. When I realized this I began to ask of everyone, returning to the first ten also, "What does this mean to you?" Great differences among individuals then became apparent. The majority explained that this meant having more money to spend, a good house, and a secure job, in other words, being rich Sicilians. But for about one-third the same initial answer meant having an opportunity to raise their social standing by increased job skills, or if it was too late for the parents, then raising the class level of their children by sending them to college and into the professions.

What this finding referred to was the massive question of social mobility aspirations. When I compared these two sets of answers to others about the public and later the private spheres, it became apparent that life styles and change patterns were falling into two very different groups. I therefore had to make a radical revision to both interviews to include questions about mobility aspirations, an important, if not crucial, factor in Sicily.

It turned out, when the study was completed, that there were in fact two patterns of social mobility which went along with the two ideas of a better future. Immigrants with low-level factory jobs felt themselves to be immensely successful since they had steady jobs which were clean and well-paid and allowed them to buy property, the major sign of increasing social status in Sicily. Others who had advanced to white-collar and other middle-class jobs also felt themselves to be successful because they had advanced in class status and they were educating their children to the university level. Thus, both groups were successful within the Sicilian system of social values. Only the latter, however, was granted higher status by the Australian system.

There are two important points to note here. The first is that the working-class immigrants felt themselves to be successful; Australian opinions mattered not at all to them. The second point is that change to an Australian model was not directly correlated with either pattern of success; the proportion of changed and unchanged individuals was about the same in both groups. Clearly, then, this is not a matter of "melting" or "assimilation." It may be a kind of "pluralism," but it is not a simple matter of matching values in some areas and not in others.

In October 1966, I returned to the University of Chicago to begin to analyze the data from the two field situations.

## ANALYSIS

When I returned, I was told about a book called *Poverty and Progress: Social Mobility in a Nineteenth Century City* by the historian Stephen Thernstrom (1964). He examined the social mobility of Irish immigrants in Newburyport, Massachusetts in the 1840s and 1850s through documents and records. He also found two patterns, identical to those I observed in Australia: one larger group worked hard in the factories, saved all their money, and bought small farms on the outskirts of town; the second, smaller, group worked hard to send at least one child on to school and into the white-collar world. Both groups were successful in their own eyes since both patterns were present and honored in Irish society. But the American residents of Newburyport recognized only the white-collar individuals as successful. Thus data from two different parts of the world, based on two culturally distinct immigrant groups, separated by 120 years, revealed the same pattern in respect to this one cluster of variables. Granted, both groups went to Anglo-Saxon countries which are culturally similar in many ways and both immigrant groups came from rural Western Europe. The point is that we can know what is similar and what is different and we can also begin to get a sense of the underlying processes at work.

Writing up my findings and analysis turned out to be by far the most difficult and also the most rewarding phase of the research. I first indexed, sorted, and re-sorted the material from Sicily. This was fairly simple, for I had a good grasp of the data from having had to organize and use it in preparing the Australian interviews. To organize the Sydney data in a nondescriptive manner I employed a simplified coding system. I took each question in turn and looked carefully at a random sample of answers to find out into what patterns the answers fell. For example, I had asked everyone if godparents become relatives. Some said "Yes," some said "No, but they become closer friends," and some said "No, but lots of Sicilians think they do." I set all the codes up on a number system based on whether the answer displayed high, medium, or low ethnicity; in other words, the answers were coded according to the degree of variance from the Sicilian norm or behavior pattern they displayed. I used a similar method with the question whether the respondent would allow his daughter to go out alone on a date, something which is never permitted in Sicily. Number one would mean high ethnicity and indicate that the respondent had replied "No." Number three would mean great change and that the respondent had replied "Yes."

Some questions were easy to code and others were extremely difficult. Job histories were simple, as were also questions which demanded simply a yes or no answer, such as "Are your godparents relatives of yours?" The difficult ones were, of course, the open-ended questions in which the respondent replied at length. These I had to read extremely carefully to try to discover all the subjects or themes touched on. For example, a question about job satisfaction could touch on salary, relations with fellow workers, relations with the boss, and enjoyment of the work itself. Each of these themes would usually be compared for Sicily and Australia and often included factors which had nothing to do with the question asked but which were important in other areas.

When all the analysis had been done I began to write. One great surprise still lay in wait. I first discovered that much analysis took place during the writing. I mentioned earlier that I had hypothesized that change would take place in two spheres of life, the public and private. In my approach I had been assuming the existence of "real change" as opposed, presumably, to some other kind of "nonreal change."

This vacuum had nagged me throughout the research, and I knew I was missing something. Finally as I wrote up the data I realized that not only were two spheres involved but there were, as well, two distinct types of change. One, which I finally called habit change ("non-real"), involves an alteration which did not matter to the respondent. The second, value change ("real change"), mattered a great deal and meant that the respondent had to give up something formerly held dear and substitute in its place something new which he or she may or may not like.

Language is a good example. In the public sphere many respondents learned and used very good English to get and keep jobs, or to advance in their places of employment. However, only a certain percentage of this group used English at home and with friends. Most did not like the English language and preferred and felt more comfortable with Italian. So, while they were perfectly willing to use it in order to gain some desired goal, they did not use it where they felt it counted—in the private sphere. Others, of course, made both habit and value changes in both spheres; these were usually the highly educated who felt they should change in an English-speaking country. There were even a few poorly educated immigrants who changed in value but not in habit; they were too old and too uneducated to learn English but they wanted to and they insisted that their children speak only English at home.

I had asked the question, "What were your very first impressions of Australia?" in an effort to find out if there was a correlation between this variable and subsequent change patterns. Fifty-four percent were impressed negatively, ten percent were neutral, and thirty-six percent were very pleased. The individuals who were pleased comprised two groups: those who related their pleasure to external factors such as work, new friends, and a beautiful city, and those who answered that it all depends on the individual and that they can be happy anywhere. Those few who were neutral had been very cautious, expecting little, and thus were neither disappointed nor delighted. The majority who were disappointed fell into the same two groups as those who were pleased. Some did not like it because of job, language problems, or poor housing. The others, who spoke of personal factors, were displeased because they were very young, because of extreme isolation, or because of loss of social status (all of these were highly educated). When I compared these answers and probable causes together with later change patterns, I discovered there was no correlation whatever between early impressions and later changes. I had thought that possibly a very good or a very bad start in a new country might predispose a person to like it and change or to hate it and resist change, but this was not the case.

The general change pattern in regard to relatives was very interesting. For a period of five to ten years relatives live with and near each other and have constant and intense contacts. This pattern is found in the Italian ghettos where almost all Italian immigrants live on arrival. This is the American stereotype of the big, happy Italian family. But for the majority of these individuals the pattern lasts for only the time it takes to get settled: to learn some English, get good jobs, learn the city, and generally be capable of managing on their own. When this stage in the process of change is reached, the nuclear family moves far away from relatives. Contact becomes limited to occasions such as weddings and funerals. The few who remain in the ghetto often resemble the Italians most Americans are familiar with from Little Italies all over the country. What I know to be true for Sydney I suspect also to be true for New York, Boston, and San Francisco. One final point—to the question "Do you think relatives change when they come to Australia?" eighty-three percent of the respondents said "yes," and in almost every case the change was said to be for the worse.

One-third of the immigrants, mainly the educated and socially mobile plus all of the second generation, revealed very high change in the parent-child relationship. Parents stopped controlling their children and began training them for independence and self-sufficiency. The rest of the parents revealed no change, but their children changed anyway: a cause of continual conflict and strife in these families. This fact was tied into the mobility aspiration, since most of the unchanged families wanted their children to be upwardly mobile. They kept them in school, paying tuition and sacrificing potential earnings, and almost all the children failed by flunking out of school. The demands of the families on their time and skills plus their lack of understanding of what it takes to succeed in a university were so at variance with the demands of a rigorous educational system that the children simply could not successfully compete, nor could they break with their families. The families thus failed in their gamble for mobility and had not been able to buy property either, and so they were the real failures in terms of both the Sicilian and the Australian systems.

The husband-wife relationship, on the other hand, had a generally happy outcome. The general tendency, especially among the less-educated, was toward greater egalitarianism. It was no longer a strain to maintain public stance of male authority that was constantly undercut by cooperation between husband and wife in private. The husbands were able to support their families and had the newly-acquired prestige of one who works steadily and for good wages. They were now able to assert some real authority openly and expect to be obeyed. At the same time, wives were now free to work outside the house, as most did, to move around the city alone, and to demonstrate publicly their talents and skills. They, too, now more openly demanded attention and an ear to their opinions. Thus, the men lost their artificial power while gaining some real authority; the women lost some of their real but secret power, but were compensated by public acclaim for their intelligence and accomplishments.

All but a few (primarily the educated) immigrants were completely satisfied with Australian public sphere institutions which were efficient, democratic, and clean. Yet most disapproved of Australian persons and their life style, the private sphere, which they perceived to be cold, unfriendly, and indifferent to family and friend alike (their perceptions were often wrong and only the educated were aware of the facts here). But since they were free to live as they wished in private, their overall satisfaction was very high. Only two respondents wished to return to Sicily (and had done so several times). Most didn't even want to visit. As with attitudes in the first year, satisfaction was not correlated with how much or how little change was evidenced.

Overall, some of the independent variables worked out, others did not. Age at emigration is not significantly correlated with any particular change pattern. In other words, it does not matter at what age a person emigrates because that age does not cause certain changes and inhibit others. The old, middle-aged, and young at emigration were totally mixed on the dependent variables. This variable is therefore not a predictor of how individuals will change.

Time in the host country was not significant as such. Longer residence in a new country does not mean that more change takes place. However, another related factor did prove important and that is the historical period in which one emigrates. The pre-World War II immigrants went to an underindustrialized country in which jobs in the city were few and those were reserved for native-born Australians. These families opened fruit and vegetable shops all over the city; this work is independent of others and takes little capital to start. The families lived in the backs of the shops. Several unintended consequences resulted. First, all family members learned very good English. Second, most shops were located in high-rent residential districts because the price of produce is higher there, and so the children became friends with upper-middle class Australians. This subsequently influenced career and marriage choices. Third, it took these families away from each other and from the Italian ghettos and thus severely reduced contact with all other Italians while promoting contact with Australians. This primarily Australian sphere of contact appears to have allowed these immigrants to know Australia well, to evaluate it better, and allow more changes to enter their lives.

By contrast, the post-World War II immigrants, with the exception of the highly educated, found abundant factory work which is steady, pays well, and which they liked. This, however, put them in contact with other southern Europeans, and since the jobs are noisy it discouraged conversation. As a result very few of this group, almost twenty years after arrival, speak more than a few sentences of English. They do not know nor do they understand Australia and Australians and I predict they never will. Many live near their work in the Italian ghettos with other southern Italians, and few value changes in the private sector are observable.

The third independent variable, education, is highly predictive of a specific change pattern among the highly educated. The sophisticated, traveled, university graduates came to Australia mainly to escape what they felt was a stultifying social scene in Italy. They have all done well occupationally and financially. In each case a reasoned, intellectualized decision to change as completely as possible was made in the first year or so in Sydney. As soon as they decided to remain they began to change, basing this decision on the idea that to live as a foreigner for the rest of one's life and to bring up one's children in two partial societies was unhealthy, wrong, and illogical. They made changes which were easy and others which were difficult and painful. Finally almost all became like other Australians in both spheres and in almost all value areas. They are indistinguishable from other educated Australians.

I found the socially mobile were the most interesting group both sociologically and psychologically. The group included educated and uneducated, young and old, newcomers and old timers. The one thing they all shared was a determination to move up socially, and although they went about it in a variety of ways, the changes which they did and did not make were almost identical. They changed where it was necessary to advance socially and occupationally, and they did not change when it was not necessary. None ever made value changes in the private sphere willingly, but they did make many such changes and made them consciously. They spoke of wearing masks while outside the home and of fooling all others into thinking them Australian. Only they and their families knew that without the mask they were the Sicilians they had always been. Though some more than others, they all were successful at what they had set out to do.

## CONCLUSION

My study should demonstrate that looking for causal variables, looking at both value systems and behavior, and ignoring the temptations to "pure" description at one point in time reveal processes and patterned regularities in change. We begin to see how changes occur, and why.

These immigrants may be unique, but I doubt it. I feel that many of the processes delineated among them will be found in other groups as well, and when they are not we will know why not. The comparison with Thernstrom's data supports this conclusion.

All change studies are not limited to classic contact or immigration situations. I am writing this chapter in Tehran, Iran, where I am doing field work for another study of change. In this case, the question is: "What happens to an old elite when the world changes around it?" The individuals and families of special interest here controlled the political, economic, and even social fortunes of Iran for almost two hundred years until about 1920. Then a new dynasty came to the throne, rapid industrialization began, and far-reaching changes in the total fabric of Iranian society began to be apparent. How successful has this old elite been in adjusting to a new Iran? If they have been able to keep up, what adaptative mechanisms have they employed? Normal, synchronic, descriptive studies of Sicilian immigrants and of these former princes and prime ministers would certainly reveal no similarities, and indeed in their unique histories there are none. Yet there are emerging similarities and differences in the processes of change found in both.

For forty years, Edward Spicer and others have lamented the slow growth and lack of theory in studies of social change. But things are now beginning to pick up. Many social scientists today are undertaking processual and causal studies of change. The recent ideas of Frederick Barth, for example, offer a very new outlook that will take us away from listing traits which change and those which do not change and into the more stimulating idea that all traits might be lost and the immigrant group can yet maintain its identity (see Selected Readings). By not viewing change as an intervening unknown between two static cultural states and by looking instead for causal relations that operate at the level of the individual as people leave one setting and adjust to another, we can perhaps begin to see the processes that would bring about the condition Barth describes. This approach would take us well beyond an understanding of immigration alone, or even of "culture change." It would take us towards an understanding of the underlying processes of formation of dispersed social groups which persist as a major part of the organization of all complex societies.

## SELECTED READINGS

Barth, Frederick, ed., 1969, *Ethnic Groups and Boundaries: The Social Organization of Cultural Difference*. Boston: Little, Brown.

Immigrants become, in some cases, members of ethnic groups. This is one of the first major attempts to recognize the special types of theoretical issues raised by the kinds of "organizations" represented by ethnic minorities and is a step toward a general theoretical framework that will include immigration and a number of related types of cultural change which lead to special types of patterns in complex societies.

Cronin, Constance, 1970, *The Sting of Change, Sicilians in Sicily and Australia*. Chicago: University of Chicago Press.

The major study that the work described above was reported in. It presents a much fuller account of the research method, interview forms and their uses, and the results.

Spicer, Edward et al., 1961, *Perspectives in American Indian Culture Change*. Chicago: University of Chicago Press.

A set of thoughtful "position papers" on the issues of culture change, contact, and assimilation as applied to American Indian groups, assessing the state of theory and, in many instances, pointing to types of change phenomena not readily taken account of in the theoretical formulations then current.

# Chapter 7

# Psychologically Oriented Studies in Comparative Cultural Behavior

**George De Vos**

Interest in the general area called "culture and personality" goes back to the 1920s. The studies lie within cultural anthropology, as the name suggests, but they also overlap with subfields of anthropology and, most importantly, link with several disciplines outside anthropology including psychology and psychiatry. The somewhat awkward term *culture and personality* is used to designate the special interest of sociol scientists in the study of psychological variables involved in cultural processes. The alternate term, *psychological anthropology*, does not as aptly suggest the multiplicity of determinants governing human social behavior.

Despite formulations about human motivation developed within the psychoanalytic tradition, there are some of us with training in anthropology as well as psychology who cannot give simplistic priority to human psychology in determining the form, content, and meaning of human social behavior. Nor can we reduce the understanding of man and view him simply as a player of roles whose behavior is determined totally by the economic, political, and other social processes operative within any given social system.

The term *culture and personality* suggests that there is some essential duality in explaining human behavior. Any general social theory *must* deal with the continuous dynamic interplay between the intrapsychic and interpersonal structures broadly conceived of as "personality" and with "culture," the complex of institutional determinants that govern behavior within society.

In recent years, an interactive or interdisciplinary approach involving psychology, sociology, and psychiatry has been developing within anthropology. Anthropologists have increasingly found that they cannot confine themselves to studying problems in narrowly conceived contexts, as the following examples of recent research amply illustrate. There are instances in which well-respected social scientists engaged in cultural studies have given an improper priority to one series of determinants over another in constructing theory. It is my contention that certain issues can be pursued more adequately only within a dual culture and personality perspective rather than single-line reasoning taken from one or another discipline.

In using the concept culture to explain human evolution, anthropologists in the beginning considered the development of culture as a universal phenomenon. Only later did a more sophisticated analysis of alternative possibilities in kinship and social organization lead to a realization that anthropology afforded a human laboratory to test out the consequences of different patterns of life as they influence the development of personality within individuals. The culture and personality approach, like other approaches in present-day anthropology, has found it possible to test social science generalizations by finding them in operation in different societies based on different premises and values.

This chapter is divided into two parts. Part One reviews the basic frontier areas for research concerning the influence of culture on human behavior. Part Two illustrates more specifically controversial issues in theory that have arisen in anthropology in respect to two culturally-structured behavioral syndromes: (1) a fear of pollution and contamination and (2) an abhorrence of incest. It is my contention that these recurrent human attitudes can only be explained through the culture and personality approach. This approach in turn is governed by a necessity to understand how both the emotional and cognitive features of human motivation have innate biological-maturational features as well as specific cultural patternings.

## THE INFLUENCE OF CULTURE ON HUMAN BEHAVIOR*

At present in anthropology there are six areas of research on the cultural patterning of human behavior. The first general area is that pertaining to the influence of culture on physical or motor development. Second, there are studies related to the influence of culture on the information processing mechanisms in personality systems: issues related to the comparative study of cognition, perception, and logical thought cross-culturally. Third, there are issues related to the study of expressive components in human behavior; seen cross-culturally, these problems are

*This section was derived from George De Vos, "Problems and Research in Comparative Human Behavior," *Proceedings of the American Philosophical Society*, Vol. 13, No. 5 (1969).

related to the nature of symbolic thought in man and its expression through myth, dreams, ritual practices, ideologies, and other forms of emotionally and affectively motivated thought embodied in cultural traditions. Fourth, there are empirical investigations of socialization within culture, the collective effects of culturally prevalent child-rearing practices, role expectations, and values on the intellectual and emotional development of members of disparate cultures. Fifth, there are the issues related to change in society or culture, psychological mechanisms underlying differential adjustments and adaptations to innovations arising within a culture, as well as to changes induced by diffusion or outside technological or ideological sources. This is an area of study that psychological anthropology shares with all the major social science disciplines at the present time. It is my strong feeling that unless there is a unified effort by social science to understand change in concert, each discipline will come back with a partial answer. Sixth, there is the set of issues related to problems of so-called mental health, issues of conformity and deviancy, as influenced by the cultural environment.

### Physical Development in a Comparative Context

Some studies in physical anthropology have been conducted on the influence of culture on physical development. Dualistic, psycho-cultural studies have focused on genetically-determined physiology as it is influenced by environmental stimulation, food, and other cultural inputs affecting physiological and psychological development.

Studies in physical anthropology are beginning to contribute to an understanding of the social nature of aggression or conflict behavior, both in culture and personality. Washburn (1965), for example, in essential agreement with Collias (1944) and with ethologists such as Wynne-Edwards (1962, 1965), suggests that in many species, including primates, group order is maintained by hierarchical organization, and between groups space is divided by habit and periodic conflict. The aggressive individual is an essential actor within the social system, and group competition seems necessary for delimiting the distribution of species and the control of local populations. Primatologists are observing that the appearance of aggressiveness in animals is not simply a physiological, hereditary issue, but rather that, among primates at least, those with more dominant mothers tend to *learn* patterns of dominance and aggression which place them higher in the pecking order. Physiological potentials can be modified even among subhuman primates. Although among male monkeys one finds differences in size of teeth, necks, and jaws that should determine advantage and disadvantage in fighting, dominance seems to derive from the complex of behavior learned in games of childhood. Dominance behavior seems to be socially developed by different play techniques among peers.

Even in such seemingly physiological areas as skeletal development, culture is a determinant. The most obvious cultural influences on physiological growth are, of course, related to cultural traditions in diet as they influence the growing body. However, other cultural-environmental influences may also be at work. The once controversial discovery of Franz Boas (1912) that convergent changes in bodily form, especially in cranial configuration, occurred in immigrant Jews and Italians in New York City, is not as shocking a finding to modern physiologists and ethologists, who are themselves now elaborating systematic studies not only of the effects of diet but also of the effects of group size and crowding on bodily size and proportions in animal groups (Wynne-Edwards, 1962). Boas had argued as a consequence of his discoveries that some concept of physiological plasticity in response to environmental conditions other than diet, such as urban versus rural living, must be superimposed upon the study of genetic transmission. In 1940, when he last wrote upon this subject, he cautioned, "No statistics will tell us what may be the disturbing elements in intrauterine or later growth that results in changes of forms." More recently published is the controversial paper by Landauer and Whiting (1964) on cross-cultural statistical comparisons of infantile stimulation and adult stature. They find a significant interrelation between some form of intense sensory stimulation in early childhood and later eventual adult stature. Included in their definitions are such stimulations as magical or cosmetic piercing of the nose, ears, or lips, circumcision, inoculation, scarification, or cauterization, the molding or stretching of arms or legs or the shaping of the head, the experience of extremes of heat or cold, or the administration of internal stresses such as emetics, irritants, or enemas. When these are found in particular cultures, they seem to be, statistically at least, associated with adult individuals who are on the average taller than those coming from cultures in which there is no evidence of such stimulation.

There are other unexplained differences concerning patterns of physiological maturation in different cultural groups. Psychiatrist Marcelle Geber (1958*a*, 1958*b*), working in Uganda, discovered remarkable differences in the comparative rates of physical maturation among African infants which she documented with films. She graphically demonstrates the physical precocity of the new-born Gandans, who shortly after birth behave like infants two or two and a half months old. These rapid rates of physical and early psychological maturation which she notes seem to become reversed after culturally determined traumatically abrupt weaning in the second year. On the other hand, differences previously reported in the United States between blacks and whites have been found to be related to environmental factors that are evidently disappearing. Knobloch and Pasamanick (1958), summarizing a great deal of this work in the United States on early motor behavior, conclude that they find no significant black-white differences and that those previously reported could not be related to innate racial characteristics.

### Cultural Influences on Information Processing

Psycho-cultural studies of the cultural influences on information processing have become increasingly concerned with how possible universal, underlying structures governing thought on the genetic side are influenced by cultural patterning. Human perception is, after all, cultural in nature. Initially, cross-cultural studies of basic cognitive perception started at the turn of the century with the Torres Straits expedition to New Guinea (see Chap. 1, p. 12). Early assumptions that primitive man would be found to be biologically different were discredited. Unfortunately for the development of research in this field, psychologists have until very recently preferred the controlled conditions of the laboratory to the difficulties of field research. Anthropologists in the field with rare exceptions have not had the training necessary for systematic studies of a psychological nature. Thus, studies of basic cognition have been neglected by both psychologists and anthropologists. In the past few years, however, some positive steps have been taken in a cross-cultural direction by several social psychologists, sometimes working collaboratively with anthropologists. Herskovits, Campbell, and Segall have analyzed differences in the perception of geometric illusions in terms of cultural differences and habits of perceptual inference which are socialized by environmental experience in given cultures.

Most clearly illustrative of the new approach to studies of cognitive growth related to the theories of psychologist Jean Piaget is the work in Africa of Jerome Brunner *et al.* (1966). In Brunner and others we see a careful consideration of the influence of cultural determinants on the development of both cognition and concepts of causality.

A comparative study of children by Laurendeau and Pinard (1962) in Canada and Dubreuil and Boisclair (1960) in Canada and Martinique found a four-year retardation of children in Martinique when compared with French Canadian norms for children of the same maturational and chronological age. The sequential stages postulated by Piaget in his theory appeared in the same order in their studies, but from their evidence one can infer that there were culturally induced impediments or the lack of a facilitative cultural atmosphere which prevented the timely appearance of expected behavior in Martinique.

Price-Williams (1967) suggests in his controlled empirical work that he found no significant difference in the development of the capacity for abstraction among the African Tiv and the French Swiss. He is aware of reported differences in other studies, and he therefore suggests that these differences are related to differences in the socialization of thought within various cultures. He also suggests that the capacity to use abstract thinking is a matter of attitude and motivation as well as process.

The work of Bruner and his associates stresses the difference in cognitive development related to the experience of formal education. In the illiterate Wolof people of Senegal, what were considered to be "immature" cognitive patterns persisted into adulthood in a good percentage of those tested. A simple minimum exposure to education or urban life tended to reduce the incidence of immature cognitive patterns. Bruner, in comparing the results with the previous research by Price-Williams among the Tiv, suggests that their disparity relates to the fact that the Tiv in their culture are generally more actively manipulative of their environment than are the Wolof.

There are necessary cautions to be exercised in interpreting results by those working in the cross-cultural study of cognition and perception. Campbell (1964), for example, suggests that one of the problems of conducting such research is very often the simple failure of communication of a frame of reference to the subject. Conklin (1962) and Frake (1962) note the extreme importance of not imposing the observer's category on native thinking. Therefore, if naively interpreted, "failure to see an object as representative of a class" might carry the implicit demand that the subject see the object as part of the observer's class for it, rather than seeing it within the subject's own classification. Suffice it to say here briefly that one will look forward in the coming decade to an increased interest among psychologists in doing psychological studies of developmental psychology cross-culturally.

### Studies of Symbolic Expressive Behavior in Culture

The term *symbolic analysis* as used by sociologists and psychologists refers to analysis of by-products of human verbal communication such as simple gestures or complex beliefs, folklore, dreams, or religious rituals. Human "expression" in this context refers to an outer social manifestation of inner motivational attitudes, emotional states, and the like. The social scientist intent on understanding social or psychological processes is interested in expressive behavior as a means of understanding the subjective meanings of social structure to the individual or of finding clues to underlying personality dynamics as these influence outward behavior. Those involved in psychological anthropology also have found particular interest in using symbolic analysis to understand the content of sacred beliefs and rituals throughout human cultures.

Most recently, students of folklore and mythology have used psychodynamic interpretations borrowed principally from psychoanalysis to unravel persisting myths and legends so as to extract from them certain variables related to particular cultural traditions. The psychodynamic approach basically involves viewing human behavior as a result of a complex, conflictful series of internally-structured, psychological processes governed by what are usually defined as defense or coping mechanisms. This approach is opposite to the behaviorist approach which simplifies human behavior as much as possible according to a limited stimulus/response paradigm. Dream analysis has been of particular interest to those involved in psychodynamic interpretation. Others have attempted systematic testing with projective psychological instruments as a means of eliciting symbolic material which can then be subjected to quantitative comparison. Noteworthy in this movement has been the work of A. Irving Hallowell (1951, 1957).

Illustrative of symbolic analysis are the earlier approaches of Abram Kardiner, who in 1939 in an innovative volume with Ralph Linton, popularized a general psychoanalytically oriented approach. Kardiner's work with Linton still stands out as a major contribution though it has been followed by numerous critiques of his concept of basic personality, some of them well taken. This term, "basic personality," was used to indicate the core of integrative personality mechanisms which characterize a prevailing number of individuals within a particular culture.

Kardiner also stressed the symbolic analysis of what he termed "secondary" institutions such as religion. He pointed out that attitudes toward supernatural beings reflect early experiences in a primary institution, the family. For example, the technique used to solicit aid from a deity or deities is an indicator of interpersonal relationships that exist in primary patterns within given cultures.

Using a more statistical approach based on material derived from the Human Relations Area Files, Spiro and D'Andrade (1959) used a more comparative approach to the symbolic analysis of religious beliefs. They concluded that cultures in which infants were indulged were significantly more likely to believe that the behavior of the gods was contingent upon the behavior of humans and that gods could be controlled by the performance of compulsive rituals. Interestingly, they found that such societies do not petition gods by sacrificial offerings. Similarly, Lambert, Triandis, and Wolf (1959) found that societies in which infants were treated relatively punitively believe in gods judged to be more aggressive and less benevolent toward human beings.

More recently the statistical survey techniques of Whiting and others have had considerable impact. Whiting and his followers have made fertile use of the comparative materials located in the human relations area files—a compilation of anthropological material that has been systematically organized under given cross-cultural categories developed by George Peter Murdock. Whiting (1959) reported that members of societies high in overall indulgence of infants tended not to see ghosts; the assumption here is that ghosts are like gods, a projection of a parental image or at least of the security experience that infants see as these projections reflect out onto subsequent experiences in the outer world.

### The Symbolic Analysis of Folklore

Symbolically, folklore—the stories that societies perpetuate—results from the underlying conflicts that are characteristic of all social-structural relations. Social scientists study folklore in order to understand the underlying conflicts of a society. Folklore as a subject for study regarding modal personalities has been approached, as Barnouw (1963) noted, in three distinct ways. First, there is the attempt either by psychoanalysts or by those congenial to the theory of psychoanalysis to establish a cross-cultural existence of symbolic motives supporting the theories of either Freud or Jung. Second, there are the attempts to relate specific aspects of folklore to other aspects of culture using statistical correlations cross-culturally. Third, there is the attempt to analyze folklore of one particular culture very intensively with implicit assumptions concerning personality.

In an effort to summarize various attempts to interpret folklore symbolically, Dorson (1963) suggests that three general approaches have been the most influential: first, theories related to the concept of survival, that is, survival of cultural traits; second, a Marxist doctrine of class struggle; third, psychoanalytic theory. In his view, the most productive approaches to date have come from the psychoanalytic approach. Also noteworthy, however, are anthropological approaches related to social structural analysis and, more recently, linguistic theory. Bascom (1954) suggests that folklore has four major functions: first, an escape valve to let off psychic pressures; second, an opportunity for fantasy acting as a defense against repressed desires; third, some symbolic validation of certain aspects of culture; fourth, a moralism used as a force toward social conformity. In Bascom's framework the individual difference in the use and retention of folklore and in its understanding and meaning become more significant. Very influential in recent years in the analysis of folklore has been the approach of Claude Lévi-Strauss (1955–1956); he uses a dialectical approach to folklore and sees inherent in many myths, legends, and folktales man's attempt to unify certain opposites or to represent the inherent dialectic in man's thought processes. The principal function of folklore in relation to social structure is to unify inherent conflicts that are characteristic of all social structural arrangements. An interesting illustrative quantitative study of folklore was done by Child, Storm, and Veroff (1958). In studying the incidence of achievement themes in twelve folktales of forty-six different cultures, they found correlations between the achievement content of the folktale and child-rearing practices related to achievement and independence.

*Dream Analysis.* In recent years there has been a continuing interest in the analysis of dreams within a given culture. The first of two basic questions that have guided much of the cross-cultural analysis of dreams has been whether one can establish cross-cultural similarity in the nature of dream symbolism. There is increasing consensus that there are indeed universals in dream analysis. Schneider and Sharp (1961) analyzed the dreams of Yir Yuront, an Australian aboriginal people. Schneider sees the manifest content as expressing the dreamer's evaluation of social situations. This awareness molds the expression of unconscious wishes so that, for example, while overt aggression in the kin group is not allowed among the Yir Yuront, 71 per cent of the aggression in dreams is against kin group members. On the other hand, the strength of the interruption in dreams of copulation varies directly with the severity of culturally defined incest prohibition of sex relations with the dream partner.

A second set of studies has emphasized the importance of handling dream content in relation to a specific cultural context. Honigmann (1961a) has cautioned that dreams must be used with other elements of culture, not in isolation, when one attempts interpretation. More recent research has shifted investigation to the form and manner in which different constellations of unconscious processes manifest themselves specifically within cultural settings. In such dreams a useful key to understanding is the culturally prevalent stresses experienced subjectively by the members of a particular group. D'Andrade (1961) in his summary of work on dreams suggests as a proposal for future research that dreams be considered basically a type of cultural content related to the structure and function of a particular society, and that their symbolic analysis makes more sense when embedded within as full a knowledge as possible of the cultural context of the dreamer. In previous research, Whiting and D'Andrade (1959) found, for example, relationships between, on the one hand, the kind of family structure and the subsistence economy of a group and, on the other, the nature of anxiety about dependency revealed in the dreams of group members. LeVine, in his book *Dreams and Deeds* (1967), demonstrated systematic differences in achievement motivation within three major ethnic groups in Nigeria. Dreams of the Ibo are significantly related to their relative actual manifest achievement (or were, prior to the present disastrous civil war in that country).

*The Use of Standardized Procedures for Evoking Symbolic Content.* The analysis of expressive behavior by means of projective test, principally the Thematic Apperception Test (TAT) and the Rorschach Test, has continued over the past twenty years. Briefly, these two tests involve having subjects develop a story-theme in response to a series of pictures (the TAT) or interpret inkblot designs (the Rorschach) in terms that reveal characteristic intellectual and emotional processes at work. There has been ample discussion of the inherent value of projective methods in cultural analysis by myself and others (De Vos 1960; De Vos and Wagatsuma 1961). Lindsey (1961) has written a comprehensive review of the use of projective techniques in anthropological research. He points out, first, that projective techniques provide a class of quantifiable control data that are highly comparable to the expressions of spontaneous material. Second, the approach usually used with projective tests is holistic or configurational; aspects of personality are not artificially separated out of their cultural and psychological context. Third, the approach to a great degree is what is now termed by linguistic anthropologists as "emic," in that such a technique directly elicits material from the informants in ways which allow them to spontaneously express themselves within a culturally specific system of thought to a degree impossible with other types of tests such as objective schedules or questionnaires. Projective tests have been extremely fruitful in the analysis of individual differences within given cultures. One of my own criticisms of previous projective testing done cross-culturally is that the analysis of these techniques is usually done without attention to how particular results compare with other results obtained from different cultures. True comparative work with new projective test materials other than the now standard Thematic Apperception Test and Rorschach Test is a task for future investigators of symbolic analysis.

### Studies of Socialization, Social Roles, and Value Orientations

Psychological theorists interested in the nature of human personality have found recently accumulating cross-cultural data on child-rearing extremely challenging. Such data are by now considered essential to test out any supposed universals postulated within developmental and educational psychology as well as within psychoanalysis. Since both psychoanalytic theory and learning theory in psychology strongly emphasize early childhood experiences as relevant to the understanding of adult behavior, it was natural to examine the available evidence brought in by anthropologists as directly relevant to understanding the childhood patterns of Western society. It is interesting to note that a recent trend has been back to a more psychodynamic analysis and away from the previous attempts to use behaviorism or learning theory as a frame of reference. John Whiting's later work is symptomatic of this shift. His earlier volume, *Becoming a Kwoma* (1951), represented a serious attempt to apply behaviorist theory to cross-cultural research. In subsequent studies of particular behavior traits and socialization practices he increasingly relied on psychoanalytic formulations as explanatory interpretations of his results. Whiting and Whiting (1960) afford us a summary of the contributions of anthropology to methods of studying childrearing. Whiting (1961) also gives us an overview of the nature of the socialization process related to personality.

A new principal area of concern in socialization studies has been that of moral development and internalization. Kohlberg (1963) summarized much of the current psychological research on moral development. It is noteworthy that this literature has incorporated a number of cross-cultural studies specifically concerned with internalization and identification. One must note that this concept, derived from psychoanalysis, has been gaining in acceptance in the general psychological literature, even among those who consider themselves averse to the general over-all framework of psychoanalysis.

*The Socialization of Role Expectations.* The concepts of *social role* and *value orientation* have also been given more systematic attention in the light of cross-cultural data. *Role expectation* as a useful concept, contrary to some impressions, has been used theoretically by certain anthropologists (Spiro 1961; Phillips 1963). Phillips has contributed to the definition of social role as it relates to a culture and personality framework. He emphasizes that many individuals undergo considerable psychic strain in the performance of expected cultural roles. He suggests that psychological defense systems function to make role behavior possible in spite of negative inclinations on the part of the individual. This view of inherent idiosyncratic personality features underlying behavioral conformity within culture is related to a very suggestive theory advanced by Wallace (1961*b*), who delineates a "mazeway" theory about the mutually predictable behavior within culture. Wallace contends that, in order to assess behavioral predictability, it is important to understand the operation of social structure rather than merely to assume a direct congruence with motives of individuals. That is to say, people can perform their role behavior in the same way from different motivational bases. Although the overt behavior of two individuals is highly similar, they may be operating within different perceptual patterns. One can therefore not directly attribute the congruence of manifest role behavior within a given culture to basic underlying similarities of personality.

### Cultural Change

In a sense, studies of culture change are most challenging of all to the problem of understanding the complex interaction between psychological and cultural variables in human behavior primarily because such studies are directly concerned with the tensions that arise between individuals and their culture rather than with static correspondences that permit patterns to continue.

Current studies of social or cultural change focus on one of two basic concerns: first, the nature of innovation in particular cultures, especially as it relates to cultural variations in achievement motivation; second, problems of acculturation that occur with various forms of cultural contact, whether or not political dominance is involved. In the first instance, in investigations of cultural change as related to human psychology, one may study directly those general predispositions found in a particular society that facilitate or inhibit indigenous change as contrasted with change induced by outside contact. In either case, one may study selectively those individuals in a particular society who are relatively prone to innovate or are amenable to acculturation; that is, we find individual differences within particular cultures related to selective permeability to change. One may also study the effects of culture change on the adaptation and adjustment of individuals. In this latter respect, studies of culture change become directed to questions of culture and mental health which we shall consider under the next general problem.

*Indigenous Innovation and Need Achievement.* One of the more controversial works in the field of culture change is that of the economist Everett Hagen (1962), who proposed a general theory to explain differential responses to economic development in different cultures. He looked for a relation between innovation within a culture and the appearance of particular social segments that for one reason or another became a minority who suffered some particular crisis in status. The response within some of these minority segments is to rigidify, but in others one finds an innovative approach that eventuates in a social or economic change affecting the total society. Very often the stimulating factor for social innovation is some form of relative deprivation of former status. The psychologist McClelland (1961) postulates a particular development of need achievement related to specific child-rearing patterns in which characteristics such as self-reliance and competition with a standard of excellence promote the general development of energetic instrumental activity toward the realization of goals. Although in general agreement with the research on need achievement, De Vos (1967) criticizes McClelland's definition of the necessary pattern of socialization and need achievement as somewhat ethnocentric, citing that the Japanese put much more emphasis on affiliation and nurturance as related positively to need achievement, whereas in the United States, need achievement and need affiliation are most characteristically inversely related in high-need achievement individuals.

*Psychological Persistence in the Face of Cultural Change.* Sometime ago, Hallowell (1945) argued against the view that it is the fixed "culture traits" that one should study in learning about cultural diffusion. He stated, rather, that since humans are never simply passive bearers of culture, one should focus one's interest on the readjustments occurring within individuals that result from culture contact. One recurring illustrative finding in several of the psychological studies of acculturation is the persistence of personality traits in spite of acculturation. Hallowell in some pioneering studies with projective tests through an analysis of Rorschach and T.A.T. scores, demonstrated the continuity of certain aspects of basic personality types among Ojibwa, even in the face of highly differential acculturation experiences. One of the aspects of culture that is the slowest to change, as noted by the Spindlers (1963), is language. Thus the manner in which people code reality may remain the same even though other aspects of the culture change. Honigmann (1961b) recently summarized the results of studies in this area by expressing the general opinion that North American Indian personality configurations have been undergoing a great deal less change than superficial evidence would suggest.

*Studies of Revivalism.* Humans who find themselves part of a defeated society or members of a culture severely challenged by change develop a variety of collective movements as preservative reactions to the stress they are experiencing. Some movements take a directly political nature; others take a religious form. Illustrative of the considerable literature on religious reactions to difficulties in acculturation is a volume by Lanternari (1963) summarizing the literature on religious reactions to culture change. He points out the very widespread appearance of nativistic movements in highly disparate cultural settings and traditions. Implicit in his survey is a recognition that much of what has been recently and properly termed "political revolt" has a very strong nativistic or revivalistic character, and that the religious commitment is a chief source of vitality within these movements which can be directed toward political change. In this field of studies, Schwartz (1962) gives a very detailed and brilliant analysis of Melanesian cargo cults which reappeared after World War II around the entire New Guinea area. He relates the stress on the sense of self-esteem to loss of a sense of economic prowess rather than to direct political domination. Whole populations would stop work and participate in magical ceremonies such as building models of docks or planes to speed the return of ships or planes bringing them the goods they had been accustomed to see accompanying United States troops during the war.

## Culture, Mental Health, and Social Deviancy

There is much theoretical controversy in studies of comparative human behavior related to the concept of mental health. It is my opinion that much disagreement could be disposed of by a careful distinction suggested earlier by Clyde Kluckhohn (1944) between social adaptation and psychological adjustment. A psychiatrist or psychologist viewing human behavior is usually concerned with adjustive mechanisms related to individual integration, whereas someone concerned with social structure or organization is most frequently concerned with social adaptation. A dualistic framework, however, makes it necessary to examine any human behavior in both contexts, whether the behavior is witchcraft, as in the case of Kluckhohn's study, or any culturally determined pattern of belief or behavioral action. Behavior is adaptive or maladaptive within an interpersonal and cultural context and at the same time it is internally adjustive or maladjustive when viewed as psychological mechanisms operating within given personality structures. Anthropologists note that various cultures do not define the same behavior as aberrant or the same idea as bizarre, and often insist on a relativistic yardstick in measuring "normal" behavior. What is defined as neuroticism in one culture may be defined as adherence to religious directives in another.

Nevertheless, in cultures where there is no profession defined as psychiatry, many forms of internal conflicts, tensions, and severely aberrant behavior must still be socially defined and responded to by members of the social group. When such aberrant behavior disturbs the group, it is usually defined as "sick" and needing intervention or help by some specialist within the culture. Such behavior may be explained as possession by a malevolent force rather than as a psychiatric problem, but therapeutic intervention may be made in an attempt to restore the individual to his social group. A general task of comparative studies in what is now termed by some *transcultural psychiatry* is to examine the various manifestations of mental illness in different cultures and the provisions made therein for dealing with them. This investigation raises a number of questions that have been dealt with by various students in this field. First, does the concept "mental health" inescapably involve value judgments that are culturally biased or are valid generalizations possible about faulty physiology or socialization that, irrespective of culture, lead to distress symptoms definable as "illness"? Second, are there culturally specific forms of mental or emotional aberration? Third, do different cultures define and treat mental illness differently, and how does this determine the behavior of the "mentally ill"? Fourth, are there differences in the incidence of internal maladjustment or social maladaptation related to culture patterns?

*Culturally Specific Symptomology.* One of the problems yet to be worked out comparatively is the nature of the structural personality mechanisms underlying the highly divergent forms of aberrant behavior. For example, there are many widely reported varieties of such behavior as possession and trance that may actually be related to the same psychological defense mechanisms. On the other hand, some peculiar forms of anxiety states may be related to culture-specific problems characteristic for given cultures. Yap (1963) describes an unusual anxiety state called "koro" among southern Chinese. Men develop an overpowering fear that their penises are being withdrawn into their bodies. Yap finds that this belief occurs among Chinese men of weak egos who come from families in which there is an absent father. They show previously poor patterns of sexual adjustment, and some have continuous obsessive fears of venereal disease. The cultural content is unique; the combination of this particular delusion and an anxiety state is also fairly unique. Why this particular kind of delusion is so widespread among Chinese has yet to be worked out.

Some attempts at finding social structural elements to explain particular disease syndromes or types of content in diseases have appeared in anthropological literature. For example, Harper (1962) describes spirit possession in southern India as a response to particular tensions in the kinship structure. He found that in one caste he examined, approximately 10 to 20 percent of the women reported some form of spirit possession, most often during their young married years. It is obvious that possession was an unconscious means of getting back at her husband for his maltreatment by the young bride who could find no other recourse when she entered her husband's family. Consciously, she had available only suicide or a hunger strike as weapon against inconsiderate treatment. If she became possessed—a culturally available idea—as a possessed person she could demand costly sacrifices as a price the spirit exacted for his departure. The girl could be sent home for a prolonged stay. Possession caused her to receive attention and deferential treatment not otherwise available, and she would in no way be punished.

Rubel (1964) notes the social advantages of coming down with magic fright or "susto," a folk illness reported in Latin American countries, especially Mexico. A male who develops the so-called "magic fright" becomes extremely helpless and incapable of action. The onset of such disease is usually some failure in meeting a role expectation. A lack of appetite may set in and the person may fail to eat; he may be subject to "soul loss," a related disease requiring a native healer to help recover the soul. This disease helps to excuse failure and evokes sympathy rather than possible condemnation for the person's manifest incapacities.

Some of the later studies in culture and mental health have been directed toward assessment of the relative incidence of various forms of mental illness in populations. Especially noteworthy are studies by Leighton *et al.* (1963) in an intensive comparative survey of Nigeria. Leighton reports among other findings that the Yoruba have more symptoms but fewer cases of obvious evident psychiatric disorder than were found in his previous studies of Nova Scotians. In Sterling County, Nova Scotia, such symptoms were more frequent among women; in Africa, they were comparatively more frequent among men. Leighton's interpretation is that the role expectations of Yoruba men cause them to feel the effects of present-day culture change more than women do; hence men are under greater stress and exhibit a greater amount of psychiatric disturbance.

*Mobility, Minority Status, and Psychological Adjustment.* The extent of present-day communication and transportation makes the possibilities and implications of movement of peoples and ideas a stark reality constraining anthropologists and other social scientists to study its effects on various peoples. Throughout the world there are rural/ urban shifts in population. Studies of the implications of mobility are appearing in anthropology as well as in other disciplines. To illustrate, there are studies interrelating social change, urban migration, acculturation, and problems of adjustment. Miner and De Vos (1960) report increased signs of intrapsychic stress in the content symbolism of a sample of Algerians living in minority status in the city of Algiers as compared with people of identical origins who remained in an oasis in the hinterlands. De Vos (1961a, 1961b) compared the Rorschach records of Japanese in Japan with two generations of minority status Japanese in the United States and found an increased amount of anatomical and sadomasochistic content in the American samples. Brody (1961) similarly stresses the high rate of admissions of blacks from the South to psychiatric hospitals and relates this to the general pathological status position of blacks within the United States. Kiev (1965) finds striking differences between West Indians moving to Britain and the indigenous British population in the age at which mental illness becomes apparent. The West Indians remaining in their home environment develop mental illness at earlier ages. This is related to the acculturation experiences of West Indians in the British environment.

In the area of social and cultural change and the earlier tradition of projective psychological testing, there is much that awaits development in the use of controlled interviewing devices. The interest awakened by the comparative exploration of a single variable, such as achievement motivation, through a systematic comparison of groups with similar stimuli will probably be extended in the future to other variables. This awaits the systematic comparative application of a number of new psychological techniques that have, up to the present, been applied only within the Western cultural area. When more systematic comparative evidence is forthcoming, there may be a large-scale shift within psychology itself toward comparative studies. With this shift may come a growing realization in the other social science disciplines that psychological evidence is necessary to strengthen the validity of possible generalizations about institutional social structural patterns. Finally, when mental-emotional and physical-medical problems are systematically compared cross-culturally, without ethnocentric blinders, it may be possible to make more valid cross-cultural generalizations about the breakdowns of psychological structure that underlie various manifestations of mental ill health. The field of psychiatry has long been concerned with the development of a truly scientific classificatory system of mental disease. A more anthropologically sophisticated examination of patterns of aberrancy cross-culturally may lead to reorganization of psychiatric theory.

In all these endeavors, an optimistic prediction would be that we may, in the next few years, leave the hunting-and-gathering evolutionary stage of field work by individual anthropologists, who, in some areas at least, will become systematic agriculturalists, and, by concerted behavior, learn to seed the soils of science more systematically, working together with colleagues from other social science traditions. Thus, by coordinated work of research teams, using similar methods in different areas, we shall be able to gather a harvest of new facts for the science of man.

The attractiveness of culture and personality is due in part not to its accomplishments but to its insistence on attempting to synthesize what others consider only partially or singly in research. It assumes that there are many levels on which human behavior is determined. It accepts within the psychic structure of man such dualities as those to be found, for example, between cognitive and affective functions in social behavior. It accepts an essential duality between what can be termed "instrumental" and "expressive" motivations[1] (De Vos, 1973). If

1. In the social science literature, "instrumental" behavior is goal-directed behavior in which the behavior considered is seen as the means to the attainment or actualization of a goal. This behavior contrasts with espressive behavior which can be considered as an end in itself—that is, the behavior is in itself the purpose. Expressive behavior serves to manifest an underlying emotional state seeking an external interpersonal outlet.

one is a dualist theoretically, he cannot give priority either to "dia-chronic" studies of change through time or synchronic, ahistorical struc-turalist forms of analysis. Societies and individuals must be viewed on the one hand as historically evolving, maturing and changing and, on the other, as complex structures to be understood in their present dy-namic tensions as well as in the context of their past development.

To become specific, I would like to illustrate in two instances dualities in behavioral determinants observed by those that work in culture and personality. The illustrations that I shall cite are fragmentary rather than exhaustive. They are derived from research experiences and theoretical interests that I have pursued. In each instance I would like to make my point by examining critically the theoretical conclusions of a well-respected social scientist which I consider to have given an im-proper priority to one series of determinants over another in constructing theory. The problems considered are examples of issues which I contend can be pursued more adequately only within a multiple culture and per-sonality perspective rather than single-line reasoning taken from one or another discipline.

## THE DANGERS OF PURE THEORY IN SOCIAL ANTHROPOLOGY

Mary Douglas' work *Purity and Danger* (1966) is an excellent ex-ample of both the possibilities and serious limitations of a certain type of theoretical formulation within contemporary social anthropology. Her book reveals how a theorist trained in the British School of Social An-thropology seeks to find symbolized in behavior or expressed attitudes, peculiarities of a given social structure governing its members. Without any attempt to summarize the virtues of Douglas' work which has had merited influence, I would like to examine her argument analyzing the dietary restrictions of traditional Judaism to illustrate how her interpre-tations and conclusions are severely limited by an unnecessary avoidance of psychological explanations of cultural behavior. As a comparative frontier science, anthropology must seek to explain complex and peculiar forms of human behavior such as culturally structured patterns of food avoidance. One cannot meet challenges to understanding social behavior by systematically excluding from consideration significant behavioral variables because they cannot be sufficiently controlled within a theoret-ical system offered by one particular segment of the anthropological discipline. It is not sufficient for example, to do what Mary Douglas and other members of the school of British social anthropology following Radcliffe-Brown would like us to do—that is, systematically exclude from consideration any variables related to what they term "individual psy-chology."

### Fear of Pollution: Symbolic Reference to Social Structure

I have found particularly insufficient in *Purity and Danger,* Mary Douglas' generalized explanations of the human avoidance of pollution insofar as she has taken them from her detailed analysis of Judaic law. The dietary prohibitions of Leviticus, she contends, are based on a fear of anomaly. Douglas argues that there is good evidence in Jewish thought that pollution adheres to those animals or objects that do not fit properly into given conceptual categories. Her evidence and arguments compel agreement. In the case of Jewish culture, at least, there is continuous implicit concern with regulation and a need for categorization. Such concerns underlie the sense of revulsion over breaches of regulations in respect to food. Nevertheless, I believe her conclusions about cognitive incongruity as the universal basis of pollution taboos is an unwarranted over-extension, whatever the merits of her symbolic explanation of the taboos of Leviticus. As I shall presently indicate, I have found it necessary in understanding the nature of caste feelings about pollution in Japanese culture to view such culturally induced patterning of fear and revulsion in a far different frame of reference involving both psychological variables as well as the type of social structural variables considered by Douglas.

In a recent article, "Self Evidence" (1972), Douglas further contends that to understand a pattern of social relations fraught with emotional power, such as pollution, the major issue is "how to rescue the notion of intuition or gut reaction" from any contrast with rationality by anchoring such experiences in "the logical properties of social forms." Her treatment tends to reduce all thought to thought which is socially, if not individually, rational, instrumental, and inherently "logical." If a thought is not rational in an individual sense, one can hope to find that it adheres in some way at least to "the logical properties of social forms." This ignores what one observes in psychological studies of changes in the maturation of thought, namely, the manner in which emotionally laden early experiences can become congealed into irrational, prelogical representations whether they are viewed from inside or outside the culture.[2] I would contend one will not find in the structuring of the social system the ultimate logical properties explaining human prelogical irrationality.

2. Jean Piaget amply illustrates the progressive stages of "prelogical" thought patterns in his various publications on the intellectual development of children. *Prelogical* refers to an early stage in the maturation of a child where he has not yet developed the ability to conceptualize a point of view apart from his own needs and intense subjective concerns. Objective logic according to Piaget and Freud occurs only at a time of completed physiological maturation. In Freud's theory, there may be psychological impediments that rigidify a person and cause him to maintain the prelogical thought even though the physical maturation would make a more mature form of thinking possible.

While there are prelogical thought processes institutionalized in all cultures, prelogical thought can in some instances refer to social processes without becoming socially "logical." Instances of social irrationality in modern as well as traditional cultures are not at all hard to find. One hears today modern rationalizations permitting belief in U.F.O.s or astrology that do not disguise the origin of such belief in underlying emotionally charged wishes for miraculous events or other-wordly contacts.

When almost any society is viewed over time one finds periods of dysfunction and disintegration in collective behavior. Many social structures do not hold together under internal or external stress assuring group survival. Collective practices based on shared beliefs rigidified into institutional or ritual behavior repeatedly become maladaptive. Many cultures die out or are modified in the course of time. To understand individual or collective behavior is not to find it necessarily "logical." It may be "prelogical" either psychologically or socially in that the symbolic representations one discovers as a result of systematic analysis may refer to previous stages of maturation or progressive differentiation in persons as well as institutions.

While Douglas contends that Judaic prohibitions related to pollution are ultimately a question of conceptual incongruity, she does not explain why. She simply assumes that the origin of a fear of pollution must be found in social structure. She makes no attempt to ask *why* or *how* Jewish culture, or any other culture evidencing similar taboos and prescriptions, *specifically* socializes human thought about being polluted in such a way to connect emotional feelings of revulsion with a socialized need for "clean" conceptualization and an avoidance of anomaly in categorization. I do not profess myself to understand the specific socialization processes, or how this might come about as a result of growing up within Jewish culture. However, I am convinced from the perspective of a long study of traditional Japanese culture—which is not similarily concerned with clean conceptualization—that the answer is to be found in a detailed examination of culturally prevalent patterns of psychosexual development which lead those socialized within to tie together thoughts and emotions in respect to what is "clean" and "unclean."

I would argue that Douglas has over-generalized in her general theory about fear of pollution from the need for conceptual clarity in the Jewish world view. There are other concerns with pollution that are more widespread cross-culturally than those socialized around cognitive control or cognitive inconsistency. Mary Douglas gives scarce heed, for example, to almost universal menstrual taboos, taboos on ingroup killing, or taboos on sexual or social congress across status barriers which are all severely polluting to violators of the taboo.

I would contend that concepts of purity and pollution are related directly to social structure only in its very broadest sense by helping in some societies at least to differentiate who belongs and who does not belong properly to society. Elsewhere (De Vos 1960) I have discussed in detail that a basic human psychological as well as social problem in group formation is conceptualizing what or who to include or exclude in one's development of a sense of identity. There are wide cultural variations attesting to the flexibility inherent in the human capacity to symbolize belonging. Man can "totemically" (see p. 123) identify with animal and plant forms. He can also narrowly identify by "dehumanizing" so as to consider subhuman all those not bound to him by some form of acknowledged kinship group. More specifically, this defining of belonging must be examined in a psycho-cultural framework utilizing more directly what we learn about "individual psychology." To illustrate I shall briefly examine taboos on killing as well as eating of flesh.

### Purity and Pollution—Man as Carnivor and Killer

The flexible human capacity to symbolically identify and include or exclude creates many psychological problems related to symbolic meaning in reconciling the human potential for functioning as carnivor, and therefore as a killer for food, as well as a killer of what or who is perceived as a threatening enemy.

Taboos on eating, such as those in respect to what is usually termed a "totemic" relationship, have to do with the acceptability or non-acceptability of partaking of flesh which can somehow be symbolically related to one's intimate associates. A frequent reason given by Indian peasants for not eating beef is that "the cow is like mother." To eat, one must first kill. One symbolically depersonalizes an object or thing as "enemy" or "nonhuman" in order to kill. Not to do so is to arouse one's sense of horror of killing a symbolized or actual object of social attachment. Humans as social animals are socialized early so that primitive aggression cannot be readily directed toward those with whom we share a collective identity. We are socialized by taboos preventing the expression of aggression toward those on whom we depend for sustenance, warmth, and basic emotional needs. We cannot tolerate the emotional conflict, or as I term it the *"affective dissonance"* which results from killing within the social group.

Even more intolerable to any socialized human are residual primitive, unconscious cannibalistic urges to destroy by eating. Humans generally are socialized so as to sense deep revulsion in the stomach and mouth at the thought of partaking of the flesh of any immediate family member or the flesh of any human. It is universally more a taboo than incest.

In analyzing the dietary restrictions found in Leviticus, Douglas neglects proper concern for other important pollution restrictions in maintaining a proper diet. Jews cannot eat *all* beef, only beef that is Kosher (clean). The act of killing a potentially edible animal must be sanctified by religious ritual, or the meat becomes hopelessly polluted by the act of killing. In the past, in ritual acts of sacrifice and communion the diety partook of the flesh following the belief that sharing together in communion takes away the implications of wanton aggressive killing and potential retribution. Also, to share in a communal feast is to bring together symbolically those who belong, whether to a church or to some kin organized community.[3]

Meateaters living in urban societies today do not witness such potentially emotion-arousing acts as the killing of animals, the shedding of crimson blood, the removal of multicolored entrails. This is performed by butchers out of sight of those buying the meat. There are periodic reports in the psychological literature of children who become vegetarians after witnessing the death and evisceration of a pet such as a rabbit. The ready arousal of emotional states involving both love and violence in childhood can be rigidified into self-imposed, noninstitutionalized dietary taboos. In some cultures, dietary taboos by becoming institutionalized can become so encompassing as to eliminate any substance defined as animal flesh. Indeed English speakers feel more comfortable about eating "meat" as opposed to "flesh," a form of semantic distantiation found in the English language.

Taboos of revulsion can be symbolically extended from dietary avoidance to avoidance of touch or contact with others who are polluted or unclean. Such mechanisms are perceptively at work in varying degrees in systems of social stratification studied in a variety of cultures by anthropologists.

## Purity and Pollution: The Problem of Status Anxiety

A subjective sense of social status is an extension of the individual's self-designation and social identity. If there is an insecurity about one's status, there is an insecurity about who one is. The individual will therefore buttress his status position with reassuring conceptualizations and soothe away underlying disruptive emotions. Let us examine by way of

3. Money-Kyrle has discussed at length the meaning of sacrifice in a psychoanalytic framework. While finding myself in general agreement, I cannot accept what I believe to be a too "orthodox" emphasis on the Oedipal relationship basic to sacrifice. Rather I would stress as involved a more existential earlier formation in the development of social belonging as part of ego development. There is not only progressive development of the me-not me, there is also the development of the we-not we sense of belonging which is the burden of my argument here.

illustration a quote from an editor of *Look Magazine* who was describing the irrationality and madness of racism in the United States. He was not describing what Douglas terms "the logical properties of social forms" in American society. He confessed frankly how he had been subject to the debilitating social and psychological disease of racism. The point at issue is that a pollution taboo is *irrational,* not logical, and can even go counter to the conscious values and social ideals of the individual subject to it. This does not argue against the social structural implications of a sense of pollution, but true comprehension must be examined psychologically as well as socially. The editor described his racism as follows:

> The madness associated with segregation takes several forms; all involve the failure of perception, the inability to make sense from the information presented to the senses. We had no trouble "understanding" our servants or our friends' servants. As long as a Negro is a servant or slave—that is to say, not a human being—we can face him. If we should confront him as a human life ourselves, however, we might feel what he feels, and that would be unbearable.
>
> Strange things pop up at us like gargoyles when we are liberated from our delusions. Madness never seems so real as when we first escape it. My own liberation came through fortunate circumstances while I was still in my teens, even before I joined the air corps in 1942. When I first began meeting Negroes as equals, I thought I was entirely prepared, emotionally and intellectually. But at the beginning, something happened, so embarrassing to me I have never before been able to tell anyone. Each time I shook hands with a Negro, I felt an urge to wash my hands. Every rational impulse, all that I considered best in myself, struggled against this urge. But the hand that had touched the dark skin had a will of its own and would not be dissuaded from signalling it was unclean.
>
> That is what I mean by madness. Because, from the day I was born, black hands had held me, bathed me, fed me, mixed dough for my biscuits. No thought *then* of uncleanliness or disease." (Quoted in De Vos and Wagatsuma (1966:381)

In a frank and honest fashion the editor reveals in his own life history the development of what is recognized in individual psychopathology as a compulsive ritual. I would suggest that to understand this case of "individual psychology" is to move toward some understanding of the institutionalization of avoidance rituals in American society. The disease described in social terms is what I would designate as "status anxiety." Shaking hands with an American black on an equal basis released conciously repressed, unresolved insecurities about social self-definition. The mechanism of revulsion has been conditioned in some American southerners to protect their dominant status. One would have to do an extensive psychoanalytic interpretation to understand all the particulars of attraction and repulsion at work. The particular psychopathological mechanisms are not our immediate concern, but the individual problem is a microcosm of a general social problem found in race relations in the United States. Seen sociologically, the individual psychodynamics shared by many American southerners can develop out of a generally shared pattern of status anxiety, which in turn, became institutionalized in legal and social patterns of segregation, leading one to contend that American society in the nineteenth century moved toward one variety of caste organization. A subjective sense of pollution was developed in some American socialization practices so as to help buttress institutions supporting caste differences, and thereby alleviating status anxiety. Self-effacing behavior on the part of blacks was reinforced by social sanctions. Low caste individuals had to learn to behave in such a way that those in a higher status did not feel socially or personally threatened. In a similar way, deferential patterning of behavior related to status differences becomes involved in the social sex roles of men and women in many societies.

Again one must note that my analysis of pollution taboos related to status anxiety is not directly in opposition with the type of analysis done by Mary Douglas and British social anthropologists. The contention that behavior symbolically reflects aspects of social organization is not being debated. However, one must go further and attempt to relate how such mechanisms and ideological representations are linked specifically to psychodynamic determinants in behavior in given societies. The editor of *Look* in washing his hands is reassuring himself psychologically and at the same time making a statement about his place in a caste society. But a statement to the effect that the hand washing compulsion in this instance is a symbolic representation of tensions over racial stratification in American society leaves out so much to become meaningless in itself. Only when we examine the determinants of this behavior in the psychological context as well as the social context can we understand this seemingly irrational act and how it is part of a yet unresolved social issue in the United States.

Rather than maintaining as Douglas does that a sense of pollution is related to the anomaly in the categorization of objects, it seems that pollution is related more broadly to abnormalities in a sense of self in interpersonal relationships in given societies. There is danger in any threat to a sense of social self-integrity. The purpose of this argument is not to reject the relevance of concern about social representations but simply to reassert that it is necessary to have a broader dualistic approach that also takes into account a kind of emotional logic that operates at the individual psychological level. One simply cannot hide behind arbitrary concepts of the limited professional competence of an anthropologist and claim no responsibility for trying to understand the operation of given psychological mechanisms as outside the province of one's discipline. If one is to undertake the understanding of such curious behavior as that related to definitions of pollution in society, one is also constrained to be responsible fully to understand the psychological dimensions involved as well as its sociological implications.

### Purity and Pollution: Cognitive or Affective Dissonance?

Another source of over-generalization in Douglas' theory becomes apparent when one compares the fear of conceptual anomaly so characteristic of Western Judeo-Christian thought and traditional Japanese thought embodied in folk religion. I can find no corresponding sense of dirtiness about cognitive incongruities, as described by Douglas, in Japanese traditional thought patterns represented in their proscriptions of unclean behavior.

Douglas' explanation about pollution combines certain features of the type of structuralism of Claude Lévi-Strauss (1962) with the psychological point of view akin to that of Leon Festinger's cognitive dissonance theory (Festinger 1957). Both these viewpoints, developed within the Western system which values rationality and clarity in thought, suffer from a structuring of human cognition as if it were ideally devoid of the influence of rigidifying emotional trauma in childhood or persisting prelogical thought processes which are not socially maladaptive or disruptive. As Festinger would have it, human beings (generalized from his own culture) have strong needs to resolve cognitive dissonance since the tension produced by cognitive inconsistency is too much for an individual to tolerate. Lévi-Strauss finds everywhere opposing representations between the "raw" and the "cooked" or between nature and culture. Unhappily for the extension of such theory to Japan, the Japanese in their eating practices as well as in their religious beliefs no more oppose the raw and the cooked categorically than do they create categorical duality between nature and culture. What is raw or natural is conjointly absorbing and is absorbed by man and bent to his purpose. Ideally there is harmony rather than opposition. Further, the Japanese can remain vague and diffuse in many areas where clarity and preciseness are categorically necessary in Western thought.

The Japanese language does not distinguish the singular and the plural. Concepts of deity remain diffuse and ill-defined. Shinto belief is full of ambiguities and careless conceptual anomalies. Western religious thinkers examining Shinto have so despaired of it as a "legitimate" religion that they would dismiss it if they could. Yet it remains a vital force among Japanese. Its tenets cannot be well translated into English because it would make the Japanese "emic"[4] subjective experience unduly precise. Translation takes away the soothing effects of a conceptual reality blurred and unfocussed. Western thinkers cannot value or give credit to a form of thought that eases away a need to define, or to catalogue or categorize. In Japanese folk belief, purity is not a matter of clean categories of conceptualization, and there is no critical examination of biblical thought in which ideas are sharpened by continual argument. Japanese mythology is a diffusely structured affirmation of life. Even the deity(s) on Mt. Inari is/are a combination of male, female sexuality and at the same time a representation of food. Any further attempts at clarification or logical explanation are put there by outsiders. They do not represent the diffused blurred sense of the sacred in the subjective experience of those who visit the shrine.

The Japanese are not worried about separating nature from culture, but as is indeed necessary and universal for human beings, they are worried about separating the social "me" and "us" from the "not me" and "not us" and making proper distinctions of what is properly inside the individual and the group from what is external. These distinctions of social belonging can become finely tuned in Japan when it comes to making out differences of social status. The Japanese language, though so imprecise in other respects, can be excruciatingly complex when applied to levels of politeness related to rank and hierarchy.

As far as I can determine from my studies a Japanese sense of ritual "cleanliness" has not been at any time related to "clean" conceptual processes. The Japanese in their thinking do not manifest the same form of conceptual concern over attempts to control nature conceptually, if not by technological means, as is manifest in the Judeo-Christian tradition. On the other hand, there is a strong sense of social barriers related to dangers of caste pollution still evident in many Japanese. The caste system of Japan which in the past did have social functions is disruptive to the present society. It serves no adequate economic or any other form of biological, instrumental function.

Concepts of purity and pollution are related to social structure, but in Japan as elsewhere, historical change can complicate this relationship so that what originated in social structure can become at another time a disruptive and disharmonious form of thought. Cultural traditions carried in childhood socialization practices that continue in spite of other changes can become out of harmony with other aspects of social life. A modern society such as Japan has no further functional use for caste

---

4. As used in anthropology, "emic" as in "phonemic" refers to a series of distinctions conscious to the user. "Etic" as in "phonetic" refers to distinctions resulting from the theoretical categorizations created by the outside observer.

feelings—yet they continue and can be readily documented as socially disruptive by social scientists, as Wagatsuma and I have reported in our volume *Japan's Invincible Race.*[5]

In Japan, as in the United States, there is still a strong sense of pollution directed toward some members of the present society on the basis of ancestry, even though caste functions have formally disappeared. In Japan as in the United States, the residues of caste feelings in large measure maintain a tenacious hold—two million Japanese live in a condition of covert social ostracism precluded from intermarrying into "proper" families and from attaining economic and occupational benefits from a supposedly open and egalitarian educational system. They show the signs of personal and social debilitation suffered by any subgroup of a society subjected to a social belief in their essential inferiority for several generations—a belief buttressed and supported by a sense of pollution which is considered to be an essential part of their genetic heritage.

Feelings of revulsion socialized from childhood in any caste society keep people apart socially—they are one form of general human structuring of groups, by processes of inclusion and exclusion which occur on the psychological level by a cultural patterning of a sense of social identity—and its opposite which I term "social distantiation."

### The Genesis of Feelings of Pollution

The present social *and* personal irrationality of caste feelings in Japan became apparent to Wagatsuma and me while we were exploring the reasons for its continuity into the modern age despite the disappearance of many of the structural features in Japanese society which gave caste meaning and substance in the past. Emotionalized and objectively irrational "prelogical" feelings about pollution are related to continuities to be found in Japanese personality dynamics which had social functions in a hierarchically structured feudal society. Today they are still very much operative as residues still serving to maintain the social barriers separating the minority outcastes living in enclosed ghettos. The major contention which we drew from our work was that caste stratification (as distinct from class stratification) is irrationally maintained by deep feelings about pollution. Whereas class differences can and do lead to payoffs in "instrumental" exploitation, usually of an economic nature, caste exploitation, where it exists, is always "expressive" as well as having possible instrumental economic gains. This "expressive" exploitation involves psychological mechanisms of displacement and the projection of what is personally disavowed to "dirty" low status outcastes who symbolically

5. De Vos and Wagatsuma, *Japan's Invisible Race: Caste in Culture and Personality,* California, 1967.

represent what is socially defined as impure, demeaned, disparaged, and even demonic.

To briefly generalize about the physiology underlying a sense of revulsion, man has an autonomic nervous system related to affective arousal. He also has basic reflexes to expel toxic substances from the mouth by regurgitation—literally a "gut level" reaction. He also has regulatory devices that withdraw blood from the skin. These are part of the mechanisms of aversion related to touch. These mechanisms of revulsion can be socialized into symbolic conceptualizations of danger, whether they are related to tabooed ideas, tabooed social contacts, or tabooed activities such as murder and incest.

This is an essential distinction in the development of age structure in human beings, whatever the culture, in the degree to which distinctions between "me" and "not me" become related to collective group designations, the "us" of the "not us." In most cultures it is necessary to represent group differences emblematically as can occur in what anthropologists call "totemic designations." The me and us—the unique feature in human personality, grouped as well as singly—demand some conscious designations. The basic distinctions therefore are not between the raw and the cooked but between the individual and collective social self, and others.

The mechanisms by which such social identity is developed and maintained are those described by Freud as copying mechanisms or defense mechanisms. What others may observe from the outside to be cognitive inconsistencies are only important to the individual in a culture when they refer to underlying irreconcilable affective states. The individual is constrained to make designations in those areas of experience that are emotionally linked. In a kinship dominated society, the kinship structure comes to carry strong emotional meaning. In such societies, anomalies in behavior related to kinship will bring on strong collective, emotional reactions.

Classification systems become important insofar as the meaning of similarity or difference is important to the individual. There is no doubt that there is a whole set of meanings of importance that are related to survival needs. In these areas, social adaptation requires perceptual differentiation leading to some form of a categorizing system. There can be no argument that conceptual systems developed by man relate to things that are important either instrumentally or emotionally in his environment. To use instrumental value or rational consistency, either social or individual, as the sole system of reference and to abjure any responsibility to determine how or why emotional experiences are important to the life history of the individual especially in early childhood in a given culture is to ignore much of the subjective meaning in human experience as it is shaped by cultural traditions.

Areas of little emotional importance to a group are not important to define or to categorize. Moreover, the degree to which the act of a "clean" categorization itself is important may differ from society to society. Some might prefer ambiguity even in areas of social importance. Mary Douglas' focus on fear of pollution as it reflects the Jewish dislike for anomaly and hybrid monsters is an outgrowth of her own society's need to control conceptually by classifying the totality of human experience. The "rational" bias to be found in some adherents is a product of cultural conditioning. They prefer not to deal with the more ambiguous areas of the emotions.

## THE UNIVERSAL APPEARANCE OF INCEST PROHIBITIONS

One of the intriguing observations of anthropologists is the universal appearance of some form of incest taboo regulating sexual expression within the primary family. Often these prohibitions are socially extended in one form or another, depending upon the kinship structure of the society, to include individuals classified through kinship as too close for legitimate marriage and/or sexual congress.

There are a number of special instances in which brother-and-sister marriage has been sanctioned to insure the continuity of a special noble caste, such as the Egyptian Pharoahs and the Polynesian *alii* or nobility. However, even in such instances taboos were strict for the general population. Nowhere is marriage between parent and child allowed (Murdock, 1949), and even though there are a few reported instances of incest, principally father-daughter liaisons, the consequences are severe. Nowhere are incestuous liaisons countenanced or left unsanctioned.

Most nonanthropological theorists who give time to a detailed analysis of this subject conclude that the enforcement of social sanctions is not sufficient to explain the cultural universality of incest prohibitions. They report the presence of self-limiting, deeply-felt repugnance which makes the act unconscionable to most individuals. Social scientists have been loathe to turn to some instinctual theory of aversion to explain the universal abhorence of sex between close-blood relatives. Instead, most of their attempts at explanation have in desperation turned back to some form of social structural theory.

### The Structural Approach to Incest Taboos

Murdock (1949:260–283) in his discussion of how social organization is structured in simple societies by the varieties of kinship organization, attempts to explain incest taboos as guarding against the possible harmful effects of inbreeding and the need to minimize disruptive forms of sexual competition within any viable continuing social structure. Such an explanation is somewhat "purposeful" in that the lack of cultural taboo is considered bad for continuity whereas its presence has survival value. In effect, the incest taboo is interpreted simply as serving a social need. However, the psychological mechanisms involved in maintaining such prohibitions have not been examined or explained.

Aberle, Bronfenbrenner, Hess, Miller, Schneider, and Spuhler (1963) in a joint summary of various anthropological theories of incest suggest that the incest taboo in humans cannot be based on any "imprinting" phenomenon, as occurs in birds, which helps to explain the competitive driving out of the young in many mammals. (It must be noted that no scientific evidence has been forwarded pro or con to indicate the basis for such an affirmation.) Although genetically beneficial, human incest taboos must perforce be culturally determined rather than instinctual in origin according to the belief of these authors. However, they do not suggest what culturally induced psychological mechanisms are operative in developing such internalized unconscious taboos. Their analysis does not go any further than affirming that sexual taboos are some form of learned behavior.

### A Bio-social Approach

Cohen (1964:160) in his summary of anthropological theories on the same subject also notes that most social scientists strongly affirm the view that there can be no biological or physical base for the incest taboo. In his attempt to explain the incest taboo, Cohen does not rule out the possibility of a biological explanation. He does not accept the argument that since incest taboos extended beyond the nuclear family are variable then the basic taboo within the primary family must be equally subject to variation. He argues that it is an error to combine the core of nuclear taboos and their socially determined extensions within a kinship system. He contends, rather that there is in man's genetic structure at least some convergence with social-structural factors leading to the universal appearance of these taboos. He therefore hypothesizes the "need for psychological privacy" as a means of controlling the volume and intensity of stimulation from others. He sees children as more vulnerable to overwhelming emotional excitation, for the child's ego is not yet completely formed and would be particularly vulnerable to the overwhelming experiences of sexual contact in childhood. Brother and sister normally grow up in intimate and intense emotional relationship as is true for mother-child experiences. A taboo on sexual contact between them seems necessary to Cohen to maintain essential emotional separateness and insularity.

Rather than hypothesizing the presence of some innate or biological need for privacy as a source of the incest taboo, while agreeing with

Cohen's focus on emotional excitation as a crucial issue, I would postulate instead that underlying the incest taboo is a condition of "affective dissonance." This condition does not involve a need for privacy but rather the psychological impossiblity, due to human physiology, of engaging over any period of time in any incompatible or inconsistent emotional attitude toward an individual with whom one has daily and continuous contact.

Although the brother-sister taboo is universal, it is quite evident that there are, depending upon social structure, highly different tensions about potential incest. There is also a greater prohibition and exercise of avoidance behavior in some societies compared with others. Schneider and Gough (1961) point out that in a matrilineal society the kinship structure defines a continuing relationship between brother and sister related to property. A brother in effect becomes the disciplinarian and mentor to his sister's children since her children will inherit from the brother. In effect, there is continual relationships around the sister's sexual and reproductive activities in a matrilineal society even though the sister herself is a heavily tabooed sexual object for the brother. Malinowski (1927) for example recounts how Trobiand mythology is permeated by actualized or attempted sibling incest. Cohen uses this and other illustrative material to argue for the existence of what he describes as the three core taboos—father-daughter, mother-son, and sibling—which arise within situations of extreme intimacy that must be counteracted to meet the innate need for privacy.

The difficulty is that Cohen's concept of the "need for privacy" as it is stated by him, cannot be related to any psychological or physiological mechanisms now understood. But, as I shall presently develop, if much the same argument were phrased in terms of affective dissonance, it could be related better both to psychoanalytic formulations and other psychological theories such as that of cognitive dissonance as expounded by Festinger.

### A Psycho-Social Regression Approach

The most subtle form of social structural approach to the subject of incest is that taken by Talcott Parsons (1954, 1958, 1964). In a brief and lucid paper (1954) he gives explicit recognition to a necessary combination of sociological and psychological considerations in what aims toward a complete explanation of this phenomenon. Whereas his exposition of the social structural elements is far more cogent than other published formulations, his explanatory extension into a psychological-physiological dimension does not provide any impression that the question has come close to being answered. His arguments are rather involved and I shall only attempt here to summarize the main features to indicate where they do not appear to resolve the ultimate questions of the nature of the psychological mechanisms supporting an incest taboo.

In developing his argument Parsons draws on his own theory of primary group organization in which four basic role positions are diagrammed for the primary family: father, son, mother, and daughter. These role positions are defined by combinations of sexual and generational dichotomies. Adult women by virtue of their primary, dominant functions with infants and children remain more concerned with feeding and other expressive need satisfactions within the primary family. Because of his physical strength the adult man is more apt to be concerned with external, protective functions. The subordinate roles of daughter and son are again directed toward expressive and instrumental specializations. This paradigm family unit provides an experiencial setting of intense, diffuse affective relationships for its members. The young derive their most formative experiences as part of their dependent relationship with parental dominant figures. Overt erotic attraction and gratification, within the primary family at least, is most carefully regulated and sanctioned by unconscious automatic processes. There need not be conscious awareness or verbalization of such incest taboos. When they are verbalized there is indication that the automatic taboos are not functioning well.

Heterosexual behavior between the adult marital pair serves to enhance the solidarity of the dominant adults, and nongenital or pregenital[6] eroticism is regulated by various proscriptions and safely patterned close contacts within dominant-subordinant, parent-child relations. Primary family units must in turn be viewed as subunits of some larger community organization which has continual influence upon how these primary family units operate.

Parsons draws heavily on Lévi-Strauss' (1949) structural analysis of kinship and marriage to analyze what can be termed the "progressive" and "regressive" features of erotic attachments as they are related to the total social structure. For example, in as far as a person marrying out of his own ethnic group is performing a social obligation held toward the social group or collectivity as a superordinate unit, he is no more free to choose than is an individual worker free to choose a job without regard to how it affects the superordinate industrial organization. In other words, the person is constrained by group membership to make a sexual choice which is determined by the structure of the group organization itself. In this sense the occurrence of incest would be a socially regressive act and the individual would have to maintain a subadult or infantile identity. (In psychological usage, "regression" refers to

6. "Pregenital" refers to sensual experiences characteristic of the maturational level prior to that at which the actual reproductive act can be performed.

the process of reverting to a more "primitive" or earlier form of relating, capacities or perceptions.) In response to stress or to unresolved internal problems, the individual returns to a less mature or less differentiated form of coping or perceiving. Incest taboos looked at from this perspective serve to propel newly matured individuals out of their nuclear families into outside adult roles and into the formation of new nuclear social units.

Parsons uses Freud's broadened concept of eroticism to explain the nature of affective ties within the primary family. According to Freud, in the early developmental stages eroticism is not organized around genital gratification. Early eroticism is diffuse and located mostly in skin and oral regions involved in early body contact care. It is sometimes difficult to resolve the intense attachment that is built up toward the person playing the maternal role. She socializes by forms of discipline while providing essential need gratification. Parson notes that erotic gratification is a particularly sensitive source of conditioning. If a socializing agent were not at the same time a principal source of gratification, the lack of gratification would cause the child to turn away from the socializing person. The socializing agent is in a position to effectively frustrate the child only to the degree she controls essential gratification. Affective gratification is the motivation matrix in which socialization takes place. In this context, direct sexual seduction as part of this experience would be disruptive to personality formation as would be the passive experience of excessive hostile and aggressive behavior.

Parsons notes that it is important that the mother as a socializing agent have possible "regressive" sexual needs and hostile feelings under control because she enters into a stronger erotic relationship with the child than does the father. From a social-structural and psychological sense "regression" as a slipping back into earlier social patterns on the part of the mother in order to seek gratification is extremely disrupting. If she cannot control her own regressive needs, the mother-child system may get stuck on one of the earlier psychosexual levels or in some form of neurotic interaction which hinders adult maturation. For instance, by over-reciprocating a child's dependency needs an overprotective mother may encourage him to an extent that she keeps the child from growing up. Her own needs may have her continue nurturing beyond the time that it is necessary. Thus, incestuous feelings especially in a mother-son relationship, whether overtly genital or covert, diffuse, and unconscious, are often an important part of a social as well as a psychological inability to grow up.

The social structural aspects of Parsons' explanations relate incest taboos to hypothesized, automatically-unconsciously operative sanctioning systems that move the individual toward proper adult status and role behavior. Psychological problems resulting from some form of culturally prevalent, incomplete socialization within the primary family may occur subsequently and hinder the development beyond the diffuse erotic dependent feelings of childhood into normal adult heterosexual interests.

## An Affective Dissonance Approach

Unfortunately, Parsons' explanation does not cover certain differences between culture groups. For example, Parsons is unconvincing when he discusses the latency period as a regular temporary repression of erotic needs for both sexes. In fact, cross-cultural studies show there are considerable differences in the degree of continuous random sexual play allowed throughout the prepubertal period. The relationship between this continuous diffuse sexual play in childhood and the instituting of subsequent adult sexual taboos needs to be better elucidated since in cultures without a well defined latency period such taboos are equally operative. Further, Parsons' exposition does not readily explain explicit taboos on sibling incest; it works best for the mother-child relationship during early childhood. One has to refer back to some other explanation such as that of Cohen based on Schneider and Gough to explain why the explicit taboos on sibling incest play a more direct and central role in matrilineal societies.

A most challenging comment related to this problem of sibling incest which is not satisfactorily explained in Parsons' theory is the observation made by Spiro in his study of the Israeli Kibbutz (1954, 1958). Spiro observes that there seems to have spontaneously developed a nonverbalized, seemingly socially unconscious and unobserved sibling incest taboo among children of the same age brought up together from birth in collective children's quarters. Instead of residing with their parents in a nuclear family pattern, children from infancy are placed in age-group domiciles supervised by special nurses. An intensity of involvement occurs among such children so that age mates take on many of the emotional attributes of siblings even though they are never so classified by the community. According to Spiro there are no reported cases of any intermarriage by young adults brought up within the same age group in any kibbutz. Yet one must stress there is absolutely no appreciable sanctioning against such marriages.[7] The families comprising the kibbutz come together from widely diverse sources and are unrelated by any kinship ties and there is no social-structural sense within the community that would make age mates feel part of a kinship pattern.

Some form of automatic marital avoidance seems to develop among

7. Spiro (personal communication) states that a recent survey of all Israeli kibbutz supports his earlier finding about the lack of marriage in age mates.

adults who were formerly age mates in a kibbutz. This suggests that one must further explore how continuous childhood interpersonal intimacy prevents adult heterosexual attraction. Further psychological exploration is necessary to understand the mechanisms involved in the transmutation of childhood sexual interests, either unconscious, semiconscious, overt or covert, into adult heterosexual interests and attachments. There must be also further exploration of the development of intense, nongenital affection based on identification and on feelings of social solidarity. These feelings are distinct and even antagonistic to any genitally-focused heterosexual affection. Adult sexual interest may involve a sharp, discrete aggressive component stimulated by strangeness, directed toward a new partner. Such a sexual stimulus would be affectively dissonant with what is experienced in childhood as feelings of diffuse, ready familiarity.

If one examines adult fantasies of childhood sweethearts, in Western culture at least, they are found to remain quite regressive and childish in tone. When strongly maintained, such fantasies represent fixations on childhood sexuality which may interfere with making a mature shift to erotic interest in other adults. In other words, an underlying fixation on a regressively toned childhood eroticism can inhibit a more genitally organized sexual performance. Intimate childhood attachments only rarely actualize into sustained adult sexual relations or marriage. Individuals who are not blood relationships but have intimate childhood associations are not discouraged from adult liaisons, but such childhood ties are experienced as part of an emotional configuration that cannot be integrated into adult heterosexual interests and obligations. Wolfe's (1966) description of difficulties within Chinese marriages in which the future wife of a son is adopted as a child into the family for the purpose of later marriage is another strong case in point. The companionship in childhood seems to lead to affective dissonance in respect to marital sexuality.

The answer to these occurrences of sustained sexual avoidance will probably not be found in any independent social structural analysis but rather will come from intensive psychological investigation into the effects of different types of childhood socialization experiences. This is where a theory of "affective dissonance" contravening Festinger's (1962) theory of cognitive dissonance seems especially necessary. An affective dissonance theory should be concerned with how the autonomic nervous system is involved. Dysfunctional affective incongruities such as those between anxiety and sexuality, eroticism and dependency, and so on may occur. Incest becomes psychologically difficult or frightening because satisfying genital sexuality may depend on balanced perceptual-autonomic body states in which there is a blending of sexual and other affective components such as a sense of strangeness or some aggressive arousal. Such sexual stimulation may be incompatible with the usual type of affectional states deeply conditioned toward particular individuals by continuous contact during childhood. Incest may occur only in rare instances when a maternal relationship has been continuously experienced as eroticized by a psychologically regressive mother, or when there has been some childhood breakthrough into continuous sexual play between sibs. More frequently such erotic wishes may be unresolved and unconscious. These are unrealizable because they would necessitate the total rearousal and reexperience of other components of an affective childhood pattern. This inaccessability leads, especially in neurotic conditions as examined by psychoanalysis, to an emphasis on erotic fantasy rather than real sexual relationship in the inner life of some individuals.

A mother who engages in genital stimulation of the son for her own satisfaction would have to be extremely aberrant and sexually disturbed herself, since the sexual satisfaction derived from an infant or a small child would in no way be equal to that derived from an adult male. It is therefore most unusual for a small child to experience the mother's active sexuality directed toward him as a means of her own direct genital gratification. There is, however, the more frequent possibility that a child senses that the mother's unsatisfied sexual needs receive some indirect, partial gratification from the sensual contact with her child. This situation does not lead to overt incest but rather to an unconscious, unresolved erotic quality in the relationship between mother and child.

In some societies there is a playful teasing of the child's genitals or even a masturbatory stimulation of the genitals by mother or caretaker, usually to "passify" the child. This genital contact is not to be viewed consciously as a direct means of experiencing genital satisfaction on the part of the stimulator, even though some diffuse pleasure may occur with the act.

A male child's witnessing of parental coitus which occurs with some frequency in many cultures is a passive experience which does not of itself prepare him to engage in genital activity with the mother. Viewing adult sexuality in others including parents usually takes place at a time of pregenital primacy in erotic organization. A passive pregenital state is not necessarily "fixating" as is sometimes suggested by psychoanalysts on the basis of experience with neurotic patients. There is not of necessity traumatic rigidification of sexual functions in cultures where such viewing is frequent. Further growth can occur so that permanent infantile desires are replaced by more satisfactory active heterosexual objects in one's cognitive schemata.

Parsons' discussion emphasizing the mother's sensual psychological state as she cares for her child, therefore, is pertinent. Only in the rarest of instances does a mother's relationship to her own child involve any form of genital eroticism. The more usual intensive diffuse erotic reciprocity between mother and child at the earliest stages of development is for the child's erotic developmental needs and may well be a normal "grooming" prerequisite for adequate heterosexual development.

An affective dissonance theory of incest does not in any way suggest the inappropriateness of erotic feelings in a mother-child relationship. On the contrary, basic satisfactions of pregenital erotic experiences with the mother prepares the child for further psychosexual growth. It is only the inappropriate specification of the relationship by the mother, either symbolically in some indirect way which would result in an aberrant psychosexual development. In mammalian research, impotency has been reported for adult primates who have not experienced the proper, sexually-satisfying acts of mothering (H. Harlow and J. F. Harlow). The grooming of the body and other acts of licking and care of erogenous areas by the mother of her infant are common to many species. Rats have shown a disturbed capacity for adult copulation when they were not properly groomed by their mothers at particular periods of infancy. Such animal research seems to be fully in accord with psychoanalytic formulations concerning the necessity for satisfying mothering experiences in childhood. That is to say, the bodily intimacy of proper mothering including pleasuarble body experiences are necessary for fully satisfactory adult sexual experiences. In humans, the lack of appropriate mothering can lead to aberrancies in an affectively consistent subjective experience of the maternal role relationship. On the other hand, culturally induced over-extension of mothering appropriate to earlier periods can produce problems of dependency which do not disappear with adulthood.

Harlow's experiments with chimpanzees and the experiments of others with rats and other mammals suggests maternal physically close grooming behavior in infancy is necessary for the appearance of adequate sexual behavior. Deprived of such behavior the adult animal does not perform adequately although he is physically capable.

### The Role of Normal Repression in the Maintenance of the Incest Taboo

Affective ties with the mother during psychosexual development through puberty and afterwards usually carry some residual components of the earlier experiences, but the psychosexual development of the individual and the transmutation taking place in his schemata gradually changes the nature of his experience of the mother with whom he nevertheless remains socially, if not physically, involved. Only if he had been actively and directly seduced by the mother could there be a breakthrough of direct genital desires in their relationship. Underlying physiological functioning interacts with evolving physiological structures to maintain cognitive-affective harmony. The mechanism of repression prevents the appearance of dissonant affective feelings which could cause a serious disruption of necessary primary relationships. Any direct conscious breakthrough of socially inappropriate fantasies causes an overwhelming level of discomfort, tension, and internal conflict.

Therapists working with delinquents in prison have reported the relatively frequent occurrence of cases in which there is a sexualized fantasy concerning the mother. In such cases the mother is invariably sexually active with several men. This attests to the fact that in some instances of childhood witnessing of promiscuity of a mother there may be a lesser degree of repression about fantasies of mother's sexuality that are stimulating to her son. A mother's frank sexuality can be a continually stimulating reality to her growing child. Nevertheless, even in such cases a son continues to demonstrate a need to maintain some level of repression. Moreover, it must be stressed that in such circumstances the relative availability of incestuous wishes is related also to the degree of attachment and sense of rejection experienced from the mother. The more giving the mother, or the warmer the relationship, even though she be sexually promiscuous, the more deeply repressed the awareness of sexual interest toward her. That is to say that those young men who experience a close maternal relationship give evidence of a more deep repression of their incestuous fantasies regardless of the mother's frank sexuality. On the other hand, those individuals who have not been emotionally rewarded in the maternal relationship have greater difficulty in repression and are more apt to have sexual and/or aggressive fantasies come to the surface of consciousness.

A theory of affective dissonance disturbing cognitive schemata would be supplementary to rather than conflict with other features of psychoanalytic theory related to repression. It could be related also to what is described in psychoanalytic theory as "transference" phenomena noted to illustrate cases of relative or complete impotency in marriage. Such cases often involve a transference of childishly toned sexualized attitudes originally held toward mother or sister to the wife. Individuals who have strong unconscious residual incestuous ties to a mother or sister are disturbed in their potency with women who are affectively equated on an unconscious level with a childhood object to which he still finds himself sexually attached.

In Japan, for example, a muted and infrequent sexual relationship between a man and his wife often develops. The wife is expected to take on a maternal role. A considerable number of Japanese males find themselves more sexually interested in, if not more potent with, professional female entertainers on whom they do not depend for other forms of gratification. For some, a mistress is a necessity for full genital satisfaction. Day by day close living rearouses childish attitudes toward the wife. These dependent attitudes are functionally equivalent to incest in that affective dissonance occurs between the maternal-like role of wife on the one hand and sexual stimulation on the other occurs. Parsons in his four role schematization of father, mother, daughter, son, neglects to consider the fact that strangeness—or infrequent, rather than daily contact—creates extra-marital sexual stimulation in all cultures. Adulterous liasons and their unsuccessful prohibition are as universal to culture as is the marriage bond.

Marital familiarity can cause active dislike and disharmony which further diminishes sexual interest. Equally often familiarity restimulates regressive dependent needs that diminish the sexual attractiveness of both partners to each other. The Japanese woman becomes reconciled to the maternal role she often plays for her husband—she, too, no longer has an active sexual interest in him. I would also hypothesize, without any first-hand contact, that the widespread appearance of the mistress in Latin American cultures has psychological causality as well as existing as a simple derivative of non-reciprocal class or sexual status relationships within the social structure of these cultures. There are reports by Mexican psycholanalysts of complex sexual disturbances between man and wife that occur after the birth of a child. The father finds himself unconsciously competing with his own child who is being gratified in its pregenital erotic relationship with the mother. The man cannot continue to relate sexually in a positive way to his wife, interpersonal disharmony develops over unsatisfied wishes, and the man takes up with another woman. At the same time the wife psychodynamically seems to retreat from genital interests in her husband and devotes herself with single-minded intensity to her infant.

An affective dissonance theory of incest taboos is also consistent with the periodic appearances in some societies of liaisons that break through formal kinship prohibitions inconsistent from the standpoint of an affective dissonance theory.

Institutionalized avoidance may actually enhance the attraction of incestuous relationships in some societies. Formal avoidance creates a sense of excitement which may be realized in an incestuous relationship even when it is severely punished. When one examines the psychosexual history of the individuals caught committing incest in our culture, the relationship may not actually have been close or positive in childhood.

Father-daughter incest sometimes takes place between an exploitative father who has previously little continuous affectional contact with a daughter. In our society in a number of reported cases found in the psychoanalytic literature, the father involved is a passive, psychologically child-like man who, in effect, plays at a form of childhood sibling incest with his own child at the expense of his wife seen in the role of deceived adult.

In such cases incest can be interpreted as the acting out of passive childhood fantasies on the part of the female which coincide with the childhood fantasies still dominating the erotic life of the father who feels safer with a non-threatening child than with a threatening adult female. There are instances reported however, where father-daughter incest is fostered unconsciously by a mother as a means of achieving for herself a vicarious experience of a childlike incestuous relationship with her own father. The complexity of the human's capacity for vicarious experience permits no simple direct explanations of the psychological states which occur in reported cases where an incest taboo is broken. Conversely, mother-son incest is extremely rare. Passive regressive fantasies on the part of a mother cannot as directly be realized by sexual congress with her own child, especially after puberty.

Both psychological and social structural forces must be considered in developing a theory of incest. Parsons' dual use of the concept of regression as developed in the social structural theory of Lévi-Strauss and in his adaptation of the psychoanalytic theory is a positive step forward. He recognizes that the secret of the incest taboo is not to be found in further analysis of social structure per se. The psychological mechanism of repression in most instances works very well to prevent the direct appearance of incest behavior within the primary family, but a general reference to that mechanism by itself tells us nothing. The more specific psychological reasons for the incest taboo are to be found somewhere in further understanding the avoidance of dissonance in man's affective structure and in specific reference to the incompatabilities existing between infantile and adult sexual or erotic experiences as they are cognitively transmuted into adult forms of psychosexual maturation. How certain features of erotic experience in the emotional investment in love objects occurs is already suggested in psychoanalytic theory, but the actual physiopsychological mechanisms operative have not as yet been fully explored by psychoanalytic procedures in other cultural settings.

### Conclusions

One cannot bring to conscious cognizance feelings that would be disruptive to an ongoing day-by-day pattern of intimate human needs and responses, either intrafamilial or general-social. That is to say, a sense of self in intimate relationships demands some degree of appropriate repression. As is often discussed in psychoanalytic literature, the human psychic apparatus has the potential of splitting off conflictful emotional attitudes originating in response to the same person and displacing them to different individuals. People also displace and project "evil," malevolence, or ritual pollution outside the social group so that either the primary group or some social group membership may be maintained more harmoniously.

In understanding how the mechanisms of repression operates in maintaining consistency in conscious life I would again suggest that affective dissonance is more generic cross-culturally than cognitive dissonance as discussed by Festinger. As I have discussed above, there are many instances in Japanese culture of juxtaposed inconsistencies in thought and behavior that can be consciously maintained without emotional discomfort. Individuals can continence within their own consciousness both inconsistencies and ambiguities to the degree that they are not thereby affectively aroused—either enraged or made anxious by the cognitive content they are contemplating. The measure of tolerance of inconsistency or ambiguity is not only to be judged in terms of direct intellectual capacities for handling complex and differentiated cognitive patterns. It is not that some Japanese men, for example, consciously equate wife with mother—hence defining sex with the wife as incestuous and forbidden. Rather it is the emotional-childish regressive tone of the relationship that makes sex less interesting or even impossible as a means of satisfaction for some men. As discussed in the context of fear of pollution in the first part of this section there is also an essential affective dimension to all cognitive structures. Some cultures, as in the case of those within the Western Judeo-Christian tradition tend to train their members to abhor illogic. They are trained to respond emotionally to logical inconsistency. Mary Douglas' arguments about Judaic concepts of pollution may pertain to an explanation of Leviticus, but the Japanese sense of pollution is not to be found in a similar abhorrence of inconsistency or illogic. It is in the socialization of the emotions in relation to thought processes that one finds the key to a sense of pollution or to the problems over dissonance or anomaly when they are experienced by those of a given culture.

Regardless of the frontier area explored in cultural anthropology —be it cognitive development, expressive symbolism, general socialization procedures, social change, or the epidemiology and treatment of personal and social malaise in various cultures as summarized in part one of this chapter—one cannot make progress in research without a multideterminant cultural discipline giving careful attention to the cultural structuring of man's emotional life as part of our genetically shared human psychology as it becomes operative in different patterns in different cultural contexts.

## SELECTED READINGS

Barnouw, Victor, 1973, rev. ed., *Culture and Personality*. Homewood, Ill.: Dorsey Press.

An excellent review of the history and methods of study of culture and personality, illustrating the pioneer approaches of Malinowski, Benedict, Mead, Kardiner, Linton, and DuBois. It also illustrates current approaches in the form of cross-cultural surveys, observational methods, interviews, life history materials, personality tests, and the analysis of folklore and art.

De Vos, George, 1973, *Socialization for Achievement: Essays on the Cultural Psychology of the Japanese.* Berkeley: University of California Press.

An exploration of those psychological features of Japanese culture that have most influenced the successful adaptation of Japanese society to modernization and social change. Both what is normative and what is deviant are examined. This approach to Japanese culture illustrates the applicability of a variety of social science methods to a study of culture. In addition to ethnographic observations, these range from an intensive analysis of literary materials and projective psychological tests to a cross-cultural statistical comparison of delinquency and suicide.

Erikson, Erik, 1964, rev. ed., *Childhood and Society.* New York: Norton.

Erikson's culturally sensitive psychoanalytic approach to childhood socialization is illustrated by studies of two American Indian tribes, the failure of ego development in a schizophrenic girl, and reflections on American, German, and Russian cultural problems influencing the maturation of individuals in these societies.

Hsu, Francis, ed., 1972, *Psychological Anthropology.* Cambridge, Mass.: Schenkman Press.

An overview which illustrates the work in depth of several cultural areas: Japanese, African, North American, and Oceania. It illustrates psycho-cultural concerns with mental illness, dreaming, and altered states of consciousness and discusses a number of topics such as the socialization process, kinship, and behavior.

Lewis, Oscar, 1959, *Five Families.* New York: Basic Books.

A case study-life history approach to the "culture of poverty" in Mexico. Lewis lets people speak for themselves without the intrusion of abstract theoretical constructs to explain their behavior. A sensitive tour de force illustrating the role of the anthropologist as listener and recorder of human life styles.

# Anthropological Linguistics

# Chapter 8

# Lexical Structures and Syntax:
# Yucatec Maya Verbal Stems

**Marlys McClaran**

Human language is an integral part of human activities, knowledge, beliefs, and values. Underlying the diversity of cultures and languages is a universal and specifically human capacity for the acquisition of the complex and tightly structured sound systems, grammatical systems, and lexical systems of the world's several thousand languages. Linguistics, the scientific study of languages, attempts to formulate a theory which will account for the universal aspects of the structure of languages.

Since language is such a pervasive part of man's behavior, it is not surprising that linguistics and anthropology have been closely affiliated. However, the relationships of language to culture, of a particular language to a particular culture, and even of linguistics to anthropology are complicated and problematic. After a brief historical characterization of these relationships, I will consider how the lexicon, the "dictionary" of meaningful elements of a language, provides an object of study from which to make direct inferences about some of the relations between language and culture. The named objects, events, and attributes of each word listed in the dictionary may vary from culture to culture, and the beliefs about them and behavior toward them also vary from culture to culture. This aspect of the dictionary may be considered its cultural side, and linguists have not traditionally concerned themselves with it. On the other hand, the sounds of the forms, the word-forming processes, the syntactic rules of combination of classes of words, and the kinds of relations among these classes may be seen as the *linguistic* side of the dictionary. This discussion is followed by the report of a project which investigated lexical items of Yucatec Maya and their structural relations.

## THE HISTORICAL DEVELOPMENT OF ANTHROPOLOGICAL LINGUISTICS

Since anthropology became an academic discipline around the turn of the century there have been two main sources of interest in linguistics: (1) the practical need for language competence as a basic field-work tool and (2) theoretical interest in language as a major product of human cultural development and a vehicle of cultural transmission. Generally, theoretical interest has been most active in North American anthropology, and was especially influenced by Franz Boas in the first, formative quarter of the century. The British tradition, by contrast, has been interested in language primarily as a field-work tool.

One of the first modern ideas to develop was the concept of the autonomy of language. Boas, and Edward Sapir after him, felt that the patterns underlying the sound and form systems were relatively independent of conscious formulation and control by their users—as opposed, for example, to systems of politeness or of government. Since the patterns operated unconsciously it further appeared that they were not subject to secondary elaborations and rationalizations or to voluntary control. For example, if an American is asked why he does not eat his food with a knife, he will most likely reply that to do so would risk cutting his mouth, or something to that effect. On the other hand, if he is asked why he refers to one male child as *boy* and more than one male child as *boys,* he will be likely to have no explanation other than "that is how you say it." He believes there are reasons for his manners but not for his language, and yet actually he is no more likely to cut his mouth with a knife than stab it with a fork.

A second contribution of these early workers was the notion that all languages are in some sense "equal." This was opposed to the prevailing view that some languages are "primitive" or more primitive than others. One implication of this new attitude is that what can be said in one langauge can be said in any other, though different things can be communicated with varying degrees of difficulty in various languages. For example, one case where this is obviously true is in the comparison of the inventory of lexical items one language has which refer to the objects and ideas of the people who speak the language with the inventory of such things and their labels in another language. The English lexical item *hamburger* cannot be "translated" into Ecuadorian Quechua because there are no hamburgers among speakers of Ecuadorian Quechua, but it could be reasonably well described and characterized by someone who knew the language.

The same principle applies to forms in languages. The elements of form are called "grammatical" as opposed to "lexical," but the differences in their inventory from language to language do not preclude translation. To take a familiar example, if I address you in Spanish I have to choose between the "familiar" *tu* and the "polite" *usted,* and my choice reflects the singularity or plurality of you and a certain range of social relationship between us. I cannot avoid the choice by using some third form, or even by omitting the pronoun, because the choice is also carried in the verb form. In English, by contrast, only one form of "you" is available, which does not specify the social relations between you and me, and only context indicates whether there is more than one of you. Examples of such differences between two languages in the grammatical categories are familiar to us as Europeans or Americans. But when we study unfamiliar languages, we are struck by the diversity among them in the concepts which are encoded into their elements of form.

Around the turn of the century interest in this kind of linguistic diversity, or "relativity" as it was called, was stimulated by the study of many of the American Indian languages. Boas and his students were leaders in this development. They also had an interest in language in its relation to thought and processes of social interaction, which was later to be taken up by Benjamin Whorf.

Prior to the Second World War, interest in establishing relativity evolved into an explicit attempt to demonstrate the internal coherence and autonomy of individual languages. The aim was to produce a self-contained description of a language as a *structural* system comprised of contrastive elements of sound, *phonemes,* ordered in sequences which have meaning, called *morphemes.* The morphemes, in turn, were the units which combined in specifiable order to form higher constructions such as words, and so on, until finally utterances of the language were described in this sense of their structure. In the linguists' use of the term *structure* there were two different but interrelated aspects. One aspect was the sequential constraints on the ordering of elements, sometimes referred to as *syntagmatic structure.* The other, sometimes called *paradigmatic* structure, refers to the similarities and differences among elements which may substitute for each other in any given environment, or linguistic context. In general, American workers during this period concentrated on sequential structures and European workers ( de Saussure, Troubetsky, the "Prague school" of linguistics) on paradigmatic structures.

The data recognized as acceptable for both sides of this basic descriptive work could consist of texts transcribed from overheard speech, texts plus the linguist's growing ability to speak the language, and texts plus informant responses to utterances created by the linguist. The analysis could be carried out, it was felt, without the need to understand the meaning of the utterances or parts of utterances, as long as one knew which items were the same in meaning to speakers and which were different. It was not thought to be necessary to describe the culture of the speakers of the language, or to consider the social interaction within which the utterances were embedded. While it was believed at this time that language was an important part of culture and that the methods developed for studying structures of language might be applicable to the study of other cultural structures, attention was directed primarily toward the development of rigorous procedures for the description of different individual languages, each in its own terms, based on units defined internally to the language and patterns in the distribution of these units.

This struggle for autonomy of method and subject matter culminated in the United States in an attempt to build algorithms (procedural models) for the induction of elements and structures from phonetic transcriptions of speech based solely on phonetic and distributional evidence. Distributional evidence refers to the patterns of appearance of a form across linguistic contexts. This tradition is often associated with the work of Bloomfield, Bloch, Trager, and Zellig Harris. Three publications are indispensable to an understanding of this period: Bloomfield's *Language* (1933); the collection of readings entitled *Reading in Linguistics*, edited by Joos (1958); and Harris's *Methods in Structural Linguistics* (1951). This tradition advocated working from the bottom (phonetics) up to the top (syntax), but it rigorously avoided the question of meaning and the role of language in human information processing, communication, and interaction.

A more balanced perspective from the 1940s through the 1960s can be found in the work of Pike and Nida and their students, who combined a somewhat more pragmatic approach to the inductive problems in describing a language, a sensitivity to the psychological side-effects of speaking a particular language, and an integration of evidence from informants' perceptions and judgments and from social interaction in order to develop hypotheses about language structure and to test these hypotheses.

At the other extreme during this period is the work of Benjamin L. Whorf who attempted to call linguists' attention to the importance of the role of language in thought and vice versa. Given the differences among languages with regard to aspects of reality which are codified in the linguistic forms, he considered the effects of these differences on the patterns of thought and "habitual behavior" of the speakers of the various languages. In pursuing this interest Whorf was picking up an earlier concern of Boas and Sapir which had gradually been excluded for purposes of rigor from the descriptions of the dominant American structuralist tradition. Whorf's concern with language and thought attracted the substantive interest of a variety of anthropologists (for example, Kluckhohn 1956) just as the rigor of the methods used in the dominant methodological tradition influenced their methodological interest.

During the late 1950s and 60s four interrelated developments took place in anthropology in response to both the contributions and deficiencies of structural analysis in linguistics: (1) fairly serious attempts were made to apply literally the current analytical methods of linguistics to the description of other cultural phenomena; (2) some tools were developed for describing semantic structures in languages as part of the ethnographic enterprise; (3) a diverse anthropological interest arose in language as communication embodied in social interaction; and (4) there was a radical reformulation of the goals and methods of linguistics, stemming from the work of Noam Chomsky.

Examples of the first development involving technical or methodological diffusion of linguistics into other areas of anthropology are the work of Birdwhistell (1952) on expression and bodily movement and the work by Norman A. McQuown (1956) and others on interviewing, and "paralanguage" or "verbal gesture." The approaches to this material share an attempt to build highly differentiated grids or multidimensional feature systems to code and notate the phenomena under consideration, for example, gestures or facial expressions. This highly differentiated grid takes the form of a transcription system sensitive enough, along the relevant dimensions—which might be those of loudness, length, eyebrow movement, head movement, mouth shape, body angle, and others—to differentiate at least each element which a native user of the language or nonverbal system might differentiate. The analyst's task then became that of lumping together different elements in the way the system does. He was to do this, as in linguistic analysis, by delineating classes of equivalent elements through lumping together those elements exhibiting physical and distributional properties which suggest that they are, in fact, equivalent—simply alternative or successive manifestations of the same thing, perhaps slightly altered either spontaneously or under the influence of context. This mechanical bottom-up approach to the description of other aspects of behavior did not prove too fruitful. The interest in the subject matter has now been resumed using other methods mentioned below.

The second approach, studying the role of language as it functions in human information processing, began with a focus on the description of lexical structures in the area of kinship (Goodenough, Lounsbury) and expanded into studies of folk classification in areas such as color (Conklin), botany (Conklin, Frake), medicine (Frake), and types and kinds of a variety of things ranging from firewood (Metzger) to legal cases (Frake, Metzger and Black). (The papers of representative authors are collected in Tyler 1969.) This area, which may be called descriptive semantics, concerned itself with developing a tool kit of techniques to help an anthropologist develop a precise understanding of the lexical structures in an unfamiliar language.

In descriptive semantics in this sense, the basic elements selected for study are *lexemes*—all the particular terms, each having a single, unpredictable (from its morphology or syntax) meaning. From such a term one can learn native interrogation procedures to go "up," "down," or "sideways" in a classification system—An X is a kind of what? What kinds of X are there? Are there any kinds of X other than Y?—to elicit lexical structures systematically. These forms are then grouped into *semantic domains* or *lexical fields* representing groups of contrasting terms differing from each other in meaning, but defining each other in their contrasts—hot, cold; color terminology; mother, father, brother, sister, uncle, aunt, and so on. A domain could be defined either through collecting terms which partition the domain demarcated by some superordinate term, such as "color," or "relatives." Or it could be defined through its terms being closely substitutable in a distributional sense and forming therefore a lexical class, though one which might have no name in the language under consideration.

After eliciting the domains of interest in a language the next step in this method of analysis was to attempt to determine the features which lead a thing to be named in a given way. These features, understood to represent collectively the referential meaning of the term, were sometimes studied intensionally, as in *boy = young + male + human*, and sometimes extensionally, as in the mapping of color terminology across color chips varying in hue, saturation, and brightness. The aim of this type of study was to see which features are necessary and sufficient for a thing to be called an X. An underlying notion of this descriptive semantics work was that regularities in naming items might correspond to regularities in behaving toward items—things named the same might tend to elicit similar behaviors and beliefs. However, the question of the importance of these lexical labels in determining how respondents behave toward items and what they believe about them was not pursued. There was also no attempt to describe a natural language in any degree of completeness using these methods. Studies usually focused on small lexical domains of no more than several hundred terms.

A third type of diffusion from linguistics come in part from the concerns with "paralanguage" and communication through bodily movement, but it adopted a very different battery of methodological procedures. This field was called *sociolinguistics* and included the study of language or languages as they vary from individual to individual in a speech community and as they manifest themselves in communication networks and social interaction. For example, Labov's and Lambert's work on social dialect differences and their perceptual consequences may provide the social matrix for language change (see Gumperz and Hymes 1972) and the structure of social interaction processes. Studies by Moerman, Sachs, and Schegloff (see Sudnow 1972) on the structure of verbal routines such as conversation, storytelling, and telephone conversation include a variety of approaches to language as communication using methods from linguistics, as well as questionnaires, other conventional behavioral science tools, and new techniques developed specifically for the study of this new terrain.

Finally, the fourth and the most important event during the late 1950s and 60s which altered the relations of anthropology and linguistics and changed some conceptions of language and culture was the development of "generative-transformational" grammatical models by Noam Chomsky. Chomsky's work made a major point of the ability of the speakers of a language to discern, for strings of words they have never heard before, which ones are grammatical and their ability to interpret these previously unheard utterances. This ability, Chomsky argued, suggests that native speakers of a language possess a finite lexicon and a finite set of syntactic rules which allow them to generate an infinite number of sentences through repeated applications of these rules. This focus on the *productivity* of natural languages represented a major contribution to the development of linguistics, which had tended to limit itself to restating specific finite texts in an elegant manner rather than developing rules based on this corpus expandable to the infinite corpus generatable by the grammar.

Chomsky's approach reflected an interest in biologically conditioned language universals, and an interest in the development of a sophisticated notational system for the succinct description of the entire grammar of a language, and of human language in general. It also entailed a reliance on introspection as a source of data. Some implications of this aspect are considered below. Some of Chomsky's early students (Lees, Postal) concentrated on reformulating the traditional problems in linguistics, while others (Katz, Fodor) expanded his approach to consider semantics. Some later students (Ross, Lakoff, and McCawley) have worked on semantic structures as the propositional input to transformational grammar, that is, they suggest that there may be a basic set of propositions of belief and knowledge which underlie the syntactic structure of a language. Along with others, they have expanded Chomsky's original concern beyond grammaticalness and synonymity to the semantic and syntactic structures functioning in the processes of text and discourse production and of social interaction.

These new turns, bringing within the linguist's frame of reference phenomena which are of interest in anthropology in both descriptive semantics and social interaction and bringing a new set of goals for individual descriptions to the anthropologist, offer new areas of both substantive and methodological rapport between linguistics and anthropology.

## BACKGROUND TO THE RESEARCH PROJECT

A research area of language which presently offers a good possibility for interaction and collaboration between linguists and anthropologists is the lexicon. As I mentioned earlier, descriptive semantics deals with systems of knowledge and beliefs manifested in structures of related vocabulary items. In modern linguistics, on the other hand, the lexicon is viewed as a component of grammar with a place within an overall theory of language structure. The viewpoint from which the present project originates is that the two areas of interest (descriptive semantic studies of vocabulary and linguistic considerations of lexicon) now overlap, though the former has emphasized methods for describing particular vocabularies and the latter has derived such structures out of the implications of theory. Focusing on the lexicon of a single language, this project combined theoretical ideas from modern linguistics and field procedures reflecting the concerns of the anthropological area called ethnosemantics in an effort to add to our knowledge of Yucatec Maya, which was already well developed in linguistics.

With the lexicon as the area of interest, I designed a research project along two lines of thought. One was a plan for training speakers of a language who were not professional linguists to provide data upon which to base a description of lexical structures—the word classes of the language and their combinatorial contraints. The other was a utilization of such a description of the lexicon to gain insight into problems of meaning and syntax.

### The Theoretical Background

The generative-transformational theory of the structure of sentences formulated in Chomsky's *Aspects of the Theory of Syntax* (1964) contained rules that state the underlying or abstract hierarchial constituency of the sentence. At the highest level, sentences consist of a noun phrase plus a verb phrase. These constructional categories in turn consist of further labeled constituents. The ultimate or lowest level constituents in this hierarchy consist of grammatical categories such as "article" (for example, *the*) and lexical categories such as "noun" and "verb." Selectional restrictions between certain lexical categories are shown by marking them with classificatory features, either inherent or in terms of co-occurrence restrictions. For example, the grammar provides for *John eats bananas,* but not for *bananas eat John,* because the noun *bananas* is inherently specified for the feature of inanimateness, and the verb *eat* is specified to occur in a sentence with an animate noun functioning as the subject.

Following Chomskyan theories, the most important kinds of relations among lexical items are class membership in lexical classes (noun, verb, etc.) and in selectional classes that cross-cut lexical classes (animate, human, etc.) and the combinational constraints among these classes in syntactic constructions, especially sentences.

But lexical and selectional classes have functions other than making sentences grammatically well or ill-formed. They are of ethnographic interest because they are a major repository for most of what a speaker knows and believes about the world. While linguists may say the sentence *bananas eat John* is ill-formed because it violates the combinatorial constraints on selectional features of animateness, ethnographers may prefer to note that it violates English speakers' knowledge and beliefs concerning which objects engage in what activities (that is, "bananas" do not "eat" "people"). But either way, the data are the lexical classes and their combinability. Whatever is wrong with *bananas eat John, apples munch Mary,* and so forth, is wrong in the same way.

During the late 1960s various statements appeared in print suggesting the impossibility in principle for an investigator to formulate an adequate grammar of a language which he did not speak natively. This point of view arose in the following way. The primary goal of a grammar, or theory of the structure of a language, was to account for, or "explicate," the language "competence" of an idealized speaker-hearer. This competence included, among other things, the speaker's intuitions about which strings of words were sentences as opposed to nonsentences, his ability to produce and understand infinitely many sentences, and his ability to recognize ambiguous sentences and anomalous or nonsense sentences. This "ability" possessed by the speaker cannot be directly observed, however, because the only manifestations of the underlying linguistic competence are to be found in the behavioral data of "performance," which is multidimensional, having biological, physical, and social constraints as well. And because this ability cannot be directly observed, the linguist does not have direct access to it. Both the notion of the "acceptability" of a sentence to a native speaker of a language and the

more general concept of the "abilities" of a speaker have a central place
in the development of the research problem.

There are in societies general categories by which speakers intuitively judge sentences to be acceptable or unacceptable. For example,
in Yucatec (Stefflre et al. 1971) speakers judged utterances as fitting in
one of the following categories:

| | |
|---|---|
| *haȼuȼ u ʔàn* | sweet his talk |
| *ȼímin ʔàn* | horse talk |
| *hah u ʔàn* | true his talk |
| *ma hah u ʔàn* | not true his talk |

These judgments, while not in one-to-one correspondence with technical
linguistic terms, are roughly comparable to the ordinary English terms
"ungrammatical," "nonsense," "true," and "false," respectively. There was
strong consensus on the application of these judgments. These categories
became the empirical starting point of my research design.

The judgment of truth, or the informants' agreement with statements, is of particular interest in the aspect of language, particularly
lexical structures, as a coding system for knowledge and beliefs. Recall
that linguistic theory addresses itself in part to the notion that speakers
can judge the grammaticalness of sentences they have never heard
before. Speakers also know and agree upon whether they believe or dis-
believe novel statements or propositions. The notion of a set of rules for
combining lexical items so as to generate all and only statements speakers
would believe to be true is therefore a useful way of conceptualizing the
problem.

Having established that the intuitions of the native speaker must
be employed in the production of data and that the linguist has notions
of what constitutes relevant data, one might conclude, as many Chom-
skyans did, that adequate data could be provided only by a person
who was both a native speaker of the language being studied and a
linguist. For an outsider who learns a language to begin to approximate
the intuitions of a person who has spoken the language since early
childhood requires many years of exposure and practice. Therefore,
this research was undertaken partly to demonstrate that speakers could
be taught to do whatever it is that linguists do when they determine
the data relevant to some aspect of their language's structure.

The linguist as native speaker has intuitive control over what words
can occur in which positions and functions. Consider the two sentences
frequently cited in the generative-transformational literature:

John is easy to please.
John is eager to please.

The native speaker of English knows that in the first sentence *John* is not the one who does the *pleasing*, while in the second sentence he is. As a linguist, the speaker also knows that another possible filler for the *easy* slot—that is, a word that has a similar distribution—is one like *difficult*, while a word such as *anxious* behaves distributionally like *eager*, rather than like *easy*. In other words, his knowledge of the language is reinforced by his professional knowledge of the technical concept of distributional similarity.

All elements which can substitute for each other in the same or approximately the same range of environments, that is, which are distributionally similar, belong to the same class by definition. This is the standard, basic position of descriptive linguistics. The concept of distribution was undoubtedly overworked in the attempt to specify mechanical discovery procedures for determining distributional patterns in raw data consisting of samples of ordinary text. For example, suppose the two sentences above had occurred in the texts collected by a linguist who was not a native speaker of English, who had a three-month field trip as his only contact with English and English-speaking people. He would probably conclude that *easy* and *eager* belong to the same distributional class because they occur in the same environment. If, however, the linguist were a native speaker of English he would realize that this conclusion is incorrect, that the two words are not substitutable in terms of keeping the syntactic roles of the other words in the sentence constant. In other words, the native speaker knows that there are actually two distinct underlying environments; in one, *John* is the subject, and in the other, *John* is the object.

The interesting fact is that the distribution of an element in a language is a property of that element—however it might be discovered —and that part of the native speaker's language competence consists in his "knowledge" of distributional classes. For the native speaker-linguist, these classes are part of the subject matter of his introspection. For a large proportion of nonlinguist native speakers, they are understood intuitively rather than consciously.

My own research project was undertaken to obtain lexical classes in a language using the intuitions of native speakers. The field procedures were developed to teach the concept of distributional similarity to speakers so they could then objectify their intuitions about their lexicon. Because I had studied the structure of Yucatec and had spent some time in the field learning the language and collecting data in the usual manner of linguists, I decided to carry out my explorations of lexical structure in this setting.

## The Yucatec Language

Yucatec is one of the languages of the Mayan family. There are about 300,000 speakers of Yucatec, sometimes called Maya proper. At the present time, over twenty-five genetically related but mutually unintelligible Mayan languages are spoken in Central America from the Pacific Coast of Guatemala north to the Gulf and Caribbean coasts of the Yucatan peninsula, east to Honduras, and west through the Mexican state of Chiapas. For many aspects of language study the Mayan area offers conditions for success matched by few language families elsewhere in the world. There is a long scholarly tradition in Mayan linguistics, both historical and descriptive. Linguistic and archeological concerns overlap in the study of hieroglyphs preserved on bark codices and stone monuments.

Previous linguistic studies of Yucatec had attained a detailed and accurate description of Yucatec morphology, which involved an enumeration of the morphemes belonging to closed classes, the grammatical morphemes, and an account of their privileges of occurrence. To illustrate this type of linguistic description, I will briefly characterize the Yucatec "verb complex" as it was represented in the literature at the time I began my research.

Yucatec, unlike English, can string together many morphemes per word. There are two kinds of morphemes in Yucatec: roots and affixes. For the most part, the roots can occur in isolation, as separate words; they can be the center of complex words consisting of a root plus affixes; or they can be compounded either with or without affixes in addition. The phonological (sound) pattern of the roots is highly restricted. It must be consonant + vowel + consonant, which we symbolize CVC. For example:

| | |
|---|---|
| *bín* | go |
| *hàč* | strike |
| *ʔóš* | ramon tree |

(The accent marks over vowels indicate tonality and may be ignored for the sake of simplicity here, although they play an important part in morphology and syntax. The symbol ʔ indicates a "glottal catch," a type of consonant.)

The affixes, on the other hand, are always dependent—they can occur only as accompaniments to roots. Their phonological pattern is overwhelmingly vowel + consonant, even though a few frequent ones are simply one consonant. A word, particularly a verb, will frequently have in addition to the root or roots, several affixes. The morphemes of a word occur in strict order relative to each other; single such complex words may function as a complete sentence.

The ordering rules of Yucatec make it possible to "define" words with respect to the distribution of the closed-class morphemes which may occur in them. Consider, for example, the following word, which is also a sentence: *bisàbih*, "he was carried off." It consists of morphemes as follows:

*bin*, "go": This is the root. For phonological reasons the *n* drops out when followed by *s*.

*s*: This suffix has been called a "transitivizer" in previous accounts, although we will see this is not the best way to describe it. It changes an inherently intransitive root into a transitive stem. Thus *bin* + *s* = *bis* can be glossed as "take" or "carry." *Transitive*, in this context, means that the action or effect denoted by the verb passes to an object. In English the same relationship, intransitive versus transitive, is accomplished by selection between distinct lexical items: *go* versus *take*.

*àb*: This is a suffix which indicates a passive relationship between the verb and the subject.

*ih*: This is the suffix indicating third person, like *he*, *she*, or *it* in English.

The suffixes must occur in this order. For example, it is part of the description of the transitivizer suffix *s* that it occurs between the stem and certain other suffixes, of the person morphemes that they occur in the final position, and so on. This is the syntagmatic dimension of distribution mentioned earlier. Another important dimension of a morpheme's distribution is its class membership, its paradigmatic aspect, which involves the question, What are the other morphemes that could occur in a given position, without changing the syntactic nature of the construction? For example, if *s* were not occupying the transitivizer slot in the verb complex, what else could be there? It was known long before this study was undertaken that some transitive verbs have an *s* transitivizer, others have a *t* transitivizer, and still others have no overt marker, which may be indicated by supposing a $\emptyset$ or "zero" transitivizer. One may say that because $\emptyset$, *s*, and *t* are mutually substitutable in a transitive verb complex they belong to the same class. What is meant by saying that such classes of morphemes as these are *closed* in membership is that a speaker of Yucatec may not invent a new transitive suffix any more than a speaker of English may invent a new noun determiner beyond *the*, *a* (or *an*), or $\emptyset$ (as before a proper noun such as *John*).

In every language, however, some kinds of classes are open. There is the possibility of making up new forms to label new things, characteristics, events, or ideas. More often than not, labels for new meanings come from older labels in a new use, but sometimes wholly new labels are invented, always obeying the sound patterns of the language. The most productive way to obtain new terms for things is by combining old morphemes, sometimes retaining the old meaning of the morpheme intact, sometimes only partially, and sometimes most tenuously. The morphemes used in such new terms may be of either the lexical or grammatical type. Thus, for the name of a new event in connection with the space program we have *splashdown*, made up of lexical morphemes. In connection with a recent fad for running around in the nude we have *streaker*, made up of a lexical morpheme with only a part of its original meaning and a grammatical morpheme, *er*, indicating agent. The English word formation processes are varied and complex; sometimes they are said to be irregular. Nevertheless, a native speaker can generally recognize the difference between a "pre-fab" term and a construction made up with the syntactic resources of the language to fulfill current needs.

An outsider, however, even one armed with a morphological description of the language such as the one discussed above for Yucatec, may not be able to make this distinction. One of the tasks facing any investigator is to determine the units of study. In the case of Yucatec, it is clear from the start that the formal entities definable was "words" will not necessarily or even usually be prefabricated terms, any more than English clauses or sentences are. Therefore, one of the major issues in this project was to define the nature of the lexical items in Yucatec, particularly in relation to the CVC root morphemes. Another key problem was to explain the use of the *s*, *t*, and *Ø* transitivizers and the syntactic nature of transitivity. The solutions to these problems rested on making a new, more refined analysis on the basis of a better collection of more uniform empirical data.

## FIELD PROCEDURES

The field procedures consisted of three parts. The purpose of the first part was to obtain classes of lexical items on the basis of distributional similarity. The purpose of the second part was to determine which two-class sequences could form the lexical basis for short simple sentences. The purpose of the third was to obtain for each acceptable two-class sequence a list of morphologically different sentences that could be formed using that combination.

To teach the concept of distributional similarity, a computer-aided training procedure was used containing four steps. The informants were literate (rural grade school), but untrained in linguistics or academic ideas about language. They were able to write Yucatec in traditional popular orthography based on fifteenth century Spanish, but from the onset they were taught the phonemic transcription used by the researcher.

The informants were asked to build a list of sentences (50 or so) that would be *hah u t'àn* ("true talk") using a selected word. This word was then deleted from these sentences, and the informants were asked to replace it with any other word of their own choosing which could go in the same slot such that the new sentence would still be "true talk." These words and frames were then written out in a matrix form, with the sentence frames as the row-labels and the list of substituted words as the column-labels. The informants' next task was to judge whether each row-column intersection was acceptable. For computational purposes, acceptable intersections were scored with a "1." Unacceptable intersections, indicating the word would not be used in that position to make a true sentence, were scored with a "0."

Figure 8.1 shows a portion of a matrix of this type built around the word *ʔoʔolkih* and the informants' judgment as to whether they agree with the combinations formed by the row-column intersection. Word 1, *totohkih*, is judged as acceptable in forming propositions this respondent agrees with in frames 1, 2, 3, 4, and so on, marked in the matrix with a "1," a total of 37 of the 50 frames. *Hač tah čič* is acceptable in 1 and 2 but not in 3 or 4. It is acceptable in 7 of the 50 frames. We can calculate the similarity distribution of each pair of words by counting the total number of matches in their acceptabilities over the total number of possible matches. For example *totohkih* (1) and *hač tah čič* (2) are acceptable in seven of the same frames: 1, 21, 9, 12, 13, 15, 30, and given their frequencies of appearance this gives them a similarity number of .31:

$$\frac{7 + 7}{37 + 7} = \frac{14}{44} = .31.$$

This same type of calculation can also be made for each pair of frames as well as each pair of words. And the computer can then rearrange the matrix putting the rows similar to each other near each other and the columns similar to each other near each other, so that clumps—the intersection of sets of words having similar distributions and sets of frames allowing similar words—can be easily seen in the matrix. (These procedures are described more fully in Stefflre et al. 1971, and McClaran 1973.)

1   Le ʔu k̆aš le š̆ǘupaloʔ ʔoʔolkih
2   ʔu yol le šáʔanoʔ ʔoʔolkih.
3   ʔu leʔ le háasoʔ, ʔoʔolkih.
4   hač ʔoʔolkih le kato.
5   Le nokoh hač tah ʔoʔolkih.
6   Le táʔanoh hač tah ʔoʔolkih.
7   hač tah ʔoʔlkih le šamboʔ.
8   Le waho? hač tah ʔoʔolkih.
9   ʔu kuʔumih Leškašoʔ ʔoʔolkih.
10  ʔu yok Le čambaloʔ hač tah ʔoʔolkih.
11  ʔu ɫoʔoɫih Le ɸimno hač tah ʔoʔolkih.
12  ʔoʔolkih ʔu leʔ Le šáʔanoʔ.
13  ʔoʔolkih Le hifoʔ ku hifik Le páaloʔ.
14  hač tah ʔoʔolkih Le bakoʔ.
15  Le ʔu ʔič Le ʔomoʔ ʔoʔolkih.
16  ʔu k̆anhoʔol Le čambalo hač tah ʔoʔolkih
17  hač tah ʔoʔolkih tuʔuʔ ku kutale máako?
18  Le Lukoʔ ʔoʔolkih tiolah Le haʔo.
19  Le piɫoʔ hač tah ʔoʔolkih ʔu LoL.
20  Le pako? hač tah ʔoʔolkih tumen tumben.
21  Le ɫak Lukoʔ hač tah ʔoʔolkih.
22  Le misiboʔ hač tah ʔoʔlkih ʔu míis.
23  hač tah ʔoʔolkih Le keweloʔ.
24  Le hučoʔ hač tah ʔoʔolkih tumen tumben.
25  hač tah ʔoʔlkih Le huunoʔ tumen haíʔ.
26  ʔu ʔič Le ɸarmuyoʔ hač tah ʔoʔolkih tumen tak̆an.
27  ʔu kuɫih Le čamaloʔ hač tah ʔoʔolkih.
28  ʔu neh Le peko hač tah ʔoʔolkih.
29  hač tah ʔoʔolkih u ɸoʔoɫih Le ʔu poL Le š̆ǘupaloʔ.
30  ʔoʔolkih ʔu tah u yik̆aL Le haʔ.
31  ʔoʔolkih ʔu haɸ Le ʔik̆oʔ tumen ma noholi.
32  Le pako hač tah ʔoʔolkih tumen tak̆an.
33  ʔu bak̆iʔ Le k̆eenoʔ hač tah ʔoʔolkih.
34  hač tah ʔoʔolkih ʔu suʔukih Le nahoʔ.
35  Le kibo hač tah ʔoʔolkih tumen ɫabaʔan.
36  hač tah ʔoʔolkih ʔu soskilih Le kihoʔ.
37  Le yašk̆ačo hač tah ʔoʔolkih ʔu winklih.
38  ʔu yom Le haʔ hač tah ʔoʔolkih tumen čul.
39  ʔu nek Le ʔošoʔ hač tah ʔoʔolkih tumen tak̆an.
40  ʔu tas ʔit Le čambalo hač tah ʔoʔolkih.
41  Le čoʔ hač tah ʔoʔolkih ʔu yok tumen mun.
42  Le putoʔ hač tah ʔoʔolkih ʔu ʔič tumen k̆an.
43  Le k̆ayomíto hač ʔoʔolkih ʔu ʔič.
44  ʔu bašah Le paloʔ hač tah ʔoʔolkih.
45  Le bola ʔu hač tah ʔoʔolkih tumen Le ʔuleh.
46  hač tah ʔoʔolkih Le sumoʔ tumen ʔučben.
47  hač tah ʔoʔolkih u ɸib Le Lapisoʔ.
48  ʔu ʔič Le pak̆aLaʔ haš tah ʔoʔolkih.
49  ʔu bač Le k̆oʔoLoLo hač tah ʔoʔolkih.
50  Le čak̆bih he u hač tah ʔoʔolkih.

**Figure 8.1**   *Input matrix with row and column tables.*

| ROW/COL | totohki·h | hač tah čič | tah ya²a·š | tah čič | šak | čokoh | nohoč | si·is | mehentak | mehentak | čič | tah ya²aš | kokočki·h | sisičkih | ma²ah kani·? | čičan | ka²anah | puuk²an | šak | čul | tam | ma²u petal | tooč kiibok | hat kalak | čuhuk | kiibok | tah | tooč | se·e? | si·is |
|---|1|2|3|4|5|6|7|8|9|10|11|12|13|14|15|16|17|18|19|20|21|22|23|24|25|26|27|28|29|30|31|
| 1 | 1|1|0|1|1|1|1|1|1|1|1|0|0|1|0|1|0|0|1|1|0|0|1|1|0|0|1|1|1|0|1 |
| 2 | 1|1|1|1|1|1|1|1|1|1|1|1|1|0|0|1|1|0|1|1|0|1|1|0|1|0|0|1|1|0|1 |
| 3 | 1|0|1|0|1|1|1|1|1|1|0|1|1|0|0|1|1|0|1|1|0|1|1|1|1|1|0|1|1|0|1 |
| 4 | 1|0|1|1|1|1|1|1|1|1|1|1|1|1|0|0|1|1|1|1|1|1|1|1|1|1|1|1|1|0|1 |
| 5 | 1|0|0|0|1|1|1|1|1|1|1|0|1|0|0|1|1|1|1|1|0|1|1|1|1|0|1|1|1|0|1 |
| 6 | 1|0|0|0|1|1|1|1|1|1|1|0|1|0|0|1|1|1|1|1|1|1|1|1|1|0|1|1|1|0|1 |
| 7 | 1|0|0|0|1|1|1|1|1|1|1|0|1|0|0|1|1|0|1|1|1|1|1|1|1|0|1|1|1|0|1 |
| 8 | 1|0|0|0|1|1|1|1|1|1|1|0|1|0|0|1|1|1|1|1|0|1|1|1|1|1|1|1|1|0|1 |
| 9 | 1|1|1|1|1|1|1|1|1|1|1|1|1|0|0|1|1|0|1|1|0|1|1|1|1|0|1|1|1|0|1 |
| 10 | 1|0|0|0|1|1|1|1|1|1|0|0|1|1|1|0|0|1|1|0|0|1|1|0|0|1|1|0|1|1|1 |
| 11 | 1|0|0|0|1|1|1|1|1|1|1|0|1|0|0|1|1|0|1|1|0|1|1|0|0|0|0|1|1|0|1 |
| 12 | 1|1|1|1|1|1|1|1|1|1|1|1|0|1|1|0|1|1|0|1|1|1|1|1|0|1|0|0|1|0|1 |
| 13 | 1|1|1|1|1|1|1|1|1|1|1|1|0|0|1|1|0|1|1|0|1|0|0|1|0|0|1|1|1|1|1 |
| 14 | 1|0|0|0|1|1|1|1|1|1|1|0|1|1|0|1|1|1|1|0|1|1|0|1|1|1|1|0|1|0|1 |
| 15 | 1|1|1|1|1|1|1|1|1|1|1|1|0|0|1|1|1|1|1|0|1|0|1|0|1|0|1|1|1|0|1 |
| 16 | 1|0|0|0|1|1|1|1|1|1|1|0|1|0|0|1|1|0|1|1|0|1|1|0|1|1|1|1|0|1|1 |
| 17 | 1|0|0|0|1|1|1|1|1|1|1|0|1|0|0|1|1|0|1|1|1|1|1|1|1|1|0|1|1|0|1 |
| 18 | 0|0|1|0|1|0|1|1|1|1|0|1|1|0|0|1|1|1|1|1|1|1|1|0|0|1|1|1|0|1 |
| 19 | 0|0|0|0|1|1|1|1|1|1|0|1|0|1|1|1|0|1|1|0|1|1|1|1|1|0|1|0|1 |
| 20 | 1|0|0|0|1|1|1|1|1|1|1|0|1|0|0|1|1|1|1|1|0|1|1|1|1|0|1|1|1|0|1 |
| 21 | 1|0|0|0|1|1|1|1|1|1|1|0|1|0|0|1|1|1|1|1|1|1|1|1|0|0|1|1|0|1|1 |
| 22 | 1|0|0|0|1|0|1|1|1|1|1|0|1|0|0|1|1|1|1|1|0|1|1|0|0|0|1|1|1|1|1 |
| 23 | 1|0|0|0|1|1|1|1|1|1|0|1|1|0|1|1|0|1|1|0|1|1|1|1|0|1|1|1|0|1 |
| 24 | 0|0|0|0|1|1|1|1|0|0|0|0|1|0|0|0|0|1|1|1|0|0|0|1|0|1|1|0|0|0|1 |
| 25 | 1|0|0|0|1|0|1|0|1|1|0|0|1|0|0|1|0|1|1|1|0|1|0|0|1|0|0|1|0|0|0 |
| 26 | 0|0|0|0|1|0|1|1|1|1|0|1|0|0|1|1|1|1|1|0|1|0|1|1|1|1|0|0|0|0 |
| 27 | 1|0|0|0|1|1|1|1|1|1|0|1|0|1|1|0|0|1|0|1|1|1|1|1|1|1|1|0|1 |
| 28 | 1|0|0|0|1|1|1|1|0|0|1|0|1|1|0|1|1|0|1|1|0|1|1|0|0|0|1|1|0|1 |
| 29 | 1|0|0|0|1|1|1|1|1|1|1|0|1|0|0|1|1|0|1|1|1|0|0|1|1|1|0|1 |
| 30 | 1|1|0|1|0|1|1|0|0|1|0|0|0|0|0|0|1|0|0|0|0|0|1|0|0|0|0|1|1|1|1 |
| 31 | 1|0|0|0|0|1|0|0|0|0|0|0|0|0|1|0|0|0|0|0|0|0|0|1|0|1|0 |
| 32 | 0|0|0|0|1|1|1|1|1|0|0|1|0|0|1|0|1|1|1|0|1|0|1|1|1|1|0|0|0|1 |
| 33 | 1|0|0|0|1|1|1|1|1|1|1|0|1|1|0|1|0|0|1|1|0|1|1|1|1|0|1|1|0|1|0|1 |
| 34 | 1|0|0|0|1|1|1|1|1|1|1|0|1|0|0|1|1|0|1|1|0|1|1|0|1|0|0|1|1|0|1 |
| 35 | 1|0|0|0|1|1|0|1|1|0|1|0|0|0|1|0|1|1|1|0|0|0|0|0|0|0|0|0 |
| 36 | 1|0|0|0|1|1|1|1|1|1|0|1|0|0|1|1|0|1|1|0|1|1|0|0|0|0|1|1|0|1 |
| 37 | 1|0|0|0|0|1|0|1|1|1|0|0|1|0|0|1|0|0|0|1|0|1|0|0|1|0|0|0|0|0|1 |
| 38 | 0|0|0|0|1|0|1|1|0|0|0|0|1|0|0|0|1|1|1|0|1|1|0|0|0|0|0|0|0|0|1 |
| 39 | 0|0|0|0|1|1|1|1|1|1|0|1|0|0|1|1|0|1|1|0|1|0|1|0|1|1|0|0|0 |
| 40 | 1|0|0|0|1|1|1|1|1|1|1|0|1|0|0|1|1|0|1|1|0|1|1|1|1|0|1|1|1|0|1 |
| 41 | 1|0|0|0|1|1|1|1|1|0|0|0|1|1|1|0|0|1|1|0|0|0|1|1|0|1|0|0|0|1 |
| 42 | 0|0|0|0|0|0|1|0|0|0|0|0|1|0|0|1|1|1|0|0|0|0|0|1|0|1|1|0|0|0|0 |
| 43 | 0|0|1|1|1|1|1|1|1|1|1|1|0|0|1|1|1|1|1|1|0|1|1|1|1|0|1|1|0|1|0|1 |
| 44 | 1|0|0|0|1|1|1|1|1|1|0|1|0|1|0|0|1|1|0|1|1|0|1|1|1|1|0|1|1|1|1|1 |
| 45 | 0|0|0|0|1|1|0|1|0|0|0|0|0|1|0|0|0|0|1|0|0|1|0|0|0|0|0|1 |
| 46 | 0|0|0|0|1|0|0|1|1|1|0|0|1|0|0|1|0|0|1|1|0|1|0|0|1|0|0|0|0|0|1 |
| 47 | 1|0|0|0|1|0|0|0|1|1|1|0|1|0|0|1|1|1|1|1|0|1|0|0|0|0|0|1|0|1|0 |
| 48 | 0|0|0|0|1|1|1|1|1|1|1|0|0|0|1|1|1|1|1|1|0|1|0|1|0|1|1|0|0|0|1 |
| 49 | 1|0|0|0|1|1|1|1|1|1|0|1|0|1|0|0|1|1|1|1|1|0|1|0|1|0|1|0|1|0|1 |
| 50 | 0|0|0|0|1|1|1|1|1|1|0|1|0|0|1|0|1|1|1|0|1|0|1|0|1|1|0|0|0|1 |
| TOTAL | 37|7|9|9|46|43|45|45|43|43|35|9|39|8|8|45|37|22|46|45|8|42|33|33|25|16|33|33|34|6|45 |

The second stage of this part of the procedure consisted of giving the informants cards containing *pairs* of words culled from the data at that point and having them rate and then rank these in terms of the amount of distributional similarity they would expect the words to exhibit in different types of matrix—that is, based on judgments of agreement, of meaningfulness, or of syntactic acceptability. These rankings could then be checked against the actual matrices containing the pair of words but built and judged by other untrained (in this aspect) informants. The informants were soon able to make very accurate estimates. Then our three principal informant-assistants were given the task of producing cards containing lexical elements and sorting these cards into piles which would distribute alike. These sorts were also spot-checked against matrices built to insure quality control in this sorting process. About 2,000 words in citation forms were sorted into 38 major classes and 422 subclasses. The classes were then put in a linear array numbered (for clerical convenience) 1.1 to 38.422.

The respondents were then asked to tell us which pairs of major classes could combine in which orders to provide us with two-class sequences that could form the basis for simple acceptable utterances. Only major classes were used because the 1444 (38 × 38) possible judgments seemed to be more feasible to describe completely than the approximately 180,000 (422 × 422) judgments if the finer-grained classes were used. Sequences longer than two words were also not used because the number of judgments required would be unworkable.

At this level—38 classes—the rules are somewhat gross and there are many exceptions, usually consisting not of individual lexemes but of entire small classes. These systematic exceptions, which we later listed exhaustively for each rule, were useful sources of hints about the semantic characteristics of the lexical classes which underlie the combinatorial structure. The 224 acceptable major class combinations out of the logically possible 1444 provided us with a data base for a description of the types of short simple sentences in Yucatec Maya.

Informants were also asked to illustrate each acceptable combination of classes with a "typical sentence" using a word from each class and they were further asked for each of these acceptable combinations to list sample sentences which followed through all of the morphosyntactic variants that could be elicited in a reasonable amount of time.

Within the 38 major classes the range of meaning is sometimes great, and the unity comes primarily from common "function" in a linguistic sense. For example, class 2. has "to open" (2.32), "to put to flight" (2.39), and "to strengthen" (2.50). The following is an example of each major class which I have selected more or less arbitrarily, but in an attempt to show a "typical" member of that class.

| | | | | |
|---|---|---|---|---|
| 1. *ȼòn* | shoot | 20. *máskab* | machete |
| 2. *kól* | pull | 21. *lùm* | earth |
| 3. *làṗ* | grab | 22. *sòy* | chicken coop |
| 4. *kàš* | tie up | 23. *sùm* | rope |
| 5. *càn* | watch | 24. *kòl* | milpa |
| 6. *tún* | taste | 25. *hán* | quickly |
| 7. *hòk* | jerk out | 26. *ʔokol* | weep |
| 8. *tiȼhaʔ* | sprinkle | 27. *ćóp* | blind person |
| 9. *mék* | embrace | 28. *bàl* | brother-in-law |
| 10. *sak* | white | 29. *mènšanab* | shoemaker |
| 11. *koʔlamak* | stony | 30. *kéken* | pig |
| 12. *takan* | ripe | 31. *ʔam* | spider |
| 13. *ʔišim* | corn | 32. *ćòm* | buzzard |
| 14. *ʔabal* | plum | 33. *sòȼ* | bat |
| 15. *ʔoš* | ramon tree | 34. *ʔaluš* | dwarf (a spirit) |
| 16. *leʔ* | leaf | 35. *ȼuʔ* | in the center |
| 17. *mayak* | table | 36. *sámal* | tomorrow |
| 18. *šéṫ* | a slice | 37. *kabašbùl* | bean soup |
| 19. *ṗúl* | jar | 38. *tùkul* | idea |

Within the 422 subclasses the semantic cohesiveness among the members is striking. For example, the members of class 2.38 are all the ways of carrying an object, differing by the body part and posture involved:

| | |
|---|---|
| *mék* | carry in the arms |
| *páhkal* | carry on the shoulders |
| *kóc* | carry on the head |
| *hénkal* | carry suspended from the shoulders |
| *kùc* | carry on the back |

The variants produced to illustrate each combinatorial rule showed few syntactic discontinuities within a single rule; that is, the functional relations between the two major lexical items in the sentence remained the same, and the variation consisted mainly in paradigmatic phenomena such as tense, person, and mode. For example, to illustrate the combination 1. × 28., the informant showed the following variants (among others) on *kins* "kill" (class 1.) and *bàl* "brother-in-law" (class 28.):

| | |
|---|---|
| *kìnsàbi ʔin bàl* | they killed my brother-in-law |
| *maʔ kìnsàb in bàliʔ* | they didn't kill my brother-in-law |
| *kìnsèš in bàl* | kill my brother-in-law |
| *kìnsàb wa ʔin bàl* | did they kill my brother-in-law? |
| *kìnsàb bìn u bàl* | his brother-in-law was allegedly killed |

The entire project is described in much more detail in McClaran (1973).

## ANALYSIS

The data produced by these procedures present evidence relevant to the two problems already raised: (1) the nature of lexical items in Yucatec, especially in relation to the CVC root morphemes, on the one hand, and "words" as morphologically defined on the other, and (2) the "explanation" of the *s, t,* and ∅ transitivizers and the syntactic nature of transitivity.

What is a lexical item in Yucatec? It is safe to assume that any utterance capable of being sufficiently abstracted from its context by speakers to be treated as a unitary item in a sorting task has some kind of psychological reality for the speakers. In the field procedure, the assistants believed that they were sorting "words." However, when they stated the permissible two-class combinations which they intended to underlie simple sentences and gave specific examples of sentences to illustrate these combinations, it was evident that a certain margin of morphological freedom (mostly variations in inflections marking distinctions of person, number, and the like) lay around each "word" within which they considered it to be the "same" word. Furthermore, the fact of having given one form, the citation form, as opposed to another within this range is significant. Forty percent of the citation forms sorted by the informants were CVC roots. Sixty percent were more complex forms. All the distributional classes sorted by the informants contained at least one CVC root. In this sense, each class could be represented by a CVC root. It was by no means evident at the start of the project that the semantic classes represented by the CVC roots were as semantically productive as this suggests. This is related to a second finding that is in many respects the most important result of the study in the context of Mayan linguistics.

This result amounted to a reconceptualization of the so-called "transitivizers," the closed class of morphemes *t, s,* and ∅, in the language. It was already known that each of these morphemes marked a single class of roots and that the roots that occurred with one did not occur with the others. It was also known that these classes correlated with other morphological characteristics, such as tone patterns and other suffixes. On the basis of this study, these disparate facts of morphology could be explained by underlying syntactic regularities. In other words, it was found that these classes are not merely arbitrary morphological groupings but that they have important differences in meaning. These differences are reflected in syntax, in the way each of the different classes is used in relation to other classes, especially nouns, in the formation of Yucatec sentences. These differences in meaning were also directly involved in the productivity of the classes, which means the ability of complex forms to take the place of morphologically simpler members of the class. In other words, a new complex verbal form might be invented. The syntactic role it would be given in the language—the way it would be combined with other elements in sentences—would depend on the class of established verbal roots, as marked by the "transitivizers," that it corresponded to in meaning.

The significant characteristics of meaning of these three verb classes involve the *number* of nouns (one or two), speaking in terms of syntax, or of "things" conceptually required by the verb, speaking in terms of meaningful entities named in the culture, and the *nature of the relationship* between the noun(s) and the verb. These classes can be indicated by the following diagram:

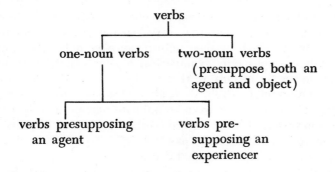

These indicate the basic relationships to noun(s) that are presupposed by the verbs of each class in their bare root form. Two-noun verbs, in bare root use, presuppose an *agent*—the "doer" of the action—and an *object* which receives the action. There are two kinds of one-noun verbs in bare root use, but they differ in that one presupposes that the noun is the *experiencer* of the state or event denoted by the verb, and the other presupposes that the noun represents the agent of the action named by the verb (which, however, in this case has no presupposed object).

These root forms can be used in constructing sentences which have noun configurations different from those conceptually required by the roots alone. There can be one- and two-noun sentences, in this sense. This is how the notion of "transitivizer" suffixes first arose. When an experiencer root is used in an experiencer sentence, no class marker is employed; similarly for the two other classes of verbs when they are used in parallel sentences. But if a one-noun verb root occurs in a two-noun sentence, it will require an *s* if it is an experiencer verb, or a *t* if it is an agent verb. The addition of the *s* to the experiencer verb marks the addition of a noun (expressed or understood) to the sentence which functions as agent; the basic relationship of the verb root to its experiencer is not thereby altered. The addition of the *t* to an agent verb marks the addition to the sentence of a noun which therein functions as the object, and does not change the underlying agent plus verb relationship. Thus the *s*, *t*, and $\emptyset$ markers preserve the underlying verb-noun(s) relationships in sentences which might be ambiguous on the basis of the surface verb-noun relationships alone. Other accomodations of roots to sentences are also possible, which need not be discussed here.

In the data, about one-fourth of the 38 classes of the word list are verbs in the linguistic sense. Of these, the inherently "transitive" classes of verbs (those that take $\emptyset$ marker in the two-noun use) have a narrowly constrained relationship to their object (viewed as either noun or "thing"). For example, the choice of the verb form from the class for slicing and cutting depends on the characteristics of the thing being sliced or cut, specified within a very narrow range. Conversely, the objects are things which by their nature can have only certain acts done to them. For example, only symmetrical objects can take certain verbs which denote an act of cutting that renders an object into equal parts. The other important generalization about the "transitive" verbs is that they name acts which must have an animate agency, mostly human.

The contrasting *t* transitivized verbs are names of activities, as "write," "jump," "pull weeds," "pay," "laugh," "rub," "scratch," "point," "care for," and "whistle," which have an animate instigator or willful agent, but they have no special effect on a particular object. In previous treatments of the language these verbs were classified as basically "intransitive," but it should now be clear why this was not an adequate description. The exact interpretation that follows from two classes is that these are one-noun verbs in which the relationship between the entity named by the noun and the act named by the verb is one of agency. In short, these name acts performed by an agent, like the $\emptyset$ verbs, but unlike them they have no special links to an object.

The third syntactically and semantically significant class, the *s* verbs, has members such as "go," "run away," "descend," "come," "pass by," "tire," various words denoting caresses, the posturative (body position) verbs, sleep, rest, awaken, and so forth. These are names of events or states which people and some animals can be said to experience and can also be caused to experience. The one noun which these verbs require is not a willful instigator but merely the experiencer of the state. When used in a two-noun sentence, the second noun therefore functions as agent. (The term "experiencer" is due to Charles Fillmore, who has explored a syntactic theory in which such "case" relationships between verbs and their nouns play a central role.)

By using native speakers' intuitions about lexical items this study was able to produce structured data in relation to both syntax and ethnographic semantics. The three classes of verbs that these data enabled us to delineate and explain are crucial to the syntax of the language, all major aspects of sentence contruction. As indicated in the preceeding discussion, several classes of nouns are directly involved with the verbal classes—animate objects, things capable of being acted upon, and so forth. What applies to the understanding of the verbs they associate with naturally also bears upon them as well.

In addition, however, the data also contained material relevant to classes of nouns that have functions in sentences other than that of acting as agents, experiencers, and objects. Examples are nouns designating units of time or place. But aside from the basic determination that these do not act as agents, experiencers, or objects, these have not yet been analyzed.

A further problem in the linguistic tradition at the time this study was undertaken consisted in the analysis of the relationship between nouns that were not linked, or mediated, by verbs. An analogy in English would be the construction "John's dog." In Yucatec, they were called "relational nouns." It had been known that there were relational suffixes linking such nouns. What was found was that the rules describing the operation of these suffixes could be related to the same general kinds of semantic considerations as the rules for the use of the verbal markers described above. This is an example of another area of linguistic analysis within this language elucidated as an indirect result of the verbal analysis and as a direct result of the data collection techniques.

While the full importance of the present data collection techniques as well as the analytical insights they provide are yet to be worked out in Mayan linguistics, the techniques have clear immediate relevance in other, more general, theoretical areas. It should be evident that these techniques enable us to deal with nuances of meaning that could not otherwise be available to nonnative speakers. It is therefore, at the very least, clearly more economical to teach native speakers to order data in a linguistically relevant way than for a linguist to try to approximate the intuitions of a native speaker. The informants' work, as described, was accomplished in six months. Learning to speak a language well enough to provide the same nuances with assurance would take many years, if it would be possible at all.

The relevance of these procedures to ethnographic semantics lies precisely in the fact that these nuances are nuances of meaning, as well as linguistic function. However, in this aspect the semantic features identified for the classes described in this analysis should be regarded as tentative. The features could be checked for cognitive reality by inventing new forms and their meanings, by predicting classes they would be placed in by native speakers on the basis of the present analysis, and finally by asking native informants to use them and classify them as a means of verifying or rejecting the prediction.

Hymes (1970) has suggested that repeatedly in the history of the linguistic method in anthropology there have been cycles in which the study of language and culture are mixed, then separated, then mixed again using new techniques, new models, and new goals. The late 1960s and early 1970s represented one such period of drawing apart while the linguists reviewed and reworked their own problems and techniques and anthropologists studied, among other things, language use in a wide variety of contexts. The mid-seventies may represent the beginnings of a new integration.

## SELECTED READINGS

Arlotto, Anthony, 1972, *An Introduction to Historical Linguistics*. New York: Houghton-Mifflin.

A good text for languages in their historical perspective.

Bolinger, Dwight, 1968, *Aspects of Language*. New York: Harcourt, Brace, and World.

This text is useful because many of its examples begin with observations an untrained observer might make.

Bright, William, 1968, "Language and Culture." International Encyclopedia of the Social Sciences, vol. 9. New York: Macmillan and The Free Press.

A concise introduction to language and culture, especially as a field of academic specialization.

Burling, Robbins, 1970, *Man's Many Voices, Language in its Cultural Context*. New York: Holt, Rinehart, and Winston.

The major textbook on language and culture.

Gleason, H. A., 1961, *Descriptive Linguistics*. New York: Holt, Rinehart, and Winston.

One of the best introductory texts in linguistics in terms of the how-to-do-it approach.

Gumperz, John, and Hymes, Dell, eds., 1972, *Directions in Sociolinguistics*. New York: Holt, Rinehart, and Winston.

This book's introductory materials and papers give a balanced overview of sociolinguistics.

Hymes, Dell, ed., 1964, *Language in Culture and Society: A Reader in Linguistics and Anthropology*. New York: Harper and Row.

Langacker, Ronald, 1968, *Language and Its Structure*. Harcourt, Brace, Jovanovich.

A text which takes into account the goals of modern linguistic theory.

McQuown, Norman, ed., 1967, *Linguistics*. Handbook of Middle American Indians, vol. 5. Austin, Texas: The University of Texas Press.

A good introduction to the study of the languages of Meso-America.

Spradley, James, and McCurdy, David, 1972, *The Cultural Experience, Ethnography in Complex Society*. Chicago: Science Research Associates.

Covers the basic hows and whys of ethnographic semantics, focusing on language.

Sudnow, David, ed., 1972, *Studies in Social Interaction*. New York: The Free Press.

One of the few collections of studies of language in social interaction.

Tyler, Stephen, ed., 1969, *Cognitive Anthropology*. New York: Holt, Rinehart, and Winston.

A collection of the classic papers in "ethnoscience" and related matters.

# Physical
# Anthropology

# Chapter 9

# An Experiment on
# the Physical Anthropology
# of Expressive Gestures

### J. H. Prost

Physical anthropology is a biological science, even though academically, for historical reasons, it is lodged among the social sciences. As a biological science, its subject matter is the morphology and physiology of humans, in all their varieties and times of life.

Morphology is the study of form, or structure. The descriptive units of morphology are organized along a spatial, or size, continuum from smaller to larger: atoms, molecules, macromolecules, organelles, cells, tissues, organs, organ systems, multicellular organisms, families, populations, subspecies, species, genera; and so forth. A prevalent research design in morphology is to explain phenomena at one size level in terms of the properties of units at a lower, or smaller, level. For example, the differences between the shapes of two muscles might be explained as the product of two different arrangements of their component fibers, or muscle cells.

Physiology is the study of change in structure. The descriptive units of physiology lie within a two-dimensional continuum, a continuum that is both spatial and temporal. The continuum includes short-term events, like a muscle twitch or nerve cell membrane depolarization, which take fractions of a second, or long term events, like the healing of bone fractures, the spread of cancerous growth, or the fixation of a favorable mutation in a population, which take weeks, months, centuries, or longer. A common research design in physiology is to explain changes at one time level as the cumulative consequence of many shorter events. For example, the contraction of a muscle might be explained as the aggregate contractile activity of its numerous motor units, that is, fibers and nerves (Handler 1970).

261

How does physical anthropology differ from other biological disciplines that study man, such as medicine? Medicine deals with the etiology, or causes, and cures of disease. The medical sciences collect data to explain disease, and they use their data to test one or another theory of disease. The theories organize the data, generate explanations, and direct research by identifying important problems.

Physical anthropology studies the nature and origin of humanity and human variability. In physical anthropology the focal theory is biological evolution. Evolutionary theory serves the same roles that the theories of disease serve in the medical sciences; that is, it organizes the data, generates explanations, and directs research.

Before the middle of the 1800s physical anthropology did not exist as a formalized and separate science. Medicine and zoology were flourishing; the former emphasized the abnormal, or pathological, side of man while the latter, being unable to rationalize the complexity of man's social and cultural adaptations, tended to dichotomize the animal kingdom into "other" animals and "the human" animal, giving man his own enigmatic niche. Explorers, zoologists, and adventurous doctors collected descriptions of superficial body and skeletal traits on a variety of peoples but intermixed these with stories of exotic habits, body mutilations, and imaginary beasts. There were almost no human or subhuman fossils, and it was held that the human condition was the result of special creation, a postulate that, of itself, gave no impetus to the collection of contradictory fossil evidence. Zoologists dissected monkey and ape specimens, noting many humanlike appearances, but they could not speculate productively on the causes of these resemblances. At that time these scattered bits of information seemed unrelated and of little consequence, compiled and classified for their esoteric worth (Eiseley 1961).

In 1858, Charles Darwin and Alfred R. Wallace presented their formulation of the theory of biological evolution before the Linnean Society of London. One year later Darwin elaborated his arguments in his book *On the Origin of Species by Means of Natural Selection*. The presentation before the Linnean Society so captured people's interest that by the end of the first day of publication 1,250 copies of Darwin's book were sold. The theoretical underpinnings of evolutionary biology, and physical anthropology, had appeared (Bell 1959; Dillon 1973).

Darwin's contention was that organisms change through time by the gradual accumulation of small, inheritable modifications; that organisms which exist in the present are the end products of change from the past; and that inheritable modifications are produced and controlled by rational and natural forces, forces which function in the present as they functioned in the past. Today, the forces which produce change are understood to be selection, hybridization, mutation, and genetic drift. Darwin described and documented selection and hybridization, although he could not thoroughly explain their underlying genetic mechanisms. The geneticists of the 1900s, building on the work of Gregor Mendel, described and documented mutation and drift and elaborated the mechanisms of selection and hybridization. From this genetic research we now know that mutations, or changes in genetic material (that is, macromolecules of deoxyribonucleic acid), are the inheritable modifications; selection increases the frequency of those modifications which adapt organisms to their unique life styles and environments; drift operates randomly to increase or decrease the frequency of modifications; and hybridization spreads genetic material among interbreeding populations. It was Darwin's formulation that gave the impetus to research in genetics—familial, populational, and biochemical—which led to current knowledge of the processes of speciation and the nature of subspecies variability (Mayr 1963).

At the time Darwin wrote the *Origin* there were practically no subhuman fossils known. Darwin, therefore, used nonhuman fossils to explicate his theory by showing that such fossils represented the ancestral strains from which the living varieties descended. The implication was clear—mankind itself ought to have originated in the same way—but he did not have fossil evidence to support this case, so he all but ignored the logical conclusion. Paleontologists began a protracted search for man's ancestors soon thereafter, a pursuit that became known as "the search for the missing link." The search was rewarded by success. The first discoveries, in the late 1800s, were of a form called Neanderthal man, which we now consider to be a close and recent relative of modern man. This was followed soon after by the discovery of *Pithecanthropus erectus*, now called *Homo erectus*, representing a group ancestral to the Neanderthals. A form more ancient than *Homo erectus*, the Australopithecines, was first unearthed in the late 1920s, although its significance was not immediately recognized except by its discoverer, Raymond Dart. Additional Australopithecine remains were found in the 1940s, 1950s, and 1960s, and these findings have brought this group its full appreciation. Darwin's suspicion that the human line evolved from lesser forms has thus been amply validated. The task which now faces human paleontologists is to reconstruct the history of the human lineage in greater detail (Howell 1965; Pfeiffer 1969; Pilbeam 1972; Jolly 1973).

Darwin's work drew attention not only to the evolutionary forces and the fossil record but also to man's nearest relatives, the Primates, a mammalian order made up of primitive forms: lemurs, lorises, galagoes, and tarsier, and advanced forms: monkeys, apes, and men. Where the nonhuman members of the order resemble man, comparative studies reveal the overall adaptive nature of these similarities. Where the non-human members differ, comparisons contrast man's unique features with other viable alternatives. Man's internal organs, such as the heart or kidney, for example, compare closely with those of the monkeys and apes, and the similarities found among these species, with their varying habits and habitats, identify the fundamental adaptive traits of these structures. Man's exclusive features, such as his bipedal locomotion and large, complexly organized central nervous system, contrast with the brachiating modes of locomotion found in some of the apes, or the quadrupedal modes of the monkeys, and the smaller, less complex, but functionally sophisticated, brains of the apes (Le Gros Clark 1959; Harrison and Montagna 1969; Simons 1972).

Darwin's concern with morphology was related to an almost equal concern with behavior. His treatment laid the foundations of ethnology, or "comparative behavior." This new science has come in the most recent decades into full bloom and public attention (Lorenz 1965; Klopfer and Hailman 1967).

Behaviors are the doings and actions of organisms, specifically, those activities which are directly monitored by other members of an organism's same-species. Behavioral events fall in the temporal mid-range of the physiological continuum, sometimes fractions of a second, usually a few seconds to several minutes, sometimes hours and even days. The longer duration behaviors are dealt with as if they were composites, being broken down into shorter units. On the spatial side, behaviors are whole body phenomena and lie in the size range of the full organism itself.

The terminology used to describe behaviors has been borrowed from man's natural language systems. Animals are said to "swim or run," "approach or withdraw," "attack or flee," "relax or fidget," "love or hate," "approve or disapprove," and so on. The modern behaviorism school of psychology has tried to rationalize this terminology by restricting its terms to the nonemotive, or nonexpressive, members of the lexicon: "We can observe *behavior—what the organism does or says* . . . such as turning toward or away . . . jumping . . . and more highly organized activities such as building a skyscraper, drawing plans, having babies, writing books, and the like" (Watson 1930:6). If expressive terms like *happiness, sadness, anger, surpise,* and such, referred only to internal states known from introspection and personal feelings, they could not be labels for externally monitored behaviors and would be of no use to behaviorism. "The objection to inner states is not that they do not exist, but that they are not relevant in a functional analysis" (Skinner 1953:35).

Darwin had taken a different approach in his book of 1872, titled

*The Expression of the Emotions in Man and Animals* (republished in 1965, with a preface by Konrad Lorenz, University of Chicago Press). He reasoned that emotional states, whatever they may be "inside" the organism, do have externally monitored manifestations. They have observed, or heard, correlates. These external correlates are products of physiology—contraction of muscles, secretion of glands, and so forth— and ought to be as subject to evolutionary explanations as any other physiological processes, irrespective of the mental states, or feelings, underlying the behaviors. There was one qualifying condition. For these external manifestations, or behaviors, to evolve, they had to be inheritable. They could not be learned anew each generation. Darwin felt the evidence showed that some behaviors were inheritable and, therefore, the kinds of modifications which were subject to the evolutionary processes. He gave his evidence accordingly: "Whenever the same movements of the features or body express the same emotions in several distinct races of man, we may infer with much probability, that such expressions are true ones—that is, are innate or instinctive. Conventional expressions or gestures, acquired by the individual during early life, would probably have differed in the different races, in the same manner as do their languages" (Darwin 1872:15, 1965 edition).

Darwin then gave his evidence of certain behaviors which (1) were inherited, (2) had changed over time in response to evolutionary forces, and (3) could be used to define and reconstruct ancestral-descendent lineages. He called these "innate," or "instinctive," to contrast them with "learned," or "adaptable," behaviors. His use of the word *innate* implied that the action, or movement, pattern of the behavior was stereotypic when it occurred, was identical from animal to animal within the same breeding community, and was probably the consequence of an internal physiological program which, when put into operation by an appropriate stimulus, played itself out to completion without interruption. Much the same meaning is meant when modern ethologists refer to "innate," or "fixed," action patterns.

The weight of his argument fell on his demonstration that similar behaviors in different species, or races, had to be the result of inheritance through common ancestry. "I have endeavoured to show in considerable detail that all the chief expressions exhibited by man are the same throughout the world. This fact is interesting, as it affords a new argument in favour of the several races being descended from a single parent-stock, which must have been almost completely human in structure, and to a large extent in mind, before the period at which the races diverged from each other. No doubt similar structures, adapted for the same purpose, have often been independently acquired through variation and natural selection by distinct species; but this view will not explain close similarity between distinct species in a multiude of unimportant details" (Darwin 1872:359, 1965 edition).

Throughout his book he compared the expressive behaviors of different human "races"—which would be called "populations" in modern terminology—with one another and with other animals, notably monkeys, apes, dogs, and cats, to discover which expressions, like fear, suffering, or rage, had great similarities across species and which like blushing, were exclusively the possession of humanity.

In the introduction to *The Expression of Emotions,* Darwin described a simple experiment: "Dr. Duchenne galvanized, as we have already seen, certain muscles in the face of an old man, whose skin was little sensitive, and thus produced various expressions which were photographed on a large scale. It fortunately occurred to me to show several of the best plates, without a word of explanation, to above twenty educated persons of various ages and both sexes, asking them, in each case, by what emotion or feeling the old man was supposed to be agitated; and I recorded their answers in the words which they used. Several of the expressions were instantly recognized by almost everyone, though described in not exactly the same terms, and these may, I think, be relied on as truthful, and will hereafter be specified. On the other hand, the most widely different judgments were pronounced in regard to some of them" (Darwin 1872:12, 1965 edition).

Darwin made the "truthful emotions" thus discovered the focus of his analyses throughout the rest of the volume. Since Duchenne had produced all the "faces" by electrically stimulating various muscles, that is, "galvanizing" them, Darwin considered that they had to be the direct, behavioral manifestations of muscular physiology. They therefore must be potentially innate, or inheritable. His analysis took no systematic account of the differing judgments for the other photographs.

## AN EXPERIMENT ON EXPRESSIVE BEHAVIOR

Given Darwin's overall interest in finding emotional expressions innate in man, the design of his experiment was incomplete in some important aspects. His design was to take a collection of photographs, show them to respondents, and identify the "truthful" ones by looking for agreement among the respondents. Darwin's recorded facial behaviors had been produced artificially and involuntarily. What Darwin did not do was to take photographs of people trying to express particular emotions and test these against the judgments of respondents. Consequently, Darwin could not compare the respondents' abilities to judge with the subjects' abilities to perform, nor could he discover how subjects structured their expressive behaviors and compare their structuring principles to the respondents' criteria for judging. Modifications of Darwin's basic design to remedy these deficiencies have subsequently been developed, particularly with facial expressions (Ekman, Friesen and Ellsworth 1972). Such modifications are basic to the strategy of the research to be described below.

The following experiment is similar to Darwin's except that the behaviors under consideration were those of the trunk and limbs, rather than the face, and instead of involuntarily producing muscular contractions, the limbs of the subjects were moved voluntarily. The subjects consciously responded to verbal commands. The purpose of the commands was to generate a variety of postural poses. Although the command words could have been of any sort that would have generated postural variety, it was found that the best words for this purpose were expressive ones—*happy, sad, angry, surprised,* and so forth.

The design was (1) to have subjects adopt a variety of postures, by giving them expressive commands, or stimuli words, (2) to photograph the behaviors performed, and (3) to show the photographs to ten respondents, who, in turn, tried to identify the emotions they thought were portrayed by the poses. The guesses of the respondents were called the "responses," ten responses for each photograph. The research strategy can be summarized by saying that it amounts to translating expressive words into postures and postures back into expressive words. The results were very much in keeping with the discoveries of Darwin, with a unique twist.

Two subjects were used, a twenty-six-year-old woman and a twelve-year-old girl. About fifty different expressive terms were selected from the literature (Darwin 1872; Allport and Vernon 1933; Davitz 1969): *sad, happy, afraid, sexy, angry, surprised, relaxed, tired, love, hate, sexless, sick, guilty, shy, courageous, vain, arrogant, tense, silly, thinking, bored, embarrassed, attractive, unattractive, feel good, pleased, disgusted, moody, confused, unhappy, emotionless, waiting,* and so on. The terms were read to the subjects, one at a time, and the subjects were asked to assume a pose which, in their opinions, would communicate the appropriate emotional state to an audience.

As the work began, it was observed that the subjects, if not directed otherwise, usually posed standing. In order to widen the range of possible expressive postures, a chair and rug were obtained, and the subjects were asked to either stand, sit on the chair, sit on the rug, or lie on the rug while they performed their postures. The sample was generated, then, by commands having two parts, an expressive part and a postural part: "happy standing," "happy chair-sitting," "happy lying," "sad standing," and so on. The sample thus obtained was composed of 599 photographs. Each subject was photographed over a two-week period, and no command was given twice on the same day, in the hope that the subjects would not remember from day to day what they had done the day before, thereby increasing the spontaneity of the poses.

The adult subject also performed 123 nonemotional poses—the face was held emotionless while the limbs were placed in positions analogous to somatotype, art, athletic, or dance positions. These additional photographs raised the total sample size to 722 photographs. It cannot be assumed that the subjects felt the emotions they tried to portray and, therefore, the nonemotional poses have to be understood merely as poses performed without the stimuli of an expressive command.

Each photograph was shown to ten respondents. The sample was too large for any one respondent to handle it all at a single sitting, so it was divided into three subsets. Each subset was shown to one group of ten respondents. The respondents were asked to guess the emotions portrayed and write down their assessments, preferably with a single word, but, if necessary, with a short sentence. No distinction was made between the 123 nonemotional poses and the 599 expressive poses, either in the presentation of the photographs or in the responses of the respondents, with one minor exception, to be noted later. It was thought the respondents would see the artificiality of the nonemotional poses, but this rarely happened.

The responses were scored rigorously. Single word responses were left unaltered. Phrases or sentences were reduced to single words. If the command words appeared in the responses, in any grammatical form, the phrases or sentences were reduced to the command word; for example, if the command had been "happy standing" and the response was "happily gazing at her hand," the answer was changed to "happy." Synonyms were always left unaltered; for example, "she is joyful" was left as "joy," even if the command had been "happy." If a response contained two or more emotional references, the command term was always given preference. If a multiple response did not contain the command term, preference was given to that word which would maximize agreement among the respondents. This scoring procedure was aimed at maximizing agreement between the commands and the responses, and, after that, maximizing agreement among the responses. There were other procedural problems which will not be discussed here; they dealt with other types of problematical responses and were designed, again, to maximize agreement with the command words, first, and among the responses, second. These two procedures were devised so that the respondents would be credited with all possible correct guesses of the command words and so that the range of postures for each expressive word would be as broad as possible.

There was a total of 7,220 responses. The frequencies of the 41 most common were: happy (523), sexy (320), nothing (302), sad (301), angry (264), posed (227), surprised (211), relaxed (201), afraid (134), bored (123), thoughtful (114), tired (111), shy (101), withdrawn (101), proud (91), dejected (89), pain (87), thinking (80), fear (76), phony (68), aggressive (64), expectant (61), disappointed (53), depressed (48), embarrassed (46), sleepy (46), defiant (46), coy (44), disgusted (44), joy (42), attentive (42), tense (42), amused (39), asleep (39), unhappy (39), playful (39), pleading (38), mad (36), pleased (35), content (34), and puzzled (34). The rest of the terms had frequencies of 20 or below. The respondents were almost all natural-born residents of Chicago, Illinois, and these terms represent a midwest, or Chicago, lexicon.

*Nothing* meant the pose showed no emotional overtones. There was no tendency to use *nothing*, or its meaning, preferentially for the 123 nonemotional poses. *Posed* meant the pose was athletic, artistic, or artificial. The term *posed* or its meaning was used more frequently for the 123 nonemotional poses; this is the exception mentioned earlier. *Phony* was used for poses that, in the minds of the viewers, were so fraudulent that the emotion was "not to be believed," to quote one respondent.

Since none of the postures in the sample was actually identical to any other posture, each slide represents a different behavior. Counting slides is the same as counting discrete behaviors. Tables 9.1 and 9.2 use slide counts to make two points about expressive postural behaviors.

Table 9.1 gives the number of slides for which the respondents interpreted the poses with words identical to the commands given the subjects. The expressive, command words are listed on the left. The number of respondents, per slide, who guessed the command word is listed across the top. The numbers in the table tell how many slides had one, two, three, or more respondents guessing correctly each different expressive, command word. Notice that the poses for only six of the expressive words were guessed with 100 percent accuracy; these were happy, sad, sexy, angry, surprised, and afraid. In these few cases the subjects were able to translate the commands into postures that could be "read" by the respondents with no statistical loss of meaning; that is, the subjects communicated perfectly with the respondents. Do these six words signify learned, cultural norms or innate behaviors? This experiment, itself, does not answer the question but a cross-cultural replication could; however, what would be replicated in a cross-cultural study—the same six emotional categories, the same poses, or both?

Table 9.2 gives the number of slides for which the respondents agreed in their interpretations, ignoring whether they did or did not, at the same time, guess the commands given the subjects. Only those

**Table 9.1**  *Number of slides for which one or more respondents guessed the command word*

| Expressive Command Word | Number of respondents guessing the command word | | | | | | | | | | Total Number of Slides |
|---|---|---|---|---|---|---|---|---|---|---|---|
| | 1 | 2 | 3 | 4 | 5 | 6 | 7 | 8 | 9 | 10 | |
| Happy | | 2 | 2 | 1 | 5 | | 6 | 8 | 8 | 4 | 36 |
| Sad | 7 | 5 | 4 | 4 | 2 | 2 | 2 | 3 | 2 | 1 | 32 |
| Sexy | 3 | 4 | 4 | 5 | 1 | 3 | 4 | 1 | | 1 | 26 |
| Angry | 3 | 2 | 3 | 5 | | 4 | | 1 | 2 | 4 | 24 |
| Surprised | 1 | 1 | 1 | 1 | 5 | 3 | 1 | 3 | 3 | 1 | 20 |
| Afraid | 4 | 1 | 6 | 1 | 1 | 1 | 1 | 1 | | 3 | 18 |
| Tired | 5 | 5 | 1 | | 1 | 2 | | | | | 14 |
| Relaxed | 3 | 3 | 1 | | 3 | 2 | | | | | 12 |
| Shy | 2 | 1 | 2 | | 1 | 1 | 1 | | | | 8 |
| Bored | 1 | 2 | 2 | 2 | 1 | | | | | | 8 |
| Thinking | 3 | 1 | 1 | 1 | | | | | | | 6 |
| Feel Good | 3 | | 3 | | | | | | | | 6 |
| Arrogant | 2 | 1 | 1 | | | 1 | | | | | 5 |
| Sick | | 3 | 1 | | | | | | | | 4 |
| Confused | 1 | | 1 | 2 | | | | | | | 4 |
| Pleased | 3 | | | | | | | | | | 3 |
| Hate | 1 | | | | | | | 1 | | | 2 |
| Love | 1 | | | | | 1 | | | | | 2 |
| Stretching | | 1 | | 1 | | | | | | | 2 |
| Pain | | | 2 | | | | | | | | 2 |
| Vain | | 1 | 1 | | | | | | | | 2 |
| Unhappy | 2 | | | | | | | | | | 2 |
| Defiant | | | | 1 | | | | | | | 1 |
| Singing | | | | 1 | | | | | | | 1 |
| Old | | | | 1 | | | | | | | 1 |
| Strong | | | | 1 | | | | | | | 1 |
| Courageous | | | 1 | | | | | | | | 1 |
| Laughing | | 1 | | | | | | | | | 1 |
| Alert | | 1 | | | | | | | | | 1 |
| Indifferent | | 1 | | | | | | | | | 1 |
| Tense | 1 | | | | | | | | | | 1 |
| Sexless | 1 | | | | | | | | | | 1 |
| Wistful | 1 | | | | | | | | | | 1 |
| Embarrassed | 1 | | | | | | | | | | 1 |
| Waiting | 1 | | | | | | | | | | 1 |
| Moody | 1 | | | | | | | | | | 1 |
| Total Number of Slides | 51 | 36 | 34 | 26 | 24 | 20 | 15 | 18 | 15 | 14 | 253 |

twenty-five words with the greatest agreements are given. This table gives a midwestern United States lexicon for the subjects' poses. It shows that postural behaviors elicit interpretations which are graded among observers, some behaviors eliciting majority agreement and others, many

**Table 9.2** *Number of slides for which the respondents agreed on the same expressive word, irrespective of the command words*

| Expressive Words Used By Respondents | Number of respondents agreeing with each other | | | | | | | | | Total Number of Slides |
|---|---|---|---|---|---|---|---|---|---|---|
| | 2 | 3 | 4 | 5 | 6 | 7 | 8 | 9 | 10 | |
| Nothing | 70 | 21 | 9 | | | | | | | 100 |
| Happy | 18 | 11 | 8 | 16 | 6 | 13 | 9 | 8 | 5 | 94 |
| Sexy | 17 | 15 | 12 | 3 | 4 | 7 | 3 | 2 | 2 | 65 |
| Sad | 17 | 11 | 6 | 5 | 4 | 2 | 3 | 3 | 1 | 52 |
| Posed | 16 | 9 | 8 | 10 | 3 | 2 | 1 | 1 | | 50 |
| Angry | 10 | 5 | 8 | 5 | 5 | 1 | 2 | 2 | 7 | 45 |
| Relaxed | 18 | 5 | 7 | 4 | 2 | 1 | | 1 | | 38 |
| Surprised | 3 | 5 | 4 | 7 | 6 | 2 | 4 | 3 | 1 | 35 |
| Bored | 13 | 10 | 4 | 1 | 1 | | | | | 29 |
| Tired | 13 | 4 | 1 | 1 | 8 | | | | | 27 |
| Afraid | 4 | 6 | 7 | 1 | 2 | 1 | | | 3 | 24 |
| Dejected | 12 | 3 | 2 | 4 | | | | | | 21 |
| Withdrawn | 6 | 7 | 2 | 2 | 2 | 1 | 1 | | | 21 |
| Thoughful | 8 | 1 | 3 | 6 | 2 | | 1 | | | 21 |
| Pained | 3 | 5 | 1 | 4 | 3 | 1 | 1 | | | 18 |
| Fear | 7 | 3 | 2 | 1 | 2 | 2 | | 1 | | 18 |
| Proud | 2 | 6 | 3 | 1 | 1 | 4 | | | | 17 |
| Thinking | 8 | 4 | 2 | | 2 | | | | | 16 |
| Shy | 3 | 6 | 3 | 1 | 1 | 1 | | 1 | | 16 |
| Aggressive | 5 | 3 | 1 | 3 | 1 | | 1 | | | 14 |
| Phony | 10 | 2 | | 1 | | | | | | 13 |
| Disappointed | 9 | 2 | | 1 | | | | | | 12 |
| Joy | 4 | 6 | 1 | 1 | | | | | | 12 |
| Depressed | 6 | 1 | 2 | | | 1 | | | | 10 |
| Sleeping | 6 | 1 | 1 | | 1 | | | | | 9 |

others, eliciting minority agreement. Since the respondents made their choices without consultation, the agreements must have been induced by the photographic portraits. The odds against ten, or nine, respondents picking, by chance, the same word for a particular pose are uncalculable, but surely very large.

Table 9.2 shows that most of the poses have only statistical meanings, that is, most poses do not mean the same thing to all people. Could some of these poses still be innate behaviors? Could there be innate behaviors which are misread by 10 percent, 20 percent, or more of the population? Could a culture use ambiguous poses for body language by arbitrarily assigning meanings to these poses? Is there an adaptive reason for the large number of ambiguous poses? Where the respondents were in high agreement but disagreed with the command words, who was in error—did the respondents misread the postures or were the subjects poor actors?

For 42 percent of the 599 photographs in the expressive sample at least one respondent guessed the command term. Out of the total of 5,990 responses only 18 percent agreed with the command terms. Some of this 18 percent might be the result of chance interpretations but the proportion would be much less than 1 percent. The best two respondents guessed 24 percent of the command terms. One of these respondents was male and the other female. The poorest respondent, a male, guessed 11 percent. With a majority rule, it could be argued that "truthful" behaviors, using Darwin's word, are those for which over 50 percent of the respondents guessed the correct command. This would give, from Table 9.1, 13.5 percent "truthful" poses. From Table 9.2 the majority rule would give 23 percent "truthful" poses, of which only 13.5 percent would agree with the expressive commands. This suggests that when a person communicates an expressive word through a posture, 23 percent of the time a panel of judges would achieve majority agreement, but they would actually guess correctly only 13.5 percent of the time and be wrong 9.5 percent of the time. The data also suggests that although someone could guess correctly 11 to 25 percent of the time, that person might have trouble persuading his or her peers that the guesses were accurate. From the standpoint of the communicator, or poser, 42 percent of the time someone would understand what the poses meant, but, overall, only 18 percent of the world would show this understanding. Some people understand better than others and the culture (13.5 percent), as a whole, is not as aware as the more sensitive people (25 percent).

The reader should remember that the scoring kept synonyms separate and, therefore, the percentages reflect the most rigorous demands for correct identifications. The photographs showed the entire body of the subjects, faces as well as limbs, and the photographs showed postures, not gestures. People use gestures, a more subtle medium of communication, as well as language (Birdwhistell 1970), to make themselves understood and are, consequently, understood better. In fact, this work implies that some people can "read" another's postures 100 percent accurately 25 percent of the time, right down to the precise word and, given all the contingencies of this experimental design, this is a surprisingly good result. When I took the sample and collapsed some of the more obvious synonyms (the reader has to trust my judgment in this respect), I was able to raise the accuracy of the better individuals to 40 percent. Still, there were glaring disagreements in 50 percent of the sample—"happy" for "hate," "contented" for "sad," and so on. Perhaps, in part, this represents the individual idiosyncracies which make us all unique and, at times, misunderstood. Such misunderstanding offers a cogent rationale for redundancy among body, face, and speech.

### Analysis of Limb Arrangements

The external appearance of the human body results from the way the soft structures at the surface are displayed in space, ignoring attributes of cosmetics and dress. Differences are mostly the consequences of the plasticity of the facial mask and the bending of the body segments at the joints. The face has been well studied (Ekman, Friesen, and Ellsworth 1972), but the trunk and limbs have not had the same kind of attention (Birdwhistell 1970; Knapp 1972). The limb arrangements pictured in the photographs were analyzed in the hope of discovering what correlations, if any, there might be between limb displays and the various commands and responses.

The limbs adopt differing spatial configurations because they are composed of rigid elements, the bones, which move on one another across discontinuities, the articulations, or joints. The bones segment the body into a series of unbending parts, such as the upper arm, forearm, and so on. Movement, or change in position, occurs when these segments are displaced relative to one another, across the joints. Postural differences result from combinations of these displacements. The displacements can be measured, or quantified, because of the anatomical properties of the joints' constructions. This amounts to the physiological "reduction" of postural states to the level of articular physiology and its measurement.

Examine, for example, your own right arm. The upper arm contains a single bone, the humerus. The forearm has two bones, the radius and ulna. The radius and ulna move on the humerus at the elbow joint. The movements of the forearm on the upper arm are called *flexions* and *extensions*. Hold the arm with the forearm in a straight line with the upper arm; this is full extension. Flexion is movement of the forearm as it returns toward the upper arm. The position of the forearm anywhere along its flexion range can be specified by measuring the angle between the forearm and upper arm at the elbow. With the arm out straight the measurement of flexion-extension would be about 180°; with the arm half-flexed, or half-extended, the measurement would be about 90°. Intermediate positions would be specified using intermediate values of angular displacement (Salter 1955; Moore 1965).

The elbow joint is a simple joint; it has only one range, or path, of movement—flexion-extension. The shoulder is more complex. Not only can the humerus move forward and backward—up toward the head and down toward the body, but it can also move from side to side—abduction-adduction range—and rotate on its long axis—move the front of the arm so it faces the body or around so it faces away from the body. This complexity can be handled with angular displacements also, but the number of variables has to be increased. There must be one variable, or measurement scale, for each of the ranges: flexion-extension, abduction-adduction, and rotation. The positions of all of the major limb joints—shoulder, elbow, wrist, hip, knee, and ankle—can be measured by using one, two, or all three of these variables (Steindler 1955; Dempster 1955, 1965; Prost 1967). Since most differences between postures are differences between the positions of the several rigid elements of the body, descriptions and comparisons of postures can be obtained by using measurements of these variables. Differences in posture due to changes in contour, that is, changes in muscle size, skin creases, or the positions of fat pads, would be ignored with this system.

Using these quantifying concepts, the photographs of the postures were viewed and, using surface landmarks, the relative positions of the bones and joints were determined (Hamilton and Simon 1958; Plagenhoef 1971; O'Connell and Gardner 1972). Where possible, measurements of the angular relations between the bones were taken directly from the photographs. Foreshortening and other perspective distortions made direct measurements of some angles difficult. For these measurements the two subjects were asked to reassume postures which mimicked those in the photographs, using the photographs as standards. Measurements which could not be taken from the photographs were then taken on the actual subjects. Because the photographs had been taken with re-posing in mind, the pictures showed all the joints and the subjects were able to retake the postures they had spontaneously assumed in the original recording sessions.

From the photographs and the reconstructed postures, measurements were obtained for each pose for the following variables: all three variables for both shoulders, flexion-extension at both elbows, rotation at both forearms, flexion-extension at both wrists, all three variables for both hips, flexion-extension at both knees, and flexion-extension at both ankles. This reduced each pose to a set of twenty-two angular measurements. These twenty-two described the limb positions and were used to compare and analyze the poses.

In a mathematical sense, the twenty-two variables conjointly taken create a twenty-two-dimensional field, or graph. Each variable is an axis of the field, and all axes meet at right angles in a point with 0 value, just as height and weight might be the two axes of a normal two-dimensional field, or graph, relating body mass to stature. Each pose would be a point locale in the total twenty-two-dimensional field, and the entire sample would form an array of points in the field. The linear distance between any two points in the graphic space would represent a measure of the total quantitative difference between the two points.

Such a field cannot be drawn, or constructed, as a physical entity but its existence can be imagined. Mathematical operations can be defined on the assumption of its existence. There are three properties of a multidimensional field which will be used to describe the postural data.

1. Point locale of the value of the complete posture of one pose. In a two-dimensional field the position of a point, or case, may be defined by two values (x and y), one for each axis of the field. In a multidimensional field the location of a point, or case, may be defined by n values ($v_1$, $v_2$, $\cdots$, $v_n$), one for each axis, or variable, of the field. In a twenty-two-dimensional field a point locale is specified with twenty-two values, one for each of the variables ($v_1$, $v_2$, $\cdots$, $v_{22}$).

2. Distance that measures the quantitative value of the difference between two poses. The linear distance between any two points may be calculated using the formula:

$$D = \sqrt{d_1{}^2 + d_2{}^2 + \cdots + d_n{}^2}$$

where D is the linear distance between the two points, $d_1$ is the difference between values for the first variable ($v_{1,2} - v_{1,1}$), $d_2$ is the difference between values for the second variable ($v_{2,2} - v_{2,1}$), and so on, to $d_n$ which is the difference between values for the last variable ($v_{22,2} - v_{22,1}$). The formula assumes that the multidimensional field, or space, has Euclidean properties throughout.

3. Direction. In two-dimensional space there are four cardinal directions—up, down, right, and left. In three-dimensional space there are six cardinal directions—up, down, right, left, front, and back. In multidimesional space the number of directions likewise increases, and this is one of the major reasons that a physical construct of space with four or more dimensions is impossible. It is only necessary, here, to understand that any two-dimensional representation of multidimensional data contains a distortion of the directional relations of the true space.

The overall organization of the sample is illustrated two-dimensionally in Figure 9.1. The marks are point locales for the different poses. The different marks identify the basic postural types: standing (dots), lying (plus signs), chair-sitting (circles), floor-sitting (Greek alphas), and kneeling (checks). Sixteen poses, falling beyond the right hand corner of the graph, have been eliminated for convenience. The scales of the two axes are in arbitrary distance units. Clusters of points were found using a mathematical program designed to discover natural groupings in multidimensional space (Prost 1973). A computer performed the tedious calculations.

The poses clustered into five groups: one containing standing poses, one containing lying poses, one containing chair-sitting poses, one containing floor-sitting poses, and one containing kneeling poses. In Figure 9.1 the clusters for standing and chair-sitting are clearly seen but, because

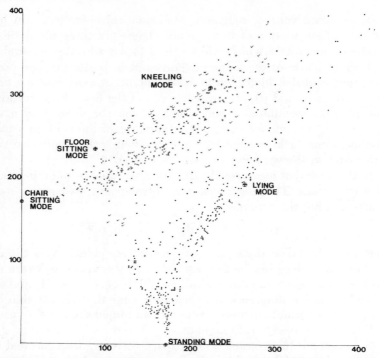

**Figure 9.1**   *A two-dimensional graph showing the overall organization of the sample.*

of the directional distortion of the two-dimensional figure, the other clusters are not as separate and distinct as they were in the twenty-two-dimensional space.

The two dense rays of points, stretching diagonally across the graph, are the standing and chair-sitting clusters. Each ray extends from a point locale. The standing ray extends out from a Standing Mode locale, and the chair-sitting ray extends out from a Chair-Sitting Mode locale. These Mode locales, which are indicated on the graph by large crosses in circles, are constructs from the statistical modes for the poses in the corresponding clusters; that is, $v_1$ for the Standing Mode point locale is the statistical mode for all the values of the right shoulder flexion-extension variable for all the standing poses, and so forth, through $v_{22}$, which is the statistical mode for all the values of the left ankle flexion-extension for all the standing poses. The other Modes were calculated in the same fashion, using the values from the poses of the corresponding postural types.

The points in Figure 9.1 are plotted with their linear distances from the Standing Mode locale on the abscissa and their linear distances from the Chair-Sitting Mode locale on the ordinate. In the twenty-two dimensional space, the Floor-Sitting Mode and its cluster, the Kneeling Mode and its cluster, and the Lying Mode and its cluster lie in different directions and, therefore, are actually separate from the standing and chair-sitting clusters. Also, in the twenty-two-dimensional space, the points of each cluster surround their Modes, like stars of a star cluster around their common gravitational center, rather than forming the raylike arrangements pictured in Figure 9.1, another effect of losing directional information through the two-dimensional representation.

Since the overall organization of the sample showed that the poses clustered into large groups: standing, chair-sitting, floor-sitting, kneeling, and lying—where are the expressive types? If all the poses generated by the command word *happy* were labeled, where would they fall in the display of Figure 9.1?

The computer was programmed to search through the expressive poses to discover, statistically, if there were any expressive groupings centering on their own unique Modal values (Prost 1973). It was found that the poses within each of the large clusters were further organized into many small, discrete groups. Each small group contained poses generated by the same command word and there was a large number of these: *happy, pleased, silly, sad, unhappy, surprised, afraid, angry, hate, disgusted, love, relaxed, tired, sick, pain, feel good, alert, sexless, sexy, shy, vain, arrogant, attractive, unattractive, courageous, emotionless, waiting, bored, thinking, puzzled, guilty, moody, tense,* and *embarrassed.* These little groups contained 69.5 percent of the expressive (599 poses) sample. The other poses, 30.5 percent of the sample, did not participate in any of these smaller groups.

There was something unique about these groups. Each major postural Mode had its own set of expressive groups. For example, contrasting only the standing and chair-sitting postures, around the Standing Mode there was a Happy group, a Sad group, a Silly group, and so on, while around the Chair-Sitting Mode there was, similarly, a Happy group, a Sad group, a Silly group, and so on. These small groups had elongated shapes, such that each group had a long axis which extended out away from its corresponding Mode. The long axes all centered on the Modes and encircled the Modes, like pins sticking out of pincushions.

Figure 9.2 is the same as Figure 9.1 except that lines have been drawn connecting poses in the same expressive group and the ungrouped poses (30.5 percent of the expressive sample) have been left out. The way the expressive groups radiate from the Modes and the elongated, or extended, shape of the groups can be seen in the figure. The connecting lines lie on top of one another, again, because the two-dimensional graph collapses the directional complexity of the true field.

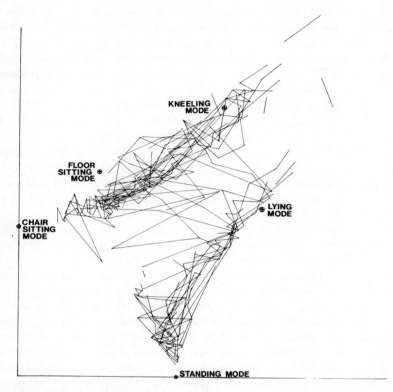

**Figure 9.2** *The same graph as in Figure 9.1 except that lines have been drawn to connect poses belonging to the same expressive group and ungrouped poses have been eliminated.*

The computer discovered the groups by assuming that points spaced close together belong together. If a point was totally isolated, surrounded by a large volume of vacant space in all directions, it was not included in any grouping. The 30.5 percent of the expressive poses that were left ungrouped were so isolated. If one pose was close to another, the two poses were grouped together. If a third pose was close to one of the others, the grouping was expanded to include all three. This is how the extended, or elongated, shapes involving the other 69.5 percent of the expressive poses were found and constructed. Fifty-two percent of all of the poses (not just the ground poses) were grouped with other poses having the same command words; for example, one Happy pose was close to two other Happy poses. Two percent of the poses grouped with the wrong poses, for example, a Sad pose close to a Happy pose; 15.5 percent of the poses lay midway between two, or more (but always less than five) other poses, only one of which had the same command term, for example, a Surprised pose lying in-between a Surprised and an Angry pose.

It is very striking that the computer sorted 52 percent of the sample neatly into the correct expressive groups while the *better* human respondents only scored 25 percent correct interpretations. This is especially so when one considers that the human respondents had the benefit of cues from the face, trunk, and hands, that is, the entire body while the computer had only the angular measurements for the major limb joints. On the other hand, the respondents had to interpret the poses with precise emotional words; synonyms did not count.

It is undoubtedly significant, in accounting for the differences, that the computer had the advantage of analyzing the entire sample. The computer was able to "see" the overall habits of the subjects. The respondents looked at the sample picture by picture without knowing anything about the subjects. The computer actually mapped the habit patterns of the subjects, without trying to correlate these behavior patterns with emotional labels. This suggests that the poses are sharply distinguished within the framework of the fields of the specific individual subjects. In this sense, what the computer analysis of the expressive groups shows is that the subjects were really structuring each of their own postural performances with reference to their other performances. Had the respondents known the rules behind the subjects' strategies they could have "read" the poses with greater accuracy.

To some extent, the computer results also tell us how individuals accomplished this structuring. For example, each of the expressive groups had a long axis which centered on their respective Modes. Why did these groups all have this kind of shape? Going back to the actors with the analysis in hand, it was discovered that the poses which lay a greater distance from the Modes were poses where the subjects had intended the more intense expressions of the emotion. When the subjects intended to be very happy, their posture locale would lie further from the Mode, along the long axis of the Happy group, than if they tried to be slightly happy. There was one exception: for the Sad groups this relation was exactly reversed; the sadder poses were closer to the Modes. For all other groups, this intensity-distance rule held. There was a definite, but not strong, paralleled tendency for the respondents to voluntarily interpret poses at the greater distance as having the greater implied intensity.

If all the groups radiate out from the Modes and the distance from the Modes correlates with interpreted or intended intensity, the Modes must be behaviors having no emotional intensity whatsoever. The respones for the poses which fell closest to the Modes were examined to see if the respondents could describe what the Modes might signify. A high proportion of the responses contained words and phrases such as: "formal standing," "military sitting," "proper sitting," "sitting as if in a dentist's office," "sitting in the principal's office of a strict girl's school," and so on. Consequently, the Modes could be called formal poses, and they seem to represent the rigid, nonemotional, or antiemotional stereotypes of the general postural attitudes standing, chair-sitting, floor-sitting, kneeling, and lying.

Plates 1 and 2 are reproductions of the poses for two of the emotional groups: Surprised and Angry. The first pose in each series is the one that is closest to its respective Mode. The last pose is the one that is farthest from its respective Mode. It was found that the closer a pose was to its Mode, the less the intensity intended by the performer. Standing and chair-sitting groups for the same expression are compared in each plate.

The computer was also given the task of searching for groups among those poses where there was better than 50 percent agreement among the respondents. The computer found groups for: *happy, sad, surprised, afraid, angry, pain, sexy, withdrawn, coy, motherly,* and *posed.* The Happy, Sad, Surprised, Angry, and Sexy groups showed the same Mode duplication that was described for the command groups. The response groups showed another characteristic: their internal organization was clinal. At the center of a group would be a pose, or poses, where the respondents had 100 percent agreement and surrounding this pose would be poses with lower percentage agreements. Most of the surrounding cases were also organized clinally—as the percentage of agreement decreased, the distance from the corresponding group increased. As the percentage of agreement decreased, cases of low agreement for another expressive term would begin to appear, until agreement for the new term became predominant. In short, the response groups were clinal and intergraded with one another; the performance, or command, groups were distinct with minor overlappings at their borders.

The 123 artificial, or nonemotional, poses were found, statistically, in two places in the field. They were found at great distances from the Modes, implying that they were composed of extreme deviations from the modal, formal postures, and they were found in directions formed by combinations having the right and left side values greatly different. The expressive poses tended to be bilaterally symmetrical—right and left limbs in almost identical positions. Asymmetry was most pronounced in the dance and art poses. Asymmetry was also somewhat more pronounced in the posed and phony poses.

This analysis indicates that: (1) for a number of basic postural attitudes the subjects had, conceptually, if not in fact, formally defined standards; (2) emotional representations deviated from these formal standards—the greater the deviation, the more the *intended* intensity of the emotion; (3) each different category of emotion deviated from the formal standard by a different combination of joint flexions and/or extensions; and (4) overlying this organization could be placed a clinal map of emotional *interpretations* of a panel of respondents. In a few places the respondents' interpretations and the subjects' performances harmonized. In many more places the respondents and the subjects were in disharmony.

## THEORETICAL IMPLICATIONS OF THE EXPERIMENT

The significance of the experiment is not in the identification of Happy, or Sad, poses. The significance is in the discovery of structure underlying the poses and responses. This discovery in turn was contingent on the research methodology and its theoretical assumption.

The main theoretical assumption was that behaviors are manifestations of physiology. Therefore, describing behaviors with physiological parameters should reveal the structuring principles generating behaviors. In this case, the positioning of the body was under consideration, so the appropriate physiological parameters were the positions of the body's articulations, measured by the angles formed at the joints. The angular variables, taken conjointly, created a mathematical field which mapped the organisms' total postural potentials. The field was an organizational scheme, a continuous theoretical background capable of containing all possible postures, against which actual performances could be compared and with which actual performances could be analyzed. The contrast between these two, potential against real, is what put the habits of the performers into focus and permitted the structure of the data to emerge.

The habits of these participants does not tell us what happy, or sad, behavior ought to look like—there were only two subjects and ten respondents, none of whom was a universal informant. The experiment tells us that people do perform expressive behaviors and do so in a highly patterned way.

Each subject had her own, different, expressive poses. Both, perhaps unconsciously, kept their poses neatly compartmentalized into separate and distinct groups. Both employed elongated groupings, letting the long axes of the groups imply emotional intensity. Both encircled their Modes with their groups and duplicated their groups from Mode to Mode. Both used, roughly, the same Modes and for a small number of emotional portrayals chose quite similar poses. The specific postures varied, but these features were shared.

**Plate 1** *Four poses from the surprised standing and surprised chair-sitting expressive groups. The percentages under the pictures are the frequencies of the more common responses given by the ten respondents who interpreted the poses.*

50% "nothing"

50% "surprised"

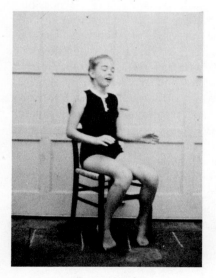

60% "surprised"

100% "surprised"

50% "surprised"

70% "surprised"

90% "surprised"

90% "surprised"

**Plate 2**   *Four poses from the angry standing and angry chair-sitting "expressive" groups. The percentages under the pictures are the frequencies of the more common responses given by the ten respondents who interpreted the poses.*

60% "excited"

60% "shocked"

20% "angry"

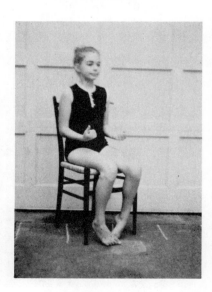

40% "angry"

30% "angry"

60% "angry"

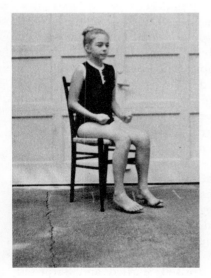

40% "angry"

40% "angry"

The respondents had varied interpretations but came into agreement on a few key poses, notably, ones that harmonized with the intentions of the subjects: Happy, Sad, Sexy, Angry, Surprised, and Afraid. The respondents could have showed their maximum agreements on poses which totally contradicted the subjects, like agreeing 100 percent to call all Silly poses Mad, but they did not. The respondents, as a group, produced interpretive clines. The clines appeared with an overview of the total behavioral variety but, also, in the overview, confusions and disharmonies became apparent.

For example, both subjects had emotional poses which the respondents never "read." One subject had neatly clustered groups for Embarrassed but the respondents never guessed the emotional command. Why did the subject perform these behaviors if no one could read the postures? Are these idiosyncratic behaviors, unique to this one subject? Might we find that the subject's immediate family could read her Embarrassed? Can we argue that the respondents never guessed Embarrassed because this subject's groups were not "truthfully" embarrassed? Why did the subject perform the poses similarly day after day, for standing as well as chair-sitting, if she was so out of step with her audience? Must we assume that the Embarrassed poses have no functional usefulness to this subject? They apparently were not social norms. They certainly were not innate. Why were they so neatly structured?

It might be contended that the reason the respondents did not guess the Embarrassed poses, or any of the other misidentified pictures, was because synonyms were not taken into account. Perhaps the "meanings" of the response words ought to have been used, instead of the explicit spellings as was done. Do *sad* and *unhappy, pleased* and *happy,* or *embarrassed* and *tense,* mean the same thing? The subjects had discrete groups for Sad, Unhappy, Pleased, Happy, Embarrassed, and Tense, so the subjects, behaviorally, did not consider these the same. How can a researcher presume to collapse categories which his subjects choose to keep distinct? To what degree can investigators distort what actually occurs in their choice of descriptive words? To what degree can people misrepresent each other when they describe their neighbors with their personal idioms?

On the other side of the coin, look at the lexicon of the respondents. The response mappings were clinal, meanings intermixed, intermediate and ambiguous poses interspersed. Language terms assume that there are neat distinctions between referenced classes, which, apparently, for body language there are not. In this sense, natural language words are poor descriptive units for body behavior. Take the case of *surprised.* One subject had two kinds of Surprised: Surprised Startled and Surprised Happy. Behaviorally there should be two types of Surprised, validated firmly by these separate groups. Does, then, the single word *surprised* accurately apply to this subject's behaviors? To what degree does a language distort by hiding variability and forcing intermediate performances into arbitrary semantic compartments (Prost 1974)?

These results have some important implications for our "common sense" knowledge about communicative behavior of all types. It is common to suppose that the message of a gesture is carried by only one, or two, body parts: "happy" is thought of as smiling, "goodby" is thought of as waving, "nervous" is thought of as fidgeting with the hands, and so on. This supposition is not supported by the data. If any of the variables had been left out of the analysis, the sorting would have been less efficacious. For example, Sad Standing had the arms down, usually somewhat in front of the body; the legs were, in most cases, quite relaxed and straight. Therefore, are the legs unimportant? Is the message, "sad," carried by the arms alone? The answer from the experiment is that the legs carry part of the message because if the legs were placed differently the message would have changed. Even though Sad legs were the same as Mad legs, the legs could not have been varied or the Sad pose would have become Tired. Reducing the number of variables would have collapsed areas of the field and, consequently, destroyed the discreteness of the groups. Neutral legs *mean* "the message is in the hands." Every part carries a message even if the meaning is "look elsewhere."

Darwin was right and behaviorism is wrong—people do behave expressively and no expurgations of vocabularies can make the realities of emotional communication disappear. But, behaviorism raised a cogent question. An investigator, himself, is no less a respondent than the respondents in this experiment. If respondents' interpretations are subject to disagreement, one with another, and with the intentions of the actors, how can a scientist be objective, or uniform, in his behavioral descriptions?

In fact, it is not the study of expressive behavior which ought to have been questioned by the behaviorists. It is the descriptive terminology, and classificatory methodology, which introduce a problem. This experiment shows that behaviors can be studied with objectivity—the joint angle descriptions are as objective as needed under the most rigorous scientific requirements. What makes a methodology subjective is the use of natural language terms, such as *happy, standing,* or *sitting,* without the recognition that the words are merely labels for some defined collection of physiological potentials. As such, they label the data adequately only when their mappings in the field are clarified. "Happy" is not a type, not a discrete identity; it labels one, or more, groups of potentially performable postures, or gestures, and it is a word used by observers to reference certain assumptions about the internal feelings of those performers who use such behaviors. An expressive group can be called Group I or Group Happy, irrespectively, as long as the field phenomena behind the term is clearly understood, either label is logically satisfactory. Behaviorism can object that we do not know what a "happy" feeling is, but it cannot eliminate Happy behaviors from the field. *Happy* is what Happy does, and the doings are proper topics of scientific scrutiny. Skinner and Watson mistook the labels for the reality, and in so doing, "misread" human behavior, just as the respondents "misread" the many well-structured, and well-intentioned, performances of these two subjects.

Even the ethologists have to be criticised. Their descriptions, too, rely on natural language categories. Lorenz tells the consequence in the clearest of statements (1935; pp. 92–93 of the reprinting of 1957): "I will readily admit that observation has one great drawback: it is hard to convey to others. If I read an observation made by my friend Horst Siewert, for instance, I know fairly well what the animal he observed was actually doing at the time. When I read Lloyd Morgan's observations, on the other hand, I have only a vague notion of what he is describing." Common words alone cannot describe the field reality of physiological phenomena, except in the vaguest way. Words can signify groups and clusters, or the structural properties of the field, but without an appropriately defined field as an anchor, the words float open-ended in a welter of semantic, connotative confusion.

The same is true of the search for innate expressions. What has been looked for are innate "happy," or "sad," faces instead of searching the habits of subjects to find what, in fact, will emerge as the stable, insensitive to learning, and universal attributes of animal performances. Some workers, like Birdwhistell (1970), doubt that there are innate, or instinctive, expressions for humans. Others, like Hass (1970) and Eibl-Eibesfeldt (1970), claim that there are such expressions, but the case they make is not too convincing because their reasoning tends to be circular. Haas and Eibl-Eibesfeldt tour the world, photographing numerous emotional acts. They note great similarities throughout the world for some emotions. But, of course, what they photograph is their own interpretations of the emotions, and these ought to look very similar. One cannot demonstrate that "happy" behaviors are the same for all mankind if the same behaviors, themselves, are used to judge whether their owners are happy. Birdwhistell's data is more carefully drawn; he took care to understand his informants and the context of their expressions and he found that in certain situations, for some people, smiling is not necessarily always "happy," and so on.

On the other hand, the Modes, the elongated expressive groups, the distance-intensity rule, and the clinal centers with 100 percent agreement between the respondents and with the subjects, are all candidates for innate status. In science, to be brief, debate never serves where research will prove, and these possibilities are best explored with a replication of this experiment with new subjects and respondents.

## SELECTED READINGS

Jolly, Allison, 1972, *The Evolution of Primate Behavior*. New York: Macmillan Co.

This book on general ethology is well illustrated. The presentation of data is drawn into a number of useful and clarifying tables and charts. It covers the field excellently, giving the reader a real grasp of this topically vogue discipline. The approach is ecological as well as ethological, and students of human society would do well to contrast human and subhuman life styles through the presentations in these pages.

Klopfer, Peter H. and Hailman, Jack P., 1967, *An Introduction to Animal Behavior: Ethology's First Century*. Englewood Cliffs, N.J.: Prentice-Hall.

There are other books more packed with data, but this text is delightful and carries the reader over the history of ethology in a most readable manner. The authors have been careful to direct the reader to other books and journals in explicit and clear fashion. The historical flow of the chapters puts the major issues of ethology into their proper perspectives.

Knapp, Mark L., 1972, *Nonverbal Communication in Human Interaction*. New York: Holt, Rinehart and Winston, Inc.

A short survey of work in human nonverbal communication which gives the reader an overall appreciation of recent research and methods and through the bibliographies explores more specific topics in detail: eye contact, body language, personal space, cultural varieties of dress and cosmetics, etc. The author gives research results as well as recording techniques which allows the reader to better evaluate the results and design his own experiments.

Lasker, Gabriel Ward, 1973, *Physical Anthropology*. New York: Holt, Rinehart and Winston, Inc.

This book surveys the entire field of physical anthropology. It is short and well written. Where necessary, the author reviews general biological principles so the reader can approach the book with no outside preparation. The author covers evolution and genetics, fossil man and race, primate evolution and behavior, integrating data and theory in a lucid and eclectic manner. He speaks forcefully for his own points of view but does no disservice to his protagonists. The beginning student could start with no better volume.

# Chapter 10

# The Physical Basis

# of Language Use

# in Primates

**Bernard G. Campbell**

Language is probably the characteristic most often been cited by philosophers and zoologists, as well as anthropologists, as distinguishing man from the animals. *"Homo symbolicus"* (Cassirer 1944) designates that animal which has evolved a means of symbolizing the components of his environment as well as his ideas about himself and his relationships to others. One of the most fascinating and elusive problems for physical anthropologists is to unravel the nature and origin of man's unique means of communication. This chapter is intended to give the reader some idea how research in a wide range of different sciences can be synthesized to create an overall view of the evolution of language.

At this time, physical anthropologists are investigating language evolution by two routes—comparative behavior and comparative anatomy. We shall first consider these two closely related routes and then demonstrate how it is possible to reach at least some conclusions about the evolution of a behavior which, unlike tool-making, leaves no trace in the fossil record.

There is a whole range of theories on the evolution of language, many of which are somewhat fatuous. They are, briefly: (1) the *interjectional* theory, that words are derived from innate animal vocalizations; (2) the *onomatopoeic* or imitative theory, that words are based on sounds made by other animals or on sounds occuring in nature, such as thunder; (3) the *work-chant* theory; (4) the *ding-dong* theory, that words are derived from the sounds made when objects are struck; (5) the *mouth-gesture* theory, that the tongue, lips, and jaws imitate the movements of the hand, etc.; (6) the *conventionalist* theory, that language is arrived at by social agreement (a kind of social-contract theory

290

applied to language); (7) the *instinctivist* theory, that language is a phenomenon arising at a certain level of cognitive or intellectual evolution (a species-specific ability); (8) the *contract* theory, that language is an outcome of man's social nature and communicative needs; (9) the *babbleluck* theory, which finds an association between infant babbling and external responses; (10) the theory of *divine origin,* which views language as a miraculous gift; and (11) the *gestural* theory, that words appear as an outcome of symbolic gestures (list taken from Hewes 1973). Before we consider any of these, however, we must consider how language differs from other means of communication.

## PRIMATE COMMUNICATION: LINGUISTIC AND NONLINGUISTIC BEHAVIOR

What is language? It has been defined in a number of ways by different people. Linguists generally use the term to imply more complex differentiation of sound systems and grammatical and syntactic mechanisms than will be discussed here. We are concerned with the simpler origins of man's very complex means of communication and will approach language primarily as a communicative code which is distinct from and more complex than that of the animals. The full meaning to be attributed to the term *language* in this chapter will be clarified in the following pages.

Norbert Weiner wrote: "Fundamentally, the social sciences are the study of the means of communication between man and man or, more generally, in a community of any sort of beings" (Weiner 1948). This comment draws our attention to the fact that any society depends for its existence and survival on an effective communication system. Without such communication a group of animals is no more than an aggregate —a random collection of individuals, such as a cluster of moths around a lamp, which only interact mechanically. In contrast, communication has been described as an interaction or relationship in which one animal stimulates a response in another at a distance. The transmitted signal triggers a response in the receiver which arises from a different energy source than that of the signal (for discussion see Altmann 1967). For example, bumping into another animal does not necessarily constitute communication, even if the second animal is pushed aside. The signal must trigger a change in the "control organizing system"—the brain— of another animal (MacKay 1972).

This idea can be taken a stage further. If the response to a signal reinforces its transmission, we have a cyclical system of information. The message is effective if it maintains the structure of its source (Leaf 1972). In other words, effective communication occurs if a response is elicited from the receiver by a transmitted message, which in turn reinforces the mental set or communication habits of the sender. This cyclical type of communication is also characterized by the maintenance of the signal code and its potential for modification through use. Clearly, language can be characterized in this way.

Communications form the relationships and bonds that create, delineate, and maintain social groups. Defined in this way, communication can take many forms. The higher primates in particular use a wide variety of channels. Signals are transmitted by whole-body posture, gesture, facial expression, vocalization, and scent. More than one channel is often used in any transmission, so that a wide range of gradation is possible.

Recent research has shown fairly conclusively that vocalizations as well as many other forms of transmission in nonhuman primates are generated by the *limbic system* of the brain—the seat of the emotions (for review see Robinson 1972)—and not by the *neocortex* of the cerebral hemispheres (Fig. 10.1). Observations of behavior and investigations of the neurophysiology of vocalizations show that most, if not all, vocalizations of nonhuman primates are in fact the expression of emotion and that such expression has evolved as an effective and vital means of communication. The expression of emotion is involuntary rather than goal-directed (on certain occasions, however, it can be repressed or directed), yet it has evolved in great variety and complexity. Such expressions are monitored by all or most other members of the social group. Other, nonvocal, signals also clearly fall into this category, such as displays of rage, cringing movements, and other responses to fear.

By contrast, there are some gestures and movements that have an important function in communication, which are clearly derived from

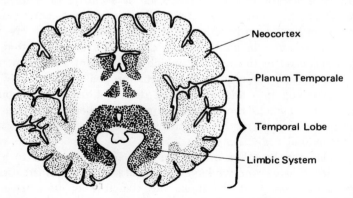

**Figure 10.1** *Cross-section of the human brain showing the relationship between the limbic system and the neocortex as well as other structures.*

the locomotor repertory and are generated by the cerebral neocortex. As such, they have a different character. A female monkey or ape may teach her young to ride on her back by pushing the young into the jockey position. The young will respond by learning, and we have to admit that communication has occurred. This behavior, in both mother and young, is controlled by the neocortex. Its special character is that it is goal-directed (MacKay 1972). Other examples of such behavior can be found in the mother-infant bond and in sexual contacts, where touch is of primary importance and is vital to the successful outcome of the relationship. Outside these two basic areas of behavior, physical contact plays an important part in establishing bonds between adults and in lowering tension levels in a social group. Among chimpanzees the hand-to-hand touch or caress seems to be as reassuring as it is among humans, and in this and many other species mutual grooming is an important means of bonding members of the group and reducing tension.

The concept of goal-directed behavior is very important. It implies the presence of intent, of behavioral options, and of choice, and it also implies that the neocortex can choose between patterns of motor output. Limbic vocalizations can be repressed or expressed: voluntary movement implies a wider selection of pathways. Goal-directed behavior, choice, and intent also imply that the imagination has made a leap to consider possible outcomes of optional behavior. The concept of the result of an action is called displacement: the displacement of conscious neural activity from present stimulus-response pathways to alternative memorized or imagined possibilities. Finally, the possibility of choice increases the information content of the signal over that of an involuntary signal (Shannon and Weaver 1964). We can summarize the two distinct categories of nonverbal communication (regardless of channel) as follows:

| *Type* | *Generated by* |
|---|---|
| 1) Involuntary, emotional | limbic system |
| 2) Voluntary, goal-directed | cerebral neocortex |

It is clear from our knowledge of animals in general and nonhuman primates in particular that the vast majority of their signalling falls into category 1. Voluntary signalling, however, is present to some degree in the communication systems of a number of groups of the higher mammals, especially the higher primates.

These two categories of communication behavior form the basis of an important distinction between primate vocalization and human language. Primate vocalization is the involuntary expression of emotion. Social animals are predisposed to monitor each other's behavior and are especially receptive to emotional expression. Emotions bring about adaptive behaviors essential for survival. The outward expression of emotional states enables all members of a group to monitor emotional levels in each other, and the survival of the group as a whole depends on the effectiveness of such monitoring by this nonverbal, involuntary means of communication.

In contrast, signals generated in the neocortex result in the voluntary movements involved in locomotion and feeding. In practice they are primarily involved in eliciting response by touch and are therefore "tight-beam" in nature. In other words, the communication channel is directed by contact to only one other individual, and the signal is not received by all members of the group. Knowing that primates communicate voluntarily by movement of the limbs in this way gives us a clue to how chimpanzees in captivity could be taught to communicate by symbolic means. Washoe, a female chimp, has learned to communicate with people using the gestures of the American Sign Language for the deaf (ASL), and her repertoire amounts to over 160 symbols (Gardner and Gardner 1971). Sarah, another female, has learned to place up to 130 magnetic plastic symbols on a magnetic board to construct simple sentences (Premack 1971).

This behavior of Washoe and Sarah demonstrate that with human to generate it and with human language as a model, chimpanzees can develop a symbolic means of communication. They can be taught to associate symbols with environmental objects and actions, and the nouns, verbs, and prepositions employed can be used to make gestural communication which has many of the properties of human language. In contrast, chimpanzees cannot be taught to speak or to use vocalization symbolically. Devoted teaching by the Hayeses could not induce the chimpanzee baby they reared with their own baby to learn to speak more than three or four poorly pronounced words (Hayes 1951, reviewed in Kellogg 1968). Though a call-system and a spoken language are both vocal-auditory means of communication, they are quite distinct in their function and physiological basis.

The distinction between these two systems of vocal communication, one emotive and the other voluntary, is also apparent in man. Laughing, crying, screaming, and exclamations of various kinds are generated by the limbic system, as are many of the accompanying facial expressions and some gestures. This is the ancestral call-system, which, although language can be superimposed upon it, is nevertheless quite distinct and involuntary. We are accustomed to inhibiting the expressions of our emotions, but we know the meaning of emotional expressions, and we monitor the call-system in others. A loud involuntary scream will attract much more attention than a verbal shout of "Help!"

The more technical differences between primate vocalizations (the call-system) and language can now be reviewed in the light of the above remarks. (For a more detailed and sophisticated discussion the reader is referred to Hockett 1960, Altmann 1967, and Thorpe 1972.)

1. Calls are mutually exclusive. An animal cannot emit a complex double call with some features of one call and some of another. Only one call can be emitted at a time. This situation is described as "closed." Language, by contrast, is "open" in the sense that we can emit utterances that are entirely novel combinations of sounds. It should be noted that, in terms of this distinction, Sarah's and Washoe's behavior qualifies as using language. Their repertoire of gestures or plastic symbols is limited, but they can combine the symbols in new ways.

2. A call is emitted only in the presence of the appropriate stimulus (external or internal); a call-system does not show temporal or spatial displacement. Language, on the other hand, does; we speak freely of things which are out of sight, in the past, in the future, or even nonexistent. This capacity of language results from its generation in the neocortex rather than in the limbic system. It is a product not of involuntary motivational processes but of voluntary intent, and intent implies displacement. In this respect as well Washoe and Sarah can be said to be using a form of language.

3. The difference between the sounds of any two calls is total. Language, on the other hand, is the elaboration of a limited number of components of sound that in themselves have no meaning but depending on their pattern may have an infinite number of meanings. In this respect the achievements of Washoe and Sarah again qualify as using language, in the same way that the use of ASL by humans qualifies.

4. The call-system is innate (generated by the limbic system), so the relationship between stimulus and response is genetically determined and somewhat inflexible. Language, on the other hand, is learned (generated by the neocortex), and its transmission and full expression must depend on a capacity to memorize symbols and their association with environmental phenomena.

5. The fact that chimpanzees cannot be taught to talk (that is, to vocalize linguistically) highlights the fact that speech is a species-specific genetic endowment of man. Man alone among living animals is able to express cortical activity in a vocal manner.

The definition of language is a complex problem and cannot be discussed here in full detail. Hockett (1960) first listed the minimum features of a communication system which could be called language; the foundations for a definition of language have been discussed by many authors since then, and further developed by Hockett himself. A useful review of the 16 design features of language now recognized has been prepared by Thorpe (1972), and the reader is referred to this paper for further details. The design features presented here fulfill the criteria not for fully evolved modern language, but for its most basic characteristics.

## HOW DID LANGUAGE EVOLVE?

Since there is no reason to discuss fully each theory of language evolution listed on page 290, I will discard numbers 2, 3, 4, 5, 9, 10 because they make assumptions which disregard the main steps in the evolution of language as we can reconstruct it from available facts. Ideas incorporated in the remaining theories have a place in our discussion.

Theory #1, which suggests that language may have evolved from the call-system, has been supported recently by Hockett and Ascher (1964), and I have discussed it favorably in an earlier paper (1970). However, there are important objections to this theory. First, as noted, language and the call-system are generated in different parts of the brain in different ways. Second, man still retains a call-system recognizably similar to that of the African great apes, that is, in man the call-system remains intact and distinct from language. On the other hand, this theory and numbers 6, 7, and 8 do suggest processes that are likely to have been important in the evolution of language, and we shall return to them.

How did the simplest form of voluntary communication first appear? In chimpanzees we already find it apparent in voluntary gestural movement. Besides the touching gestures already mentioned, we see chimpanzees using begging and soliciting gestures, extending the arm as a request for social acceptance and warning things away. Much of the behavior of a mother chimpanzee towards her offspring seems to fall into the same category. There is a whole range of greeting behavior which may also be at least partially voluntary. The learned repertoire of gestures is clearly quite extensive, even if still ill-defined. Since neocortical mechanisms underlie these gestures and since their meaning can easily be interpreted as symbolic, we have here behavior which is not really very different from the ASL behavior of Washoe. It already has many of the properties of linguistic communication.

Because we share a relatively recent common ancestor with the chimpanzee, we can adopt as the most economical hypothesis the view that the earliest form of voluntary, goal-directed, and symbolic communication among man's ancestors, the Hominidae, was gestural rather than vocal.

At this point we should note again that among higher primates many communications are multimodal—that is, they are expressed in more than one channel simultaneously. A human scream or cry is accompanied by a facial expression and in many cases a bodily gesture. Among nonhuman primates, the balance between modes is appropriate for the function of the call and the environment in which it is made. Some transmissions, such as calls, are more suitable for a forest environment where vision is restricted, while some, such as gestures and displays, are appropriate for communication in open country where predators are a threat. The channel and the transmitting and receiving organs selected are always approapriate to the environment of the species concerned.

It is not a great step from this stage of development to a multimodal symbolic and voluntary system of communication. In particular, it is commonly necessary to attract attention to a gesture by making a sound, especially if no physical contact is involved. From this observation we can predict that the first voluntary vocalizations would have the function or goal of drawing the attention of a number of individuals to a voluntary gesture. To the extent that the original gesture was voluntary in the first place, the sound itself could in due course be made to stand in for it alone.

What sounds were available to our own early ancestor? The kinds of sound made by higher primates—the screams, hoots, whimpers, pants, and barks—are the physical equivalent to human vowel sounds; they are created by the expiration of air through the mouth without interruption by the tongue and lips. The special character of human verbal language is that the expiration of vowel sounds is interpreted by the consonants of speech. Movements of the mouth involved in speech are not greatly different from those involved in sucking or swallowing. Just as the sucking reflex involves the lips and tongue, so consonants are formed: *p, b, m* at the lips; *d, n, t* at the tip of the tongue; *g, k* at the tongue base. The proximity of the tongue to the larynx and sides of the mouth may also form gutturals and clicks in certain languages.

Baboons show us how this way of producing speech may have begun. In baboons a common form of communication is lipsmacking—a display derived from movements of the lips and tongue that they use in grooming. Lipsmacking is not an uncommon greeting among higher primates and occurs among chimpanzees, but baboons alone emit grunts at the same moment. These grunts, modulated by tongue and lip movements, sound very much like human vowels and are produced in exactly the same way. The plains-dwelling baboons and the plains-dwelling ancestors of man shared a way of life that depended on group cohesion and structure. It is perhaps not a coincidence, therefore, that baboons share with man the ability to make vowel sounds modulated by tongue and lip as an aid to communication within a group.

This theory of the evolution of language suggests that an entirely new type of cortically generated vocalization was derived from a combination of a basic form of symbolic gesturing with the addition of voluntary vocalizations, which are basically vowel sounds and are generated in the same manner as primate vocalizations. In this new and restricted sense, theory #1 holds and can be incorporated into our general theory.

Hewes (1973) has discussed the gestural origin of language in a slightly different manner and has pointed out that tool-making may have facilitated this origin. It seems evident that any voluntary manual activity which is observed by other individuals and which is important for survival will enhance this gestural channel of communication. Manual skills were passed on from generation to generation by observation in this manner, as gestures and later as words. Holloway (1969) has argued that tool-making, like language, involves the imposition of arbitrary form upon the environment. It implies a cognitive structure which is at least necessary for language and harmonious with it. Hewes, however, suggests that the vocal aspect of language was very late in making its appearance, which I doubt; I will discuss the evidence in a later section of this chapter. I will now review the anatomical evidence on the evolution of language.

## EVIDENCE OF COMPARATIVE ANATOMY

### The Brain and Endocast

There are many minor differences between the head (where vocalizations are generated) of a man and that of a chimpanzee, but few major ones. One of the most striking differences lies in the relative size and form of the brain. Cranial capacity alone, however, is no guide to linguistic ability. The elephant and the whale, with brains vastly bigger than our own (5000 cc and 6700 cc respectively), do not "talk," while human so-called "bird-headed" (nanocephalic) dwarfs, whose brains are no bigger than those of chimpanzees or early hominids (varying from 400–600 cc), can talk like five-year-old children (Sekel 1960). Evidently they carry the anatomical correlates of language acquisition and use. We can assume that the foundations of language in the form of new intracortical connections may have appeared well before the brain expanded, but that the immense memory bank and the extensive ability to associate between modalities which language requires both provided a role for and necessitated an increase in brain size. This increase represents not the inception but the flowering of the specifically human adaptation.

The general increase in size is found in all parts of the brain, but is especially obvious in the cerebral cortex, which in man is deeply folded (64 percent of the surface of the human cortex is hidden in the folds or sulci, as compared to 25 to 30 percent in apes). This implies a great elaboration of the cortex and its components—the cortical nerve cells and intracortical connections.

The human brain is roughly three times as large as the chimpanzee brain and is slightly asymmetrical. Unlike the chimpanzee brain, the human brain is larger on the left side in the area of the *planum temporale* (see Fig. 10.1) (Geschwind 1972). There is evidence that the parts of the cortex concerned with the source of speech symbols and concepts almost always lie on the larger, so-called dominant hemisphere of the brain—usually the left hemisphere. (Damage to that hemisphere in early life will result in displacement of the so-called speech areas to the right hemisphere.) These speech areas are shown in Figure 10.2. They include *Wernicke's area* apparently the most important, which lies on

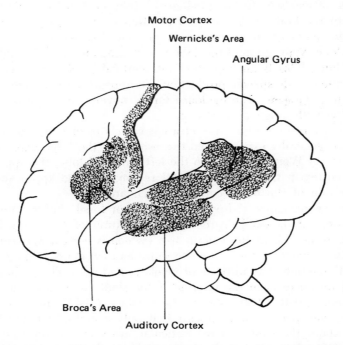

Motor Cortex

Wernicke's Area

Angular Gyrus

Broca's Area

Auditory Cortex

**Figure 10.2** *View of the left side of the human brain showing the main areas of the neocortex concerned with speech production.*

the temporal lobe, and includes the planum temporale. Damage to this area results in loss not of verbal fluency, but of sense. The victim's speech seems to be lacking in content; the appropriate words are frequently replaced by others, sometimes related in meaning and sometimes not; and in some victims the sound components of words are incorrectly integrated. Second, there is *Broca's area* on the frontal lobe; damage here results in forgetting words and difficulties with grammar, rather than failure of sense. Between them, these two areas of the cortex create the program for speech (Geschwind 1972). This program is synthesized in a third area, the supplementary motor cortex, where the appropriate muscle patterns are planned. The plan evolved in this area is then fed into the adjacent motor gyrus, where muscle contractions are effected. (For a recent review of neurolinguists see Whitaker 1971.) It is of great interest that Wernicke's area is closely linked to the angular gyrus —the inferior parietal association area. Only man seems to have this particular part of the cortex, and its development is recent in man's evolution (see Von Bonin and Bailey 1961; Geschwind 1964; Campbell 1970).

The idea that the angular gyrus is a recent development in the evolution of man's brain (its phylogeny) is supported by studies of the growth of the brain in infants and children (ontogeny). Here we find that those parts of the brain which develop last include the inferior parietal lobe. Maturation of this lobe is not complete until the eighteenth year or later. This is an important intracortical association area which is associated with speech production: it appears late in ontogeny as well as in phylogeny. The evidence for its novelty in evolution and its association with language is strong.

Thus we can see some very clearcut correlates of language in man's brain: the generally expanded cortex, especially the large expansion on the surface of Wernicke's area in the left temporal lobe, the appearance of new cortex in the inferior parietal region, and the appearance and specialization of the other cortical speech areas.

Can we recognize those developments in fossil skulls? The inside of the bones of the skull do reflect some features of the brain. Besides giving us some indication of brain size (which is not exactly equivalent to cranial capacity), they indicate considerably more folding in the cortex of hominids than in those of monkeys and apes. The earliest work of this kind on casts of the interior of the skull (endocasts) was done by Schepers (1946, 1950) and Le Gros Clark (1947). In spite of the claims by Schepers, it now appears that only a limited amount can be learned about the evolution of particular areas of the hominid brain. Dart (1926) claimed that the brain of *Australopithecus* was already reorganized in a human direction in spite of its chimpanzee-like size, and Holloway has recently argued (1972) that the expansion of the parietal cortex (which we see clearly in man) was well underway, perhaps to the extent that some gestural or even verbal voluntary communication was possible.

A newly discovered skull from Kenya (East Rudolf No. 1470), dating from over 2 million years ago, shows on the internal surface of the cranial bones signs of a very well developed third inferior frontal gyrus in the region of Broca's speech area. This is highly suggestive of a human-like reorganization and expansion of the frontal lobes, which would make linguistic behavior possible.

Scientists in the USSR claim that in the skull of *Homo erectus* (the species of hominid which precedes *Homo sapiens*), in which the endo-cranial capacity varies from 850–1200 cc, we can recognize prominences which coincide with all three speech areas described above (Kotchet-kova 1960). If these observations are confirmed, the neuroanatomical correlates of speech itself may have been quite fully evolved at least half a million years ago.

My own inclination is to accept these observations and their im-plications. There is no question that the reorganization and development in the brain associated with human speech is quite profound in its ex-tent and is likely to have evolved over a considerable period. The key reorganization may be quite ancient and may even have preceded the rapid expansion of the brain, which began perhaps two-and-one-half to three million years ago. The expansion was undoubtedly associated with the evolution of language and the vast memory store which this implies, but it was probably associated with other hominid adaptations as well. Thus the evidence of the evolution of the brain obtained from endo-casts, though not as precise as we would wish, is suggestive of a reasonably slow evolution of those parts of the cortex which in modern man are involved in speech production.

### The Pharynx

Like those of the other higher primates, the vowel sounds of humans are generated in the larynx, but only in humans do they then pass through an extension of the alimentary canal called the pharynx before entering the oral cavity (Fig. 10.3). This part of the vocal tract above the larynx in humans appears to have been selected for only one func-tion—phonetic differentiation. The distance of the cross-sectional area of the vocal tract from the laryngeal source determines the formant frequencies of the vowel sounds (Lieberman 1973). The form of the vocal tract can be varied by raising and lowering the larynx or the tongue. The resonance of the nasal cavity can be altered by raising or lowering the soft palate. The presence of the pharynx is unique to man (Negus 1949) and is clearly associated with the evolution of speech.

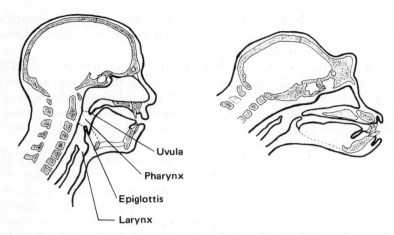

Uvula

Pharynx

Epiglottis

Larynx

**Figure 10.3** *The vocal tracts of man and chimpanzee compared, demonstrating the presence of the pharynx in the human tract. (After Lieberman et al., 1972)*

Do we have any evidence of this anatomical novelty in the fossil record?

Lieberman et al. (1972) claim that it is possible to reconstruct the vocal tract of fossil hominids by deducing the position of the hyoid bone (never preserved in fossilization) which supports the larynx. The hyoid bone is supported by the geniohyoid muscles which arise on the genial tubercles on the inner surface of the jaw in the mid-line and the style-hyoid ligament which arises from the styloid process on the base of the skull. As indicated in Figure 10.4, the intersection of lines projected from these bony anchor points is taken to indicate the position of the hyoid bone and larynx. While the accuracy of this supposition may be questionable, the overall result of these investigations is interesting and probably valid. We find that the position of the larynx in mature modern humans is almost unique and only shared by a limited number of fossil hominid skulls, such as Cro Magnon, Skhul V, and perhaps Steinheim, though the latter may be 200,000 years old. Some of the more recent fossils of Neanderthal man do not have the modern pharynx. This evidence suggests that the modern long pharynx evolved gradually during the last quarter-million years of man's evolution and was not well evolved in the large-jawed Neanderthal man. Evidently the neural mechanisms for linguistic communication had been established for a long time, as we have seen, but the evolution of the pharynx was a later development which allowed the production of optimal acoustic signals—vowel sounds that are varied, efficient, easy to produce and to distinguish, and therefore allow rapid information transfer (Lieberman 1973).

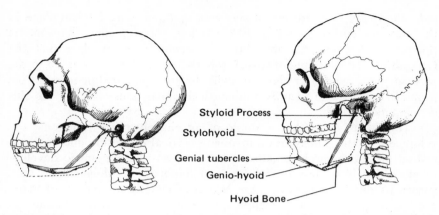

Styloid Process
Stylohyoid
Genial tubercles
Genio-hyoid
Hyoid Bone

**Figure 10.4** *Differences in the vocal tract are associated with the different positions of the hyoid bone in modern man and other related forms (e.g. Neanderthal man). In fossil forms, the position of the hyoid can be estimated by reference to the form of the genial tubercles and the angle of the styloid process on which the genial-hyoid and stylohyoid muscles originate. (After Lieberman, 1973)*

### The Tongue

The human tongue has an important part to play in generating speech, as the word *language,* from the Latin *lingua* ("tongue"), implies. Man's tongue is somewhat larger than that of some other higher primates, and its musculature is well developed. It has been claimed that the presence of certain small, bony protuberances on the inside of the jaw of fossil hominids is an indication that they possessed tongues similar to human tongue, whose muscles are anchored there. However, these prominences are present not only in man, but can be found in other living primates. We have seen that it is the direction in which they point rather than their presence alone which is significant in the evolution of verbalization.

### The Auditory Apparatus

The auditory apparatus receives and decodes vocalization and verbalization and thus is an essential component in vocal communication. The ear itself is highly evolved among primates and shows little evidence of change in man's evolution. The brain analyzes auditory input and makes possible the recognition of vocalization, as well as other sounds relevant to survival: these are all distinguished from background noise. The recognition of primate calls, however, is very different from the decoding process involved in language comprehension. Because of the closed nature of the call-system and the total differences among individual calls, the process of recognizing them, which takes place in the auditory cortex (see Fig. 10.2), is less complex than the analytic process of decoding the meaning of speech. It seems clear that the recognition and decoding of speech sounds are functionally related to the cortical areas where productive symbolization and coding occur (see p. 299), and we can identify intracortical connections which make this development possible.

This, then, is another example of an entirely novel functional development in the human brain involving cortical expansion and reorganization. Much research remains to be done on neurolinguistic development, which is no less fascinating and important a phenomenon than speech production (for review see Masland 1968). Both aspects of man's use of language present complex questions which will continue to challenge neurophysiologists and neuroanatomists.

## CONCLUSIONS

The distinction between language and the primate call-system of vocalizations seems well established. It is, however, not absolutely watertight. The limbic system has been shown to be a factor in facilitating the linguistic operations of the neocortex (Robinson 1972). Although intracortical connections are essential and primary in the production of speech, language is rarely entirely free of emotional overtones, and the limbic system continues to generate emotional signals which affect all cortical activity. Speech allows man his rational detachment and makes possible his concern with matters not directly related to his immediate biological goals. But this detachment, however desirable it may appear, is incomplete, and complete detachment is forever beyond man's reach. This is not so much a human defect as a biological need: natural selection has evolved a mechanism in which the limbic system still controls biological priorities.

The "detachment" between the limbic system and neocortex does seem, however, to be associated with the possibility of voluntarism, goal-direction, and displacement in language, and these are perhaps its key characteristics. Displacement makes possible the evolution of environmental reference—the possibility of object naming—and allows symbolization and classification. As Lancaster (1968) has argued, this is clearly an important stage in language evolution. Symbolization allows displacement and therefore reference to objects out of sight. More than this, symbolization and displacement make possible concepts of the first and second person—concepts of I and you. The concept of role interchange implies the recognition that I and you are in the same class of object, though each of us is quite distinct. It makes possible the recognition of the social identity of others and of self as an independent functioning object as well as subject.

This recognition of the first, second, and ultimately third person and of their social roles entails a rudimentary linguistic grammar (person), just as object (noun) and intention (verb) do. Possibly, collective exploitation of this kind of potential—of displacement with reference to persons as well as objects—is the key to the evolution of language and grammar. It is not so much the naming of objects in the environment—though this was an important first stage in the process—as the recognition of social identity that lifted verbalization from its earliest phase of social use among groups of interdependent individuals into language as we know it today.

We have postulated that the beginnings of goal-directed symbolic communication took the form of a repertoire of gestures generated by the neocortex. That such gestures are possible in nonhuman primates has been demonstrated by the work done with Washoe. Insofar as these gestures became symbolic, they required expanded memory and intracortical associations between sensory association areas and motor action patterns. This idea is somewhat close to that developed by Hewes (1973) and listed in this chapter as theory #11. We can then postulate that certain calls equivalent to vowel sounds would have been used to attract attention to these gestures. Here the vocal apparatus evolved for limbic expression comes under the control of the cortex. [The interjectional theory (#1) can in this limited sense be associated with our general theory.] We can also note that this evolutionary development was obviously a response to man's social nature and communication needs (theory #8), though it is also species-specific and depends for its further evolution on characteristics unique to the hominid brain. (Though not exactly theory #7, this observation does bear some slight relationship to it.) As the sound-gesture system of communication evolved, the meaning of the sounds and gestures must necessarily have become symbolic and in turn arbitrary. In this sense they were surely subject to social agreement (at some level of consciousness), and so we can absorb some of the ideas of the conventionalist theory, #6.

We can suppose that the greater importance assumed by the vocal aspect of our primitive language was due partly to the fact that the hands became more useful and valuable as organs of manipulation rather than communication, and partly to the fact that the information content of simple gestures was extremely limited and would soon have resulted in ambiguity. Silence is still needed in a few vital human activities, such as when hunters stalk their prey, and Bushmen still use a detailed and complex range of hand signals to communicate when hunting. Many of these symbols are pictorial, but some are quite abstract, if not fully arbitrary (Howell 1965). In general, however, man has become a talker, and a somewhat noisy creature: his means of communication is primarily by verbalization. Instead of using sound to reinforce gesture, we now use gesture to reinforce words.

The possibility of verbal communication—the development of an open system—brought with it the possibility of a rapid expansion in vocabulary and syntax, so that language was now in the position to carry the evolving hominid a long way beyond the level of adaptation found in any other animal. When the environment put more stress on these hominids, when selection pressures increased, language was a behavior which enabled man not only to survive as a uniquely well socialized species, but to spread and diversify his adaptations to just about every part in the world. Because our system of communication is symbolic and open there is virtually no limit to what we can do with it and no end to the cultural adaptations possible for man in the future. The limitations come from elsewhere; not from man's potential as an adaptive species, but from the environment which cannot carry for long any species which exploits the bases of its own subsistence—the environmental "capital." Biological limitations are now reversed: it is no longer a question so much of the adaptation of a species as of the integrity and limits of its environment. Adaptation to limit environmental exploitation in an absolute sense is a new type of evolutionary adaptation now required of the species *Homo sapiens*. The survival of the symbolic animal will depend upon it.

## SELECTED READINGS

Altmann, Stuart A., 1967, *Social Communication Among Primates*. Chicago: University of Chicago Press.

A useful collection of papers on primate communication.

Hewes, G. W., 1973, "Primate Communication and the Gestural Origin of Language," *Curren. Anthrop.*, 14:5–24.

A paper on the evolution of language.

Hinde, Robert, ed., 1972, *Non-Verbal Communication*. Cambridge: Cambridge University Press.

A recent review of non-verbal communication in animals and man.

Hockett, C. F. and Ascher, R., 1964, "The Human Revolution," *Curren. Anthrop.*, 5:135–168.

A paper on the evolution of language.

Lancaster, Jane B., 1968, "Primate Communication Systems and the

Emergence of Human Language," in *Primates—Studies in Adaptation and Variability*, P. Jay, ed. New York: Holt, Rinehart and Winston.

A paper on the evolution of language.

Sebeok, Thomas A., 1968, *Animal Communication*. Bloomington: Indiana University Press.

A general survey of animal communication systems.

Washburn, S. L. and Dolinhow, P. eds., 1971, *Perspectives on Human Evolution 2*. New York: Holt, Rinehart and Winston.

# Conclusion

# Chapter 11

# Anthropology In The Year 2000

**Murray J. Leaf**

The year 2000 seems a long way off. Yet it is no farther ahead of us than the year 1950 is behind us. In important respects, 1950 is not yet part of the anthropological past at all—it is part of the present. Issues raised then, and even before then, are now being debated as current issues. Opinions expressed then are still being quoted, not as background, but as viable argument to be agreed with or rejected. This suggests that if we keep the developments between 1950 and the present in mind as a guide and look for developing issues analogous to those that turned out to be important in the early 1950s, it should be possible to project ahead an equal space of time.

The natural procedure for this projection is to review the preceding chapters for common major themes, then review these themes for the pattern they seem to be converging toward, and then to consider the likely effects of this convergence in the overall context of the discipline.

## THE MAJOR COMMON THEMES

A high level of technical expertise is a remarkably common and constant element throughout the preceding chapters. Whether the knowledge is in computer programming, statistics, anatomy, language and language history, ceramic techniques, ecology, information theory, philosophy of science, psychology, or simple ethnography, it is clear that these authors are working with more specialized knowledge than their counterparts of twenty years ago—and far more than their speculative academic ancestors of fifty years ago. To my mind, however, this difference now appears as but a part of a larger system of differences, some of which are quite surprising.

311

The most obvious and far-reaching common theme of these essays involves the combination of three ideas, most forcefully expressed by Professors Prost, Cronin, and De Vos. These are the ideas of the use of logical models of potential configurations of variables, of causality, and of explanations involving not one but rather two or more independent types of variables. Together they make up a specific conception of the nature of anthropological research and explanation that is quite different from previous major formulations. The approach can be called "methodological generalization" in place of the older and more common idea that can be described as "substantive generalization."

All anthropologists, indeed most all scholars, would probably agree that some sort of generalization was the aim of their activity. In some way or other, scholars look into a specific corpus of data for information that will apply not only to that corpus but to an indefinite amount of further data as well. Disagreements arise when one tries to define "further" and when one tries to say what aspect of the data on hand is generally relevant.

The idea of substantive generalization in modern academic anthropology represents a carry-over from the nineteenth century. Basically, it is the idea that in building a theory one builds a system of abstract statements that directly describe, in abstract terms, features of the phenomenon under review. For cultural anthropology, the idea was to provide some general definition of culture, then to define major subtypes, and so on. Ruth Benedict's general division between "Dionysian" and "Apollonian" cultures was a very famous example and a prototype of many similar thematic or stylistic schemes. The most popular and widely used version of this approach is more technologically and organizationally oriented, and it borrows its major subtypes directly from nineteenth-century evolutionary theory: divisions among hunting and gathering, pastoral, peasant/agricultural, and industrial and/or urban cultures or societies. "Society" was another general category, divided in some views into types such as "patrilineal and patrilocal," "patrilineal and matrilocal," "matrilineal and matrilocal," and so forth. Archeologists used schemes based on a general idea of "cultures," and divided them like cultural anthropologists: pastoralism, agriculture, and so on. They also used thematic schemes of their own, like "formative," "preclassic," "classic," and so on. In all these schemes, analysis consisted of demonstrating that specific societies or communities fitted into one category rather than another, or into none. This is the approach E. R. Leach called "butterfly collecting" (1961:3, 4).

The present authors are not against classificatory schemes, and most of them make use of some of the traditional categories. However, none uses such schemes to identify his or her explanatory mechanisms directly or equates such categorization itself with explanation. Most of the authors develop new systems of categories to expose the general features of their data. But these categories are not substantive in the same sense, and simply applying them is not explanation in its own right. Prost's mathematical space of twenty-two dimensions is not a general definition of posture of which the separate postures he describes are subcategories. It is rather a kind of logical or conceptual background against which postures can be uniformly placed and grouped, no matter how they are qualitatively labeled. Longacre's conception of a random distribution of stylistic traditions serves the same function in his arguments; Plog's conception of geographical space with "populations" dispersed across it serves the same in his; Wagner's conception of a kind of logical blank slate that is filled in by native category distinctions that flow from their most general conceptual divisions serves for him; the concept of a communication cycle and the underlying apparatus of the mathematical concept of information serves the same function in my argument; "dualism" as a general pattern of interaction among variables serves for De Vos; McClaran uses the idea of a matrix of frames with items than can fill them; and Campbell seems to work mainly with a generalized conception of primate physiology and its behavioral potentials. Cronin was less explicit than the others about developing such a background scheme as a general point of method, but her orientation toward hypothesis testing, with its implications of interacting variables, fulfilled a similar role in her arguments. It is precisely in erecting such background systems that the largest part of the technical interests of the authors makes itself evident.

Once the background systems are erected and the phenomena of interest are described against them, the actual explanations follow from the phenomena themselves and represent "generalized" features of the phenomena only in the sense that they are what appear to be basic aspects of them. In other words, important or constant phenomena are identified to account for the less important or derivative ones. Facts are explained by more important facts, not by abstract categories as such.

This use of abstract schemes as background rather than as direct substantive categorizations of the phenomena under consideration is what the term "methodological generalization" is meant to convey. The generalization is not the phenomenon itself but a way of getting at it.

Although the authors have generally concentrated more on the method for making the explanatory variables appear than on fully describing the variables themselves, there do seem to be some common substantive trends or themes emerging. The most obvious is a concern with learning and the specific assumption that learning is a kind of scarce commodity. Learning in this sense involves not only how-to-do-it information but also ways of saying who is to do it: the organization as well as the content of work. The second obvious theme is a concern with survival, or adaptation, at an individual level that involves exploiting many kinds of resources that interact and shift in a constantly difficult and challenging way. These two themes are interrelated. Exploiting resources requires a great deal of learning, and learning requires resources to exploit and adaptive problems to solve. Learning is a means of survival, and survival both permits and requires continuing learning.

Of course, the idea that culture is some sort of learned system or system of learned patterns is a stock phrase in cultural anthropology, and one with which all traditional archeologists and social anthropologists would probably agree. Moreover, there is nothing radically new about a focus on adaption at the individual level, although most treatments do not focus on it as distinct from general social or cultural evolution quite so sharply as do the present treatments. The latter try, however, to introduce unusual and empirical content into both these concepts. "Learning" is not simply assumed to have happened in relation to everything that is known. Rather it is assumed that only some known things were actually learned, while others were either acquired from what was learned indirectly or self-generated in some way. There is a focus on exactly how learning occurs—that is, on *teaching*, or training. This is viewed as a complex and fairly intensive interaction between specific individuals, involving the transfer of quite restricted kinds of information rather than of "culture" in general. Longacre thinks in terms of a close interaction between older women and younger women who teach such matters as the preparation of temper, slip, design, firing, and decoration. The questions are which older women teach to which younger women and, assuming that such patterns are so complex they must become habitual for those who learn them, what happens to the early association in the later life of the younger women. Plog assumes that the resources of the environment known to him were recognized and exploited by the prehistoric people he studies, given the needs and limitations imposed by their population, seed, and basic technology (allowing for high levels of innovation and interchange of available knowledge between areas). That is, he assumes people study their environments and learn from them whatever they can use, while they pass on an internal tool kit of basic devices and techniques—from seeds to knowledge of water control. Population concentrations reflect this knowledge. Not arguing for universal categories of mind but rather for implications of key categories that differ from society to society, Wagner is assuming that people learn these key categories from their group, learn how to use them, and then proceed to work with them in constantly creative and flexible ways. In other words, he is reducing social structure to a few key building-blocks that can be shown to be taught by one person in the community to another. My own conception of the items of information that make up the "social contracts" of rituals is quite similar. The ritual as "contract" does not specify detailed attributes of each of the roles involved, but rather only vague core ideas, broad general parameters which people then use in discussing their relationships with each other. People "fill in" these ideas to further specify their relationships as they go along, day to day and minute to minute. No one knows precisely what a husband or wife should be, but everyone has a general conception along with some related ideas: a wife is also to be a mother, is dependent, needs protection and support, and must herself protect her children and their interests. A woman may engage in some specific actions that she considers to fit this general pattern, but other people may disagree about their appropriateness. Domestic arguments often turn on such points. It may even be that the woman does something for quite unrelated reasons and will still argue that it fits the required pattern. In this way, the detailed "meaning" of the core ideas is constantly being negotiated and thus is constantly changing, yet the pattern of the core ideas remains a general framework encompassing the negotiations. A ritual is a special type of culturally evolved teaching machine: it says what the basic ideas are and gives dramatic instruction in how they are applied and acted out.

Although the negotiation around such vague concepts could logically go on forever, there are practical limits to the time and energy people can devote to it. These limits are suggested best by Professor Cronin's paper, especially by the slippage she described between the ways in which success was perceived by the two groups of Sicilians and the Australians. Why do these "discrepancies" exist? Because they do not matter—in fact because they probably seldom if ever are made explicit for most individuals in the normal course of their daily affairs. People with each set of ideas work productively and achieve their own ends while they interact in a restricted context where their business relations are foremost. Agreement limited to general ideas of success as a desirable goal and some concept of material achievement is quite sufficient for this interaction, and they need dig no deeper into each other's beliefs. Each person can evidently interpret his position in the general society as consistent with his own conception of what success can be, and in the normal course of business he has little or no occasion to discover that other people he deals with hold quite different conceptions.

McClaran is also concerned with teaching and makes it a direct aspect of her analytic method. The skills she teaches—resting on abstract concepts of contrast or similarity of distribution of elements— provide interesting and important support to Wagner's argument for equally abstract concepts of quite a different sort, and the two essays taken together raise many important long-range issues.

Professor De Vos deals with learning and teaching from a more subjective perspective. He asks the question: What would make a child want to learn the social concepts of his community? What gives seemingly abstract social symbols their apparent force and emotive importance for individuals? The questions are complicated in the way he poses them and tries to argue abstractly that they are logically related, but the gist of his answer seems simple and important. He assumes, and to some extent argues, that a newborn child has a bundle of inherited reaction patterns which are related to its survival. The patterns have both emotional and behavioral aspects: revulsion coupled with vomiting and withdrawal; a vague fear coupled with crying and retreat or withdrawal; happiness or contentment together with attraction and feeding, and so forth. None of the reactions are clearly differentiated or consciously labeled, but all are very strong and important as perceptions and physiological experiences. From this point, the argument seems to be that as a person ages, certain of these complex reactions are recognized and developed in cultural learning. They become institutionalized and institutionally fixed and differentiated from other institutionalized features—like knots formed by ribbons tied in a pattern of separate points on a ball of yarn. From the actor's point of view, the institutionalization is adopted because it provides recognition for his own internal needs and action-orientations. Learning a label for hunger is useful to a person who is hungry. From a social point of view, the action-orientations thus tagged provide a motivational, emotive, context to the tags that can be exploited for important social purposes, tying the individual's feelings and desires to the concepts in ways that make him much more than a detached reciter of cultural lessons. In the end, the action-orientations related to basic emotional drives tied to individual survival become an aspect of the social symbols for those who learn them, and the symbols become aspects of the internal organization of one's cognitive/emotive conceptions of self and of one's surroundings.

Professor Prost's results and the methods that underlie them strongly reinforce the idea that what one learns from one's culture is not a complete complex system of rules, but rather a system of minimal tags that have in common mainly the property that they are understood to be different from each other. To the learner, it isn't clear what "anger" is in detail, but it is clear that whatever it is must be different from "happy." On the basis of this understanding, each person works out a system of postures that is largely personal, elaborating the little bit of information he has genuinely been taught. This is why the human interpreters did less well than the computers. The computer simply asked for different groups within the postures of each person. The humans looked for general stances or postures apart from the other postures of each actor—which were unknown to them. Anger for one person was not closely similar to anger for the second, but anger for each person was clearly different from his own happy, sad, and so on. Prost's data indicate the kind of physiological/cultural "bundle" that is created in the learning process more simply than De Vos's arguments do. The stances involve training of muscles, proprioceptors, and presumably some emotional component on the physiological side, and these are intertwined with the verbal labels that serve as commands and their social significance on the side of culture. The idea of "intensity" attaching to the labels for emotions on the cultural side is intertwined with the internal sensations of imbalance, or deviation from a rest posture, on the physiological side and with perceptions of more extreme extensions of the limbs.

It is astonishing how well Professor Campbell's explanation of the physiological and evolutionary basis of language use applies directly to Prost's results and indirectly to De Vos's conceptions of learning. Although Prost concentrates on the postures, he is in fact describing very much the sort of behavior Campbell made central to his evolutionary reconstruction: vocal expression that calls attention to a voluntary gesture. It is quite reasonable to consider Prost's command just such a verbal means of calling attention to a gesture and to consider postures as the learned, variable gestures which Campbell discusses. This means, in effect, that the physiological and evolutionary basis of language described by Campbell also underlies postural behavior as analyzed by Prost and to some degree the kind of learning of cultural symbols in a behaviorally oriented and emotive context that De Vos was calling attention to. Perhaps I should also add that Campbell's concept of a language fits quite well with my own concept of an information system and also with Wagner's concept of a set of basic cultural distinctions involving words associated with vague, imagistic forms. Both are vocalized systems that allow choice of elements, allow recombination of elements, are used in planning and in "displaced" description, and, most importantly, allow individuals to imaginatively interchange role positions in a grammatical way—they have categories for "I" and "you," where it is understood that if two parties are speaking, each can be "I" to the other "you." It might be added that such restricted information systems do not seem to depend on the existence of elaborate grammatical languages of the sort McClaran is concerned with, and they might therefore quite possibly predate such languages in the course of human evolution.

In short, the picture we have emerging is of the creation of social forms by the training of evolved symbolic and emotional mechanisms at an individual level, and we seem to see the full range of relevant factors in a descending chain from the pressures on individuals in responding to their environment with their levels of population and technology down through the structure of the symbolism of day-to-day interaction, the way it is implanted in the cultural setting of the growing individual, and finally to a conception of the exact physiological mechanisms that carry the training and physically connect the emotional, verbal, and behavioral memories and reactions in the individual.

## THE POINT OF CONVERGENCE

The point that all these themes seem to be converging toward is a kind of revised version of Malinowski's "functionalism"—an approach that explains society in relation to the individual and not the reverse (and without insisting that society is a single monolithic entity). The fundamental difference between this view and the original theory is that Malinowski could not find a viable alternative to the idea of a fixed set of biological "needs," and his position was thus untenable. With the new approach we have a way of seeing how needs can be created, but without recourse to the idea that they are created *by* society. Society—or conceptions of society and of the world in general—is created as part of the processes of differentiating and organizing needs, and needs, conversely, are thereby built into the concepts as they are learned and acted upon. The fundamental processes are those of differentiation for organization and for communication. These processes occur at the level of human interaction and are passed on by use from generation to generation through mechanisms as diverse as mothers washing babies, groups engaging in complex rituals, or hunting parties where young men follow older men. This new conception is a major step further removed from common-sense social theory than Malinowski's was because its major parameters are no longer those of ordinary discourse, but those whose reality has been demonstrated through technical research. It is not really founded on distinctions like that between society and the individual, but rather on differences among types of adaptive strategies, conceptions of symbolism and symbolic process, and detailed ideas of how the human organism actually works. Methods of proof and modes of argument demand far more rigor and comprehensiveness than those found in social thought in ordinary discourse.

## RELATION TO ANTHROPOLOGY AS A WHOLE

The best way to review the possible effects of these ideas on the field of anthropology as a whole, as it might develop in the next twenty-five years, is to return to the original distinction between the academic, professional, and intellectual organizations of the discipline.

There are three major uncertainties in the academic organization at present. Will the trend toward increasing undergraduate instruction in proportion to graduate instruction continue? Will departments of anthropology break up along subdisciplinary lines, as has apparently been happening in the case of linguistics? Will the overall size of the discipline in comparison with other disciplines continue to increase?

The trend toward expanding undergraduate enrollment and consequent concentration on undergraduate teaching has been underway now for almost thirty-five years, and it responds to many factors apart from the theoretical content of the discipline. Accordingly, acceptance of the drift in thinking represented in these chapters would not be expected to exert a dominant influence in the future. But I think that to the extent that the subject matter does become more technical and demand genuine knowledge of a number of difficult areas, anthropology should become less accessible or desirable as a general education course and relatively stronger as a graduate training field and a pure research field. I think it is possible to predict that graduate instruction and research, contrary to some present indications, will remain lively.

In the face of the vision of the future that emerges from these chapters and the fact that their detailed interrelations arose without prior arrangement, it seems to me impossible to believe that there will be a serious tendency for division of the present field into significantly more independent subfields, which would be reflected in departments of anthropology breaking up into departments of social anthropology, departments of physical anthropology, and the like. What we see here instead is an interweaving of subdisciplines, with each focusing the task of the other and providing explanatory mechanisms that help cope with the problems that others can not solve. The essays argue for a gradual filling in of at least most of the gaps between the present subfields, and this we would expect to see reflected in departmental curricula and in staffing. Of course, the fact that most subdisciplines now overlap with other fields outside anthropology will not be affected. Indeed, it seems evident from what has been written here that the intimacy of these connections can be expected to increase, with physical anthropologists becoming more knowledgeable in physiology, linguists more knowledgeable in language theory, at least some archeologists more knowledgeable in economics, perhaps others in aspects of technology, and so forth. These trends suggest a pattern of fairly large departments with many joint appointments with other schools and departments, a diversified research program, and active graduate teaching and research. This in turn probably means that major training of Ph.D's will continue to be concentrated in relatively few large departments.

Like the trend toward undergraduate teaching, the trend toward the increasing size of the discipline as a whole is a response to many factors outside the theoretical content of the discipline and in large measure beyond the organized control of the discipline. In fact, the two trends are related, since undergraduate teaching constitutes the major source of economic demand for anthropologists. Increased graduate demand and research demand are also factors. I would say that the perspective suggested by these chapters, if adopted, would 'tend to ensure continued growth, stimulating new work in new areas and requiring new research money. Although the present convergence carries a new sense of accomplishment, it also carries a powerful sense of the need for much more work—precisely because it is responsive to higher standards of technical rigor.

In the area of the professional organization of the discipline, the present trends would seem to fit very closely with wider institutional changes underway. Responding to its greatly increased size, the American Anthropological Association has recently inaugurated a series of subfield journals for articles of narrower interest and has adopted a policy of making the *American Anthropologist* a vehicle for articles of general theoretical relevance that cross subdisciplinary lines. At the same time, it is moving toward an internal structure consisting of overlapping subgroups composed of memberships of the more specialized societies that roughly parallels the structures of these chapters. Each rests on its own technical literature, but there is an overlapping and interlocking of techniques, results, and subject matter among them—a chain of theoretical areas concerned with a chain of phenomena in the world. Unquestionably, these organizational changes will involve many difficulties. I suspect, however, that eventually there will be formal international anthropological societies with strong continental subunits, strong regional conferences under them, and probably some sort of indirect electoral control—the council of fellows of the American Anthropological Association has already ceased to be effective as a body for making scholarly policy. Individuals will nonetheless undoubtedly continue to belong to multiple associations reflecting their particular technical skills and interests.

The area of research support, depending as it does on government policy to a large degree, is difficult to predict. At present, there is a tendency to prefer research with national applications of a fairly direct sort. In my opinion, this tendency partly reflects the absence of a framework of theory that would permit anthropologists to explain forcefully the need for more basic research in clear terms. My feeling is that the present convergence does frame such an ability, and as it pays off more and more spectacularly (if it does) it should reawaken funding interest in farther-reaching problem areas. It also seems evident that as the subdisciplines within anthropology draw more closely together, each of the speciality areas will have relatively more to offer its nonanthropological counterpart. As physical anthropology becomes more integrated with linguistics and social anthropology, it will have more to offer comparative anatomy in biology, for example. This too should increase the interest of funding agencies.

But *will* the present themes be developed in the future? It is best to break up this question into some component elements.

Many of the major themes of these essays are already being adopted on a broad front. Technical skills are widely demanded—sometimes for their own sake with no relation to the substantive problems they are applied to. The search for overarching deterministic theories is becoming increasingly old-fashioned and is being criticized from many perspectives. This dissatisfaction is bound to grow. There is a widespread trend to focus more on the individual as an explanatory variable in relation to society. All these drifts may be expected to continue to develop. These trends would not necessarily lead to a convergence of theory and subject matter, however. In fact, many anthropologists have taken increasing technical proficiency as implying that the field will eventually break up into increasing numbers of pockets of experts who do not speak to or interest each other. It is often supposed that the choice will be between being experts or being "generalists"—broad speculative thinkers without thorough grounding in any area. The rejection of deterministic theory is considered to fit into this pattern, amounting to a rejection of any general theory at all, since it is thought that a nondeterministic theory complex enough to deal with society and culture would be too complex to codify and use.

In each subfield, there are theoretical persuasions that point away from convergence and toward fragmentation of the field as a whole. In each subfield, there are generally good reasons for each of these developments. In archeology, for example, there are many problems of chronology, of reconstructing technology, and of simply acquiring more information on the historical record which do not have direct, or at least obvious, relations to other subfields, and many archeologists who work on them do not see any clear benefit from a theory that would unite their work with others, especially if that theory was more complicated than one directly tailored to their concerns. Indeed, there is probably a measure of comfort to be obtained from the knowledge that such relevance does not exist. In social anthropology, much of the current work in symbolic analysis would be embarrassed, and not aided, by demands for broad relevance. In cultural anthropology, strong developments in several areas, notably "ethnoscience" and "componential analysis," have no obvious relation to other work in other subfields, but they do involve important issues in their own immediate contexts and are bound to continue to grow. Some important work in physical anthropology is undertaken without clear use of a framework of general relevance—most notably in genetics, as indicated. And in linguistics, many of the claims for new insight into the general nature of thought have no bearing on knowledge about thought as it appears in other subfields and no concrete prospect of developing any. If one considers the reasons for each of these developments, and especially if one also takes a dim view of human nature to the effect that an easier approach that reduces the quarters from which criticism might come will be adopted even if it promises less so long as it promises enough to justify continuing work, then the prospects for the present convergence would seem rather dim.

It seems to me, however, there is a major flaw in this reasoning. It assumes people are "in" subfields just as the traditional cultural and social models assume natives are "in" their families, lineages, or other local groups. In reality, this is not the case. Anthropologists merely use the ideas of subfields, as they also use other ideas. They could use the idea of anthropology as a whole, and it can have as direct a bearing on what they do as the idea of a narrow specialization deep "within" the field. Subfields are a kind of myth, and myths can be forgotten or replaced by other myths.

It seems obvious that people adopt myths which provide compelling justifications for their actions and give them the strongest possible claim on the attention and respect of others. Accordingly, if an archeologist has to choose between a theoretical outlook that applies to his work alone and another that relates his work to others, he will eventually either choose the latter or lose out to someone who does. To choose the former, even if it provides better protection from external criticism, is to choose the weaker general justification for his work. The same may be said for any other "subfield." Eventually, if the sorting of competing overviews goes on in an orderly manner, we would expect a common general rationale to emerge.

Based on the past history of anthropology and of other scientific fields, I would guess that the present conception of a set of overlapping issues ranging from ecological adaptation to the relation of the brain to speech and manual behavior will not constitute a major theory by itself. It is too complicated, and for any person to grasp all the links requires a level of training and thinking not generally found or needed for the normal work in the field. I would rather see this convergence as a pattern in the data and research results that will continue to develop, although some much simpler general theoretical model will be required to account for it and bring it into full prominence. However, simpler models are likely to be comparatively vague, and thus, at least initially, there are likely to be several competing ways to account for the same more concrete results.

My own candidate for the general ruling conception that is likely to be fastened upon is some sort of cyclical model of cultural interaction in different major forms: individuals with individuals, groups with their environments, and individuals with their environments. My preference would be for the kind of communication model used in the conclusion of my analysis of Sikh rituals and in my 1972 monograph, but it is more likely that a simpler and vaguer notion will be more widely accepted.

In any event, as more anthropologists begin to work with the idea of communication or interaction cycles and with the idea of the choice of perceptual and behavioral options that they imply, it will become clear that a more fundamental problem is yet to be solved and a more fundamental theoretical model still to be developed. This is a conception of minimal differences, a theory of how an individual perceives, or creates, contrast itself—for contrast is at the basis of differences, and differences are the basis of choice. This problem has already been recognized in connection with theories of perception for several decades, and it is a main focus of Professor Wagner's interests. One cannot define the basis of contrast without a sense of the uses to which contrasts are put and of the perceptual and expressive apparatus of the organisms employing them. For this reason I think that eventually the concern with contrast and differences will come together with communication theory and with a physiological model of the integration of verbal, physical, and emotive behavior to form a general empirical model of the social stabilization of individual thought and perception. Beyond this, it is not possible to predict.

To judge by the changes from 1950 to the present, it would not be surprising if the year 2000 saw only the beginning of the second step imagined here, the theory of perceivable contrast. But it should be remembered that these chapters represent not bare beginnings of trends, but work already well under way. My guess is that some sort of well-developed idea of communication cycles will be widely accepted within ten years and that the rudiments of an idea of how the individual sees contrasts and uses them in learning and teaching will be emerging at about the same time. The rest of the time will be spent in testing these formulations against older ones and refining them. This will have to include a great deal of work on language and language learning; at this point the kind of work Professor McClaran is doing should fit in and add great force to the developing trend.

Before beginning this project, I was not so optimistic. It is still possible these projections are wrong. But my own present conviction after editing these chapters and discussing them with their authors and many other people in the field is that anthropology in the year 2000 will be stronger and healthier than it is now. It will survive the present crisis posed by the idea that one must choose between being a narrow and irrelevant "expert" or a vague "generalist" and will move toward a more hierarchical type of structure where it is clearer that leading work is done by those who are more technically expert and have a broader vision of the field as a whole which permits them to choose crucial areas of research with more decisive and far-reaching implications—as in the biological and physical sciences at present. All this will involve a qualitatively new conception of how one studies man, and yet it will still be a beginning. It is my belief that the discoveries of the past will grow small and pale before the discoveries of the present and future.

# Bibliography

Aberle, D., *et al.*, **1963**, "The Incest Taboo and the Mating of Animals," *American Anthropologist*, 65:253–265.

Adams, Robert McC., **1960**, "Early Civilizations, Subsistence and Environment," in *City Invincible: An Oriental Institute Symposium*, C. H. Kraeling and R. McC. Adams, eds. Chicago: University of Chicago Press.

———, **1965**, *Land Behind Baghdad: A History of Settlement on the Diyala Plains*. Chicago: University of Chicago Press.

Allison, A. C., **1954**, "Protection Afforded Sickle-Cell Trait Against Subtertion Malarial Infection," *British Medical Journal*, I:290–294.

Allport, G. W., and P. E. Vernon, **1933**, *Studies in Expressive Movement*. New York: Macmillan.

Altmann, Stuart A., **1967**, "The Structure of Primate Social Communication," in *Social Communication Among Primates*, S. A. Altmann, ed. Chicago: University of Chicago Press, pp. 325–363.

Arlotto, Anthony, **1972**, *Introduction to Historical Linguistics*. Boston: Houghton Mifflin.

Bailey, Fredrick G., **1960**, *Tribe, Case and Nation*. Manchester: Manchester University Press.

Barnes, J., **1962**, "African Models in the New Guinea Highlands," *Man*, 62:5–9.

Barnett, H. G. *et al.*, **1954**, "Acculturation: An Exploratory Formulation," Social Science Research Council Summer Seminar on Acculturation, 1953, *American Anthropologist*, 56:973–995.

Barnouw, Victor, **1963**, *Culture and Personality*. Homewood, Ill.: Dorsey Press.

Barth, Frederick, ed., **1969**, *Ethnic Groups and Boundaries: The Social Organization of Cultural Difference*, Series in Anthropology. Boston: Little, Brown.

**Bascom, William R.,** 1954, "Four Functions of Folklore," *Journal of American Folklore,* 67:266 ff.

**Bateson, Gregory,** 1958, *Naven,* 2d printing. Stanford: Stanford University Press.

**Bell, P. R.,** 1959, *Darwin's Biological Work.* New York: John Wiley.

**Birdwhistell, R. L.,** 1952, *Introduction to Kinesics: An Annotation System for Analysis of Body Motion and Gesture.* Washington, D.C.: Department of State, Foreign Service Institute.

———, 1970, *Kinesics and Context.* Philadelphia: University of Pennsylvania Press.

**Bloomfield, Leonard,** 1933, *Language.* New York: Holt, Rinehart and Winston.

**Boas, Franz,** 1905, Boas' selection in Boas and J. Powell, *Introduction to Handbook of American Indian Languages and Indian Lingustic Families of America North of Mexico,* Preston Holder, ed. Lincoln: University of Nebraska Press, 1966.

———, 1912, "Changes in Bodily Form of Descendants of Immigrants," *American Anthropologist,* 14, 3:530–562.

———, 1916, "The Origin of Totemism," *American Anthropologist,* 18:319–326.

———, 1936, "The Aims of Anthropological Research (1932)," in *Race, Language, and Culture.* Glencoe, Ill.: Free Press, 1966.

———, 1936, "History and Science in Anthropology, A Reply," reprinted in *Race, Language, and Culture.* Glencoe, Ill.: Free Press, 1966.

———, 1940, *Race, Language and Culture.* New York: Macmillan.

**Bolinger, Dwight,** 1968, *Aspects of Language.* New York: Harcourt, Brace and World.

**Bonin, G. von,** and **P. Bailey,** 1961, "Pattern of the Cerebral Isocortex," *Primatologia,* 2: part 2, chap. 10.

**Borrie, W. D.,** *et al.,* 1959, *The Cultural Integration of Immigrants,* Survey based upon the Papers and Proceedings of the UNESCO Conference held in Havana, April, 1956. Paris: UNESCO.

**Bright, William,** 1968, *Language and Culture,* International Encyclopedia of the Social Sciences. New York: Macmillan and Free Press, Vol. 9, pp. 18–22.

**Brody, Eugene R.,** 1961, "Social Conflict and Schizophrenic Behavior in Young Negro Adult Males," *Psychiatry: Journal for the Study of Interpersonal Processes,* 24, 4:337–346.

**Bruner, J. S.,** *et al.,* 1966, *Studies in Cognitive Growth.* New York: John Wiley.

**Buettner-Janusch, John,** 1966, *Origin of Man, Physical Anthropology.* New York: John Wiley.

**Burling, Robbins,** 1970, *Man's Many Voices. Language in Its Cultural Context.* New York: Holt, Rinehart and Winston.

**Campbell, Bernard G.,** 1966, *Human Evolution, An Introduction to Man's Adaptations.* Chicago: Aldine.

———, 1970, "The Roots of Language," in *Psycholinguistics,* J. Morton, ed. London: Logos Press.

Campbell, Donald T., 1964, "Distinguishing Differences of Perception from Failures of Communication in Cross-Cultural Studies," in *Cross-Cultural Understanding: Epistemology in Anthropology*, F. S. C. Northrop and Helen H. Livingston, eds. New York: Harper and Row, pp. 308–333.

Carroll, John B., ed., 1956, *Language, Thought, and Reality. Selected Writings of Benjamin Lee Whorf*. New York: John Wiley.

Cassirer, E., 1944, *An Essay on Man*. New Haven: Yale University Press.

Chang, K. C., 1967, *Rethinking Archeology*. New York: Random House.

———, 1968, *Settlement Archeology*. Palo Alto, Cal.: National Press.

———, 1972, *Settlement Patterns in Archeology*. Reading, Mass.: Addison-Wesley.

Child, I. L., T. Storm, and J. Veroff, 1958, "Achievement Themes in Folk Tales Related to Socialization Practice," in *Motives in Fantasy, Action, and Society*, J. W. Atkinson, ed. New York: Van Nostrand, pp. 479–492.

Childe, V. Gordon, 1962, *The Prehistory of European Society*. London: Cassell.

Chomsky, Noam, 1957, *Aspects of the Theory of Syntax*. Cambridge, Mass.: MIT Press.

———, 1964, *Aspects of the Theory of Syntax*. Cambridge, Mass.: MIT Press.

———, 1964, *Syntactic Structures*. Paris: Mouton.

Clark, W. E., Le Gros, 1947, "Observations on the Anatomy of the Fossil Australopithecinae," *J. Anat.* (London), 81:300–333.

———, 1959, *The Antecedents of Man*. New York: Harper and Row.

Cohen, Yehudi, 1964, *The Transition from Childhood to Adolescence*. Chicago: Aldine.

Collias, M. E., 1944, "Aggressive Behavior Among Vertebrate Animals," *Physiological Zoology* 17, 1:83–123.

Conklin, Harold C., 1962, "Comment," in *Anthropology and Human Behavior*, Thomas Gladwin and W. C. Sturtevant eds. Washington, D.C.: The Anthropological Society of Washington, pp. 86–91.

Cronin, Constance, 1962, "An Analysis of Pottery Design Elements, Indicating Possible Relationships Between Three Decorated Types," in *Fieldiana: Anthropology*, 53:105–114. Chicago: Field Museum of Natural History.

D'Andrade, Roy G., 1961, "Anthropological Study of Dreams," in *Psychological Anthropology*, F. L. K. Hsu, ed. Homewood, Ill.: Dorsey Press, pp. 296–332.

Darling, Sir Malcolm, 1947, *The Punjab Peasant in Prosperity and Debt*, 4th ed. Bombay: Oxford University Press (first printing 1925).

Dart, Raymond A., 1926, "Taungs and its Significance," *Nat. Hist.*, 26:315–327.

Darwin, Charles, 1871, *The Descent of Man*. London: J. Murray.

———, 1872, *The Expression of Emotions in Man and Animals*. Chicago: University of Chicago Press (reprinted, 1965).

Davitz, J. R., 1969, *The Language of Emotion*. New York: Academic Press.

Deetz, James, 1965, "The Dynamics of Stylistic Change in Arikara Ceramics," *Illinois Studies in Anthropology*, Number 4. Urbana: University of Illinois Press.

De Lepervanche, M., 1967, "Descent, Residence, and Leadership in the New Guinea Highlands," *Oceania*, 38.2:134–158.

Dempster, W. T., 1955, "The Anthropology of Body Action," *Ann. N. Y. Acad. Sci.*, 63:559–585.

———, 1965, "Mechanisms of Shoulder Movement," *Arch. Phys. Med. Rehabil.*, 42:49–70.

De Vos, George, 1961, "Symbolic Analysis in the Cross-Cultural Study of Personality," in *Studying Personality Cross-Culturally*, Bert Kaplan, ed. Evanston, Ill.: Powe-Peterson, pp. 599–634.

———, and Hiroshi Wagatsuma, 1966, *Japan's Invisible Race, Caste in Culture and Personality*. Berkeley: University of California Press.

———, 1967, "Achievement in Culture and Personality," in *The Study of Personality: An Interdisciplinary Appraisal*, Rice University Symposium, Edward Norbeck, ed. New York: Holt, Rinehart and Winston.

———, and Arthur Hippler, 1969, "Cultural Psychology: Comparative Studies of Human Behavior," in *Handbook of Social Psychology*, Gardner Lindsey and Elliot Aronson, eds. Reading, Mass.: Addison-Wesley, revised.

———, and Hiroshi Wagatsuma, n. d. *Heritage of Endurance*.

Dillon, L. S., 1973, *Evolution: Concepts and Consequences*. St. Louis: C. V. Mosby.

Dorson, Richard, 1963, "Current Folklore Theories," *Current Anthropology*, 4:93–112.

Douglas, Mary, 1962, *Purity and Danger: An Analysis of Concepts of Pollution and Taboo*. London: Routledge and Kegan Paul.

———, 1970, *Natural Symbols: Explorations in Cosmology*. London: Barrie and Rockliff.

———, 1972, "Self Evidence," in *Proceedings of the Royal Anthropological Institute of Great Britain and Ireland*, p. 27.

Dozier, Edward P., 1966, *Mountain Arbiters, The Changing Life of a Philippine Hill People*. Tucson: University of Arizona Press.

Dubreuil, Guy, and Cecile Boisclair, 1960, "Le Realisme Enfant à la Martinique et au Canada Français: Etude Genetique et Experimentale," *Thoughts from the Learned Societies of Canada*, pp. 83–95.

Durkheim, Emile, 1915, *Elementary Forms of the Religious Life*. London: George Allen & Unwin Ltd.

———, 1966, *The Division of Labor in Society*, G. Simpson, tr. New York: Free Press.

———, 1966, *The Rules of Sociological Method*, S. A. Solovay and J. H. Mueller, tr. New York: Free Press.

———, 1967, *Suicide: A Study in Sociology*, J. A. Spaulding and G. Simpson, tr. New York: Free Press.

———, 1967, *The Elementary Forms of the Religious Life*, J. W. Swain, tr. New York: Free Press.

Durkheim, E., and M. Mauss, 1963, *Primitive Classification*, R. Needham, tr. Chicago: University of Chicago Press.

Eggan, Fred, ed., 1955, *Social Anthropology of North American Tribes*, 2d ed. Chicago: University of Chicago Press.

Eiseley, L., 1961, *Darwin's Century*. Garden City, N. Y.: Doubleday.

Ekman, P., W. W. Friesen, and P. Ellsworth, 1972, *Emotion in the Human Face*. New York: Pergamon Press.

Epstein, T. Scarlett, 1962, *Economic Development and Social Change in South India*. Manchester: Manchester University Press.

Festinger, Leon, 1962, "Cognitive Dissonance," *Scientific American*, 207:93–102.

Fillmore, Charles, 1968, "The Case for Case," in *Universals in Linguistic Theory*, Bach and Harms, eds. New York: Holt, Rinehart and Winston.

Fortes, M., 1945, *The Dynamics of Clanship among the Tallensi*. London: Oxford University Press.

———, 1949, *The Web of Kinship among the Tallensi*. London: Oxford University Press.

———, 1953, "The Structure of Unilineal Descent Groups," *American Anthropologist*, 55.1:7–41.

———, 1959a, "Descent, Filiation and Affinity: A Rejoinder to Dr. Leach," 2 parts, *Man*, 59 (309):193–197, and 59 (331):206–212.

Frankfort, Henri, 1950, *The Birth of Civilization in the Near East*. Garden City, N. Y.: Doubleday.

Gardner, R. A., and B. T. Gardner, 1971, "Two-way Communication with an Infant Chimpanzee," in *Behavior of Non-Human Primates*, A. Schrier and F. Stollnitz, eds. New York: Academic Press, Vol. 4, pp. 117–184.

Geber, Marcelle, 1958, "Psychomotor Development in African Children: The Effects of Social Class and the Need for Improved Tests," *Bulletin Organization Mondial Sante*, 18:471–476.

Geschwind, N., 1964, "The Development of the Brain and the Evolution of Language," in *Report of the 15th Annual R. T. M. on Linguistic and Language Studies*, C. I. J. M. Stuard, ed. Monogr. Ser. Languages and Linguistics, No. 17, pp. 155–169.

Glasse, R. M., and M. J. Meggitt, eds., 1969, *Pigs, Pearlshells, and Women: Marriage in the New Guinea Highlands*. Englewood Cliffs, N.J.: Prentice-Hall.

Gleason, H. A., 1961, *Descriptive Linguistics*. New York: Holt, Rinehart and Winston.

Gluckman, M., 1953, *Custom and Conflict in Africa*. Oxford: Blackwell.

———, 1954, *Rituals of Rebellion in South-East Africa*. Manchester: Manchester University Press.

———, 1964, *Closed Systems and Open Minds: The Limits of Naivety in Social Anthropology*. Edinburgh: Oliver and Boyd.

———, 1965, *Politics, Law, and Ritual in Tribal Society*. Chicago: Aldine.

———, 1968, *Essays on the Ritual of Social Relations*, Manchester: Manchester University Press.

———, 1971, *Order and Rebellion in Tribal Africa*. London: Routledge and Kegan Paul.

———, ed., 1972, *The Allocation of Responsibility*. Manchester: Manchester University Press.

Goldenweiser, Alexander, 1910, "Totemism, An Analytical Study," *Journal of American Folklore*, 23:178–298.

Goody, J., 1959, "The Mother's Brother and the Sister's Son in West Africa," *Journal of the Royal Anthropological Institute*, 89.

———, 1962, *Death, Property, and Ancestors*. Stanford: Stanford University Press.

Gumperz, John, and Dell Hymes, eds., 1972, *Directions in Sociolinguistics, The Ethnography of Communication*. New York: Holt, Rinehart and Winston.

Hagen, Everett, 1962, *On the Theory of Social Change: How Economic Growth Begins*. Homewood, Ill.: Dorsey Press.

Haggett, P., 1966, *Locational Analysis in Human Geography*. New York: St. Martin's Press.

Hallowell, A. I., 1942, "Acculturation Process and Personality Changes as Indicated by the Rorschach Technique," *Rorschach Research Exchange*, 6:42–50.

———, 1945, "'Popular' Responses and Cultural Differences: An Analysis Based on Frequencies in a Group of American Indian Subjects," *Rorschach Research Exchange*, 9:153–168.

———, 1951, "The Use of Projective Techniques and the Study of Sociopsychological Aspects of Acculturation," *Journal of Projective Techniques*, 15:27–44.

———, 1957, *Culture and Experience*. Philadelphia: University of Pennsylvania Press.

Hamilton,W. J., and G. Simon, 1958, *Surface and Radiological Anatomy for Students and General Practitioners*. Cambridge: W. Heffer and Sons.

Handler, P., 1970, *Biology and the Future of Man*. London: Oxford University Press.

Harlow, H., and J. I. Harlow, 1964, "Early Deprivation and Later Behavior in the Monkey," in *Unfinished Tasks in the Behavioral Sciences*, A. Abrams, et al. Baltimore: Williams and Wilkins, pp. 154–173.

Harper, E. B., 1962, "Spirit Possession and Social Structure," in *Anthropology on the March*, B. Ratman, ed. Madras: Thompson and Co.

Harris, Zellig, 1951, *Methods in Structural Linguistics*. Chicago: University of Chicago Press.

Harrison, R. and W. Mantagna, 1969, *Man*. New York: Appleton-Century-Crofts.

Hass, H., 1970, *The Human Animal*. New York: G. P. Putnam's Sons.

Hayes, C., 1951, *The Ape in Our House*. London: Victor Gollancz.

Held, G. J., 1951, *De Papoea. Cultuurimprovisator*. 's Gravenhage/Bandung: N. V. Uitgeverij W. van Hoeve.

Herskovits, Melville, *et al.*, 1963, "Cultural Differences in the Perceptions of Geometric Illusion," *Science*, 139:769–771.

Hewes, G. W., 1973, "Primate Communication and the Gestural Origin of Language," *Curr. Anthrop.*, 14:5–24.

Hill, James N., 1970, "Broken K Pueblo: Prehistoric Social Organization in the

American Southwest," in *Anthropological Papers of the University of Arizona*, Number 18. Tucson: University of Arizona Press.

Hockett, C. F., 1960, "Logical Considerations in the Study of Animal Communication," in *Animal Sounds and Communication*, W. E. Lanyon and W. N. Tavolga, eds. Washington, D.C.: American Institute of Biological Sciences, pp. 392–430.

———, and R. Asher, 1964, "The Human Revolution," *Curr. Anthrop.*, 5:35–168.

Hole, F. and R. F. Heizer, 1973, *An Introduction to Prehistoric Archeology*. New York: Holt, Rinehart and Winston.

Holloway, Ralph L., 1972, "Australopithecine Endocasts, Brain Evolution in the Hominoidea, and a Model of Hominid Evolution," in *The Function and Evolutionary Biology of Primates*, R. Tuttle, ed. Chicago: Aldine-Atherton, pp. 85–204.

Honigmann, John J., 1961, "The Interpretation of Dreams in Anthropological Field Work: A Case Study," in *Studying Personality Cross-Culturally*, Bert Kaplan, ed. Evanston, Ill.: Rowe-Peterson, pp. 579–586.

———, 1961, "North America," in *Psychological Anthropology*, F. L. K. Hsu, ed. Homewood, Ill.: Dorsey Press.

Howell, F. C., 1965, *Early Man*. New York: Time-Life Books.

Hymes, Dell, ed., 1964, *Language in Culture and Society, A Reader in Linguistics and Anthropology*. New York: Harper and Row.

———, 1970, "Linguistic Method in Ethnography. Its Development in the United States," in *Method and Theory in Linguistics*, Paul Garvin, ed. The Hague: Mouton.

Jesperson, Otto, 1924, *Language, Its Nature, Development and Origin*. New York: Henry Holt & Company.

Jessor, Richard, Theodore D. Graves, and Robert C. Hanson, 1968, *Society, Personality and Deviant Behavior: A Social-Psychological Study of a Tri-Ethnic Community*. New York: Holt, Rinehart and Winston.

Jolly, A., 1972, *The Evolution of Primate Behavior*. New York: Macmillan.

Jolly, C. J., 1973, "Changing Views of Hominid Origins," *Yearbook of Physical Anthropology*, 1972:1–17.

Joos, Martin, ed., 1958, *Readings in Linguistics*. New York: American Council of Learned Societies.

Kardiner, Abram, 1939, *The Individual and His Society: The Psychodynamics of Primitive Social Organization*. New York: Columbia University Press.

———, and Edward Prekle, 1961, *They Studied Man*. Cleveland: World Publishing.

Kellogg, W. N., 1968, "Communication and Language in the Home-raised Chimpanzee," *Science*, 162:423–427.

Kiev, Ari, 1964, *Magic, Faith, and Healing, Studies in Primitive Psychiatry Today*. New York: Glencoe Free Press.

Klopfer, P. H. and J. P. Hailman, 1967, *An Introduction to Animal Behavior*. Englewood Cliffs, N. J.: Prentice-Hall.

Kluckhohn, Clyde, 1940, "The Conceptual Structure in Middle American Studies," in *The Maya and Their Neighbors*, C. L. Hay *et al.*, eds. New York: Appleton-Century, pp. 41–51.

———, 1944, *Navaho Witchcraft*. Cambridge: Peabody Museum.

———, 1956, "Review of Language in Culture," H. Hoijer, ed., *American Anthropologist*, 58:569–574.

Knapp, M. L., 1972, *Nonverbal Communication in Human Interaction*. New York: Holt, Rinehart and Winston.

Knobloch, Hilda, and Benjamin Pasamanick, 1958, "The Relationship of Race and Socioeconomic Status to the Development of Motor Behavior Patterns in Infancy," *Psychiatric Research Reports*, 10:123–133.

Kohlberg, Lawrence, *et al.*, 1963, *Child Psychology*. Chicago: University of Chicago Press.

Kotchetkova, V. I., 1960, "L'évolution des regions specifiquement humaine de l'écorce cerebrale chez les Hominidés," in *Proceedings, Sixth International Congress of Anthropological and Ethnological Sciences*. Paris. Vol. 1:623–630.

Lambert, William W., Leigh M. Triandis, and Margery Wolf, 1959, "Some Correlates of Beliefs in the Malevolence and Benevolence of Supernatural Beings, a Cross-Cultural Study," *Journal of Abnormal and Social Psychology*, 58, 2:162–169.

Lancaster, Jane B., 1968, "Primate Communication Systems and the Emergence of Human Language," in *Primates—Studies in Adaptation and Variability*, P. Jay, ed. New York: Holt, Rinehart and Winston, pp. 439–457.

Landauer, Thomas K., and John W. M. Whiting, 1964, "Infantile Stimulation and Adult Stature of Human Males," *American Anthropologist*, 66, 5:1007–1028.

Lang, Andrew, 1911, "Totemism," *Encyclopedia Brittanica*, 11th ed., Vol. 28, pp. 79–91.

Langacker, Ronald, 1968, *Language and Its Structure*. New York: Harcourt, Brace.

Langness, L. L., 1964, "Some Problems in the Conceptualization of Highlands Social Structure," in *New Guinea: the Central Highlands, American Anthropologist*, Special Issue, 66.4, part 2:162–182.

Lanternari, Vittorio, 1963, *The Religions of the Oppressed: A Study of Modern Messianic Cults*. New York: Alfred A. Knopf.

Laurendeau, M., and A. Pinard, 1962, *Causal Thinking in the Child*. New York: International Universities Press.

Leach, E. R., 1961, *Rethinking Anthropology*. London School of Economics Monographs in Social Anthropology 22. London: Athlone Press.

———, 1965, *Political Systems of Highland Burma: A Study of Kachin Social Structure*. Boston: Beacon Press.

———, 1967, *The Structural Study of Myth*, Cambridge Papers in Social Anthropology No. 4.

Leaf, Murray J., 1972, *Information and Behavior in a Sikh Village: Social Organization Reconsidered*. Berkeley: University of California Press.

Leakey, L. S. B., Jack Prost and Stephanie Prost, eds., 1971, *Adam or Ape.* Cambridge, Mass.: Schenkman.

Leighton, Alexander, *et al.,* 1963, *Psychiatric Disorder Among the Yoruba.* Ithaca, New York: Cornell University Press.

Leone, M., 1968, "Economic Autonomy and Social Distance: Archeological Evidence," Ph.D. dissertation, University of Arizona.

LeVine, Robert A., 1966, "Outsiders' Judgments: An Ethnographic Approach to Group Differences in Personality," *Southwestern Journal of Anthropology,* 22, 2:101–116.

Lévi-Strauss, Claude 1955, "The Structural Study of Myth," *American Journal of Folklore,* 68:428 ff.

——, 1962, "Social Structure," in *Anthropology Today,* Sol Tax, ed. Chicago: Chicago University Press.

——, 1962, *Totemism,* R. Needham, tr. Boston: Beacon Press.

——, 1966, *The Savage Mind,* anon. tr. London: Weidenfeld and Nicolson.

——, 1969, *The Elementary Structures of Kinship,* rev. ed., J. H. Bell, J. R. von Sturmer, and R. Needham, ed. and tr. Boston: Beacon Press.

——, 1969, *The Raw and the Cooked.* New York: Harper and Row.

Lieberman, P., E. S. Crelin, and D. H. Klatt, 1972, "Phonetic Ability and Related Anatomy of the Newborn, Adult Human, Neanderthal Man and the Chimpanzee," *American Anthropologist,* 74:287–307.

——, 1973, "On the Evolution of Language: A Unified View," *Cognition,* 2:59–94.

Longacre, William A., 1970a, "Archeology as Anthropology: A Case Study," in *Anthropological Papers of the University of Arizona,* Number 17. Tucson: University of Arizona Press.

——, 1970b, *Reconstructing Prehistoric Pueblo Society.* Albuquerque: University of New Mexico Press.

——, ed., 1974, "Multi-Disciplinary Research at Grasshopper," in *Anthropological Papers of the University of Arizona.* Tucson: University of Arizona Press.

Lorenz, D., 1935, "Companionship in Bird Life," reprinted 1957 in *Instinctive Behavior,* C. H. Schiller, ed. New York: International Universities Press.

Lorenz, K., 1965, *Evolution and Modification of Behavior.* Chicago: University of Chicago Press.

Lowie, Robert H., 1937, *History of Ethnological Theory.* New York: Holt, Rinehart and Winston.


MacKay, D. M., 1972, "Formal Analysis of Communicative Processes," in *Non-Verbal Communication,* R. Hinde, ed. Cambridge: Cambridge University Press.

Malinowski, B., 1913, *The Family among the Australian Aborigines.* London: University of London Press.

——, 1922, *Argonauts of the Western Pacific.* London: Routledge & Kegan Paul.

——, 1926, *Crime and Custom in Savage Society.* London: Kegan Paul, Trench, Trubner.

————, 1927, *Sex and Repression in Savage Society*. London: Kegan Paul, Trench, Trubner.

————, 1929, *The Sexual Life of Savages in Northwestern Melanesia*. London: G. Routledge & Sons.

————, 1935, *Coral Gardens and Their Magic*. 2 vols. New York: American Book.

Masland, Richard L., 1968, "Some Neurological Processes Underlying Language," in *Perspectives on Human Evolution 2*, S. L. Washburn and P. Dolinow, eds. New York: Holt, Rinehart and Winston.

Mayr, E., 1963, *Animal Species and Evolution*. Cambridge, Mass.: Harvard University Press.

McClaran, Marlys, 1973, "Lexical and Syntactic Structures in Yucatec Maya." Ph.D. dissertation, Harvard University.

McClelland, David C., 1961, *The Achieving Society*. New York: D. Van Nostrand.

McQuown, Norman A., 1956, *The Natural History of an Interview*. Chicago: University of Chicago Microfilm.

————, ed., 1967, *Linguistics. Handbook of Middle American Indians*, Vol. 5; Wauchope, gen ed. Austin: University of Texas Press.

Mauss, M., 1954, *The Gift: Forms and Functions of Exchange in Archaic Societies*, I. Cunnison, tr. Glencoe, Ill.: Free Press.

Mead, M. and Ruth Buzel, 1960, *The Golden Age of American Anthropology*. New York: Geo. Braziller.

Miner, Horace, and George DeVos, 1960, "Oasis and Casbah, Algerian Culture and Personality in Change," *Michigan Anthropological Papers*, No. 15, entire issue.

Money-Kyrle, Roger Ernle, 1968, *The Meaning of Sacrifice*. New York: Johnson Reprint.

Moore, M. L., 1965, "Clinical Assessment of Joint Motion," in *Therapeutic Exercise*, S. Licht, ed. New Haven: Elizabeth Licht, Publ.

Morrill, R., 1969, *The Spatial Organization of Society*. Belmont, Cal.: Wadsworth.

Murdock, G. P., 1949, *Social Structure*. New York: Macmillan.

Negus, V. W., 1949, *The Comparative Anatomy and Physiology of the Larynx*. New York: Hafner.

O'Connell, A. L. and E. B. Gardner, 1972, *Understanding the Scientific Basis of Human Movement*. Baltimore: Williams and Wilkins.

Parsons, Talcott, 1954, "The Incest Taboo in Relation to Social Structure and the Socialization of the Child," *British Journal of Sociology*, 15:278–328.

————, 1964, "Social Structure and the Development of Personality," *Psychiatry*, 21:328–340.

————, 1964, *Social Structure and Personality*. New York: Free Press.

Penniman, T. K., 1965, *A Hundred Years of Anthropology*. London: Gerald Duckworth.

Pfeiffer, J. E., 1969, *The Emergence of Man.* New York: Harper & Row.

Phillips, Herbert, 1963, "Relationships between Personality and Social Structure in a Siamese Peasant Community," *Human Organization,* 22:105–108.

Piaget, Jean, 1954, *The Construction of Reality in the Child.* New York: Basic Books.

———, 1930, *The Child's Concept of Physical Causality.* London: Kegan Paul.

Pike, Kenneth, 1954, *Language in Relation to a Unified Theory of the Structure of Human Behavior.* Glendale, Calif.: Summer Institute of Linguistics.

Pilbeam, D., 1972, *The Ascent of Man.* New York: Macmillan.

Plagenhoef, S., 1971, *Patterns of Human Motion.* Englewood Cliffs, N.J.: Prentice-Hall.

Plog, S., 1973, "Variability in Ceramic Design Frequencies as a Measure of Prehistoric Social Organization," (manuscript). Ann Arbor: University of Michigan.

Pouwer, J., 1960, "Loosely Structured Societies in Netherlands New Guinea," *Bijdragen tot de taal-, land-, en Volkenkunde,* 116:109–118.

———, 1966, "Toward a Configurational Approach to Society and Culture in New Guinea," *Journal of the Polynesian Society,* 75.1:67–84.

Premack, D., 1971, "On the Assessment of Language Competence in the Chimpanzee," in *Behavior of Nonhuman Primates,* A. M. Schrier and F. Stollinitz, eds. New York: Academic Press, Vol. 4, pp. 185–228.

Price-Williams, Douglass R., 1967, "Ethnopsychology II: Comparative Psychological Processes," in *Introduction to Cultural Anthropology: Essays in the Scope and Methods of the Science of Man,* James A. Clifton, ed. Boston: Houghton Mifflin, pp. 317–335.

Prost, J. H., 1967, "Bipedalism of Man and Gibbon Compared Using Estimates of Joint Motion," *Amer. J. Phys. Anthrop.,* 26:135–148.

———, 1973, "Natural Groups in Multidimensional Space," *Communication Channel,* March/April:6–8.

———, 1974, "Varieties of Human Posture," *Human Biology,* in press.

Radcliffe-Brown, A. R., 1952, *Structure and Function in Primitive Society.* Glencoe, Ill.: Free Press.

Robinson, B. W., 1972, "Anatomical and Physiological Contrasts Between Human and Other Primate Vocalizations," in *Perspectives on Human Evolution 2,* S. L. Washburn and P. Dolinow, eds. New York: Holt, Rinehart and Winston.

Rosen, Bernard C., 1962, "Socialization and Achievement Motivation in Brazil," *American Sociological Review,* 27, 5:612–626.

Rubel, Arthur J., 1964, "The Epidemiology of a Folk Illness: Susto in Hispanic America," *Ethnology,* 3:268–283.

Ruppé, R., 1966, "The Archeological Survey: A Defense," *American Antiquity,* 31:313–333.

Russell, D. A., et al., 1971, "Blood Groups and Salivary ABH Secretion of Inhabitants of the Karimui Plateau and Adjoining Areas of the New Guinea Highlands," *Human Biology in Oceania,* I, 2.

Sahlins, M. D., 1965, "On the Sociology of Primitive Exchange," in ASA Monograph No. 1: *The Relevance of Models for Social Anthropology*, M. Banton, ed. New York: Praeger.

Salisbury, R. F., 1956, "Asymmetrical Marriage Systems," *American Anthropologist*, 58:639–655.

———, 1956, "Unilineal Descent Groups in the New Guinea Highlands, *Man*, 56:2–7.

———, 1964, "New Guinea Highlands Models and Descent Theory," *Man*, 64:168–171.

Salter, N., 1955, "Methods of Measurement of Muscle and Joint Function," *J. Bone Jt. Surg.*, 37B:474–491.

Sapir, Edward, 1949, *Language*. New York: Harcourt, Brace, Jovanovich.

Schepers, G. W. H., 1946, "The South African Fossil Ape-men, Part 2," in *Transvaal Mus. Mem.*, No. 2., R. Broom and G. W. H. Schepers, eds.

Schneider, David M., 1965, "Some Muddles in the Models: or, How the System Really Works," in ASA Monograph No. 1: *The Relevance of Models for Social Anthropology*, M. Banton, ed. New York: Praeger.

———, and Kathleen Gough, 1959, *Matrilineal Kinship*. Berkeley: University of California Press.

Seckel, H. P. G., 1960, *Bird-Headed Dwarfs*. Basel: Karger.

Shannon, C. and W. Weaver, 1964, *The Mathematical Theory of Communication*. Urbana: University of Illinois Press.

Simons, E. L., 1972, *Primate Evolution*. New York: Macmillan.

Skinner, B. F., 1953, *Science and Human Behavior*. New York: Macmillan.

Smith, William R., 1907, *Lectures on the Religion of the Semites*, 2d ed., reissued. London: Adam and Charles Black.

Spicer, Edward *et al.*, 1961, *Perspectives in American Indian Culture Change*. Chicago: University of Chicago Press.

Spindler, George and Louise Spindler, 1963, "Psychology in Anthropology: Applications to Culture Change," in *Psychology, A Study of a Science 6*, Sigmund Koch, ed. New York: McGraw-Hill, pp. 510–551.

Spiro, Melford E., 1951, "Culture and Personality: The Natural History of a False Dichotomy," *Psychiatry*, 14:19–46.

———, 1954, "Is the American Family Universal?" *American Anthropologist*, 56:839–846.

———, 1958, *Children of the Kibbutz*. Cambridge, Mass.: Harvard University Press.

———, and R. G. D'Andrade, 1958, "A Cross-Cultural Study of Some Supernatural Beliefs," *American Anthropologist*, 60:456–466.

Spradley, James and David McCurdy, 1972, *The Cultural Experience, Ethnography In Complex Society*. Chicago: Science Research Associates.

Stefflre, Volney J., Peter Reich, and Marlys McClaran-Stefflre, 1971, "Some Eliciting and Computational Procedures for Descriptive Semantics," in *Explorations in Mathematical Anthropology*, Paul Kay, ed. Cambridge, Mass.: MIT Press.

Steindler, S., 1955, *Kinesiology and the Human Body*. Springfield, Ill.: Charles C. Thomas.

Strathern, A. J., 1969, "Descent and Alliance in the New Guinea Highlands: Some Problems of Comparison," *Royal Anthropological Institute Proceedings* for 1968, 37–52.

————, 1971, *The Rope of Moka: Big Men and Ceremonial Exchange in Mount Hagen, New Guinea.* Cambridge: Cambridge University Press.

Struever, S., 1968, "Woodland Subsistence-Settlement Systems in the Lower Illinois Valley, in *New Perspectives in Archeology*, S. R. Binford and L. R. Binford, eds. Chicago: Aldine.

Sturtevant, A. H., 1967, "Mendel and the Gene Factory," in *Heritage From Mendel*, Alexander Brink, ed. Milwaukee: University of Wisconsin Press.

Sudnow, David, ed., 1972, *Studies in Social Interaction.* New York: Free Press.

Taylor, Walter W., 1948, "A Study of Archeology," *American Anthropological Association Memoir*, No. 69. Kenosha: American Anthropological Association.

Thernstron, Stephen, 1964, *Poverty and Progress: Social Mobility in a Nineteenth Century City.* Cambridge, Mass.: Harvard University Press.

Thompson, R. H., and W. A. Longacre, 1966, "The University of Arizona Archaeological Field School at Grasshopper, East-Central Arizona," *The Kiva*, 31; 4:255–275. Tucson: Arizona Archaeological and Historical Society, Inc.

Thorpe, W. H., 1972, "The Comparison of Vocal Communication in Animals and Man," in *Non-Verbal Communication*, R. Hinde, ed. Cambridge: Cambridge University Press.

Trigger, B., 1968, "The Determinants of Settlement Patterns," in *Settlement Archeology*, K. C. Chang, ed. Palo Alto, Calif.: National Press.

Turner, V. W., 1957, *Schism and Continuity in an African Society: A Study of Ndembu Village Life.* Manchester: Manchester University Press.

————, 1967, *The Forest of Symbols: Aspects of Ndembu Ritual.* Ithaca, N. Y.: Cornell University Press.

————, 1968, *The Drums of Affliction: A Study of Religious Process among the Ndembu of Zambia.* Oxford: Clarendon Press.

————, 1969, *The Ritual Process: Structure and Antistructure.* Chicago: Aldine.

Tyler, Stephen, ed., 1969, *Cognitive Anthropology.* New York: Holt, Rinehart and Winston.

Wagner, Roy, 1967, *The Curse of Souw: Principles of Daribi Clan Definition and Alliance in New Guinea.* Chicago: University of Chicago Press.

————, 1972, *Habu: The Innovation of Meaning in Daribi Religion.* Chicago: University of Chicago Press.

Warner, W. Lloyd, 1937, *A Black Civilization, A Social Study of an Australian Tribe.* New York: Harper & Row.

Washburn, Sherwood L., 1965, "Conflict in Primate Society," unpublished manuscript, University of California.

Watson, J. B., 1930, *Behaviorism.* Chicago: University of Chicago Press.

————, 1964, "Introduction: Anthropology in the New Guinea Highlands," *American Anthropologist*, 66.4, Pt. 2:1–19.

————, 1970, "Society as Organized Flow," *Southwestern Journal of Anthropology*, 26.1:107–124.

Whitaker, Harry A., 1971, "Neurolingustics," in *A Survey of Linguistic Science*, W. O. Dingwall, ed. College Park: University of Maryland Press, pp. 136–244.

Whiting, John W. M., 1941, *Becoming a Kwoma*. New Haven: Yale University Press.

————, 1959, "Sorcery, Sin and the Superego: A Cross-Cultural Study of Some Mechanisms of Social Control," *Symposium on Motivation*, 174–195.

————, 1961, "Socialization Process and Personality," in *Psychological Anthropology*, F. L. K. Hsu, ed. Homewood, Ill.: Dorsey Press, pp. 355–380.

————, and R. G. D'Andrade, 1959, "Sleeping Arrangements and Social Structure: A Cross-Cultural Study," paper presented at the American Anthropological Meeting, Mexico City, December.

————, and Beatrice Whiting, 1960, "Contributions to the Methods of Studying Child Rearing," in *Handbook of Research Methods in Child Development*, P. H. Mussen, ed. New York: John Wiley, pp. 918–944.

Whorf, Benjamin Lee, 1956, *Language, Thought, and Reality, Selected Writings of B. L. Whorf*, John B. Carroll, ed. Cambridge, Mass.: MIT Press.

Wiener, Norbert, 1948, "Time, Communication, and the Nervous System," *Ann. N. Y. Acad. Sci.*, 50:197–220.

Willey, G., 1953, "Prehistoric Settlement Patterns in the Viru Valley, Peru," Bulletin 155, Bureau of American Ethnology.

Wittfogel, K., 1957, *Oriental Despotism*. New Haven: Yale University Press.

Wolf, Arthur D., 1966, "Childhood Association, Sexual Attraction, and the Incest Taboo," *American Anthropologist*, Vol. 68, No. 4.

Wolfe, Peter, 1960, *The Developmental Psychologies of Jean Piaget and Psychoanalysis*. New York: International Universities Press.

Wynne-Edwards, V. C., 1962, *Animal Dispersion in Relation to Social Behavior*. New York: Hafner.


Yap, P. M., 1963, "Koro or Suk-yeong—An Atypical Culture-Bound Psychogenic Disorder Found in Southern Chinese," paper presented at the Joint Meetings of the Japanese Society of Neurology and Psychiatry and the American Psychiatric Association, Tokyo, May, 1963.

# Index